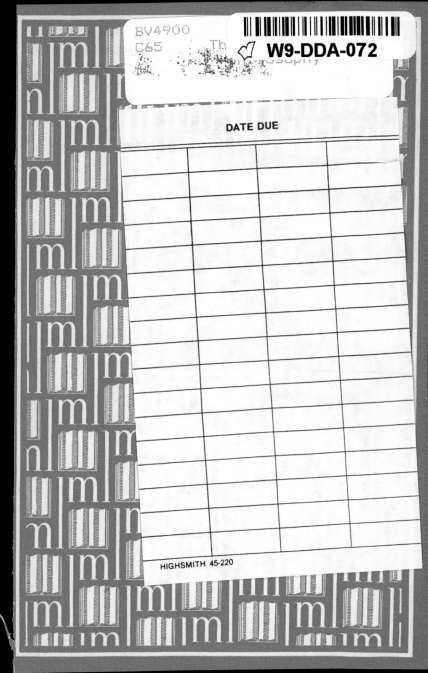

THE MODERN LIBRARY
OF THE WORLD'S BEST BOOKS

THE CONSOLATION
OF PHILOSOPHY

*The publishers will be pleased to send, upon request, an
illustrated folder setting forth the purpose and scope of
THE MODERN LIBRARY, and listing each volume
in the series. Every reader of books will find titles he
has been looking for, handsomely printed, in definitive
editions, and at an unusually low price.*

The Consolation of Philosophy

BOETHIUS

THE CONSOLATION OF PHILOSOPHY

THOMAS À KEMPIS

THE IMITATION OF CHRIST

SIR THOMAS BROWNE

RELIGIO MEDICI

With an Introduction by IRWIN EDMAN

Professor of Philosophy, Columbia University

THE MODERN LIBRARY · NEW YORK

Random House IS THE PUBLISHER OF

THE MODERN LIBRARY

BENNETT A. CERF · DONALD S. KLOPFER · ROBERT K. HAAS

Manufactured in the United States of America

By H. Wolff

CONTENTS

INTRODUCTION

BY IRWIN EDMAN

THROUGH the centuries certain books have been sources of consolation and fortitude for troubled spirits in troublous times, in personal crisis or in public calamity; they have been both anodyne and refreshment. Notable in such wisdom literature are the three classics included in this volume. Each has served again and again as a resource for men shaken by inner scepticism, or by outer violence tempted to despair. They all three exhibit, in different forms and in different accents, the "consolation of philosophy."

The philosophy in each case is close to religion, for all three authors believed in God. But the God they believed in was in each instance the God whom reason might assent to as well as faith credit. The consolation each book affords is to the mind as well as to the heart. All three authors lived in troubled times, though only Boethius lived a troubled life. All three still speak with curiously timely, curiously timeless, directness to those perplexed about the future or anxious about the perpetual issues of life and destiny.

The "consolation" in each of these books is not solely, or perhaps primarily, a matter of argument. Indeed it is only the first, *The Consolation of Philosophy,* that argues on the basis of a considered dialectic. The healing is communicated not least by what one might call the "music" of the discourse and the enchantment of mood shining through the discussion. It is not without point that the second of the three books here included, *The Imitation of Christ,* had as an alternative title "Musica Ecclesiastica"—"Ecclesiastical Music," and music did not refer to the mere sound; it connoted the melody of the doctrine itself.

In each case it is as if, or rather it is in fact that, a composed spirit by the contagion of his own native rhetoric soothes and edifies our own psyches. Boethius, a scholar and public official, Thomas à Kempis, a retiring monk, Sir Thomas Browne, a comfortable soliloquizing physician, keep on rhythmically whispering in the ears of each generation that it is possible during distraction or defeat or despair, in the face of public violence or private uncertainty, in the face of inner turbulences or external disasters, to achieve equableness of life and serenity of spirit.

Boethius speaks in the sixth century from the prison near Rome where he actually writes the *Consolation* several months before his execution as a traitor. Thomas à Kempis in the fifteenth century writes *The Imitation of Christ* from a monastic retreat in the Low Countries in the midst of the barbarities and violences of the religious and secular wars. Thomas Browne, in the seventeenth century in England, fortunate in his personal circumstances of wealth and position, stands aside and half quizzically dreams his bravura prose meditations, the *Religio Medici,* while a revolution is going on.

The times and the tempers of each are different. But what each says in the way each says it has a perennial appeal to men trying to find stability in other crises in civilization or in their own souls.

It is hard to say whether any one of these three books ought to be classified primarily as religion or philosophy. All three authors were Christians, but none of them could be classed as simple or conventional in his piety. Boethius had a belief that was buttressed by, and indeed almost made possible by, the pagan philosophies he was humanistically interested in preserving and transmuting. Thomas à Kempis was a subtle mystic rather than an orthodox routine theologian. Sir Thomas Browne himself acknowledges that the "scandal of his profession" (his book is the "religion of a physician") made his piety suspect, but his piety, about which there is no doubt, has a deliberate complexity; he likes to believe not least what is mysterious and paradoxical.

All three books are in different fashion philosophical. *The Consolation of Philosophy* is the most professional in tone and in organization, though cast in the graceful form of a dialogue between Boethius, the doubting and downcast prisoner, and the Lady Philosophy appearing to him in his cell. The arguments are by no means original with Boethius. The trained student recognizes Plato, Aristotle, Plotinus. Themes familiar in the Greek and Roman schools of philosophy, down even to detailed turns of arguments, echo in Boethius' pages. There are passages almost plagiarized from Plato and from Cicero. But the note remains Boethius' own. And the note is that of a passionate brief for the identity of goodness with God and the omnipresence of God in the universe, whatever the embittering appearances of evil may seem to be.

Thomas à Kempis' work, too, despite its specifically religious title, its identifying Christian name, *The Imitation* (or the following) *of Christ,* is a philosophical tract. It is philosophy in the sense not of sustained objective argument but of an uttered spiritual mood, of an inner soliloquy. It is philosophy as meditation. It is the lyric thought of a soul which, in monastic walls, has renounced the world and sought the quiet eventual ecstasy of union with God. It is philosophy, too, in the sense of considered reflections upon the inroads upon serenity, the distractions of worldliness and the world, which hinder such a union. It is, finally, a reflection on the inner armor we have against worldliness and the world.

Sir Thomas Browne, too, is a philosopher in almost a quaint sense. He has no system; he has no fixed order of principles. But he is a roving mind, curiously exploring all the oddities and paradoxes of faith and feeling. He has no hierarchy of ideas, but his miscellany of notions is fused in a genial, sceptic and tolerant faith. In his circuitous and mouth-filling phrases he touches depths and scales altitudes. An oddly engaging mixture of the simple and the sophisticated, he, too, suggests, though by an eccentric path, the union of the meditative soul with its God.

Here, then, are three writers, one in the sixth century, writing in a prison near Rome, another in the fifteenth, presumably writing in a monastery in the Low Countries, one in the seventeenth century privately scribbling in the retired residence of a wealthy physician in the English countryside town of Norwich. Boethius is a cultivated semi-expert in the philosophies of Greece and Rome, Thomas à Kempis is a meditative poet and mystical psychologist, Sir Thomas Browne, a man of wide and curious learning with a taste for the singular and the intellectually perplexing. They are different in culture, temper and training. But they are all members of that timeless sodality who turn the minds of men from "the politics of time to the politics of eternity" and by so doing bring them peace.

Each of them has his own secret of charm and persuasion. In the case of *The Imitation of Christ,* the magic is almost inexpressible in other than the mystical sentences of the writer himself. Each wrote a book which says more about itself than anything that could be said about it. But an introduction can perhaps help to place each book for the modern reader and define the region in which each makes its timeless appeal. It can indicate the time and place out of which, and the person out of whom, each of these consoling classics arose.

It is fitting that Boethius should have been so long a favorite book not only among professional philosophers and ecclesiastics, but among men of the world. For he was not a recluse philosopher. He was a man of affairs, of an aristocratic family, an ardent humanist and an active Roman official. He wrote philosophy by snatching moments of speculation from a busy life devoted to the state. Though neither Christ nor the Holy Bible is mentioned in *The Consolation of Philosophy,* there is every presumption that, as an official in the sixth century in the reign of the pagan-hating Theodoric, he was a Christian. He is assumed, indeed, to have written a few theological tracts. He is a man of the world who is a philosopher, and a Christian whose real religion is philosophy.

He was apparently an adviser to Theodoric on the most varied matters: the construction of a water clock, the appointment of a harpist; he was even—it is suggested by some scholars—for a time director of the mint. In 510 he was made a consul. In 522 his two sons were made consuls. In 523 he was created *magister officiorum*, a position involving constant attendance upon the king. In 524 he was convicted of high treason. In the following year he was put to death.

In the dungeon of Alvanzano, near Milan, during his imprisonment, he composed, as a kind of singing in the dark, *The Consolation of Philosophy*. It has been a saving music for many others, in actual prisons or the prisons of their own doubts. It saved Boethius' faith (and possibly his reason), if it did not save his life. He was executed a year later. The charges that he had communication with the Eastern Empire seem highly dubious. It is more probable that his Catholic conservatism made him suspect to Theodoric who had espoused the Arian heresy.

Boethius' imprisonment was a misfortune for Boethius. But the very fact of it is responsible for a remarkable piece of prose literature as well as philosophy. It is doubtful whethei anything less than the agony of incarceration, under what seemed the most unjust charges after the most honorable public life, could have evoked in him the intimate sense of evil in the world with which the *Consolation* begins. Out of this sense emerged reflection on fortune and misfortune, on justice and injustice, on good and evil, which are the central themes of the book. It is doubtful, too, that the form of the book would have been just what it is, or that, though these things are of course pure speculation, this particular work would have been undertaken. For Boethius, who had planned a complete translation of Plato and Aristotle, was a professional scholar. He had as his ambition the reconciliation of Platonism and Aristotelianism. He wrote a commentary on Porphyry's introduction to the *Categories* of Aristotle. He wrote a treatise "on Music," used for hundreds of years at

Oxford. He wrote long letters to friends, treatises, in the form of letters, on theology.

The Consolation of Philosophy, though it is full of evidences of philosophical learning (learning, by the way, *remembered* by a scholar parted from his library), is not an academic philosophical work. It is a work of belles lettres. Though it raises some of the most persistent technical questions in philosophy, it is completely free of technical jargon. It is in the style of an urbane essayist. It is a Platonic dialogue, or, more strictly, a Ciceronian dialogue, for it has the qualities of Roman elegance rather than of Greek feeling. It is a long conversation between Lady Philosophy and the writer. Philosophy appears to recall him from his doubts and despairs by reminding him of her own teaching, of which his doubts and despairs are betrayals and forgetfulness.

The dialogue is interrupted, or, more accurately, carried forward, by short poems which are both summaries and intellectual choruses. They are celebrations of points that have been or are about to be argued. The book is, as Dr. E. K. Rand points out, prison literature. It is also consolation literature, and in the category also of those introductions and encouragements to philosophy such as had been written by both Aristotle and by Cicero. But it is also an attempt to answer in terms of the whole system of the universal good those doubts as to goodness which arise in the mind of the imprisoned and mistreated philosopher, or of any imprisoned or mistreated human being. Where fate seems unkind, where Providence seems to bless the wicked, where deserved happiness is snatched away, where violence triumphs over reason: under such circumstances nothing less will answer these horrors to the mind and heart than a theory of the universe in which all adds up to a system of good, a system of God. It is toward a demonstration of this that Boethius' compact work is designed, and for all the passion animating the whole and the poetry interrupting the parts, the argument is closely knit.

It is increasingly tightly woven as it progresses, when philosophy feels that her patient is sufficiently recovered to bear her more stringent discipline of dialectic. What begins as persuasive medicine ends as severe demonstration. The patient, Boethius, is ill. He is broken down by the weight of his unintelligible misfortunes. Like Job he feels himself to be a good man badly wronged. He is bemoaning his miseries, surrounded by the Muses echoing his miseries. Lady Philosophy enters and drives away the false comforters. More is needed than poetry; philosophy must clear the vapors of sentiment from the patient's mind. Fortune has treated him unjustly? Philosophy has deserted him?

Fortune is by nature fickle; other men before him have suffered for the truth. Reason would teach to him to scorn what he has lost, to cease to pine for what most men, misled by passion, hold dear. Philosophy listens to Boethius' complaints: he protests at the fickleness of human chance in a world of nature where all is order. Philosophy seizes upon the fact that though he thinks chances are randomly disposed in this world, there is an ordered governance in nature. It is a sign, this recognition of reasonableness in things, that there is a spark of reason in Boethius. By this he may be cured of his confusions and despairs; the poem with which Book I closes is characteristic:

"When the stars are hidden by black clouds, no light can they afford. When the boisterous south wind rolls along the sea and stirs the surge, the water, but now as clear as glass, bright as the fair sun's light, is dark, impenetrable to sight, with stirred and scattered sand. The stream, that wanders down the mountain's side, must often find a stumbling-block, a stone within its path torn from the hill's own rock. So too shalt thou: if thou wouldst see the truth in undimmed light, choose the straight road, the beaten path; away with passing joys! away with fear! put vain hopes to flight! and grant no place to grief! Where these distractions reign, the mind is clouded o'er, the soul is bound in chains."

Boethius makes Philosophy (in the second book) suggest one of the resources the mind can have when the chances of Fortune turn fickle or hostile. The nature of Fortune itself is fickleness. One who knows her nature should not have expected more. This is hardly consolation in real trouble and Philosophy gives warmer comfort in reminding Boethius of the goods that remain: his wife, his sons, his friend Symmachus. But it is hardly a distinctively philosophical consolation to be told that one still has something good left. The really speculative reassurance begins when Philosophy questions the absoluteness of the goods which men enjoy (or think they enjoy) when they possess them, which they mourn when they lose them. One of the uses of Fortune is indeed her very fickleness. By taking away illusory goods she shows us how illusory they are. Relieving the mind from immersion in false attachments, she shows it where its true devotions lie. The mind discovers that what it truly loves is the good.

Boethius is neither the first nor the last to indicate with mournful exactitude the transiency, the precariousness and the vanity of earthly goods, riches, luxurious objects that delight the senses, and above all, fame, a deception to desire which the ancients were all fond of analyzing because it was so favorite an object of ancient ambition.

Men, at least not philosophically-minded men, have never been satisfied to be told merely that the usual goods were illusions. They will not, without bitterness or regret, give these up without some proof that there is another, less deceptive, good. Philosophy attempts to prove to the imprisoned Boethius that such true good does exist. For what all men desire, even when they err, is *the* good; all that *is* good in the illusory goods of fame, and riches, power and sensual satisfaction, is the highest good of which these are at best "broken lights," when they are not obscuring darkness. It is to the highest goods of which all other goods are aspects or of which they are instruments or precursors, toward which men aspire.

This highest good exists, it is unified, it is perfect, it is God. One addresses it by prayer and analyzes it by reason. One prays to the Good, for it is the Good which one longs for. One prays to it also because it is the very source of all other goods and of one's own being. One analyzes it to define its reality and distinguish it from the illusions to which emotion rather than understanding, passion unenlightened by reason, lead mortal man.

Parts of the argument of the *Consolation* read like Marcus Aurelius or any Stoic arguing away the importance, demonstrating the illusoriness, of pleasure and wealth and fame. Succeeding parts read, especially in Boethius' complaints, like Job. The answers made are those that convinced faith has always tried, when it resorted to argument, in answer to the question: Why does a good God permit evil in the world; why, if the universe is all good, is there evil in it?

The traditional theological answer is that, completely understood, evil is but a partial aspect of the good. There is order, unity, goodness in Providence; they are, indeed, its other name. Fate, which is Providence, as it were, operative in the world, seems to be helter skelter, willful and random. The chances it distributes are, however, only apparently without reason. They are the only half-understood manifestations of good itself.

The answers that Boethius the writer makes Philosophy give Boethius the prisoner are not altogether satisfactory. Theological answers never have been quite conclusive even to the faithful but inquiring spirit. There are neat apparent solutions, such as that God can foresee all although at any moment man has free choice. Boethius pictures Philosophy as giving none of these. But the dialogue is not cherished these hundreds of years because it successfully argues evil out of the world. It has been welcomed because it breathes, in the face of adversity, a sense of the relativity of both goods and evils in life. It communicates a profound sense of the good at the heart of the things and the love which can bring us back to union with the principle of love itself from which all else flows. It is the human spirit committed in prayer and virtue to the highest good it can envisage, convinced, even when evil seems to triumph, that good is ultimately and eternally triumphant in the nature of things. Without such conviction it would be difficult for good men to go on struggling against chaos and the dark. Fortified by such a conviction, in Boethius' closing words, one may "possess one's mind with worthy hopes."

The author of *The Imitation of Christ* was not a prisoner. Thomas à Kempis (1380–1471) was, one has good reason to believe, a priest and a monk. He lived in an order such as that of the Brothers of the Common Life, free from most of the complications of theology and elaborate organization. His voice is that of a man who has renounced the world but feels no loss because he has found a vocation and a goal: the union of the soul with God.

The world is almost absent from Thomas à Kempis' pages, that is, the "great world," the marketplace, the sphere of major events. Such events as there are, are interior ones, and the world is bounded by the relations of confederates in piety, members of a free society of simple, godly men. It is the book of a man dreaming of a "world elsewhere," a realm to be discovered by interior meditation. Like Augustine, Thomas à Kempis finds his union with God through the exploration of his own soul, which derives its very being from God.

It is not hard to see why this unaffected little masterpiece has had its devotees not only among pious mystics but among meditative men everywhere. Philosophers and theologians may argue away the evil of the world. But it may be that *the* evil is existence itself and our absorption in it, our distraction by it. Men everywhere, not least men who, like the author of the *Imitation*, seem once to have known the outside world, have sought at one time or another for interior quietude, for the peace that is the avenue to rapture. "Blessed are those eyes that are closed to outward things and attend to the inward things. Blessed are they that pierce to inward things and study to make themselves ready by daily exercise, more and more to take heavenly secrets. Blissful are they that take heed to God and cast themselves out from all impediments of the world."

This is what the *Imitation* is really about: the way (to use its closing phrase) to "the land of everlasting clearness." The book consists of audible meditations, musing confessions and enraptured exhortations. The confessions are of distractions from the path, from the "upward way." The exhortations are reminders of what man's felicity is, the direction one must take toward grace. The author is content to be God's fool, but he is no man's fool. It is clear that he recognizes quite candidly the assaults of lust, the insistence of ambition, the corruptions of petulance, pride of impatience. Even in a monastery he is aware that these and subtler things are distractions from "the everlasting clearness": private loves, for instance, self-absorption or absorption in this one object, that one person; busyness, too, and preoccupation. We are constantly lost among things; we are mastered by the external; we are blinded by the immediate. We do not see the eternal vision; we do not hear the eternal music because we are blinded by the here and now, deafened by loud and alien noises. And it is our lusts, our little loves, our small ambitions, our trivial irritations, our pains and our pleasures even, that prevent us from being filled with the lucidity of Heaven, that keep us from the rapture of clear union with the Divine.

Thomas à Kempis counsels obedience, patience, continence, poverty, not for their own sake, but because they free the spirit for its sheerest joy. Like all mystics he does not counsel these things because he cannot have wealth, power, luxury, but because he profoundly distrusts them. It is not that the world fails to satisfy him, but that at its best it cannot satisfy the spirit. It can only distract the soul; hence the necessity of a "rule" by which these distractions may be conquered. Distraction once conquered, the joy of vision will follow. That vision will be peace. To "keep holiday and rest from every external care" is to find felicity added to us.

It is the fashion in the modern world to decry this kind of mysticism as a form of escape, as if escape itself were necessarily evil. Escape may be an avenue to good. It is wisdom to escape from evil. Thomas à Kempis is simply one of that long line of quietists who feel that it is external existence itself

that is the great disaster. We are but strangers here; heaven
is our home. No improvement in temporal conditions can
overcome the essential disease of time itself. The *Imitation*
is the little Bible of those who would go home, and find themselves in the quiet ecstasy of union with the eternal. All this
monk's comments on life and the world are simply suggestions
as to how to overcome the obstacles that hold us here, that
hold us back, that keep us blindfolded.

We know much more about Sir Thomas Browne than we
do about Thomas à Kempis. Furthermore, unlike *The Imitation of Christ,* the *Religio Medici* is not the only great book he
wrote. It happens to be the one that, in this connection, concerns us. It is not the book of a schematically trained thinker
like Boethius, nor does it have the simple mystical piety of
Thomas à Kempis. It is the meandering and meditative credo
of a half credulous, half sophisticated mind.

It was written by its author when he was thirty years old,
and intended for private circulation among his friends. When
news of its printed publication reached the good doctor, he
published a corrected version himself. The book has been
persuasive for rather different reasons than the two others
included in this volume. It is, in the first place, of course, a
classic in its own right in its deliberately towering and gran-
diose prose. It is secular church music. It is also a secular piece
of theology which its author himself knew could well be suspect
to orthodox believers. It is subtle and simple all at once. It is
full of philosophical insight and of current superstition. It
is packed with curious and also with debatable learning. It is
both tolerant and impatient.

But what gives it an appeal more than that of quaintness
or meditative music is the sense it communicates of a genu-
inely religious mind, too religious to be the slave of any narrow
orthodoxy, too sophisticated to condition its faith on the
demonstration of logic. Finally, the book has both an urbane
tolerance of rival sects and, particularly strange in the England of the period, of Catholicism, and of infidels. It has also

an almost smug Anglicanism, and Sir Thomas Browne (though rather more so in his other works) reveals the most childish superstitions. Yet he can also rise, in his own phrase, to an *O Altitudo!* There are a plumbing of mystical depths, a scaling of heights of speculation, a range of cosmic imagination that are an elevation to the soul of the reader carried along by the glories of the latinized and long-cadenced prose.

Sir Thomas Browne's *Religio Medici* is read for many reasons. Some read it, and justly enough, for the sheer magic of its prose sublimities, full of idiosyncrasy, but as grand and moving rhythms as exist in the English language. They remind one, with their swellings of passion, their modulations of tone and of feeling, of something that belongs almost more to the history of music than to the history of literature.

But the *Religio Medici* is read, too, for its enlightening intellectual eccentricity. It follows no marked line of orthodoxy or of scepticism. It explores the paradoxes familiar to all human beings who have felt they cannot be taken in by reason any more than they can by superstition. Thomas Browne was a physician and had caught the experimental habit of mind current in that Royal Society which never quite trusted his experimental habit of mind sufficiently to make him a member of it. For he realized that what reason can explore is a narrow land bounded by the oceans of mystery which it cannot fathom. A less agonized Pascal, he was not so much frightened by the finite as intrigued by it. Like Tertullian, he says he wishes to believe because it is impossible. And his soul is delighted with the mysteries transcending common sense.

It is not often that one finds in one personality the mystic and the man of the world, the tolerant sceptic and the almost conventional pietist. Perhaps the combination could have occurred nowhere save in England, and in no circumstances save in those of a man as fortunately placed in life as Sir Thomas Browne. Englishmen have recurrently displayed a conventional acceptance of the Anglican forms of religion and religious practice, and privately uttered or espoused a mystical intensity not native to English church mores. Tolerance is bred by happy personal circumstances. Where one is free, intellectual scepticism can almost amusedly consort, as it does in Sir Thomas Browne, with the greatest regularity of outward, and even considerable inward, conformity.

Sir Thomas Browne was born in 1605, and lived until 1682. Through the Civil War he lived in retirement (his strong royalist sentiments never actively expressed) in the country town of Norwich. In his youth he was a student in France and Italy, studied medicine at Montpellier and Padua, and took his medical degree at Leiden. He lived for most of his life at Norwich and practised medicine there. He devoted his leisure to the exploration of the antiquities of the city, and also, in Baconian fashion, of the fauna of the district. Like Bacon, he mixed "science" with the oddest superstitions, which are evident in him even when he is presumably critically examining the *Vulgar Errors* (the title of one of the most famous and characteristic of his works). He corresponded with many of the learned of the time both in England and abroad, but he himself did not make, and was not by his competent contemporaries thought to have made, any real contribution to science. He married and had ten children, one of whom became a distinguished physician. There seem to be no dramatic or tragic events in his life, and the history of his being is largely the history of his mind as revealed in his books.

That mind is an amalgam whose elements are noted above. But the quality of it can hardly be identified by its elements, and the contagion of it is the temper of the expression, the range of the metaphors and associations, the curious paradox and the musing "agreeable melancholy," as one contemporary French critic put it, of the whole. There have been better statements of both piety and scepticism, or even of the possible reconciliation of the two. But there have been few books which, like the *Religio Medici,* so convey the sense of mystery, the insistence of paradox, the intimations of both eternity and of oblivion in the most ordinary of human experiences. Even the "music of taverns" carries him—and the reader—off into cosmic dimensions:

> There is in it something of divinity, more than the ear discovers: it is an hieroglyphical and shadowed lesson on the whole world, and creatures of God, such a melody to the ear as the whole world, well understood, would afford to the understanding.

It is for this note of mystical sublimity, harmonized somehow with a humorous curiosity and worldliness, that Browne is most cherished. We know that he was an obstinate anti-Copernican, that he believed in witchcraft, that, in the light of that belief, he gave testimony at a trial which sent two women to their deaths. One forgets the eccentric and the reactionary in the mystical soliloquist, in the rhapsodist of the infinite. In the *Garden of Cyrus* and *Urn Burial* he has much to say about tombs and about oblivion. He is forever, like John Donne (of whom in some respects he is a prose analogue), meditating on the singular connections and interweavings of death and immortality.

> This is that mystical philosophy, from whence no true scholar becomes an atheist, but from the visible effects of nature grows up a real divine, and beholds, not in a dream, as Ezekiel, but in an ocular and visible object, the types of his resurrection.

The writers of mystical philosophy generally fly off in their prose to the most abstract regions of the empyrean. But what makes Sir Thomas Browne so engaging is that he can connect the grandest reaches of cosmic speculation with the minutiae of creation, and loves to watch the habits of bees and ants and spiders. He finds that "in these narrow engines there is more curious mathematics and that the civility of these little citizens more neatly sets forth the wisdom of their maker."

What makes the book most endearing is that Browne furthermore finds (not altogether unlike Thomas à Kempis) the lesson of Heaven in the text of himself. Emerson and St. Augustine could both have written the following sentences:

> We carry with us the wonders we seek without us; there is all Africa and her prodigies in us. We are that bold and adventurous piece of nature he that studies wisely learns in a compendium that others labor at in a divided piece and endless volume.

And the compendium of his own soul is wonderfully attractive in its whimsical tolerance, its oddities of lore and learning, its revelation of an equable, exploring, and sensitive mind:

> I perceive [says our author] that every man is his best Oedipus, and will find a way to loose those bonds wherewith the subtleties of error have enchained more flexible and tender judgments.

The rotund phrases do not conceal a generosity of temper that is no less attractive now when new fanaticisms have assailed the world. In the very orotundity, too, is an escape into a grand and retrieving music.

Here, then, are three books, of three different periods, by different personalities. One is an argument; the second a set, almost, of spiritual exercises; the third the diary of a serene but acute spirit. Each in its own way provides the "consolation of philosophy"—of philosophy not in the sense of professional argument, but that wisdom the soul finds when it succeeds in speaking to itself with clarity and candor. Our three authors each succeeded in thus speaking to himself and therefore to all and for all troubled spirits everywhere, in their times and in ours. The beauty of their expression, moreover, illustrates the comment Socrates makes in the *Phaedo*, that philosophy is perhaps "a finer kind of music." That music amid the terrifying clamors of war has its special healing power.

New York
December, 1942

THE CONSOLATION OF PHILOSOPHY

BY BOETHIUS

TRANSLATED BY
W. V. COOPER

THE CONSOLATION OF PHILOSOPHY

BOOK ONE

(Boethius bewails his changed circumstances.)

"To pleasant songs my work was erstwhile given, and bright were all my labours then; but now in tears to sad refrains am I compelled to turn. Thus my maimed Muses guide my pen, and gloomy songs make no feigned tears bedew my face. Then could no fear so overcome to leave me companionless upon my way. They were the pride of my earlier bright-lived days: in my later gloomy days they are the comfort of my fate; for hastened by unhappiness has age come upon me without warning, and grief hath set within me the old age of her gloom. White hairs are scattered untimely on my head, and the skin hangs loosely from my worn-out limbs.

"Happy is that death which thrusts not itself upon men in their pleasant years, yet comes to them at the oft-repeated cry of their sorrow. Sad is it how death turns away from the unhappy with so deaf an ear, and will not close, cruel, the eyes that weep. Ill is it to trust to Fortune's fickle bounty, and while yet she smiled upon me, the hour of gloom had well-nigh overwhelmed my head. Now has the cloud put off its alluring face, wherefore without scruple my life drags out its wearying delays.

"Why, O my friends, did ye so often puff me up, telling me that I was fortunate? For he that is fallen low did never firmly stand."

(Philosophy approaches Boethius:
the form of her appearance is allegorical.)

While I was pondering thus in silence, and using my pen to set down so tearful a complaint, there appeared standing over

my head a woman's form, whose countenance was full of majesty, whose eyes shown as with fire and in power of insight
surpassed the eyes of men, whose colour was full of life, whose
strength was yet intact though she was so full of years that
none would ever think that she was subject to such age as ours.
One could but doubt her varying stature, for at one moment
she repressed it to the common measure of a man, at another
she seemed to touch with her crown the very heavens: and
when she had raised higher her head, it pierced even the sky
and baffled the sight of those who would look upon it. Her
clothing was wrought of the finest thread by subtle workman-
ship brought to an indivisible piece. This had she woven with
her own hands, as I afterwards did learn by her own shewing.
Their beauty was somewhat dimmed by the dulness of long
neglect, as is seen in the smoke-grimed masks of our ancestors.
On the border below was inwoven the symbol Π, on that above
was to be read a θ.[1] And between the two letters there could
be marked degrees, by which, as by the rungs of a ladder,
ascent might be made from the lower principle to the higher.
Yet the hands of rough men had torn this garment and
snatched such morsels as they could therefrom. In her right
hand she carried books, in her left was a sceptre brandished.

When she saw that the Muses of poetry were present by
my couch giving words to my lamenting, she was stirred a
while; her eyes flashed fiercely, and said she, "Who has suffered these seducing mummers to approach this sick man?
Never do they support those in sorrow by any healing remedies, but rather do ever foster the sorrow by poisonous sweets.
These are they who stifle the fruit-bearing harvest of reason
with the barren briars of the passions: they free not the minds
of men from disease, but accustom them thereto. I would think
it less grievous if your allurements drew away from me some
uninitiated man, as happens in the vulgar herd. In such an
one my labours would be naught harmed, but this man has
been nourished in the lore of Eleatics and Academics; and to

[1] Π and θ are the first letters of the Greek words denoting Practical
and Theoretical, the two divisions of philosophy.

him have ye reached? Away with you, Sirens, seductive unto destruction! leave him to my Muses to be cared for and to be healed."

Their band thus rated cast a saddened glance upon the ground, confessing their shame in blushes, and passed forth dismally over the threshold. For my part, my eyes were dimmed with tears, and I could not discern who was this woman of such commanding power. I was amazed, and turning my eyes to the ground I began in silence to await what she should do. Then she approached nearer and sat down upon the end of my couch: she looked into my face heavy with grief and cast down by sorrow to the ground, and then she raised her complaint over the trouble of my mind in these words.

"Ah me! how blunted grows the mind when sunk below the o'erwhelming flood! Its own true light no longer burns within, and it would break forth to outer darkness. How often care, when fanned by earthly winds, grows to a larger and unmeasured bane. This man has been free to the open heaven: his habit has it been to wander into the paths of the sky: his to watch the light of the bright sun, his to inquire into the brightness of the chilly moon; he, like a conqueror, held fast bound in its order every star that makes its wandering circle, turning its peculiar course. Nay, more, deeply has he searched into the springs of nature, whence came the roaring blasts that ruffle the ocean's bosom calm: what is the spirit that makes the firmament revolve; wherefore does the evening star sink into the western wave but to rise from the radiant East; what is the cause which so tempers the season of Spring that it decks the earth with rose-blossoms; whence comes it to pass that Autumn is prolific in the years of plenty and overflows with teeming vines: deeply to search these causes was his wont, and to bring forth secrets deep in Nature hid.

"Now he lies there; extinct his reason's light, his neck in heavy chains thrust down, his countenance with grievous weight downcast; ah! the brute earth is all he can behold.

"But now," said she, "is the time for the physician's art, rather than for complaining." Then fixing her eyes wholly on me, she said, "Are you the man who was nourished upon the milk of my learning, brought up with my food until you had won your way to the power of a manly soul? Surely I had given you such weapons as would keep you safe, and your strength unconquered; if you had not thrown them away. Do you know me? Why do you keep silence? Are you dumb from shame or from dull amazement? I would it were from shame, but I see that amazement has overwhelmed you."

When she saw that I was not only silent, but utterly tongue-tied and dumb, she put her hand gently upon my breast, and said, "There is no danger: he is suffering from drowsiness, that disease which attacks so many minds which have been deceived. He has forgotten himself for a moment and will quickly remember, as soon as he recognises me. That he may do so, let me brush away from his eyes the darkening cloud of thoughts of matters perishable." So saying, she gathered her robe into a fold and dried my swimming eyes.

Then was dark night dispelled, the shadows fled away, and my eyes received returning power as before. 'Twas just as when the heavenly bodies are enveloped by the west wind's rush, and the sky stands thick with watery clouds; the sun is hidden and the stars are not yet come into the sky, and night descending from above o'erspreads the earth: but if the north wind smites this scene, launched forth from the Thracian cave, it unlocks the imprisoned daylight; the sun shines forth, and thus sparkling Phœbus smites with his rays our wondering eyes.

(Boethius gains power to address Philosophy.)

In such a manner were the clouds of grief scattered. Then I drew breath again and engaged my mind in taking knowledge of my physician's countenance. So when I turned my eyes towards her and fixed my gaze upon her, I recognised my nurse, Philosophy, in whose chambers I had spent my life from earliest manhood. And I asked her, "Wherefore have you, mistress of all virtues, come down from heaven above to visit my lonely place of banishment? Is it that you, as well as I, may be harried, the victim of false charges?" "Should I," said she, "desert you, my nursling?

(Philosophy chides his lack of courage.)

Should I not share and bear my part of the burden which has been laid upon you from spite against my name? Surely Philosophy never allowed herself to let the innocent go upon their journey unbefriended. Think you I would fear calumnies? That I would be terrified as though they were a new misfortune? Think you that this is the first time that wisdom has been harassed by dangers among men of shameless ways? In ancient days before the time of my child, Plato, have we not as well as nowadays fought many a mighty battle against the recklessness of folly? And though Plato did survive, did not his master, Socrates, win his victory of an unjust death, with me present at his side? When after him the followers of Epicurus, and in turn the Stoics, and then others did all try their utmost to seize his legacy, they dragged me, for all my cries and struggles, as though to share me as plunder; they tore my robe which I had woven with mine own hands, and snatched away the fragments thereof: and when they thought I had altogether yielded myself to them, they departed. And since among them were to be seen certain signs of my outward bearing, others ill-advised did think they wore my livery: thus were many of them undone by the errors of the herd of uninitiated. But if you have not heard of the exile of Anaxagoras,[1] nor the poison drunk by Socrates,[2] nor the torture of Zeno,[3] which all were of foreign lands, yet you may know of Canius,[4] Seneca,[5] and

---

[1] Anaxagoras went into exile from Athens about 450 B.C.
[2] Socrates was executed by the Athenian state, B.C. 309.
[3] Zeno of Elea was tortured by Nearchus, tyrant of Elea, about 440 B.C.
[4] Canius was put to death by Caligula, *c.* A.D. 40.
[5] Seneca was driven to commit suicide by Nero, A.D. 65.

Soranus,[1] whose fame is neither small nor passing old. Naught else brought them to ruin but that, being built up in my ways, they appeared at variance with the desires of unscrupulous men. So it is no matter for your wonder if, in this sea of life, we are tossed about by storms from all sides; for to oppose evil men is the chief aim we set before ourselves. Though the band of such men is great in numbers, yet it is to be contemned: for it is guided by no leader, but is hurried along at random only by error running riot everywhere. If this band when warring against us presses too strongly upon us, our leader, Reason, gathers her forces into her citadel, while the enemy are busied in plundering useless baggage. As they seize the most worthless things, we laugh at them from above, untroubled by the whole band of mad marauders, and we are defended by that rampart to which riotous folly may not hope to attain.

"He who has calmly reconciled his life to fate, and set proud death beneath his feet, can look fortune in the face, unbending both to good and bad: his countenance unconquered he can shew. The rage and threatenings of the sea will not move him though they stir from its depths the upheaving swell: Vesuvius's furnaces may never so often burst forth, and he may send rolling upwards smoke and fire; the lightning, whose wont it is to smite down lofty towers, may flash upon its way, but such men shall they never move. Why then stand they wretched and aghast when fierce tyrants rage in impotence? Fear naught, and hope naught: thus shall you have a weak man's rage disarmed. But whoso fears with trembling, or desires aught from them, he stands not firmly rooted, but dependent: thus has he thrown away his shield; he can be rooted up, and he links for himself the very chain whereby he may be dragged.

"Are such your experiences, and do they sink into your soul?" she asked. "Do you listen only as 'the dull ass to the

---

[1] Soranus was condemned to death by Nero, A.D. 66.

lyre'? Why do you weep? Wherefore flow your tears? 'Speak, nor keep secret in thine heart.' If you expect a physician to help you, you must lay bare your wound."

(Boethius complains to Philosophy of his sufferings after his just life.)

Then did I rally my spirit till it was strong again, and answered, "Does the savage bitterness of my fortune still need recounting? Does it not stand forth plainly enough of itself? Does not the very aspect of this place strike you? Is this the library which you had chosen for yourself as your sure resting-place in my house? Is this the room in which you would so often tarry with me expounding the philosophy of things human and divine? Was my condition like this, or my countenance, when I probed with your aid the secrets of nature, when you marked out with a wand the courses of the stars, when you shaped our habits and the rule of all our life by the pattern of the universe? [1] Are these the rewards we reap by yielding ourselves to you? Nay, you yourself have established this saying by the mouth of Plato, that commonwealths would be blessed if they were guided by those who made wisdom their study, or if those who guided them would make wisdom their study.[2] By the mouth of that same great man did you teach that this was the binding reason why a commonwealth should be governed by philosophers, namely that the helm of government should not be left to unscrupulous or criminal citizens lest they should bring corruption and ruin upon the good citizens.[3] Since, then, I had learned from you in quiet and inaction of this view, I followed it further, for I desired to practise it in public government. You and God Himself, who has grafted you in the minds of philosophers, are my witnesses that never have I applied myself to any office of state except that I might work for the common welfare of all good men.

[1] Boethius means that his chief "philosophical" studies had been physics, astronomy, and ethics.
[2] Plato, *Repub.* v. 473.
[3] Plato, *Repub.* vi. 488, 489.

Thence followed bitter quarrels with evil men which could not be appeased, and, for the sake of preserving justice, contempt of the enmity of those in power, for this is the result of a free and fearless conscience. How often have I withstood Conigastus [1] to his face, whenever he has attacked a weak man's fortune! How often have I turned by force Trigulla, [1] the overseer of the Emperor's household, from an unjust act that he had begun or even carried out! How many times have I put my own authority in danger by protecting those wretched people who were harried with unending false charges by the greed of barbarian Goths which ever went unpunished! Never, I say, has any man depraved me from justice to injustice. My heart has ached as bitterly as those of the sufferers when I have seen the fortunes of our subjects ruined both by the rapacity of persons and the taxes of the state. Again, in a time of severe famine, a grievous, intolerable sale by compulsion was decreed in Campania, and devastation threatened that province. Then I undertook for the sake of the common welfare a struggle against the commander of the Imperial guard; though the king was aware of it, I fought against the enforcement of the sale, and fought successfully. Paulinus was a man who had been consul: the jackals of the court had in their own hopes and desires already swallowed up his possessions, but I snatched him from their very gaping jaws. I exposed myself to the hatred of the treacherous informer Cyprian, that I might prevent Albinus, also a former consul, being overwhelmed by the penalty of a trumped-up charge. Think you that I have raised up against myself bitter and great quarrels enough? But I ought to have been safer among those whom I helped; for, from my love of justice, I laid up for myself among the courtiers no resource to which I might turn for safety. Who, further, were the informers upon whose evidence I was banished? One was Basilius: he was formerly expelled from the royal service, and was driven by debt to inform

---

[1] Conigastus and Trigulla were favourite officers of the Emperor, Theodoric, the Goth: they used their influence with him for the oppression of the weak.

against me. Again, Opilio and Gaudentius had been con-·
demned to exile by the king for many unjust acts and crimes:
this decree they would not obey, and they sought sanctuary in
sacred buildings, but when the king was aware of it, he declared that if they departed not from Ravenna before a certain
day, they should be driven forth branded upon their fore-
heads. What could be more stringent than this? Yet upon that
very day information against me was laid by these same men
and accepted. Why so? Did my character deserve this treatment? Or did my prearranged condemnation give credit and
justification to my accusers? Did Fortune feel no shame for
this? If not for innocence calumniated, at any rate for the
baseness of the calumniators?

"Would you learn the sum of the charges against me? It
was said that 'I had desired the safety of the Senate.' You
would learn in what way. I was charged with 'having hindered
an informer from producing papers by which the Senate could
be accused of treason.' What think you, my mistress? Shall I
deny it lest it shame you? Nay, I did desire the safety of the
Senate, nor shall ever cease to desire it. Shall I confess it?
Then there would have been no need to hinder an informer.
Shall I call it a crime to have wished for the safety of that
order? By its own decrees concerning myself it has established
that this is a crime. Though want of foresight often deceives
itself, it cannot alter the merits of facts, and, in obedience to
the Senate's command, I cannot think it right to hide the
truth or to assent to falsehood.

"However, I leave it to your judgment and that of philosophers to decide how the justice of this may be; but I have
committed to writing for history the true course of events,
that posterity may not be ignorant thereof. I think it unnecessary to speak of the forged letters through which I am accused
of 'hoping for the freedom of Rome.' Their falsity would have
been apparent if I had been free to question the evidence of
the informers themselves, for their confessions have much
force in all such business.

"But what avails it? No liberty is left to hope for. Would

there were any! I would answer in the words of Canius, who
was accused by Gaius Cæsar,[1] Germanicus's son, of being
cognisant of a plot against himself: 'If I had known of it, you
would not have.'

"And in this matter grief has not so blunted my powers that
I should complain of wicked men making impious attacks
upon virtue: but at this I do wonder, that they should hope
to succeed. Evil desires are, it may be, due to our natural fail-
ings, but that the conceptions of any wicked mind should prevail against innocence while God watches over us, seems to me
unnatural. Wherefore not without cause has one of your own
followers asked, 'If God is, whence come evil things? If He
is not, whence come good?'

"Again, let impious men, who thirst for the blood of the
whole Senate and of all good citizens, be allowed to wish for
the ruin of us too whom they recognise as champions of the
Senate and all good citizens: but surely such as I have not
deserved the same hatred from the members of the Senate too?

"Since you were always present to guide me in my words
and my deeds, I think you remember what happened at
Verona. When King Theodoric, desiring the common ruin of
the Senate, was for extending to the whole order the charge
of treason laid against Albinus, you remember how I laboured
to defend the innocence of the order without any care for my
own danger? You know that I declare this truthfully and with
no boasting praise of self. For the secret value of a conscience,
that approves its own action, is lessened somewhat each time
that it receives the reward of fame by displaying its deeds. But
you see what end has fallen upon my innocency. In the place of
the rewards of honest virtue, I am suffering the punishments
of an ill deed that was not mine. And did ever any direct confession of a crime find its judges so well agreed upon exercising
harshness, that neither the liability of the human heart to err,
nor the changeableness of the fortune of all mankind, could
yield one dissentient voice? If it had been said that I had
wished to burn down temples, to murder with sacrilegious

[1] The Emperor Caligula.

sword their priests, that I had planned the massacre of all good citizens, even so I should have been present to plead guilty or to be convicted, before the sentence was executed. But here am I, nearly five hundred miles away, without the opportunity of defending myself, condemned to death and the confiscation of my property because of my too great zeal for the Senate. Ah! well have they deserved that none should ever be liable to be convicted on such a charge! Even those who laid information have seen the honour of this accusation, for, that they might blacken it with some criminal ingredient, they had need to lie, saying that I had violated my conscience by using unholy means to obtain offices corruptly. But you, by being planted within me, dispelled from the chamber of my soul all craving for that which perishes, and where your eyes were looking there could be no place for any such sacrilege. For you instilled into my ears, and thus into my daily thoughts, that saying of Pythagoras, 'Follow after God.' Nor was it seemly that I, whom you had built up to such excellence that you made me as a god, should seek the support of the basest wills of men. Yet, further, the innocent life within my home, my gathering of most honourable friends, my father-in-law Symmachus,[1] a man esteemed no less in his public life than for his private conscientiousness, these all put far from me all suspicion of this crime. But—O the shame of it!—it is from you that they think they derive the warrant for such a charge, and we seem to them to be allied to ill-doing from this very fact that we are steeped in the principles of your teaching, and trained in your manners of life. Thus it is not enough that my deep respect for you has profited me nothing, but you yourself have received wanton contumely from the hatred that had rather fallen on me. Yet besides this, is another load added to my heap of woes: the judgment of the world looks not to the deserts of the case, but to the evolution of chance, and holds that only this has been intended which good fortune may chance to foster: whence it comes that the good opinion of the world is the first to desert the unfortunate. It

[1] Symmachus was executed by Theodoric at the same time as Boethius.

is wearisome to recall what were the tales by people told,
or how little their many various opinions agreed. This alone
I would fain say: it is the last burden laid upon us by unkind
fortune, that when any charge is invented to be fastened upon
unhappy men, they are believed to have deserved all they have
to bear. For kindness I have received persecutions; I have
been driven from all my possessions, stripped of my honours,
and stained for ever in my reputation. I think I see the intoxi-
cation of joy in the sin-steeped dens of criminals: I see the
most abandoned of men intent upon new and evil schemes of
spying: I see honest men lying crushed with the fear which
smites them after the result of my perilous case: wicked men
one and all encouraged to dare every crime without fear of
punishment, nay, with hope of rewards for the accomplishment thereof: the innocent I see robbed not merely of their
peace and safety, but even of all chance of defending themselves. So then I may cry aloud:—

"Founder of the star-studded universe, resting on Thine
eternal throne whence Thou turnest the swiftly rolling sky,
and bindest the stars to keep Thy law; at Thy word the moon
now shines brightly with full face, ever turned to her brother's
light, and so she dims the lesser lights; or now she is herself
obscured, for nearer to the sun her beams shew her pale horns
alone. Cool rises the evening star at night's first drawing nigh:
the same is the morning star who casts off the harness that she
bore before, and paling meets the rising sun. When winter's
cold doth strip the trees, Thou settest a shorter span to day.
And Thou, when summer comes to warm, dost change the
short divisions of the night. Thy power doth order the seasons
of the year, so that the western breeze of spring brings back
the leaves which winter's north wind tore away; so that the
dog-star's heat makes ripe the ears of corn whose seed Arcturus watched. Naught breaks that ancient law: naught leaves
undone the work appointed to its place. Thus all things Thou
dost rule with limits fixed: the lives of men alone dost Thou
scorn to restrain, as a guardian, within bounds. For why does

Fortune with her fickle hand deal out such changing lots? The hurtful penalty is due to crime, but falls upon the sinless head: depraved men rest at ease on thrones aloft, and by their unjust lot can spurn beneath their hurtful heel the necks of virtuous men. Beneath obscuring shadows lies bright virtue hid: the just man bears the unjust's infamy. They suffer not for forsworn oaths, they suffer not for crimes glozed over with their lies. But when their will is to put forth their strength, with triumph they subdue the mightiest kings whom peoples in their thousands fear. O Thou who dost weave the bonds of Nature's self, look down upon this pitiable earth! Mankind is no base part of this great work, and we are tossed on Fortune's wave. Restrain, our Guardian, the engulfing surge, and as Thou dost the unbounded heaven rule, with a like bond make true and firm these lands."

(*Philosophy reassures him.*)

While I grieved thus in long-drawn pratings, Philosophy looked on with a calm countenance, not one whit moved by my complaints. Then said she, "When I saw you in grief and in tears I knew thereby that you were unhappy and in exile, but I knew not how distant was your exile until your speech declared it. But you have not been driven so far from your home; you have wandered thence yourself: or if you would rather hold that you have been driven, you have been driven by yourself rather than by any other. No other could have done so to you. For if you recall your true native country, you know that it is not under the rule of the many-headed people, as was Athens of old, but there is one Lord, one King, who rejoices in the greater number of his subjects, not in their banishment. To be guided by his reins, to bow to his justice, is the highest liberty. Know you not that sacred and ancient law of your own state by which it is enacted that no man, who would establish a dwelling-place for himself therein, may lawfully be put forth? For there is no fear that any man should merit exile, if he be kept safe therein by its protecting walls. But any man that may no longer wish to dwell there, does equally no longer deserve to be there. Wherefore it is your looks rather than the aspect of this place which disturb me.[1] It is not the walls of your library, decked with ivory and glass, that I need, but rather the resting-place in your heart, wherein I have not stored books, but I have of old put that which gives value to books, a store of thoughts from books of mine. As to your services to the common weal, you have spoken truly, though but scantily, if you consider your manifold exertions. Of all wherewith you have been charged either truthfully or falsely, you have but recorded what is well known. As for the crimes and wicked lies of the informers, you have rightly thought fit to touch but shortly thereon, for they are better and more fruitfully made common in the mouth of the crowd that discusses all matters. You have loudly and strongly upbraided the unjust ingratitude of the Senate: you have grieved over the charges made against myself, and shed tears over the insult to my fair fame: your last outburst of wrath was against Fortune, when you complained that she paid no fair rewards according to deserts: finally, you have prayed with passionate Muse that the same peace and order, that are seen in the heavens, might also rule the earth. But you are overwhelmed by this variety of mutinous passions: grief, rage, and gloom tear your mind asunder, and so in this present mood stronger measures cannot yet come nigh to heal you. Let us therefore use gentler means, and since, just as matter in the body hardens into a swelling, so have these disquieting influences, let these means soften by kindly handling the unhealthy spot, until it will bear a sharper remedy.

"When the sign of the crab doth scorch the field, fraught with the sun's most grievous rays, the husbandman that has freely intrusted his seed to the fruitless furrow, is cheated by the faithless harvest-goddess; and he must turn him to the oak tree's fruit.

"When the field is scarred by the bleak north winds, wouldst thou seek the wood's dark carpet to gather violets?

[1] *Cp.*, p. 9.

If thou wilt enjoy the grapes, wouldst thou seek with clutching hand to prune the vines in spring? 'Tis in autumn Bacchus brings his gifts. Thus God marks out the times and fits to them peculiar works: He has set out a course of change, and lets no confusion come. If aught betake itself to headlong ways, and leaves its sure design, ill will the outcome be thereto.

"First then," she continued, "will you let me find out and make trial of the state of your mind by a few small questions, so that I may understand what should be the method of your treatment?"

"Ask," said I, "what your judgment would have you ask, and I will answer you."

Then said she, "Think you that this universe is guided only at random and by mere chance? Or think you there is any rule of reason constituted in it?"

"No, never would I think it could be so, nor believe that such sure motions could be made at random or by chance. I know that God, the founder of the universe, does overlook His work; nor ever may that day come which shall drive me to abandon this belief as untrue."

"So is it," she said, "and even so you cried just now, and only mourned that mankind alone has no part in this divine guardianship: you were fixed in your belief that all other things are ruled by reason. Yet, how strange! how much I wonder how it is that you can be so sick though you are set in such a health-giving state of mind! But let us look deeper into it: I cannot but think there is something lacking. Since you are not in doubt that the universe is ruled by God, tell me by what method you think that government is guided?"

"I scarcely know the meaning of your question; much less can I answer it."

"Was I wrong," said she, "to think that something was lacking, that there was some opening in your armour, some way by which this distracting disease has crept into your soul? But tell me, do you remember what is the aim and end of all things? What the object to which all nature tends?"

"I have heard indeed, but grief has blunted my memory."

"But do you not somehow know whence all things have their source?"

"Yes," I said; "that source is God."

"Is it possible that you, who know the beginning of all things, should not know their end? But such are the ways of these distractions, such is their power, that though they can move a man's position, they cannot pluck him from himself or wrench him from his roots. But this question would I have you answer: do you remember that you are a man?"

"How can I but remember that?"

"Can you then say what is a man?"

"Need you ask? I know that he is an animal, reasoning and mortal; that I know, and that I confess myself to be."

"Know you naught else that you are?" asked Philosophy.

"Naught," said I.

"Now," said she, "I know the cause, or the chief cause, of your sickness. You have forgotten what you are. Now therefore I have found out to the full the manner of your sickness, and how to attempt the restoring of your health. You are overwhelmed by this forgetfulness of yourself: hence you have been thus sorrowing that you are exiled and robbed of all your possessions. You do not know the aim and end of all things; hence you think that if men are worthless and wicked, they are powerful and fortunate. You have forgotten by what methods the universe is guided; hence you think that the chances of good and bad fortune are tossed about with no ruling hand. These things may lead not to disease only, but even to death as well. But let us thank the Giver of all health, that your nature has not altogether left you. We have yet the chief spark for your health's fire, for you have a true knowledge of the hand that guides the universe: you do believe that its government is not subject to random chance, but to divine reason. Therefore have no fear. From this tiny spark the fire of life shall forthwith shine upon you. But it is not time to use severer remedies, and since we know that it is the way of all minds to clothe themselves ever in false opinions as they throw off the true, and these false ones breed a dark distraction which confuses the true insight, therefore will I try to lessen this darkness for a while with gentle applications of easy remedies, that so the shadows of deceiving passions may be dissipated, and you may have power to perceive the brightness of true light."

"When the stars are hidden by black clouds, no light can they afford. When the boisterous south wind rolls along the sea and stirs the surge, the water, but now as clear as glass, bright as the fair sun's light, is dark, impenetrable to sight, with stirred and scattered sand. The stream, that wanders down the mountain's side, must often find a stumbling-block, a stone within its path torn from the hill's own rock. So too shalt thou: if thou wouldst see the truth in undimmed light, choose the straight road, the beaten path; away with passing ioys! away with fear! put vain hopes to flight! and grant no place to grief! Where these distractions reign, the mind is clouded o'er, the soul is bound in chains."

BOOK TWO

(Philosophy would prove that his opinions and his griefs are not justified in one of her followers.)

THEN for a while she held her peace. But when her silence, so discreet, made my thoughts to cease from straying, she thus began to speak: "If I have thoroughly learned the causes and the manner of your sickness, your former good fortune has so affected you that you are being consumed by longing for it. The change of this alone has overturned your peace of mind through your own imagination. I understand the varied disguises of that unnatural state. I know how Fortune is ever most friendly and alluring to those whom she strives to deceive, until she overwhelms them with grief beyond bearing, by deserting them when least expected. If you recall her nature, her ways, or her deserts, you will see that you never had in her, nor have lost with her, aught that was lovely. Yet, I think, I shall not need great labour to recall this to your memory. For then too, when she was at your side with all her flattery, you were wont to reproach her in strong and manly terms; and to revile her with the opinions that you had gathered in worship of me with my favoured ones. But no sudden change of outward affairs can ever come without some upheaval in the mind. Thus has it followed that you, like others, have fallen somewhat away from your calm peace of mind. But it is time now for you to make trial of some gentle and pleasant draught, which by reaching your inmost parts shall prepare the way for yet stronger healing draughts. Try therefore the assuring influence of gentle argument which keeps its straight path only when it holds fast to my instructions. And with this art of orators let my handmaid, the art of song, lend her aid in chanting light or weighty harmonies as we desire.

"What is it, mortal man, that has cast you down into grief and mourning? You have seen something unwonted, it would seem, something strange to you. But if you think that Fortune has changed towards you, you are wrong. These are ever her ways: this is her very nature. She has with you preserved her own constancy by her very change. She was ever changeable at the time when she smiled upon you, when she was mocking you with the allurements of false good fortune. You have discovered both the different faces of the blind goddess. To the eyes of others she is veiled in part: to you she has made herself wholly known. If you find her welcome, make use of her ways, and so make no complaining. If she fills you with horror by her treachery, treat her with despite; thrust her away from you, for she tempts you to your ruin. For though she is the cause of this great trouble for you, she ought to have been the subject of calmness and peace. For no man can ever make himself sure that she will never desert him, and thus has she deserted you. Do you reckon such happiness to be prized, which is sure to pass away? Is good fortune dear to you, which is with you for a time and is not sure to stay, and which is sure to bring you unhappiness when it is gone? But seeing that it cannot be stayed at will, and that when it flees away it leaves misery behind, what is such a fleeting thing but a sign of coming misery? Nor should it ever satisfy any man to look only at that which is placed before his eyes. Prudence takes measure of the results to come from all things. The very changeableness of good and bad makes Fortune's threats no more fearful, nor her smiles to be desired. And lastly, when you have once put your neck beneath the yoke of Fortune, you must with steadfast heart bear whatever comes to pass within her realm. But if you would dictate the law by which she whom you have freely chosen to be your mistress must stay or go, surely you will be acting without justification; and your very impatience will make more bitter a lot which you cannot change. If you set your sails before the wind, will you not move forward whither the wind drives you, not whither your will may choose to go? If you intrust your seed to the furrow, will you not weigh the rich years and the barren against each other? You have given yourself over to Fortune's rule, and you must bow yourself to your mistress's ways. Are you trying to stay the force of her turning wheel? Ah! dull-witted mortal, if Fortune begin to stay still, she is no longer Fortune.

"As thus she turns her wheel of chance with haughty hand, and presses on like the surge of Euripus's tides, fortune now tramples fiercely on a fearsome king, and now deceives no less a conquered man by raising from the ground his humbled face. She hears no wretch's cry, she heeds no tears, but wantonly she mocks the sorrow which her cruelty has made. This is her sport: thus she proves her power; if in the selfsame hour one man is raised to happiness, and cast down in despair, 'tis thus she shews her might.

(Philosophy shews how Fortune may plead her justification.)

"Now would I argue with you by these few words which Fortune herself might use: and do you consider whether her demands are fair. 'Why, O man,' she might say, 'do you daily accuse me with your complainings? What injustice have I wrought upon you? Of what good things have I robbed you? Choose your judge whom you will, and before him strive with me for the right to hold your wealth and honours. If you can prove that any one of these does truly belong to any mortal man, readily will I grant that these you seek to regain were yours. When nature brought you forth from your mother's womb, I received you in my arms naked and bare of all things; I cherished you with my gifts, and I brought you up all too kindly with my favouring care, wherefore now you cannot bear with me, and I surrounded you with glory and all the abundance that was mine to give. Now it pleases me to withdraw my hand: be thankful, as though you had lived upon my loans. You have no just cause of complaint, as though you had really lost what was once your own. Why do you rail against me? I have wrought no violence towards you. Wealth, honours, and all such are within my rights. They are my handmaids; they know their mistress; they come with me and go when I depart. Boldly will I say that if these, of whose loss you complain, were ever yours, you would never have lost them at all. Am I alone to be stayed from using my rightful power? The heavens may grant bright sunlit days, and hide the same beneath the shade of night. The year may deck the earth's countenance with flowers and fruits, and again wrap it with chilling clouds. The sea may charm with its smoothed surface, but no less justly it may soon bristle in storms with rough waves. Is the insatiate discontent of man to bind me to a constancy which belongs not to my ways? Herein lies my very strength; this is my unchanging sport. I turn my wheel that spins its circle fairly; I delight to make the lowest turn to the top, the highest to the bottom. Come you to the top if you will, but on this condition, that you think it no unfairness to sink when the rule of my game demands it. Do you not know my ways? Have you not heard how Crœsus,[1] king of Lydia, who filled even Cyrus with fear but a little earlier, was miserably put upon a pyre of burning faggots, but was saved by rain sent down from heaven? Have you forgotten how Paulus shed tears of respect for the miseries of his captive, King Perses?[2] For what else is the crying and the weeping in tragedies but for the happiness of kings overturned by the random blow of fortune? Have you never learnt in your youth the ancient allegory that in the threshold of Jove's hall there stand two vessels, one full of evil, and one of good? What if you have received more richly of the good? What if I have not ever withheld myself from you? What if my changing nature is itself a reason that you should hope

---

[1] The proverbially rich and happy king; defeated and condemned to death by Cyrus, king of Media, in 546 B.C., but spared by him.

[2] The last king of Macedonia, defeated at Pydna, 168 B.C., by L. Æmilius Paulus.

for better things? In any way, let not your spirit eat itself away: you are set in the sphere that is common to all, let your desire therefore be to live with your own lot in life, a subject of the kingdom of the world.

" 'If Plenty with o'erflowing horn scatter her wealth abroad, abundantly, as in the storm-tossed sea the sand is cast around, or so beyond all measure as the stars shine forth upon the studded sky in cloudless nights; though she never stay her hand, yet will the race of men still weep and wail. Though God accept their prayers freely and give gold with ungrudging hand, and deck with honours those who deserve them, yet when they are gotten, these gifts seem naught. Wild greed swallows what it has sought, and still gapes wide for more. What bit or bridle will hold within its course this headlong lust, when, whetted by abundance of rich gifts, the thirst for possession burns? Never call we that man rich who is ever trembling in haste and groaning for that he thinks he lacks.'

(Philosophy proceeds to justify Fortune in the balance of accounts with Boethius.)

"If Fortune should thus defend herself to you," said Philosophy, "you would have naught, I think, to utter on the other part. But if you have any just defence for your complaining, you must put it forward. We will grant you the opportunity of speaking."

Then I answered, "Those arguments have a fair form and are clothed with all the sweetness of speech and of song. When a man listens to them, they delight him; but only so long. The wretched have a deeper feeling of their misfortunes. Wherefore when these pleasing sounds fall no longer upon the ear, this deep-rooted misery again weighs down the spirit."

"It is so," she said. "For these are not the remedies for your sickness, but in some sort are the applications for your grief which chafes against its cure. When the time comes, I will apply those which are to penetrate deeply. But that you may not be content to think yourself wretched, remember how many and how great have been the occasions of your good fortune. I will not describe how, when you lost your father, men of the highest rank received you into their care: how you were chosen by the chief men in the state to be allied to them by marriage;[1] and you were dear to them before you were ever closely related; which is the most valuable of all relationships. Who hesitated to pronounce you most fortunate for the greatness of your wives' families, for their virtues, and for your blessings in your sons too? I need not speak of those things that are familiar, so I pass over the honours which are denied to most old men, but were granted to you when yet young. I choose to come to the unrivalled crown of your good fortune. If the enjoyment of anything mortal can weigh at all in the balance of good fortune, can your memory of one great day ever be extinguished by any mass of accumulated ills? I mean that day when you saw your two sons proceed forth from your house as consuls together, amid the crowding senators, the eager and applauding populace: when they sat down in the seats of honour and you delivered the speech of congratulation to the king, gaining thereby glory for your talent and your eloquence: when in the circus you sat in the place of honour between the consuls, and by a display of lavishness worthy of a triumphing general, you pleased to the full the multitude who were crowded around in expectation.

"While Fortune then favoured you, it seems you flaunted her, though she cherished you as her own darling. You carried off a bounty which she had never granted to any citizen before. Will you then balance accounts with Fortune? This is the first time that she has looked upon you with a grudging eye. If you think of your happy and unhappy circumstances both in number and in kind, you will not be able to say that you have not been fortunate until now. And if you think that you were not fortunate because these things have passed away

[1] Boethius's first wife was Elpis, daughter of Festus: his second was Rusticiana, daughter of Symmachus, a senator and consul, A.D. 485. His second wife was the mother of the two sons mentioned below.

which then seemed to bring happiness, these things too are passing away, which you now hold to be miserable, wherefore you cannot think that you are wretched now. Is this your first entrance upon the stage of life? Are you come here unprepared and a stranger to the scene? Think you that there is any certainty in the affairs of mankind, when you know that often one swift hour can utterly destroy a man? For though the chances of life may seldom be depended upon, yet the last day of a lifetime seems to be the end of Fortune's power, though it perhaps would stay. What, think you, should we therefore say; that you desert her by dying, or that she deserts you by leaving you?"

"When o'er the heaven Phœbus from his rose-red car begins to shed his light abroad, his flames oppress the paling stars and blunt their whitened rays. When the grove grows bright in spring with roses 'neath the west wind's warming breath, let but the cloudy gale once wildly blow, and their beauty is gone, the thorns alone remain. Often the sea is calmly glistening bright with all untroubled waves, but as often does the north wind stir them up, making the troubling tempest boil. If then the earth's own covering so seldom constant stays, if its changes are so great, shalt thou trust the brittle fortunes of mankind, have faith in fleeting good? For this is sure, and this is fixed by everlasting law, that naught which is brought to birth shall constant here abide."

(Boethius pleads that "sorrow's crown of sorrows is remembering happier things," and Philosophy answers him.)

Then I answered her, "Cherisher of all the virtues, you tell me but the truth: I cannot deny my rapid successes and my prosperity. But it is such remembrances that torment me more than others. For of all suffering from Fortune, the unhappiest misfortune is to have known a happy fortune."

"But," said Philosophy, "you are paying the penalty for your mistaken expectations, and with this you cannot justly charge your life's circumstances. If you are affected by this empty name of Fortune's gift of happiness, you must listen while I recall how many and how great are your sources of happiness: and thus, if you have possessed that which is the most precious among all Fortune's gifts, and if that is still safe and unharmed in your possession, you will never, while you keep these better gifts, be able to justly charge Fortune with unkindness. Firstly, your wife's father, Symmachus, is still living and hale; and what more precious glory has the human race than him? And he, because your worth is undiminished and your life still so valuable, is mourning for the injustice you suffer, this man who is wholly made up of wisdom and virtue. Again, your wife lives, a woman whose character is full of virtue, whose modesty excels its kind; a woman who (to put in a word the gifts she brought you) is like her father. She lives, and, hating this life, for your sake alone she clings to it. Herein only will I yield to allow you unhappiness; she pines with tears and grief through her longing for you. Need I speak of your sons who have both been consuls, and whose lives, as when they were boys, are yet bright with the character of their grandfather and their father? Wherefore, since mortals desire exceedingly to keep a hold on life, how happy you should be, knew you but your blessings, since you have still what none doubts to be dearer than life itself? Wherefore now dry your tears. Fortune's hatred has not yet been so great as to destroy all your holds upon happiness: the tempest that is fallen upon you is not too great for you: your anchors hold yet firm, and they should keep ever nigh to you confidence in the present and hope for future time."

"And may they continue to hold fast," said I, "that is my prayer: while they are firm, we will reach the end of our voyage, however things may be. But you see how much my glory has departed."

And she answered, "We have made some progress, if you are not now weary entirely of your present lot. But I cannot bear this dallying so softly, so long as you complain that your happiness lacks aught, so long as you are full of sorrow and care. Whose happiness is so firmly established that he has no quarrel from any side with his estate of life? For the condition of our welfare is a matter fraught with care: either its completeness never appears, or it never remains. One man's wealth is abundant, but his birth and breeding put him to shame. Another is famous for his noble birth, but would rather be unknown because he is hampered by his narrow means. A third is blessed with wealth and breeding, but bewails his life because he has no wife. Another is happy in his marriage, but has no children, and saves his wealth only for an heir that is no son of his. Another is blessed with children, but weeps tears of sorrow for the misdeeds of son or daughter. So none is readily at peace with the lot his fortune sends him. For in each case there is that which is unknown to him who has not experienced it, and which brings horror to him who has experienced it. Consider further, that the feelings of the most fortunate men are the most easily affected, wherefore, unless all their desires are supplied, such men, being unused to all adversity, are cast down by every little care: so small are the troubles which can rob them of complete happiness.

"How many are they, think you, who would think themselves raised to heaven if the smallest part of the remnants of your good fortune fell to them? This very place, which you call a place of exile, is home to those who live herein. Thus there is nothing wretched unless you think it to be so: and in like manner he who bears all with a calm mind finds his lot wholly blessed. Who is so happy but would wish to change his estate, if he yields to impatience of his lot? With how much bitterness is the sweetness of man's life mingled! For even though its enjoyment seem pleasant, yet it may not be surely kept from departing when it will. It is plain then how wretched is the happiness of mortal life which neither endures for ever with men of calm mind, nor ever wholly delights the care-ridden. Wherefore, then, O mortal men, seek ye that happiness without, which lies within yourselves? Ye are confounded by error and ignorance. I will shew you as shortly as I may, the pole on which turns the highest happiness. Is there aught that you value more highly than your own self? You will answer that there is nothing. If then you are master of yourself, you will be in possession of that which you will never wish to lose, and which Fortune will never be able to take from you. Yet consider this further, that you may be assured that happiness cannot be fixed in matters of chance: if happiness is the highest good of a man who lives his life by reason, and if that which can by any means be snatched away, is not the highest good (since that which is best cannot be snatched away), it is plain that Fortune by its own uncertainty can never come near to reaching happiness. Further, the man who is borne along by a happiness which may stumble, either knows that it may change, or knows it not: if he knows it not, what happiness can there be in the blindness of ignorance? If he knows it, he must needs live in fear of losing that which he cannot doubt that he may lose; wherefore an ever-present fear allows not such an one to be happy. Or at any rate, if he lose it without unhappiness, does he not think it worthless? For that, whose loss can be calmly borne, is indeed a small good. You, I know well, are firmly persuaded that men's understandings can never die; this truth is planted deep in you by many proofs: since then it is plain that the happiness of fortune is bounded by the death of the body, you cannot doubt that, if death can carry away happiness, the whole race of mortals is sinking into wretchedness to be found upon the border of death. But we know that many have sought the enjoyment of happiness not only by death, but even by sorrow and sufferings: how then can the presence of this life make us happy, when its end cannot make us unhappy?

"He that would build on a lasting resting-place; who would be firm to resist the blasts of the storming wind; who seeks, too, safety where he may contemn the surge and threatening of the sea; must leave the lofty mountain's top, and leave the thirsting sands. The hill is swept by all the might of the headstrong gale: the sands dissolve, and will not bear the load upon them. Let him fly the danger in a lot which is pleasant rest unto the eye: let him be mindful to set his house surely upon the lowly rock. Then let the wind bellow, confounding

wreckage in the sea, and thou wilt still be founded upon un-
moving peace, wilt be blessed in the strength of thy defence:
thy life will be spent in calmness, and thou mayest mock the
raging passions of the air.

(*Philosophy examines more carefully the value of things highly
prized by men.*)

"But now," she continued, "the first remedies of reasoning
are reaching you more deeply, and I think I should now use
those that are somewhat stronger. If the gifts of Fortune fade
not nor pass quickly away, even so, what is there in them
which could ever be truly yours, or which would not lose its
value when examined or thought upon?

"Are riches valuable for their own nature, or on account
of your and other men's natures? Which is the more valuable,
the gold itself or the power of the stored up-money? Surely
wealth shines more brightly when spent than when put away
in masses. Avarice ever brings hatred, while generous spending
brings honour. But that cannot remain with one person which
is handed over to another: therefore money becomes valuable
to its possessor when, by being scattered, it is transferred to
others, and ceases to be possessed. And if all that is heaped
together among mankind comes to one man, it makes the others
all poor. A voice indeed fills equally the ears of all that hear:
but your riches cannot pass to others without being lessened:
and when they pass, they make poor those whom they leave.
How strait then and poor are those riches, which most men
may not have, and which can only come to one by making
others poor!

"Think again of precious stones: does their gleam attract
your eyes? But any excellence they have is their own brilliance, and belongs not to men: wherefore I am amazed that
men so strongly admire them. What manner of thing can that
be which has no mind to influence, which has no structure of
parts, and yet can justly seem to a living, reasoning mind to
be beautiful? Though they be works of their creator, and by
their own beauty and adornment have a certain low beauty,

yet are they in rank lower than your own excellence, and have in no wise deserved your admiration.

"Does the beauty of landscape delight you?"

"Surely, for it is a beautiful part of a beautiful creation: and in like manner we rejoice at times in the appearance of a calm sea, and we admire the sky, the stars, the sun, and the moon."

"Does any one of these," said she, "concern you? Dare you boast yourself of the splendid beauty of any one of such things? Are you yourself adorned by the flowers of spring? Is it your richness that swells the fruits of autumn? Why are you carried away by empty rejoicing? Why do you embrace as your own the good things which are outside yourself? Fortune will never make yours what Nature has made to belong to other things. The fruits of the earth should doubtless serve as nourishment for living beings, but if you would satisfy your need as fully as Nature needs, you need not the abundance of Fortune. Nature is content with very little, and if you seek to thrust upon her more than is enough, then what you cast in will become either unpleasing or even harmful.

"Again, you think that you appear beautiful in many kinds of clothing. But if their form is pleasant to the eyes, I would admire the nature of the material or the skill of the maker. Or are you made happy by a long line of attendants? Surely if they are vicious, they are but a burden to the house, and full of injury to their master himself; while if they are honest, how can the honesty of others be counted among your possessions?

"Out of all these possessions, then, which you reckon as your wealth, not one can really be shown to be your own. For if they have no beauty for you to acquire, what have they for which you should grieve if you lose them, or in keeping which you should rejoice? And if they are beautiful by their own nature, how are you the richer thereby? For these would have been pleasing of themselves, though cut out from your possessions. They do not become valuable by reason that they have come into your wealth; but you have desired to count them among your wealth, because they seemed valuable. Why then do you long for them with such railing against Fortune? You seek, I believe, to put want to flight by means of plenty. But you find that the opposite results. The more various is the beauty of furniture, the more helps are needed to keep it beautiful, and it is ever true that they who have much, need much; and on the other hand, they need least who measure their wealth by the needs of nature, not by excess of display.

"Is there then no good which belongs to you and is implanted within you, that you seek your good things elsewhere, in things without you and separate from you? Have things taken such a turn that the animal, whose reason gives it a claim to divinity, cannot seem beautiful to itself except by the possession of lifeless trappings? Other classes of things are satisfied by their intrinsic possessions; but men, though made like God in understanding, seek to find among the lowest things adornment for their higher nature: and you do not understand that you do a great wrong thereby to your Creator. He intended that the human race should be above all other earthly beings; yet you thrust down your honourable place below the lowest. For if every good thing is allowed to be more valuable than that to which it belongs, surely you are putting yourselves lower than them in your estimation, since you think precious the most worthless of things; and this is indeed a just result. Since, then, this is the condition of human nature, that it surpasses other classes only when it realises what is in itself; as soon as it ceases to know itself, it must be reduced to a lower rank than the beasts. To other animals ignorance of themselves is natural; in men it is a fault. How plainly and how widely do you err by thinking that anything can be adorned by ornaments that belong to others! Surely that cannot be. For if anything becomes brilliant by additions thereto, the praise for the brilliance belongs to the additions. But the subject remains in its own vileness, though hidden and covered by these externals.

"Again, I say that naught can be a good thing which does

harm to its possessor. Am I wrong? 'No,' you will say. Yet many a time do riches harm their possessors, since all base men, who are therefore the most covetous, think that they themselves alone are worthy to possess all gold and precious stones. You therefore, who now go in fear of the cudgel and sword of the robber, could laugh in his face if you had entered upon this path with empty pockets.[1] How wonderful is the surpassing blessing of mortal wealth! As soon as you have acquired it, your cares begin!

"O happy was that early age of men, contented with their trusted and unfailing fields, nor ruined by the wealth that enervates. Easily was the acorn got that used to satisfy their longwhile fast. They knew not Bacchus' gifts, nor honey mixed therewith. They knew not how to tinge with Tyre's purple dyes the sheen of China's silks. Their sleep kept health on rush and grass; the stream gave them to drink as it flowed by: the lofty pine to them gave shade. Not one of them yet clave the ocean's depths, nor, carrying stores of merchandise, had visited new shores. Then was not heard the battle's trump, nor had blood made red with bitter hate the bristling swords of war. For why should any madness urge to take up first their arms upon an enemy such ones as knew no sight of cruel wounds nor knew rewards that could be reaped in blood? Would that our times could but return to those old ways! But love of gain and greed of holding burn more fiercely far than Ætna's fires. Ah! who was the wretch who first unearthed the mass of hidden gold, the gems that only longed to lie unfound? For full of danger was the prize he found.

"What am I to say of power and of the honours of office, which you raise to heaven because you know not true honoured power? What fires belched forth from Ætna's flames, what overwhelming flood could deal such ruin as these when

[1] This is an application of Juvenal's lines (*Sat*. x. 19) which contrast the terror of the money-laden traveller with the careless happiness of the man who meets a highwayman with no purse and empty pockets.

they fall into the hands of evil men? I am sure you remember how your forefathers wished to do away with the consular power, which had been the very foundation of liberty, because of the overbearing pride of the consuls, just as your ancestors had too in earlier times expunged from the state the name of king on account of the same pride. But if, as rarely happens, places of honour are granted to honest men, what else is delightful in them but the honesty they practise thereby? Wherefore honour comes not to virtue from holding office, but comes to office from virtues there practised.

"But what is the power which you seek and esteem so highly? O creatures of the earth, can you not think over whom you are set? If you saw in a community of mice, one mouse asserting his rights and his power over the others, with what mirth you would greet the sight! Yet if you consider the body, what can you find weaker than humanity? Cannot a tiny gnat by its bite, or by creeping into the inmost parts, kill that body? How can any exercise right upon any other except upon the body alone, or that which is below the body, whereby I mean the fortunes? Can you ever impose any law upon a free spirit? Can you ever disturb the peculiar restfulness which is the property of a mind that hangs together upon the firm basis of its reason? When a certain tyrant thought that by tortures he would compel a free man[1] to betray the conspirators in a plot against his life, the philosopher bit through his tongue and spat it out in the tyrant's face. Thus were the tortures, which the tyrant intended to have cruel results, turned by the philosopher into subjects of high courage. Is there aught that one man can do to another, which he may not suffer from another in his turn? We have heard how Busiris, who used to kill strangers, was killed by Hercules when he came to Egypt. Regulus,[2] who had cast into chains many a Carthaginian captive, soon yielded himself a prisoner to their chains. Do you

---

[1] This story is told of Anaxagoras and Nicocreon, king of Cyprus, *c.* B.C. 323.

[2] Regulus was the Roman general in Sicily in the first Punic War, taken prisoner in 255 B.C., and put to death in 250.

think that power to be any power, whose possessor cannot ensure his own escape from suffering at another's hands what he inflicts upon some other?

"Further, if there were any intrinsic good in the nature of honours and powers themselves, they could never crowd upon the basest men. For opposites will not be bound together. Nature refuses to allow contraries to be linked to each other. Wherefore, while it is undoubted that for the most part offices of honour are enjoyed by bad men, it is also manifest that those things are not by nature good, which allow themselves to cling to evil men. And this indeed may worthily be held of all the gifts of fortune which come with the greatest success to the most unscrupulous. And in this matter we must also think on this fact, that no one doubts a man to be brave in whom he has found by examination that bravery is implanted: and whoever has the quality of swiftness is plainly swift. So also music makes men musical, medicine makes men physicians, oratory makes men orators. The nature of each quality acts as is peculiar to itself: it is not confused with the results of contrary qualities, but goes so far as to drive out those qualities which are opposed to it. Wealth cannot quench the insatiable thirst of avarice: nor can power ever make master of himself the man whom vicious passions hold fast in unbreakable chains. Honours, when joined to dishonest men, so far from making them honourable, betray them rather, and show them to be dishonourable. Why is this so? It is because you rejoice to call things by false names which belong not to them; their names are refuted by the reality of their qualities: wherefore neither riches, nor that kind of power, nor these honours, can justly so be called. Lastly, we may come to the same conclusion concerning all the aspects of Fortune: nothing is to be sought in her, and it is plain she has no innate good, for she is not always joined with good men, nor does she make good those with whom she is joined."

"We have heard what ruin Nero wrought when Rome was burnt and senators were slain. We know how savagely he did to death his brother,[1] how he was stained by the spilling of his own mother's blood, and how he looked upon her cold body and yet no tear fell upon his cheek: yet could this man be judge of the morals that were dead? Nay, he was ruler of the peoples whom the sun looks upon from the time he rises in the east until he hides his rays beneath the waves, and those whom the chilling northern Wain o'errules, and those whom the southern gale burns with its dry blast, as it heats the burning sands. Say, could great power chasten Nero's maddened rage? Ah! heavy fate, how often is the sword of high injustice given where is already most poisonous cruelty!"

Then I said, "You know that the vain-glory of this world has had but little influence over me; but I have desired the means of so managing affairs that virtue might not grow aged in silence."

(*Philosophy discusses Fame, "that last infirmity of noble minds."*)

"Yes," said she, "but there is one thing which can attract minds, which, though by nature excelling, yet are not led by perfection to the furthest bounds of virtue; and that thing is the love of fame and reputation for deserving well of one's country. Think then thus upon it, and see that it is but a slight thing of no weight. As you have learnt from astronomers' shewing, the whole circumference of the earth is but as a point compared with the size of the heavens. That is, if you compare the earth with the circle of the universe, it must be reckoned as of no size at all. And of this tiny portion of the universe there is but a fourth part, as you have learnt from the demonstration of Ptolemæus,[2] which is inhabited by living beings known to us. If from this fourth part you imagine subtracted all that is covered by sea and marsh, and all the vast regions of thirsty desert, you will find but the narrowest space left for

---

[1] Britannicus, son of Nero's father, the Emperor Claudius, put to death A.D. 55.

[2] A mathematician, astronomer, and geographer of Alexandria. Fl. 140-160 A.D. Boethius translated one of his works.

human habitation. And do you think of setting forth your fame and publishing your name in this space, which is but as a point within another point so closely circumscribed? And what size or magnificence can fame have which is shut in by such close and narrow bounds? Further, this narrow enclosure of habitation is peopled by many races of men which differ in language, in customs, and in their whole scheme of living; and owing to difficulty of travelling, differences of speech, and rareness of any intercourse, the fame of cities cannot reach them, much less the fame of men. Has not Cicero written somewhere that in his time the fame of Rome had not reached the mountains of the Caucasus, though the Republic was already well grown and striking awe among the Parthians and other nations in those parts? Do you see then how narrow and closely bounded must be that fame which you wish to extend more widely? Can the fame of a Roman ever reach parts to which the name of Rome cannot come?

"Further, the manners and customs of different races are so little in agreement, that what is considered praiseworthy among one people may be punished by another. Wherefore it may not be to a man's advantage in many lands to make his name known, because he takes pleasure in a glorious fame. So each man shall be content if his fame travels throughout his own countrymen, and the immortality of his name shall be bounded by the limits of one nation. But how many men, the most famous of their times, are wiped out by oblivion because no man has written of them![1] And yet what advantage is there in much that is written? For with their authors these writings are overwhelmed in the length and dimness of age. Yet when you think upon your fame in future ages, you seem to think

[1] Boethius is thinking of Horace, *Odes* iv. 9.

> Ere Agamemnon saw the light,
>   There lived brave men : but tearless all
> Enfolded in eternal night,
>   For lack of sacred minstrels, fall.
>   (Mr. Gladstone's translation.)

that you are prolonging it to immortality. But if you think upon the unending length of eternity, what enjoyment do you find in the long endurance of your name? For though one moment bears but the least proportion to ten thousand years, yet there is a definite ratio, because both are limited spaces of time. But even ten thousand years, or the greatest number you will, cannot even be compared with eternity. For there will always be ratio between finite things, but between the finite and the infinite there can never be any comparison. Wherefore, however long drawn out may be the life of your fame, it is not even small, but it is absolutely nothing when compared with eternity. You know not how to act rightly except for the breezes of popular opinion and for the sake of empty rumours; thus the excellence of conscience and of virtue is left behind, and you seek rewards from the tattle of other men. Listen to the witty manner in which one played once upon the shallowness of this pride. A certain man once bitterly attacked another who had taken to himself falsely the name of philosopher, not for the purpose of true virtue, but for pride of fame; he added to his attack that he would know soon whether he was a philosopher, when he saw whether the other bore with meekness and patience the insults he heaped upon him. The other shewed patience for a while and took the insults as though he scoffed at them, until he said, 'Do you now see that I am a philosopher?' 'I should have, had you kept silence,' said the other stingingly. But we are speaking of great men: and I ask, what do they gain from fame, though they seek glory by virtue? What have they after the body is dissolved at death? For if men die utterly, as our reason forbids us to believe, there is no glory left to them at all, since they whose it is said to be, do not exist. If, on the other hand, the mind is still conscious and working when it is freed from its earthly prison, it seeks heaven in its freedom and surely spurns all earthly traffic: it enjoys heaven and rejoices in its release from the things of this world.

"The mind that rushes headlong in its search for fame, thinking that is its highest good, should look upon the spreading regions of the air, and then upon the bounded tracts that are this world: then will shame enter it; that, though fame grow, yet can it never fill so small a circle. Proud men! Why will ye try in vain to free your necks from the yoke mortality has set thereon? Though fame may be wide scattered and find its way through distant lands, and set the tongues there talking; though a splendid house may draw brilliance from famous names and tales; yet death regards not any glory, howsoever great. Alike he overwhelms the lowly and the lofty head, and levels high with low.

"Where are Fabricius's [1] bones, that honourable man? What now is Brutus? [2] or unbending Cato? [3] Their fame survives in this: it has no more than a few slight letters shewing forth an empty name. We see their noble names engraved, and only know thereby that they are brought to naught. Ye lie then all unknown, and fame can give no knowledge of you. But if you think that life can be prolonged by the breath of mortal fame, yet when the slow time robs you of this too, then there awaits you but a second death.

"But," she said, "do not think that I would urge implacable war upon Fortune. There are times when her deception of men has certain merits: I mean when she discovers herself, unveils her face, and proclaims her ways. Perhaps you do not yet understand what I would say. It is a strange thing that I am trying to say, and for that reason I can scarcely explain myself in words. I think that ill fortune is of greater advantage to

[1] Fabricius was the Roman general whom Pyrrhus could neither bribe nor intimidate, B.C. 280.

[2] L. Junius Brutus, who led the Romans to expel the last of the kings, and was elected the first consul, B.C. 509.

[3] Probably Cato Major, the great censor, B.C. 184, the rigid champion of the stern old Roman morals; or possibly Cato Minor, who committed suicide at Utica after the battle of Thapsus, B.C. 46, because he considered that Cæsar's victory was fatal to the Republic and the liberty of Rome.

men than good fortune. Good fortune is ever lying when she seems to favour by an appearance of happiness. Ill fortune is ever true when by her changes she shews herself inconstant. The one deceives; the other edifies. The one by a deceitful appearance of good things enchains the minds of those who enjoy them: the other frees them by a knowledge that happiness is so fragile. You see, then, that the one is blown about by winds, is ever moving and ever ignorant of its own self; the other is sober, ever prepared and ever made provident by the undergoing of its very adversities. Lastly, good fortune draws men from the straight path of true good by her fawning: ill fortune draws most men to the true good, and holds them back by her curved staff.

"And do you think that this should be reckoned among the least benefits of this rough, unkind, and terrible ill fortune, that she has discovered to you the minds of your faithful friends? Fortune has distinguished for you your sure and your doubtful friends; her departure has taken away her friends and left you yours. At what price could you have bought this benefit if you had been untouched and, as you thought, fortunate? Cease then to seek the wealth you have lost. You have found your friends, and they are the most precious of all riches.

"Through Love[1] the universe with constancy makes changes all without discord: earth's elements, though contrary, abide in treaty bound: Phœbus in his golden car leads up the glowing day; his sister rules the night that Hesperus brought: the greedy sea confines its waves in bounds, lest the earth's borders be changed by its beating on them: all these are firmly bound by Love, which rules both earth and sea, and has its empire in the heavens too. If Love should slacken this its hold, all mutual love would change to war; and these would strive to undo the scheme which now their glorious movements carry

---

[1] Boethius in this passage is probably thinking of Empedocles's doctrine of Love which unites, and Strife which divides, the two primal forces in the universe.

out with trust and with accord. By Love are peoples too kept bound together by a treaty which they may not break. Love binds with pure affection the sacred tie of wedlock, and speaks its bidding to all trusty friends. O happy race of mortals, if your hearts are ruled as is the universe, by Love!"[1]

[1] *Cp.* Bk. i. Prose iv. p. 10.

BOOK THREE

When she finished her lay, its soothing tones left me spell-bound with my ears alert in my eagerness to listen. So a while afterwards I said, "Greatest comforter of weary minds, how have you cheered me with your deep thoughts and sweet singing too! No more shall I doubt my power to meet the blows of Fortune. So far am I from terror at the remedies which you did lately tell me were sharper, that I am longing to hear them, and eagerly I beg you for them."

Then said she, "I knew it when you laid hold upon my words in silent attention, and I was waiting for that frame of mind in you, or more truly, I brought it about in you. They that remain are indeed bitter to the tongue, but sweet to the inner man. But as you say you are eager to hear, how ardently you would be burning, if you knew whither I am attempting to lead you!"

"Whither is that?" I asked.

"To the true happiness, of which your soul too dreams; but your sight is taken up in imaginary views thereof, so that you cannot look upon itself."

Then said I, "I pray you shew me what that truly is, and quickly."

"I will do so," she said, "for your sake willingly. But first I will try to picture in words and give you the form of the cause, which is already better known to you, so that, when that picture is perfect and you turn your eyes to the other side, you may recognise the form of true happiness.

"When a man would sow in virgin soil, first he clears away the bushes, cuts the brambles and the ferns, that the corn-

42

goddess may go forth laden with her new fruit. The honey, that the bee has toiled to give us, is sweeter when the mouth has tasted bitter things. The stars shine with more pleasing grace when a storm has ceased to roar and pour down rain. After the morning star has dispersed the shades of night, the day in all its beauty drives its rosy chariot forth. So thou hast looked upon false happiness first; now draw thy neck from under her yoke: so shall true happiness now come into thy soul."

(*Philosophy discusses "the highest good."*)

She lowered her eyes for a little while as though searching the innermost recesses of her mind; and then she continued:— "The trouble of the many and various aims of mortal men bring them much care, and herein they go forward by different paths but strive to reach one end, which is happiness. And that good is that, to which if any man attain, he can desire nothing further. It is that highest of all good things, and it embraces in itself all good things: if any good is lacking, it cannot be the highest good, since then there is left outside it something which can be desired. Wherefore happiness is a state which is made perfect by the union of all good things. This end all men seek to reach, as I said, though by different paths. For there is implanted by nature in the minds of men a desire for the true good; but error leads them astray towards false goods by wrong paths.

"Some men believe that the highest good is to lack nothing, and so they are at pains to possess abundant riches. Others consider the true good to be that which is most worthy of admiration, and so they strive to attain to places of honour, and to be held by their fellow-citizens in honour thereby. Some determine that the highest good lies in the highest power; and so they either desire to reign themselves, or try to cleave to those who do reign. Others think that renown is the greatest good, and they therefore hasten to make a famous name by the arts of peace or of war. But more than all measure the fruit of good by pleasure and enjoyment, and these think that the happiest man is abandoned to pleasure.

"Further, there are those who confuse the aims and the causes of these good things: as those who desire riches for the sake of power or of pleasure, or those who seek power for the sake of money or celebrity. In these, then, and other things like to them, lies the aim of men's actions and prayers, such as renown and popularity, which seem to afford some fame, or wife and children, which are sought for the pleasure they give. On the other hand, the good of friends, which is the most honourable and holy of all, lies not in Fortune's but in Virtue's realm. All others are adopted for the sake of power or enjoyment.

"Again, it is plain that the good things of the body must be accounted to those false causes which we have mentioned; for bodily strength and stature seem to make men more able and strong; beauty and swiftness seem to give renown; health seems to give pleasure. By all these happiness alone is plainly desired. For each man holds that to be the highest good, which he seeks before all others. But we have defined the highest good to be happiness. Wherefore what each man desires above all others, he holds to be a state of happiness.

"Wherefore you have each of these placed before you as the form of human happiness: wealth, honours, power, glory, and pleasure. Epicurus[1] considered these forms alone, and accordingly determined upon pleasure as the highest good, because all the others seemed but to join with it in bringing enjoyment to the mind.

"But to return to the aims of men: their minds seem to seek to regain the highest good, and their memories seem to dull their powers. It is as though a drunken man were seeking his home, but could not remember the way thither. Can those

---

[1] Epicurus (B.C. 342-270) was the famous founder of the Epicurean school of philosophy. His school had a large following of Romans under the Empire. His own teaching was of a higher nature than might be supposed from this bare statement that he thought "pleasure was the highest good."

people be altogether wrong whose aim it is to lack nothing? No, there is nothing which can make happiness so perfect as an abundant possession of good things, needing naught that belongs to others, but in all ways sufficing for itself. Surely those others too are not mistaken who think that what is best is also most worthy of reverence and respect. It cannot be any cheap or base thing, to attain which almost all men aim and strive. And is power not to be accounted a good thing? Surely it is: can that be a weak thing or forceless, which is allowed in all cases to excel? Is renown of no value? We cannot surrender this; that whatever is most excellent, has also great renown. It is hardly worth saying that happiness has no torturing cares or gloom, and is not subject to grief and trouble; for even in small things, the aim is to find that which it is a delight to have and to enjoy. These, then, are the desires of men: they long for riches, places of honour, kingdoms, glory, and pleasure; and they long for them because they think that thereby they will find satisfaction, veneration, power, renown, and happiness. It is the good then which men seek by their different desires; and it is easy to shew how great a force nature has put therein, since in spite of such varying and discordant opinions, they are all agreed in the goal they seek, that of the highest good.

"I would to pliant strings set forth a song of how almighty Nature turns her guiding reins, telling with what laws her providence keeps safe this boundless universe, binding and tying each and all with cords that never shall be loosed. The lions of Carthage, though they bear the gorgeous bonds and trappings of captivity, and eat the food that is given them by hand, and though they fear their harsh master with his lash they know so well; yet if once blood has touched their bristling jaws, their old, their latent wills return; with deep roaring they remember their old selves; they loose their bands and free their necks, and their tamer is the first torn by their cruel teeth, and his blood is poured out by their rage and wrath.

"If the bird who sings so lustily upon the high tree-top, be caught and caged, men may minister to him with dainty care, may give him cups of liquid honey and feed him with all gentleness on plenteous food; yet if he fly to the roof of his cage and see the shady trees he loves, he spurns with his foot the food they have put before him; the woods are all his sorrow calls for, for the woods he sings with his sweet tones.

"The bough which has been downward thrust by force of strength to bend its top to earth, so soon as the pressing hand is gone, looks up again straight to the sky above.

"Phœbus sinks into the western waves, but by his unknown track he turns his car once more to his rising in the east.

"All things must find their own peculiar course again, and each rejoices in his own return. Not one can keep the order handed down to it, unless in some way it unites its rising to its end, and so makes firm, immutable, its own encircling course.

(*Philosophy shews the vanity of riches.*)

"And you too, creatures of the earth, do dream of your first state, though with a dim idea. With whatsoever thinking it may be, you look to that goal of happiness, though never so obscure your thoughts: thither, to true happiness, your natural course does guide you, and from the same your various errors lead you. For I would have you consider whether men can reach the end they have resolved upon, namely happiness, by these ways by which they think to attain thereto. If money and places of honour and such-like do bring anything of that sort to a man who seems to lack no good thing, then let us acknowledge with them that men do become happy by the possession of these things. But if they cannot perform their promises, and there is still lack of further good things, surely it is plain that a false appearance of happiness is there discovered. You, therefore, who had lately abundant riches, shall first answer me. With all that great wealth, was your mind never perturbed by torturing care arising from some sense of injustice?"

"Yes," I said; "I cannot remember that my mind was ever free from some such care."

"Was it not because something was lacking, which you missed, or because something was present to you which you did not like to have?"

"Yes," I answered.

"You desired, then, the presence of the one, and the absence of the other?"

"I acknowledge it."

"Then," said she, "such a man lacks what he desires."

"He does."

"But while a man lacks anything, can he possibly satisfy himself?"

"No," said I.

"Then, while you were bountifully supplied with wealth, you felt that you did not satisfy yourself?"

"I did indeed."

"Then," said she, "wealth cannot prevent a man from lacking or make him satisfied. And this is what it apparently professed to do. And this point too I feel is most important: money has in itself, by its own nature, nothing which can prevent its being carried off from those, who possess it, against their will."

"It has not," I said.

"No, you cannot deny that any stronger man may any day snatch it from them. For how come about the quarrels of the law-courts? Is it not because people try to regain money that has been by force or by fraud taken from them?"

"Yes," I answered.

"Then," said she, "a man will need to seek from the outside help to guard his own money."

"That cannot be denied," I said.

"And a man will not need that unless he possesses money which he can lose."

"Undoubtedly he will not."

"Then the argument turns round the other way," she said. "The riches which were thought to make a man all-sufficient for himself, do really put him in need of other people's help. Then how can need be separated from wealth? Do the rich never feel hunger nor thirst? Do the limbs of moneyed men never feel the cold of winter? You will say, 'Yes, but the rich have the wherewithal to satisfy hunger and thirst, and drive away cold.' But though riches may thus console wants, they cannot entirely take them away. For, though these ever crying wants, these continual requests, are satisfied, yet there must exist that which is to be satisfied. I need not say that nature is satisfied with little, greed is never satisfied. Wherefore, I ask you, if wealth cannot remove want, and even creates its own wants, what reason is there that you should think it affords satisfaction to a man?

"Though the rich man with greed heap up from ever-flowing streams the wealth that cannot satisfy, though he deck himself with pearls from the Red Sea's shore, and plough his fertile field with oxen by the score, yet gnawing care will never in his lifetime leave him, and at his death his wealth will not go with him, but leave him faithlessly."

(*The vanity of high places.*)

"But," I urged, "places of honour make the man, to whom they fall, honoured and venerated."

"Ah!" she answered, "have those offices their force in truth that they may instil virtues into the minds of those that hold them, and drive out vices therefrom? And yet we are too well accustomed to see them making wickedness conspicuous rather than avoiding it. Wherefore we are displeased to see such places often falling to the most wicked of men, so that Catullus called Nonius 'a diseased growth,'[1] though he sat in the highest chair of office. Do you see how great a disgrace high honours can add to evil men? Their unworthiness is less con-

[1] Probably Boethius makes a mistake in his interpretation of Catullus (*Carm.* 52), as Nonius's surname was very likely "Struma" (which also means a wen); in which case Catullus cannot at most have intended more to be understood than a play upon the man's true name.

spicuous if they are not made famous by honours. Could you yourself have been induced by any dangers to think of being a colleague with Decoratus,[1] when you saw that he had the mind of an unscrupulous buffoon, and a base informer? We cannot consider men worthy of veneration on account of their high places, when we hold them to be unworthy of those high places. But if you see a man endowed with wisdom, you cannot but consider him worthy of veneration, or at least of the wisdom with which he is endowed. For such a man has the worth peculiar to virtue, which it transmits directly to those in whom it is found. But since honours from the vulgar crowd cannot create merit, it is plain that they have not the peculiar beauty of this worth. And here is a particular point to be noticed: if men are the more worthless as they are despised by more people, high position makes them all the worse because it cannot make venerable those whom it shews to so many people to be contemptible. And this brings its penalty with it: wicked people bring a like quality into their positions, and stain them with their infection.

"Now I would have you consider the matter thus, that you may recognise that true veneration cannot be won through these shadowy honours. If a man who had filled the office of consul many times in Rome, came by chance into a country of barbarians, would his high position make him venerated by the barbarians? Yet if this were a natural quality in such dignities, they would never lose their effective function in any land, just as fire is never aught but hot in all countries. But since they do not receive this quality of veneration from any force peculiar to themselves, but only from a connexion in the untrustworthy opinions of men, they become as nothing as soon as they are among those who do not consider these dignities as such.

"But that is only in the case of foreign peoples. Among the very peoples where they had their beginnings, do these dignities last for ever? Consider how great was the power in Rome

[1] Decoratus was a minion of Theodoric.

of old of the office of Præfect: now it is an empty name and a heavy burden upon the income of any man of Senator's rank. The præfect then, who was commissioner of the corn-market, was held to be a great man. Now there is no office more despised. For, as I said before, that which has no intrinsic beauty, sometimes receives a certain glory, sometimes loses it, according to the opinion of those who are concerned with it. If then high offices cannot make men venerated, if furthermore they grow vile by the infection of bad men, if changes of time can end their glory, and, lastly, if they are held cheaply in the estimation of whole peoples, I ask you, so far from affording true beauty to men, what beauty have they in themselves which men can desire?

"Though Nero decked himself proudly with purple of Tyre and snow-white gems, none the less that man of rage and luxury lived ever hated of all. Yet would that evil man at times give his dishonoured offices to men who were revered. Who then could count men blessed, who to such a villain owed their high estate?

(*The vanity of kingdoms.*)

"Can kingdoms and intimacies with kings make people powerful? 'Certainly,' some may answer, 'in so far as their happiness is lasting.' But antiquity and our times too are full of examples of the contrary; examples of men whose happiness as kings has been exchanged for disaster. What wonderful power, which is found to be powerless even for its own preservation! But if this kingly power is really a source of happiness, surely then, if it fail in any way, it lessens the happiness it brings, and equally causes unhappiness. However widely human empires may extend, there must be still more nations left, over whom each king does not reign. And so, in whatever direction this power ceases to make happy, thereby comes in powerlessness, which makes men unhappy; thus therefore there must be a greater part of unhappiness in every king's estate. That tyrant[1] had learnt well the dangers of his lot, who likened the fear which goes with kingship to the terror inspired by a sword ever hanging overhead. What then is such a power, which cannot drive away the bite of cares, nor escape the stings of fear?

"Yet these all would willingly live without fear, but they cannot, and yet they boast of their power. Think you a man is powerful when you see that he longs for that which he cannot bring to pass? Do you reckon a man powerful who walks abroad with dignity and attended by servants? A man who strikes fear into his subjects, yet fears them more himself? A man who must be at the mercy of those that serve him, in order that he may seem to have power?

"Need I speak of intimacies with kings when kingship itself is shewn to be full of weakness? Not only when kings' powers fall are their friends laid low, but often even when their powers are intact. Nero compelled his friend and tutor, Seneca,[2] to choose how he would die. Papinianus,[3] for a long while a powerful courtier, was handed over to the soldiers' swords by the Emperor Antoninus. Yet each of these was willing to surrender all his power. Seneca even tried to give up all his wealth to Nero, and to seek retirement. But the very weight of their wealth and power dragged them down to ruin, and neither could do what he wished.

"What then is that power, whose possessors fear it? In desiring to possess which, you are not safe, and from which you cannot escape, even though you try to lay it down? What help are friends, made not by virtue but by fortune? The friend gained by good fortune becomes an enemy in ill-fortune.

[1] Dionysius, tyrant of Syracuse, shewed his flattering courtier Damocles, what it was to be a tyrant, by setting him in his own seat at a sumptuous banquet, but hung a sword above him by a hair.

[2] Seneca, the philosopher and wise counsellor of Nero, was by him compelled to commit suicide, A.D. 65.

[3] Papinianus, the greatest lawyer of his time, was put to death by the Emperor Antoninus Caracalla, A.D. 212.

And what plague can more effectually injure than an intimate enemy?

"The man who would true power gain, must needs subdue his own wild thoughts: never must he let his passions triumph and yoke his neck by their foul bonds. For though the earth, as far as India's shore, tremble before the laws you give, though Thule bow to your service on earth's farthest bounds, yet if thou canst not drive away black cares, if thou canst not put to flight complaints, then is no true power thine.

(*The vanity of earthly glory, fame.*)

"How deceitful is fame often, and how base a thing it is! Justly did the tragic poet cry out,[1] 'O Fame, Fame, how many lives of men of naught hast thou puffed up!' For many men have got a great name from the false opinions of the crowd. And what could be baser than such a thing? For those who are falsely praised, must blush to hear their praises. And if they are justly won by merits, what can they add to the pleasure of a wise man's conscience? For he measures his happiness not by popular talk, but by the truth of his conscience. If it attracts a man to make his name widely known, he must equally think it a shame if it be not made known. But I have already said that there must be yet more lands into which the renown of a single man can never come; wherefore it follows that the man, whom you think famous, will seem to have no such fame in the next quarter of the earth.

"Popular favour seems to me to be unworthy even of mention under this head, for it comes not by any judgment, and is never constant.

(*The vanity of noble birth.*)

"Again, who can but see how empty a name, and how futile, is noble birth? For if its glory is due to renown, it belongs not

---

[1] Euripides, *Andromache*, l. 319-320.

to the man. For the glory of noble birth seems to be praise for the merits of a man's forefathers. But if praise creates the renown, it is the renowned who are praised. Wherefore, if you have no renown of your own, that of others cannot glorify you. But if there is any good in noble birth, I conceive it to be this, and this alone, that the highborn seem to be bound in honour not to show any degeneracy from their fathers' virtue.

"From like beginning rise all men on earth, for there is one Father of all things; one is the guide of everything. 'Tis He who gave the sun his rays, and horns unto the moon. 'Tis He who set mankind on earth, and in the heavens the stars. He put within our bodies spirits which were born in heaven. And thus a highborn race has He set forth in man. Why do ye men rail on your forefathers? If ye look to your beginning and your author, which is God, is any man degenerate or base but he who by his own vices cherishes base things and leaves that beginning which was his?

(The vanity of the lusts of the flesh.)

"And now what am I to say of the pleasures of the body? The desires of the flesh are full of cares, their fulfilment is full of remorse. What terrible diseases, what unbearable griefs, truly the fruits of sin, do they bring upon the bodies of those who enjoy them! I know not what pleasure their impulse affords, but any who cares to recall his indulgences of his passions, will know that the results of such pleasures are indeed gloomy. If any can shew that those results are blest with happiness, then may the beasts of the field be justly called blessed, for all their aims are urged toward the satisfying of their bodies' wants. The pleasures of wife and children may be most honourable; but nature makes it all too plain that some have found torment in their children. How bitter is any such kind of suffering, I need not tell you now, for you have never known it, nor have any such anxiety now. Yet in this matter

I would hold with my philosopher Euripides,[1] that he who has no children is happy in his misfortune.

"All pleasures have this way: those who enjoy them they drive on with stings. Pleasure, like the winged bee, scatters its honey sweet, then flies away, and with a clinging sting it strikes the hearts it touches.

(All these vanities are actually harmful.)

"There is then no doubt that these roads to happiness are no roads, and they cannot lead any man to any end whither they profess to take him. I would shew you shortly with what great evils they are bound up. Would you heap up money? You will need to tear it from its owner. Would you seem brilliant by the glory of great honours? You must kneel before their dispenser, and in your desire to surpass other men in honour, you must debase yourself by setting aside all pride. Do you long for power? You will be subject to the wiles of all over whom you have power, you will be at the mercy of many dangers. You seek fame? You will be drawn to and fro among rough paths, and lose all freedom from care. Would you spend a life of pleasure? Who would not despise and cast off such servitude to so vile and brittle a thing as your body? How petty are all the aims of those who put before themselves the pleasures of the body, how uncertain is the possession of such? In bodily size will you ever surpass the elephant? In strength will you ever lead the bull, or in speed the tiger? Look upon the expanse of heaven, the strength with which it stands, the rapidity with which it moves, and cease for a while to wonder at base things. This heaven is not more wonderful for those things than for the design which guides it. How sweeping is the brightness of outward form, how swift its movement, yet more fleeting than the passing of the flowers of spring. But if, as Aristotle says, many could use the eyes of lynxes to see through that which meets the eye, then if they saw into the

[1] Referring to lines in the *Andromache* (419-420), where Euripides says: "The man who complains that he has no children suffers less than he who has them, and is blest in his misfortune."

organs within, would not that body, though it had the most fair outside of Alcibiades,[1] seem most vile within? Wherefore it is not your own nature, but the weakness of the eyes of them that see you, which makes you seem beautiful. But consider how in excess you desire the pleasures of the body, when you know that howsoever you admire it, it can be reduced to nothing by a three-days' fever. To put all these points then in a word: these things cannot grant the good which they promise; they are not made perfect by the union of all good things in them; they do not lead to happiness as a path thither; they do not make men blessed.[2]

"Ah! how wretched are they whom ignorance leads astray by her crooked path! Ye seek not gold upon green trees, nor gather precious stones from vines, nor set your nets on mountain tops to catch the fishes for your feast, nor hunt the Umbrian sea in search of goats. Man knows the depths of the sea themselves, hidden though they be beneath its waves; he knows which water best yields him pearls, and which the scarlet dye. But in their blindness men are content, and know not where lies hid the good which they desire. They sink in earthly things, and there they seek that which has soared above the star-lit heavens. What can I call down upon them worthy of their stubborn folly? They go about in search of wealth and honours; and only when they have by labours vast stored up deception for themselves, do they at last know what is their true good.

"So far," she continued, "we have been content to set forth the form of false happiness. If you clearly understand that, my next duty is to shew what is true happiness."

"I do see," said I, "that wealth cannot satisfy, that power comes not to kingdoms, nor veneration to high offices; that true renown cannot accompany ambition, nor true enjoyment wait upon the pleasures of the body."

[1] Alcibiades was the most handsome and brilliantly fascinating of all the public men of Athens in her most brilliant period.

[2] Compare Philosophy's first words about the highest good, p. 43.

"Have you grasped the reasons why it is so?" she asked.

"I seem to look at them as through a narrow chink, but I would learn more clearly from you."

(Philosophy begins to examine true happiness.)

"The reason is to hand," said she; "human error takes that which is simple and by nature impossible to divide, tries to divide it, and turns its truth and perfection into falsity and imperfection. Tell me, do you think that anything which lacks nothing, can be without power?"

"Of course not."

"You are right; for if anything has any weakness in any part, it must lack the help of something else."

"That is so," I said.

"Then perfect satisfaction and power have the same nature?"

"Yes, it seems so."

"And do you think such a thing contemptible, or the opposite, worthy of all veneration?"

"There can be no doubt that it is worthy."

"Then let us add veneration to that satisfaction and power, and so consider these three as one."

"Yes, we must add it if we wish to proclaim the truth."

"Do you then think that this whole is dull and of no reputation, or renowned with all glory? For consider it thus: we have granted that it lacks nothing, that it has all power and is worthy of all veneration; it must not therefore lack the glory which it cannot supply for itself, and thereby seem to be in any direction contemptible."

"No," I said, "I must allow that it has glory too."

"Therefore we must rank this glory equally with the other three."

"Yes, we must."

"Then that which lacks nothing from outside itself, which is all-powerful by its own might, which has renown and veneration, must surely be allowed to be most happy too?"

"I cannot imagine from what quarter unhappiness would creep into such a thing, wherefore we must grant that it is full of happiness if the other qualities remain existent."

"Then it follows further, that though perfect satisfaction, power, glory, veneration, and happiness differ in name, they cannot differ at all in essence?"

"They cannot."

"This then," said she, "is a simple, single thing by nature, only divided by the mistakes of base humanity; and while men try to gain a part of that which has no parts, they fail both to obtain a fraction, which cannot exist, and the whole too after which they do not strive."

"Tell me how they fail thus," I said.

"One seeks riches by fleeing from poverty, and takes no thought of power," she answered, "and so he prefers to be base and unknown, and even deprives himself of natural pleasures lest he should part with the riches which he has gathered. Thus not even that satisfaction reaches the man who loses all power, who is stabbed by sorrow, lowered by his meanness, hidden by his lack of fame. Another seeks power only: he scatters his wealth, he despises pleasures and honours which have no power, and sets no value upon glory. You see how many things such an one lacks. Sometimes he goes without necessaries even, sometimes he feels the bite and torture of care; and as he cannot rid himself of these, he loses the power too which he sought above all things. The same argument may be applied to offices, glory, and pleasure. For since each one of these is the same as each other, any man who seeks one without the others, gains not even that one which he desires."

"What then?" I asked.

"If any man desires to obtain all together, he will be seeking the sum of happiness. But will he ever find that in these things which we have shewn cannot supply what they promise?"

"No."

"Then happiness is not to be sought for among these things

which are separately believed to supply each thing so sought."

"Nothing could be more plainly true," I said.

"Then you have before you the form of false happiness, and its causes; now turn your attention in the opposite direction, and you will quickly see the true happiness which I have promised to shew you."

"But surely this is clear even to the blindest, and you shewed it before when you were trying to make clear the causes of false happiness. For if I mistake not, true and perfect happiness is that which makes a man truly satisfied, powerful, venerated, renowned, and happy. And (for I would have you see that I have looked deeply into the matter) I realize without doubt that that which can truly yield any one of these, since they are all one, is perfect happiness."

"Ah! my son," said she, "I do see that you are blessed in this opinion, but I would have you add one thing."

"What is that?" I asked.

"Do you think that there is anything among mortals, and in our perishable lives, which could yield such a state?"

"I do not think that there is, and I think that you have shewn this beyond the need of further proof."

"These then seem to yield to mortals certain appearances of the true good, or some such imperfections; but they cannot give true and perfect good."

"No."

"Since, then, you have seen what is true happiness, and what are the false imitations thereof, it now remains that you should learn whence this true happiness may be sought."

"For that," said I, "I have been impatiently waiting."

"But divine help must be sought in small things as well as great (as my pupil Plato says in his *Timæus* [1]); so what, think you, must we do to deserve to find the place of that highest good?"

---

[1] Plato, *Timæus*, 27 C. (ch. v.)—"All those who have even the least share of moderation, on undertaking any enterprise, small or great, always call upon God at the beginning."

"Call," I said, "upon the Father of all, for if we do not do so, no undertaking would be rightly or duly begun."

"You are right," said she; and thus she cried aloud [1]:—

(Philosophy invokes God's guidance.)

"Thou who dost rule the universe with everlasting law, founder of earth and heaven alike, who hast bidden time stand forth from our Eternity, for ever firm Thyself, yet giving movement unto all. No causes were without Thee which could thence impel Thee to create this mass of changing matter, but within Thyself exists the very idea of perfect good, which grudges naught, for of what can it have envy? Thou makest all things follow that high pattern. In perfect beauty Thou movest in Thy mind a world of beauty, making all in a like image, and bidding the perfect whole to complete its perfect functions. All the first principles of nature Thou dost bind together by perfect orders as of numbers, so that they may be balanced each with its opposite: cold with heat, and dry with moist together; thus fire may not fly upward too swiftly because too purely, nor may the weight of the solid earth drag it down and overwhelm it. Thou dost make the soul as a third between mind and material bodies: to these the soul gives life and movement, for Thou dost spread it abroad among the members of the universe, now working in accord. Thus is the soul divided as it takes its course, making two circles, as though a binding thread around the world. Thereafter it returns unto itself and passes around the lower earthly mind; and in like manner it gives motion to the heavens to turn their course. Thou it is who dost carry forward with like inspiration these souls and lower lives. Thou dost fill these weak vessels with lofty souls, and send them abroad throughout the heavens and earth, and by Thy kindly law dost turn them again to Thyself and bring them to seek, as fire doth, to rise to Thee again.

[1] This hymn is replete with the highest development of Plato's theory of ideas, as expressed in the *Timæus,* and his theory of the ideal good being the moving spirit of the material world. Compare also the speculative portion of Virgil, *Æneid,* vi.

"Grant them, O Father, that this mind of ours may rise to Thy throne of majesty; grant us to reach that fount of good. Grant that we may so find light that we may set on Thee unblinded eyes; cast Thou therefrom the heavy clouds of this material world. Shine forth upon us in Thine own true glory. Thou art the bright and peaceful rest of all Thy children that worship Thee. To see Thee clearly is the limit of our aim. Thou art our beginning, our progress, our guide, our way, our end.

(*Philosophy discourses on the union of the highest good with God.*)

"Since then you have seen the form both of the imperfect and the perfect good, I think I should now shew you where lies this perfection of happiness. In this I think our first inquiry must be whether any good of this kind can exist in the very nature of a subject; for we must not let any vain form of thought make us miss the truth of this matter. But there can be no denial of its existence, that it is as the very source of all good. For if anything is said to be imperfect, it is held to be so by some loss of its perfection. Wherefore if in any kind of thing a particular seems imperfect, there must also be a perfect specimen in the same kind. For if you take away the perfection, it is impossible even to imagine whence could come the so-called imperfect specimen. For nature does not start from degenerate or imperfect specimens, but starting from the perfect and ideal, it degenerates to these lower and weaker forms. If then, as we have shewn above, there is an uncertain and imperfect happiness to be found in the good, then there must doubtless be also a sure and perfect happiness therein." [1]

"Yes," said I, "that is quite surely proved to be true."

"Now consider," she continued, "where it lies. The universally accepted notion of men proves that God, the fountain-head of all things, is good. For nothing can be thought of better than God, and surely He, than whom there is nothing better, must without doubt be good. Now reason shews us that God

---

[1] This reasoning hangs upon Plato's theory of ideas, and so is the opposite of the theory of evolution.

is so good, that we are convinced that in Him lies also the perfect good. For if it is not so, He cannot be the fountain-head; for there must then be something more excellent, possessing that perfect good, which appears to be of older origin than God: for it has been proved that all perfections are of earlier origin than the imperfect specimens of the same: wherefore, unless we are to prolong the series to infinity, we must allow that the highest Deity must be full of the highest, the perfect good. But as we have laid down that true happiness is perfect good, it must be that true happiness is situated in His Divinity."

"Yes, I accept that; it cannot be in any way contradicted."

"But," she said, "I beg you, be sure that you accept with a sure conscience and determination this fact, that we have said that the highest Deity is filled with the highest good."

"How should I think of it?" I asked.

"You must not think of God, the Father of all, whom we hold to be filled with the highest good, as having received this good into Himself from without, nor that He has it by nature in such a manner that you might consider Him, its possessor, and the happiness possessed, as having different essential existence. For if you think that good has been received from without, that which gave it must be more excellent than that which received it; but we have most rightly stated that He is the most excellent of all things. And if you think that it is in Him by His nature, but different in kind, then, while we speak of God as the fountain-head of all things, who could imagine by whom these different kinds can have been united? Lastly, that which is different from anything cannot be the thing from which it differs. So anything which is by its nature different from the highest good, cannot be the highest good. And this we must not think of God, than whom there is nothing more excellent, as we have agreed. Nothing in this world can have a nature which is better than its origin, wherefore I would conclude that that which is the origin of all things, according to the truest reasoning, is by its essence the highest good."

"Most truly," I said.

"You agree that the highest good is happiness?"

"Yes."

"Then you must allow that God is absolute happiness?"

"I cannot deny what you put forward before, and I see that this follows necessarily from those propositions."

"Look then," she said, "whether it is proved more strongly by this too: there cannot be two highest goods which are different. For where two good things are different, the one cannot be the other; wherefore neither can be the perfect good, while each is lacking to the other. And that which is not perfect cannot be the highest, plainly. Therefore if two things are highest good, they cannot be different. Further, we have proved to ourselves that both happiness and God are each the highest good. Therefore the highest Deity must be identical with the highest happiness."

"No conclusion," I said, "could be truer in fact, or more surely proved by reason, or more worthy of our God."

"Besides this let me give you corollary, as geometricians do, when they wish to add a point drawn from the propositions they have proved. Since men become happy by acquiring happiness, and happiness is identical with divinity, it is plain that they become happy by acquiring divinity. But just as men become just by acquiring the quality of justice, and wise by wisdom, so by the same reasoning, by acquiring divinity they become divine. Every happy man then is divine. But while nothing prevents as many men as possible from being divine, God is so by His nature, men become so by participation."

"This corollary," I said, "or whatever you call it, is indeed beautiful and very precious."

"Yes, but nothing can be more beautiful than this too which reason would have us add to what we have agreed upon."

"What is that?" I asked.

"Happiness seems to include many things: do all these join it together as into a whole which is happiness, as though each thing were a different part thereof, or is any one of them a good which fulfils the essence of happiness, and do the others merely bear relations to this one?"

"I would have you make this plain by the enunciation of these particulars."

"Do we not," she asked, "hold that happiness is a good thing?"

"Yes," I answered, "the highest good."

"But you may apply this quality of happiness to them all. For the perfect satisfaction is the same, and the highest power, and veneration, and renown, and pleasure; these are all held to be happiness."

"What then?" I asked.

"Are all these things, satisfaction, power, and the others, as it were, members of the body, happiness, or do they all bear their relation to the good, as members to a head?"

"I understand what you propose to examine, but I am waiting eagerly to hear what you will lay down."

"I would have you take the following explanation," she said. "If these were all members of the one body, happiness, they would differ individually. For this is the nature of particulars, to make up one body of different parts. But all these have been shewn to be one and the same. Therefore they are not as members; and further, this happiness will then appear to be joined together into a whole body out of one member, which is impossible."

"That is quite certain," said I, "but I would hear what is to come."

"It is plain that the others have some relation to the good. It is for that reason, namely because it is held to be good, that this satisfaction is sought, and power likewise, and the others too; we may suppose the same of veneration, renown, and pleasure. The good then is the cause of the desire for all of these, and their consummation also. Such a thing as has in itself no real or even pretended good, cannot ever be sought. On the other hand, such things as are not by nature good, but seem to be so, are sought as though they were truly good. Wherefore we may justly believe that their good quality is the cause of the desire for them, the very hinge on which they turn, and their consummation. The really important object of a desire, is that for the sake of which anything is sought, as a means. For instance, if a man wishes to ride for the sake of his health, he does not so much desire the motion of riding, as the effect, namely health. As, therefore, each of these things is desired for the sake of the good, the absolute good is the aim, rather than themselves. But we have agreed that the other things are desired for the sake of happiness, wherefore in this case too, it is happiness alone which is the object of the desire. Wherefore it is plain that the essence of the good and of happiness is one and the same."

"I cannot see how any one can think otherwise."

"But we have shewn that God and true happiness are one and the same."

"Yes."

"Therefore," said she, "we may safely conclude that the essence of God also lies in the absolute good and nowhere else.

"Come hither all who are the prey of passions, bound by their ruthless chains; those deceiving passions which blunt the minds of men. Here shall you find rest from your labours; here a haven lying in tranquil peace; this shall be a resting-place open to receive within itself all the miserable on earth. Not all the wealth of Tagus's golden sands, nor Hermus's gleaming strand,[1] nor Indus, nigh earth's hottest zone, mingling its emeralds and pearls, can bring light to the eyes of any soul, but rather plunge the soul more blindly in their shade. In her deepest caverns does earth rear all that pleases the eye and excites the mind. The glory by which the heavens move and have their being, has nought to do with the darknesses which bring ruin to the soul. Whosoever can look on this true light will scarce allow the sun's rays to be clear."

"I cannot but agree with that," I said, "for it all stands woven together by the strongest proofs."

[1] The modern Sarabat, in Asia Minor, formerly auriferous.

Then she said, "At what would you value this, namely if you could find out what is the absolute good?"

"I would reckon it," I said, "at an infinite value, if I could find out God too, who is the good."

"And that too I will make plain by most true reasoning, if you will allow to stand the conclusions we have just now arrived at."

"They shall stand good."

(Philosophy discourses upon the unity which is the highest good.)

"Have I not shewn," she asked, "that those things which most men seek are for this reason not perfect goods, because they differ between themselves; they are lacking to one another, and so cannot afford full, absolute good? But when they are gathered together, as it were, into one form and one operation, so that complete satisfaction, power, veneration, renown, and pleasure are all the same, then they become the true good. Unless they are all one and the same, they have no claim to be reckoned among the true objects of men's desires."

"That has been proved beyond all doubt."

"Then such things as differ among themselves are not goods, but they become so when they begin to be a single unity. Is it not then the case these become goods by the attainment of unity?"

"Yes," I said, "it seems so."

"But I think you allow that every good is good by participation in good?"

"Yes, I do."

"Then by reason of this likeness both unity and good must be allowed to be the same thing; for such things as have by nature the same operation, have the same essence."

"Undeniably."

"Do you realise that everything remains existent so long as it keeps its unity, but perishes in dissolution as soon as it loses its unity?"

"How so?" I asked.

"In the case of animals," she said, "so long as mind and

body remain united, you have what you call an animal. But as soon as this unity is dissolved by the separation of the two, the animal perishes and can plainly be no longer called an animal. In the case of the body, too, so long as it remains in a single form by the union of its members, the human figure is presented. But if the division or separation of the body's parts drags that union asunder, it at once ceases to be what it was. In this way one may go through every subject, and it will be quite evident that each thing exists individually, so long as it is one, but perishes so soon as it ceases to be one."

"Yes, I see the same when I think of other cases."

"Is there anything," she then asked, "which, in so far as it acts by nature, ever loses its desire for self-preservation, and would voluntarily seek to come to death and corruption?"

"No," I said; "while I think of animals which have volition in their nature, I can find in them no desire to throw away their determination to remain as they are, or to hasten to perish of their own accord, so long as there are no external forces compelling them thereto. Every animal labours for its preservation, shunning death and extinction. But about trees and plants, I have great doubts as to what I should agree to in their case, and in all inanimate objects."

"But in this case too," she said, "you have no reason to be in doubt, when you see how trees and plants grow in places which suit them, and where, so far as nature is able to prevent it, they cannot quickly wither and perish. For some grow in plains, others on mountains; some are nourished by marshes, others cling to rocks; some are fertilised by otherwise barren sands, and would wither away if one tried to transplant them to better soil. Nature grants to each what suits it, and works against their perishing while they can possibly remain alive. I need hardly remind you that all plants seem to have their mouths buried in the earth, and so they suck up nourishment by their roots and diffuse their strength through their pith and bark: the pith being the softest part is always hidden away at the heart and covered, protected, as it were, by the strength of the wood; while outside, the bark, as being the defender who endures the best, is opposed to the unkindness of the weather. Again, how great is nature's care, that they should all propagate themselves by the reproduction of their seed; they all, as is so well known, are like regular machines not merely for lasting a time, but for reproducing themselves for ever, and that by their own kinds. Things too which are supposed to be inanimate, surely do all seek after their own by a like process. For why is flame carried upward by its lightness, while solid things are carried down by their weight, unless it be that these positions and movements are suitable to each? Further, each thing preserves what is suitable to itself, and what is harmful, it destroys. Hard things, such as stones, cohere with the utmost tenacity of their parts, and resist easy dissolution; while liquids, water, and air, yield easily to division, but quickly slip back to mingle their parts which have been cut asunder. And fire cannot be cut at all.

"We are not now discussing the voluntary movements of a reasoning mind, but the natural instinct. For instance, we unwittingly digest the food we have eaten, and unconsciously breathe in sleep. Not even in animals does this love of self-preservation come from mental wishes, but from elementary nature. For often the will, under stress of external causes, embraces the idea of death, from which nature revolts in horror.[1] And, on the other hand, the will sometimes restrains what nature always desires, namely the operation of begetting, by which alone the continuance of mortal things becomes enduring. Thus far, then, this love of self-preservation arises not from the reasoning animal's intention, but from natural instinct. Providence has given to its creatures this the greatest cause of permanent existence, the instinctive desire to remain existent so far as possible. Wherefore you have no reason to doubt that all things, which exist, seek a permanent existence by nature, and similarly avoid extinction."

[1] Boethius is possibly thinking here of passages in Plato's *Republic*, Bk. iv. (439-441), where Socrates points out the frequent opposition of reason and instinct.

"Yes," I said, "I confess that I see now beyond all doubt what appeared to me just now uncertain."

"But," she continued, "that which seeks to continue its existence, aims at unity; for take this way, and none will have any chance of continued existence."

"That is true."

"Then all things desire unity," she said, and I agreed.

"But we have shewn unity to be identical with the good?"

"Yes," said I.

"Then all things desire the good; and that you may define as being the absolute good which is desired by all."

"Nothing could be more truthfully reasoned. For either everything is brought back to nothing, and all will flow on at random with no guiding head; or if there is any universal aim, it will be the sum of all good."

"Great is my rejoicing, my son," said she, "for you have set firmly in your mind the mark of the central truth. And hereby is made plain to you that which you a short time ago said that you knew not."

"What was that?"

"What was the final aim of all things," she said, "for that is plainly what is desired by all: since we have agreed that that is the good, we must confess that the good is the end of all things.

"If any man makes search for truth with all his penetration, and would be led astray by no deceiving paths, let him turn upon himself the light of an inward gaze, let him bend by force the long-drawn wanderings of his thoughts into one circle; let him tell surely to his soul, that he has, thrust away within the treasures of his mind, all that he labours to acquire without. Then shall that truth, which now was hid in error's darkening cloud, shine forth more clear than Phœbus's self. For the body, though it brings material mass which breeds forgetfulness, has never driven forth all light from the mind. The seed of truth does surely cling within, and can be roused as a spark by the fanning of philosophy. For if it is not so, how do ye men make answers true of your own instinct when teachers question you? Is it not that the quick spark of truth lies buried in the heart's low depths? And if the Muse of Plato sends through those depths the voice of truth, each man has not forgotten and is but reminding himself of what he learns." [1]

When she made an end, I said, "I agree very strongly with Plato; for this is the second time that you have reminded me of these thoughts. The first time I had lost them through the material influence of the body; the second, when overwhelmed by this weight of trouble."

(*Philosophy shews that God rules the universe for the highest good.*)

"If," said she, "you look back upon what we have agreed upon earlier, you will also soon recall what you just now said you knew not."

"What is that?" I asked.

"The guidance by which the universe is directed."

"Yes, I remember confessing my ignorance, and though I think I foresee the answer you will offer, I am eager to hear you explain it more fully."

"This world," she said, "you thought a little while ago must without doubt be guided by God."

"And I think so now," I said, "and will never think there is any doubt thereof; and I will shortly explain by what reasoning I arrive at that point. This universe would never have been suitably put together into one form from such various and opposite parts, unless there were some One who joined such different parts together; and when joined, the very variety of their natures, so discordant among themselves, would break their harmony and tear them asunder unless the One held together what it wove into one whole. Such a fixed order of nature could not continue its course, could not develop motions taking such various directions in place, time, operation, space, and attributes, unless there were One who, being immutable, had the disposal of these various changes. And this cause of

[1] Plato's doctrine of remembrance is chiefly treated of in his *Phædo* and *Meno*.

their remaining fixed and their moving, I call God, according to the name familiar to all."

Then said she, "Since these are your feelings, I think there is but little trouble left me before you may revisit your home with happiness in your grasp. But let us look into the matter we have set before ourselves. Have we not shewn that complete satisfaction exists in true happiness, and we have agreed that God is happiness itself, have we not?"

"We have."

"Wherefore He needs no external aid in governing the universe, or, if He had any such need, He would not have this complete sufficiency."

"That of necessity follows," I said.

"Then He arranges all things by Himself."

"Without doubt He does."

"And God has been shewn to be the absolute good."

"Yes, I remember."

"Then He arranges all things by good, if He arranges them by Himself, whom we have agreed to be the absolute good. And so this is the tiller and rudder by which the ship of the universe is kept sure and unbreakable."

"I feel that most strongly," I said; "and I foresaw that you would say so before, though I had a slight uncertainty."

"I believe you," she said, "for now you bring your eyes more watchfully to scan the truth. But what I am going to say is no less plain to the sight."

"What is that?"

"Since we may reasonably be sure that God steers all things by the helm of goodness, and, as I have shewn you, all things have a natural instinct to hasten towards the good, can there be any doubt that they are guided according to their own will: and that of their own accord they turn to the will of the supreme disposer, as though agreeing with, and obedient to, the helmsman?"

"That is so," I said, "and the government would not seem happy if it was a yoke upon discontented necks, and not the salvation of the submissive."

"Then nothing need oppose God's way for its own nature's preservation."

"No."

"But if it try to oppose Him, will it ever have any success at all against One whom we have justly allowed to be supremely powerful in matters of happiness?"

"Certainly not."

"Then there is nothing which could have the will or the power to resist the highest good?"

"I think not."

"Then it is the highest good which is guiding with strength and disposing with gentleness?"

Then said I, "How great pleasure these things give me! Not only those which have been proved by the strongest arguments, but still more the words in which you prove them, which make me ashamed that my folly has bragged so loudly."

"You have heard in mythology how the giants attacked heaven. It was this kindly strength which overthrew them too, as was their desert. But would you care to put these arguments at variance? For perhaps from such a friction, some fair spark of truth may leap forth."

"As you hold best," I said.

"Nobody would care to doubt that God is all-powerful?"

"At any rate, no sane man would doubt it."

"Being, then, all-powerful, nothing is beyond His power?"

"Nothing."

"Can, then, God do evil?"

"No."

"Then evil is nothing, since it is beyond His power, and nothing is beyond His power?"

"Are you playing with me," I asked, "weaving arguments as a labyrinth out of which I shall find no way? You may enter a labyrinth by the way by which you may come forth: come now forth by the way you have gone in: or are you folding your reason in some wondrous circle of divine simplicity? A little while ago you started from happiness, and said that happiness was the highest good; and you shewed how that rested in the highest Deity. And you reasoned that God too was the highest good, and the fullest happiness; and you allowed, as though granting a slight gift, that none could be happy except such as were similarly divine. Again, you said that the essence of God and of happiness was identical with the very form of good; and that that alone was good which was sought by all nature. And you argued, too, that God guided this universe by the helm of goodness; and that all creatures with free will obeyed this guidance, and that there was no such thing as natural evil; and all these things you developed by no help from without, but by homely and internal proofs, each gaining its credence from that which went before it."

Then she answered, "I was not mocking you. We have worked out the greatest of all matters by the grace of God, to whom we prayed. For the form of the divine essence is such that it is not diffused without, nor receives aught into itself from without. But as Parmenides says of it, "It is a mass well rounded upon all sides." [1] But if you examine it with reasoning, sought for not externally but by lying within the sphere of the very thing we are handling, you will not wonder at what you have learnt on Plato's authority,[2] that our language must be akin to the subjects of which we speak.

"Happy the man who could reach the crystal fount of good: happy he who could shake off the chains of matter and of earth. The singer of Thrace in olden time lamented his dead wife: by his tearful strains he made the trees to follow him, and bound the flowing streams to stay: for him the hind would fearlessly go side by side with fiercest lions, and the hare would

[1] This is a verse from the poems in which Parmenides embodied his philosophy: this was the doctrine of the unity which must have been in Boethius's mind above. Parmenides, the founder of the Eleatic school (495 B.C.), was perhaps, considering his early date, the greatest and most original of Greek philosophers. Boethius probably did not make a clear distinction between the philosopher's own poems and the views expressed in Plato's *Parmenides*.

[2] Plato in the *Timæus* says, "The language must also be akin to the subjects of which its words are the interpreters"—(29 B.).

look upon the hound, nor be afraid, for he was gentle under the song's sway. But when the hotter flame burnt up his inmost soul, even the strains, which had subdued all other things, could not soothe their own lord's mind. Complaining of the hard hearts of the gods above, he dared approach the realms below. There he tuned his songs to soothing tones, and sang the lays he had drawn from his mother's [1] fount of excellence. His unrestrained grief did give him power, his love redoubled his grief's power: his mourning moved the depths of hell. With gentlest prayers he prayed to the lords of the shades for grace. The three-headed porter [2] was taken captive with amazement at his fresh songs. The avenging goddesses,[3] who haunt with fear the guilty, poured out sad tears. Ixion's [4] wheel no longer swiftly turned. Tantalus,[5] so long abandoned unto thirst, could then despise the flowing stream. The vulture, satisfied by his strains, tore not a while at Tityos's [6] heart. At last the lord of the shades [7] in pity cried: "We are conquered; take your bride with you, bought by your song; but one condition binds our gift: till she has left these dark abodes, turn not your eyes upon her." Who shall set a law to lovers? Love is a greater law unto itself. Alack! at the very bounds of darkness Orpheus looked upon his Eurydice; looked, and lost her, and was lost himself.

"To you too this tale refers; you, who seek to lead your thoughts to the light above. For whosoever is overcome of desire, and turns his gaze upon the darkness 'neath the earth, he, while he looks on hell, loses the prize he carried off."

[1] Orpheus's mother was the Muse Calliope, mistress of the Castalian fount.

[2] The dog Cerberus.

[3] The Furies.

[4] Ixion for his crimes was bound upon a rolling wheel.

[5] Tantalus for his crimes was condemned to perpetual hunger and thirst though surrounded by fruits and water which ever eluded his grasp.

[6] Tityos for his crimes was for ever fastened to the ground, while a vulture devoured his entrails.

[7] Pluto.

BOOK FOUR

(They discuss the possibility of evil in God's world.)

THUS gently sang the Lady Philosophy with dignified mien and grave countenance; and when she ceased, I, who had not thoroughly forgotten the grief within me, interrupted her as she was about to speak further. "Herald of true light," I said, "right clear have been the outpourings of your speech till now, seeming inspired as one contemplates them, and invincible through your reasonings. And though through grief for the injustices I suffer, I had forgotten them, yet you have not spoken of what I knew not at all before. But this one thing is the chief cause of my grief, namely that, when there exists a good governor of the world, evils should exist at all, or, existing, should go unpunished. I would have you think how strange is this fact alone. But there is an even stranger attached thereto: ill-doing reigns and flourishes, while virtue not only lacks its reward, but is even trampled underfoot by wicked doers, and pays the penalties instead of crime. Who can wonder and complain enough that such things should happen under the rule of One who, while all-knowing and all-powerful, wills good alone?"

Then she answered: "Yes, it would be most terrible, monstrous, and infinitely amazing if it were as you think. It would be as though in a well-ordered house of a good master, the vilest vessels were cared for while the precious were left defiled. But it is not so. If our former conclusions are unshaken, God Himself, of whose government we speak, will teach you that the good are always powerful, the evil are always the lowest and weakest; vice never goes unpunished; virtue never goes without its own reward; happiness comes to the good, misfortune to the wicked: and when your complaints are set

74

at rest, many such things would most firmly strengthen you in this opinion. You have seen now from my teaching the form of true happiness; you know now its place: let us go quickly through all that must be lightly passed over, and let me shew you the road which shall lead you to your home. I will give wings to your mind, by which it shall raise itself aloft: so shall disquiet be driven away, and you may return safe to your home by my guidance, by the path I shall shew you, even by myself carrying you thither.

"Yea, airy wings are mine to scale the heights of heaven; when these the mind has donned, swiftly she loathes and spurns this earth. She soars above the sphere of this vast atmosphere, sees the clouds behind her far; she passes high above the topmost fires which seethe above the feverish tur- moil of the air,[1] until she rises to the stars' own home, and joins her path unto the sun's; or accompanies on her path the cold and ancient Saturn, maybe as the shining warrior Mars; or she may take her course through the circle of every star that decks the night. And when she has had her fill of journey- ing, then may she leave the sky and tread the outer plane of the swift moving air, as mistress of the awful light. Here holds the King of Kings His sway, and guides the reins of the uni- verse, and Himself unmoved He drives His winged chariot, the bright disposer of the world. And if this path brings thee again hither, the path that now thy memory seeks to recall, I tell thee, thou shalt say, 'This is my home, hence was I de- rived, here shall I stay my course.' But if thou choose to look back upon the earthly night behind thee, thou shalt see as exiles from light the tyrants whose grimness made wretched peoples so to fear."

"Wondrous," I cried; "what vast things do you promise! And I doubt not that you can fulfil them. I only beg that you

---

[1] This and some of the following lines allude to some of the theories of the early Physicists.

will not hold me back with delays, now that you have excited me thus far."

(Philosophy argues that the good are powerful, the bad are weak.)

"First, then, you must learn that power is never lacking to the good, while the wicked are devoid of all strength. The proofs of these two statements hang upon each other. For good and bad are opposites, and therefore, if it is allowed that good is powerful, the weakness of evil is manifest: if the weakness and uncertainty of evil is made plain, the strength and sureness of good is proved. To gain more full credit for my opinion, I will go on to make my argument sure by first the one, then the other of the two paths, side by side.

"It is allowed that there are two things upon which depend the entire operation of human actions: they are will and power. For if the will be wanting, a man does not even attempt that which he has no desire to perform; if the power be wanting, the will is exercised in vain. Wherefore, if you see a man wish for that which he will in no wise gain, you cannot doubt that he lacks the power to attain that which he wishes."

"That is plain beyond doubt."

"And if you see a man gain that which he wishes, can you doubt that he has the power?"

"No."

"But wherein a man has power, he is strong; wherein he has not power, he must be counted weak?"

"Yes."

"Do you remember that we agreed from our earlier reasonings, that the instinct of all human will, though acted upon by different aims, does lead with eagerness towards happiness?"

"Yes," said I, "I remember that that too was proved."

"Do you remember that happiness is the absolute good, and that the good is desired of all, when in that manner happiness is sought?"

"I need not recall that," I said, "since it is present fixedly in my memory."

"Then all men, good and bad alike, seek to arrive at the good by no different instincts?"

"Yes, that follows necessarily."

"But it is certain that the good become so by the attainment of good?"

"Yes."

"Then the good attain that which they wish?"

"Yes," said I, "it seems so."

"But if evil men attain the good they seek, they cannot be evil?"

"No."

"Since, then, both classes seek the good, which the good attain, but the evil attain not, it is plain that the good are powerful, while the evil are weak?"

"If any doubt that, he cannot judge by the nature of the world, nor by the sequence of arguments."

Again she said, "If there are two persons before whom the same object is put by natural instinct, and one person carries his object through, working by his natural functions, but the other cannot put his natural instinct into practice, but using some function unsuitable to nature he can imitate the successful person, but not fulfil his original purpose, in this case, which of the two do you decide to be the more capable?"

"I think I guess what you mean, but I would hear more explicitly."

"You will not, I think, deny that the motion of walking is a natural one to mankind?"

"No, I will not."

"And is not that the natural function of the feet?"

"Yes."

"If, then, one man walks, being able to advance upon his feet, while another, who lacks the natural function of feet, uses his hands and so tries to walk, which of these two may justly be held the more capable?"

"Weave me other riddles!" I exclaimed, "for can any one doubt that a man who enjoys his natural functions, is more capable than one who is incapable in that respect?"

"But in the case of the highest good," she said, "it is equally the purpose set before good and bad men; good men seek it by the natural functions of virtue, while bad men seek to attain the same through their cupidity, which is not a natural function for the attainment of good. Think you not so?"

"I do indeed," said I; "this is plain, as also is the deduction which follows. For it must be, from what I have already allowed, that the good are powerful, the wicked weak."

"Your anticipation is right; and as doctors are wont to hope, it shews a lively nature now fit to withstand disease. But I see that you are very ready in understanding, and I will multiply my arguments one upon another. See how great is the weakness of these wicked men who cannot even attain that to which their natural instinct leads them, nay, almost drives them. And further, how if they are deprived of this great, this almost invincible, aid of a natural instinct to follow? Think what a powerlessness possesses these men. They are no light objects which they seek; they seek no objects in sport, objects which it is impossible that they should achieve. They fail in the very highest of all things, the crown of all, and in this they find none of the success for which they labour day and night in wretchedness. But herein the strength of good men is conspicuous. If a man could advance on foot till he arrived at an utmost point beyond which there was no path for further advance, you would think him most capable of walking: equally so, if a man grasps the very end and aim of his search, you must think him most capable. Wherefore also the contrary is true; that evil men are similarly deprived of all strength. For why do they leave virtue and follow after vice? Is it from ignorance of good? Surely not, for what is weaker or less compelling than the blindness of ignorance? Do they know what they ought to follow, and are they thrown from the straight road by passions? Then they must be weak too in self-control if they cannot struggle with their evil passions. But they lose thus not only power, but existence all together. For those who abandon the common end of all who exist, must equally cease to exist. And this may seem strange, that we should say that evil men, though the majority of mankind, do not exist at all; but it is so. For while I do not deny that evil men are evil, I do deny that they 'are,' in the sense of absolute existence. You may say, for instance, that a corpse is a dead man, but you cannot call it a man. In a like manner, though I grant that wicked men are bad, I cannot allow that they are men at all, as regards absolute being. A thing exists which keeps its proper place and preserves its nature; but when anything falls away from its nature, its existence too ceases, for that lies in its nature. You will say, 'Evil men are capable of evil': and that I would not deny. But this very power of theirs comes not from strength, but from weakness. They are capable of evil; but this evil would have no efficacy if it could have stayed under the operation of good men. And this very power of ill shews the more plainly that their power is naught. For if, as we have agreed, evil is nothing, then, since they are only capable of evil, they are capable of nothing."

"That is quite plain."

"I would have you understand what is this strength of power. We have a little while ago laid down that nothing is more powerful than the highest good?"

"Yes," I said.

"But the highest good can do no evil?"

"No."

"Is there any one who thinks that men are all-powerful?"

"No one," I said, "unless he be mad."

"And yet those same men can do evil."

"Would to heaven they could not!" I cried.

"Then a powerful man is capable only of all good; but even those who are capable of evil, are not capable of all: so it is plain that those who are capable of evil, are capable of less. Further, we have shewn that all power is to be counted among objects of desire, and all objects of desire have their relation to the good, as to the coping-stone of their nature. But the power of committing crime has no possible relation to the good. Therefore it is not an object of desire. Yet, as we said, all power is to be desired. Therefore the power of doing evil is no power at all. For all these reasons the power of good men and the weakness of evil men is apparent. So Plato's opinion [1] is plain that 'the wise alone are able to do what they desire, but unscrupulous men can only labour at what they like, they cannot fulfil their real desires.' They do what they like so long as they think that they will gain through their pleasures the good which they desire; but they do not gain it, since nothing evil ever reaches happiness.

"Kings you may see sitting aloft upon their thrones, gleaming with purple, hedged about with grim guarding weapons, threatening with fierce glances, and their hearts heaving with passion. If any man take from these proud ones their outward covering of empty honour, he will see within, will see that these great ones bear secret chains. For the heart of one is thus filled by lust with the poisons of greed, or seething rage lifts up its waves and lashes his mind therewith: or gloomy grief holds them weary captives, or by slippery hopes they are tortured. So when you see one head thus labouring beneath so many tyrants, you know he cannot do as he would, for by hard task-masters is the master himself oppressed.

(The good and the evil have their own rewards.)

"Do you see then in what a slough crimes are involved, and with what glory honesty shines forth? It is plain from this that reward is never lacking to good deeds, nor punishment to crime. We may justly say that the reward of every act which is performed is the object for which it is performed. For instance, on the racecourse the crown for which the runner strives is his reward. But we have shewn that happiness is

[1] From Plato's *Gorgias* (466). Boethius in this and several other passages in this book has the *Gorgias* in mind; for Plato there discusses the strength and happiness of good men, and the impotence and unhappiness of bad men. Socrates is also there represented as proving that the unjust man is happier punished than unpunished, as Boethius does below.

the identical good for the sake of which all actions are performed. Therefore the absolute good is the reward put before all human actions. But good men cannot be deprived of this. And further, a man who lacks good cannot justly be described as a good man; wherefore we may say that good habits never miss their rewards. Let the wicked rage never so wildly, the wise man's crown shall never fail nor wither. And the wickedness of bad men can never take away from good men the glory which belongs to them. Whereas if a good man rejoiced in a glory which he received from outside, then could another, or even he, may be, who granted it, carry it away. But since honesty grants to every good man its own rewards, he will only lack his reward when he ceases to be good. And lastly, since every reward is sought for the reason that it is held to be good, who shall say that the man, who possesses goodness, does not receive his reward? And what reward is this? Surely the fairest and greatest of all. Remember that corollary[1] which I emphasised when speaking to you a little while ago; and reason thus therefrom. While happiness is the absolute good, it is plain that all good men become good by virtue of the very fact that they are good. But we agreed that happy men are as gods. Therefore this is the reward of the good, which no time can wear out, no power can lessen, no wickedness can darken; they become divine. In this case, then, no wise man can doubt of the inevitable punishment of the wicked as well. For good and evil are so set, differing from each other just as reward and punishment are in opposition to each other: hence the rewards, which we see fall to the good, must correspond precisely to the punishments of the evil on the other side. As, therefore, honestly is itself the reward of the honest, so wickedness is itself the punishment of the wicked. Now whosoever suffers punishment, doubts not that he is suffering an evil: if, then, they are ready so to judge of themselves, can they think that they do not receive punish-

[1] P. 62.

ment, considering that they are not only affected but thoroughly permeated by wickedness, the worst of all evils?

"Then, from the other point of view of the good, see what a punishment ever goes with the wicked. You have learnt a little while past that all that exists is one, and that the good itself is one; it follows therefrom that all that exists must appear to be good. In this way, therefore, all that falls away from the good, ceases also to exist, wherefore evil men cease to be what they were. The form of their human bodies still proves that they have been men; wherefore they must have lost their human nature when they turned to evil-doing. But as goodness alone can lead men forward beyond their humanity, so evil of necessity will thrust down below the honourable estate of humanity those whom it casts down from their first position. The result is that you cannot hold him to be a man who has been, so to say, transformed by his vices. If a violent man and a robber burns with greed of other men's possessions, you say he is like a wolf. Another fierce man is always working his restless tongue at lawsuits, and you will compare him to a hound. Does another delight to spring upon men from ambushes with hidden guile? He is as a fox. Does one man roar and not restrain his rage? He would be reckoned as having the heart of a lion. Does another flee and tremble in terror where there is no cause of fear? He would be held to be as deer. If another is dull and lazy, does he not live the life of an ass? One whose aims are inconstant and ever changed at his whims, is in no wise different from the birds. If another is in a slough of foul and filthy lusts, he is kept down by the lusts of an unclean swine. Thus then a man who loses his goodness, ceases to be a man, and since he cannot change his condition for that of a god, he turns into a beast.

"The east wind wafted the sails which carried on the wandering ships of Ithaca's king to the island where dwelt the fair goddess Circe, the sun's own daughter. There for her new guests she mingled cups bewitched by charms. Her hand, well skilled in use of herbs, changed these guests to different forms.

One bears the face of a boar; another grows like to an African lion with fangs and claws; this one becomes as a wolf, and when he thinks to weep, he howls; that one is an Indian tiger, though he walks all harmless round about the dwelling-place. The leader alone, Ulysses, though beset by so many dangers, was saved from the goddess's bane by the pity of the winged god, Mercury. But the sailors had drunk of her cups, and now had turned from food of corn to husks and acorns, food of swine. Naught is left the same, speech and form are gone; only the mind remains unchanged, to bewail their unnatural sufferings.

"How weak was that hand, how powerless those magic herbs which could change the limbs but not the heart! Within lies the strength of men, hidden in deep security. Stronger are those dread poisons which can drag a man out of himself, which work their way within: they hurt not the body, but on the mind their rage inflicts a grievous wound." [1]

Then I answered: "I confess that I think it is justly said that vicious men keep only the outward bodily form of their humanity, and, in the attributes of their souls, are changed to beasts. But I would never have allowed them willingly the power to rage in the ruin of good men through their fierce and wicked intentions."

"They have not that power," said she, "as I will shew you at a convenient time. But if this very power, which you believe is allowed to them, were taken from them, the punishment of vicious men would be to a great extent lightened. For, though some may scarcely believe it, evil men must be more unhappy when they carry out their ill desires than when they cannot fulfil them. For if it is pitiable to have wished bad things, it is more pitiable to have had the power to perform them, without which power the performance of this pitiable will would never have effect. Thus, when you see men with the will and the power to commit a crime, and you see them

[1] *Cf.* St. Matthew x. 28.

perform it, they must be the victims of a threefold misfortune, since each of those three things brings its own misery."

"Yes," said I, "I agree; but I do wish from my heart that they may speedily be rid of one of these misfortunes, being deprived of this power of doing evil."

"They will be rid of it," she said, "more speedily even than you wish perhaps, and sooner than they think they will be rid thereof. There is in the short course of life naught which is so long coming that an immortal mind can think it has long to wait for it. Many a time are their high hopes and great plans for evil-doing cut short by a sudden and unlooked-for end. This indeed it is that sets a limit to their misery. For if wickedness makes a man miserable, the longer he is wicked, the more miserable must he be; and I should hold them most miserable of all, if not even death at last put an end to their evil-doing. If we have reached true conclusions concerning the unhappiness of depravity, the misery, which is said to be eternal, can have no limit."

"That is a strange conclusion and hard to accept. But I see that it is suited too well by what we have agreed upon earlier."

"You are right," she said; "but when one finds it hard to agree with a conclusion, one ought in fairness to point out some fault in the argument which has preceded, or shew that the sequence of statements is not so joined together as to effectively lead to the conclusion; otherwise, if the premises are granted, it is not just to cavil at the inference. This too, which I am about to say, may not seem less strange, but it follows equally from what has been taken as fact."

"What is that?" I asked.

"That wicked men are happier when they pay the penalty for their wickedness than when they receive no penalty at the hands of justice.[1] I am not going to urge what may occur to any one, namely, that depraved habits are corrected by penalties, and drawn towards the right by fear of punishment, and that an example is hereby given to others to avoid all that

[1] Plato, *Gorgias*, 472 and ff.

deserves blame. But I think that the wicked who are not punished are in another way the more unhappy, without regard to the corrective quality of punishment, nor its value as an example."

"And what way is there other than these?"

"We have allowed, have we not," she said, "that the good are happy, but the bad are miserable?"

"Yes."

"Then if any good be added to the misery of any evil man, is he not happier than the man whose miserable state is purely and simply miserable without any good at all mingled therewith?"

"I suppose so."

"What if some further evil beyond those by which a man, who lacked all good things, were made miserable, were added to his miseries? Should not he be reckoned far more unhappy than the man whose misfortune was lightened by a share in some good?"

"Of course it is so."

"Therefore," she said, "the wicked when punished have something good added to their lot, to wit, their punishment, which is good by reason of its quality of justice; and they also, when unpunished, have something of further evil, their very impunity, which you have allowed to be an evil, by reason of its injustice."

"I cannot deny that," said I.

"Then the wicked are far more unhappy when they are unjustly unpunished, than when they are justly punished. It is plain that it is just that the wicked should be punished, and unfair that they should escape punishment."

"No one will gainsay you."

"But no one will deny this either, that all which is just is good; and on the other part, all that is unjust is evil."

Then I said: "The arguments which we have accepted bring us to that conclusion. But tell me, do you leave no punishment of the soul to follow after the death of the body?"

"Yes," she answered, "heavy punishments, of which some,

I think, are effected by bitter penalties, others by a cleansing mercy.[1] But it is not my intention to discuss these now. My object has been to bring you to know that the power of evil men, which seems to you so unworthy, is in truth nothing; and that you may see that those wicked men, of whose impunity you complained, do never miss the reward of their ill-doing; and that you may learn that their passion, which you prayed might soon be cut short, is not long-enduring, and that the longer it lasts, the more unhappiness it brings, and that it would be most unhappy if it endured for ever. Further, I have tried to shew you that the wicked are more to be pitied if they escape with unjust impunity, than if they are punished by just retribution. And it follows upon this fact that they will be undergoing heavier penalties when they are thought to be unpunished."

"When I hear your arguments, I feel sure that they are true as possible. But if I turn to human opinions, I ask what man would not think them not only incredible, but even unthinkable?"

"Yes," she said, "for men cannot raise to the transparent light of truth their eyes which have been accustomed to darkness. They are like those birds whose sight is clear at night, but blinded by daylight. So long as they look not upon the true course of nature, but upon their own feelings, they think that the freedom of passion and the impunity of crime are happy things. Think upon the sacred ordinances of eternal law. If your mind is fashioned after better things, there is no need of a judge to award a prize; you have added yourself to the number of the more excellent. If your mind sinks to worse things, seek no avenger from without: you have thrust yourself downward to lower things. It is as though you were

---

[1] It must not be supposed from the words "cleansing mercy" (*purgatoria clementia*) that Boethius held the same views as were held by the Church later concerning purgatory, and as are now taught by the Roman Catholic Church. It is true that St. Augustine had in 407 A.D. hinted at the existence of such a state, but it was not dogmatically inculcated till 604, in the Papacy of Gregory the Great.

looking at the squalid earth and the heavens in turn; then take away all that is about you; and by the power of sight, you will seem to be in the midst now of mud, now of stars. But mankind looks not to such things. What then shall we do? Shall we join ourselves to those whom we have shewn to be as beasts? If a man lost utterly his sight, and even forgot that he had ever seen, so that he thought he lacked naught of human perfection, should we think that such a blind one can see as we do? Most people would not even allow another point, which rests no less firmly upon strong reasons, namely, that those who do an injury are more unhappy than those who suffer one." [1]

"I would hear those strong reasons," I said.

"You do not deny that every wicked man deserves punishment?"

"No."

"It is plain for many reasons that the wicked are unhappy?"

"Yes."

"Then you doubt not that those who are worthy of punishment are miserable?"

"No, I agree."

"If then you were sitting as a judge, upon which would you consider punishment should fall—the man who did the injury, or the man who suffered it?"

"I have no hesitation in saying that I would make amends to the sufferer at the expense of the doer of the injustice."

"Then the doer of the injustice would seem to you more miserable than the sufferer?"

"That follows."

"Then from this," said she, "and other causes which rest upon the same foundation, it is plain that, since baseness makes men more miserable by its own nature, the misery is brought not to the sufferer of an injustice, but to the doer thereof. But the speakers in law-courts take the opposite course: they try to excite the pity of the judges for those who

[1] Plato, *Gorgias*, 474 and ff.

have suffered any heavy or bitter wrong; but more justly their pity would be due to those who have committed the wrong. These guilty men ought to be brought, by accusers kindly rather than angry, to justice, as patients to a doctor, that their disease of crime may be checked by punishment. Under such an arrangement the occupation of advocates for defence would either come to a complete standstill, or if it seemed more to the advantage of mankind, it might turn to the work of prosecution. And if the wicked too themselves might by some device look on virtue left behind them, and if they could see that they would lay aside the squalor of vice by the pain of punishment, and that they would gain the compensation of achieving virtue again, they would no longer hold it punishment, but would refuse the aid of advocates for their defence, and would intrust themselves unreservedly to their accusers and their judges. In this way there would be no place left for hatred among wise men. For who but the most foolish would hate good men? And there is no cause to hate bad men. Vice is as a disease of the mind, just as feebleness shews ill-health in the body. As, then, we should never think that those, who are sick in the body, deserve hatred, so are those, whose minds are oppressed by a fiercer disease than feebleness, namely wickedness, much more worthy of pity than of persecution.

"To what good end do men their passions raise, even to drag from fate their deaths by their own hands? If ye seek death, she is surely nigh of her own will; and her winged horses she will not delay. Serpents and lions, bears, tigers and boars, all seek your lives with their fangs, yet do ye seek them with swords? Is it because your manners are so wide in variance that men raise up unjust battles and savage wars, and seek to perish by each other's darts? Such is no just reason for this cruelty. Wouldst thou apportion merit to merit fitly? Then love good men as is their due, and for the evil shew your pity."

(*Boethius still feels dissatisfied with the world's government.*)

Then said I, "I see how happiness and misery lie insep-arably in the deserts of good and bad men. But I am sure that there is some good and some bad in the general fortune of men. For no wise man even would wish to be exiled, impoverished, and disgraced rather than full of wealth, power, veneration, and strength, and flourishing securely in his own city. The operation of wisdom is shewn in this way more nobly and clearly, when the happiness of rulers is in a manner trans-mitted to the people who come into contact with their rule; and especially when prisons, bonds, and other penalties of the law become the lot of the evil citizens for whom they were designed. I am struck with great wonder why these dues are interchanged; why punishments for crimes fall upon the good, while the bad citizens seize the rewards of virtue; and I long to learn from you what reason can be put forward for such unjust confusion. I should wonder less if I could believe that everything was the confusion of accident and chance. But now the thought of God's guidance increases my amaze-ment; He often grants happiness to good men and bitterness to the bad, and then, on the other hand, sends hardships to the good and grants the desires of the wicked. Can we lay our hands on any cause? If not, what can make this state different in any way from accidental chance?"

"It is no wonder," she answered, "if one who knows not the order and reasons of nature, should think it is all at random and confused. But doubt not, though you know not the cause of such a great matter of the world's government, doubt not, I say, that all is rightly done, because a good Governor rules the universe.

"If any man knows not that the star Arcturus[1] has his course nearest the topmost pole, how shall he not be amazed

---

[1] Arcturus, the star in Boötes nearest to the Bear, used to be thought the nearest star to our pole. Boötes was also known as the Arctophylax, or Bearward, and so also as the driver of the Wain.

that Boötes so slowly takes his wain and is so late to dip his brightness in the ocean, and yet so swiftly turns to rise again? The law of heaven on high will but bewilder him. When the full moon grows dim to its horns, darkened by the shadow of dull night, when Phœbe thus lays bare all the varying bands of the stars, which she had hidden by the power of her shining face: then are the nations stirred by the errors of the vulgar, and beat without ceasing brazen cymbals.[1] No man is surprised when the blasts of the wind beat a shore with roaring waves, nor when a solid mass of frozen snow is melted by the warmth of Phœbus's rays; for herein the causes are ready at hand to be understood. But in those other matters the causes are hidden, and so do trouble all men's hearts, for time does not grant them to advance with experience in such things as seldom recur: the common herd is ever amazed at all that is extraordinary. But let the cloudy errors of ignorance depart, and straightway these shall seem no longer marvellous."

"That is true," I said; "but it is your kind office to unravel the causes of hidden matters, and explain reasons now veiled in darkness; wherefore I beg of you, put forth your decree and expound all to me, since this wonder most deeply stirs my mind."

Then said she, smiling, "Your question calls me to the greatest of all these matters, and a full answer thereto is well-nigh impossible. For this is its kind: if one doubt be cut away, innumerable others arise, as the Hydra's heads; and there can be no limit unless a man restrains them by the most quick fire of the mind. For herein lie the questions of the directness of Providence, the course of Fate, chances which cannot be foreseen, knowledge, divine predestination, and freedom of judgment. You can judge for yourself the weight of these questions. But since it is a part of your treatment to know some of these, I will attempt to make some advantage there-

---

[1] The old superstition was that an eclipse meant the withdrawal of the moon, and that by a noise of beaten brass, etc., she could be saved.

from, though we are penned in by our narrow space of time. But if you enjoy the delights of song, you must wait a while for that pleasure, while I weave together for you the chain of reasons."

"As you will," said I.

Then, as though beginning afresh, she spake thus:

(*Philosophy discusses Providence and Fate.*)

"The engendering of all things, the whole advance of all changing natures, and every motion and progress in the world, draw their causes, their order, and their forms from the allotment of the unchanging mind of God, which lays manifold restrictions on all action from the calm fortress of its own directness. Such restrictions are called Providence when they can be seen to lie in the very simplicity of divine understanding; but they were called Fate in old times when they were viewed with reference to the objects which they moved or arranged. It will easily be understood that these two are very different if the mind examines the force of each. For Providence is the very divine reason which arranges all things, and rests with the supreme disposer of all; while Fate is that ordering which is a part of all changeable things, and by means of which Providence binds all things together in their own order. Providence embraces all things equally, however different they may be, even however infinite: when they are assigned to their own places, forms, and times, Fate sets them in an orderly motion; so that this development of the temporal order, unified in the intelligence of the mind of God, is Providence. The working of this unified development in time is called Fate. These are different, but the one hangs upon the other. For this order, which is ruled by Fate, emanates from the directness of Providence. Just as when a craftsman perceived in his mind the form of the object he would make, he sets his working power in motion, and brings through the order of time that which he had seen directly and ready present to his mind. So by Providence does God dispose all that is to be done, each thing by itself and unchangeably; while these same things which Providence has arranged are worked out by Fate in many ways and in time. Whether, therefore, Fate works by the aid of the divine spirits which serve Providence, or whether it works by the aid of the soul, or of all nature, or the motions of the stars in heaven, or the powers of angels, or the manifold skill of other spirits, whether the course of Fate is bound together by any or all of these, one thing is certain, namely that Providence is the one unchangeable direct power which gives form to all things which are to come to pass, while Fate is the changing bond, the temporal order of those things which are arranged to come to pass by the direct disposition of God. Wherefore everything which is subject to Fate is also subject to Providence, to which Fate is itself subject. But there are things which, though beneath Providence, are above the course of Fate. Those things are they which are immovably set nearest the primary divinity, and are there beyond the course of the movement of Fate. As in the case of spheres moving round the same axis, that which is nearest the centre approaches most nearly the simple motion of the centre, and is itself, as it were, an axis around which turn those which are set outside it. That sphere which is outside all turns through a greater circuit, and fulfils a longer course in proportion as it is farther from the central axis; and if it be joined or connect itself with that centre, it is drawn into the direct motion thereof, and no longer strays or strives to turn away. In like manner, that which goes farther from the primary intelligence, is bound the more by the ties of Fate, and the nearer it approaches the axis of all, the more free it is from Fate. But that which clings without movement to the firm intellect above, surpasses altogether the bond of Fate. As, therefore, reasoning is to understanding; as that which becomes is to that which is; as time is to eternity; as the circumference is to the centre: so is the changing course of Fate to the immovable directness of Providence. That course of Fate moves the heavens and the stars, moderates the first principles in their turns, and alters their forms by balanced interchangings. The same course renews all things that are born and wither away by like advances of offspring and seed. It constrains, too, the actions and fortunes of men by an unbreakable chain of causes: and these causes must be unchangeable, as they proceed from the beginnings of an unchanging Providence. Thus is the world governed for the best if a directness, which rests in the intelligence of God, puts forth an order of causes which may not swerve. This order restrains by its own unchangeableness changeable things, which might otherwise run hither and thither at random. Wherefore in disposing the universe this limitation directs all for good, though to you who are not strong enough to comprehend the whole order, all seems confusion and disorder. Naught is there that comes to pass for the sake of evil, or due to wicked men, of whom it has been abundantly shewn that they seek the good, but misleading error turns them from the right course; for never does the true order, which comes forth from the centre of the highest good, turn any man aside from the right beginning.

"But you will ask, 'What more unjust confusion could exist than that good men should sometimes enjoy prosperity, sometimes suffer adversity, and that the bad too should sometimes receive what they desire, sometimes what they hate?' Are then men possessed of such infallible minds that they, whom they consider honest or dishonest, must necessarily be what they are held to be? No, in these matters human judgment is at variance with itself, and those who are held by some to be worthy of reward, are by others held worthy of punishment. But let us grant that a man could discern between good and bad characters. Can he therefore know the inmost feelings of the soul, as a doctor can learn a body's temperature? For it is no less a wonder to the ignorant why sweet things suit one sound body, while bitter things suit another; or why some sick people are aided by gentle draughts, others by sharp and bitter ones. But a doctor does not wonder at such things, for he knows the ways and constitutions of health and sickness. And what is the health of the soul but virtue? And what the sickness, but vice? And who is the preserver of the good and banisher of the evil, who but God, the guardian and healer of minds? God looks forth from the high watch-tower of His Providence, He sees what suits each man, and applies to him that which suits him. Hence then comes that conspicuous cause of wonder in the order of Fate, when a wise man does that which amazes the ignorant. For, to glance at the depth of God's works with so few words as human reason is capable of comprehending, I say that what you think to be most fair and most conducive to justice's preservation, that appears different to an all-seeing Providence. Has not our fellow-philosopher Lucan told us how 'the conquering cause did please the gods, but the conquered, Cato?' [1] What then surprises you when done on this earth, is the true-guided order of things; it is your opinion which is perverted and confused. But if there is any one whose life is so good that divine and human estimates of him agree, yet he must be uncertain in the strength of his mind; if any adversity befall him, it may always be that he will cease to preserve his innocence, by which he found that he could not preserve his good fortune. Thus then a wise dispensation spares a man who might be made worse by adversity, lest he should suffer when it is not good for him to be oppressed. Another may be perfected in all virtues, wholly conscientious, and very near to God: Providence holds that it is not right such an one should receive any adversity, so that it allows him to be troubled not even by bodily diseases. As a better man [2] than I has said, 'The powers of virtues build up the body of a good man.' It often happens that the duty of a supreme authority is assigned to good men for the purpose of pruning the insolent growth of wickedness. To some, Providence grants a mingled store of

[1] Lucan, *Pharsalia*, i. 128. This famous line refers to the final triumph of Cæsar at Thapsus, B.C. 46, when Cato considered that the Republican cause was finally doomed and he committed suicide at Utica rather than survive it.

[2] The author is supposed to be Hermes Trismegistus, who wrote in the third century after Christ. The word "powers" was used by many Neo-Platonic philosophers for those beings in the scale of nature, with which they filled the chasm between God and man. But Boethius does not seem to intend the word to have that definite meaning here.

good and bad, according to the nature of their minds. Some she treats bitterly, lest they grow too exuberant with long-continued good fortune; others she allows to be harassed by hardships that the virtues of their minds should be strengthened by the habit and exercise of patience. Some have too great a fear of sufferings which they can bear; others have too great contempt for those which they cannot bear: these she leads on by troubles to make trial of themselves. Some have brought a name to be honoured for all time at the price of a glorious death. Some by shewing themselves undefeated by punishment, have left a proof to others that virtue may be invincible by evil. What doubt can there be of how rightly such things are disposed, and that they are for the good of those whom we see them befall? The other point too arises from like causes, that sometimes sorrows, sometimes the fulfilment of their desires, falls to the wicked. As concerns the sorrows, no one is surprised, because all agree that they deserve ill. Their punishments serve both to deter others from crime by fear, and also to amend the lives of those who undergo them; their happiness, on the other hand, serves as a proof to good men of how they should regard good fortune of this nature, which they see often attends upon the dishonest. And another thing seems to me to be well arranged: the nature of a man may be so headstrong and rough that lack of wealth may stir him to crime more readily than restrain him; for the disease of such an one Providence prescribes a remedy of stores of patrimony: he may see that his conscience is befouled by sin, he may take account with himself of his fortune, and will perhaps fear lest the loss of this property, of which he enjoys the use, may bring unhappiness. Wherefore he will change his ways, and leave off from ill-doing so long as he fears the loss of his fortune. Again, good fortune, unworthily improved, has flung some into ruin. To some the right of punishing is committed that they may use it for the exercise and trial of the good, and the punishment of evil men. And just as there is no league between good and bad men, so also the bad cannot either agree among themselves: nay, with their vices tearing their own consciences asunder, they cannot agree with themselves, and do often perform acts which, when done, they perceive that they should not have done. Wherefore high Providence has thus often shewn her strange wonder, namely, that bad men should make other bad men good. For some find themselves suffering injustice at the hands of evil men, and, burning with hatred of those who have injured them, they have returned to cultivate the fruits of virtue, because their aim is to be unlike those whom they hate. To divine power, and to that alone, are evil things good, when it uses them suitably so as to draw good results therefrom. For a definite order embraces all things, so that even when some subject leaves the true place assigned to it in the order, it returns to an order, though another, it may be, lest aught in the realm of Providence be left to random chance. But 'hard is it for me to set forth all these matters as a god,'[1] nor is it right for a man to try to comprehend with his mind all the means of divine working, or to explain them in words. Let it be enough that we have seen that God, the Creator of all nature, directs and disposes all things for good. And while He urges all, that He has made manifest, to keep His own likeness, He drives out by the course of Fate all evil from the bounds of His state. Wherefore if you look to the disposition of Providence, you will reckon naught as bad of all the evils which are held to abound upon earth.

"But I see that now you are weighed down by the burden of the question, and wearied by the length of our reasoning, and waiting for the gentleness of song. Take then your draught, be refreshed thereby and advance further the stronger.

"If thou wouldst diligently behold with unsullied mind the laws of the God of thunder upon high, look to the highest point of heaven above. There, by a fair and equal compact, do the stars keep their ancient peace. The sun is hurried on by its whirl of fire, but impedes not the moon's cool orb. The Bear

[1] Homer, *Iliad*, xii. 176.

turns its rushing course around the highest pole of the universe, and dips not in the western depths, and though it sees the other constellations sink, it never seeks to quench its flames in the ocean stream. In just divisions of time does the evening star foretell the coming of the late shadows, and, as Lucifer, brings back again the warming light of day. Thus does the interchanging bond of love bring round their never-failing courses; and strife is for ever an exile from the starry realms. This unity rules by fair limits the elements, so that wet yields to dry, its opposite, and it faithfully joins cold to heat. Floating fire rises up on high, and matter by its weight sinks down. From these same causes in warm spring the flowering season breathes its scents; then the hot summer dries the grain; then with its burden of fruits comes autumn again, and winter's falling rain gives moisture. This mingling of seasons nourishes and brings forth all on earth that has the breath of life; and again snatches them away and hides them, whelming in death all that has arisen. Meanwhile the Creator sits on high, rules all and guides, King and Lord, fount and source of all, Law itself and wise judge of justice. He restrains all that stirs nature to motion, holds it back, and makes firm all that would stray. If He were not to recall them to their true paths, and set them again upon the circles of their courses, they would be torn from their source and so would perish. This is the common bond of love; all seek thus to be restrained by the limit of the good. In no other manner can they endure if this bond of love be not turned round again, and if the causes, which He has set, return not again.

(Philosophy shews that all fortune is good.)

"Do you see now," she continued, "what follows upon all that we have said?"

"What is it?" I asked.

"That all fortune is plainly good," she answered.

"How can that be?" said I.

"Consider this," she said: "all fortune, whether pleasant or difficult, is due to this cause; it is for the sake of rewarding the good or exercising their virtue, and of punishing and correcting bad men: therefore it is plain that all this fortune which is allowed to be just or expedient, must be good."

"Yes," I said, "that is a true argument, and when I think of the Providence or Fate about which you have taught me, the conclusion rests upon strong foundations. But if it please you, let us count it among those conclusions which you a little while ago set down as inconceivable."

"Why?" she asked.

"Because it is a commonplace saying among men—indeed an especially frequent one—that some people have bad fortune."

"Would you then have us approach more nearly the common conversation of men, lest we should seem to withdraw too far from human ways?"

"If you will," I said.

"Do you not think that that, which is advantageous, is good?"

"Yes."

"And that fortune, which exercises or corrects, is advantageous?"

"I agree," said I.

"Then it is good, is it not?"

"It must be so."

"This is the fortune of those who are either firmly set in virtue and struggling against their difficulties, or of those who would leave their vices and take the path of virtue?"

"That is true," I said.

"But what of that pleasant fortune which is granted as a reward to good men? Do most people perceive that it is bad? No; but, as is true, they esteem it the best. And what of the last kind of fortune, which is hard and which restrains bad men by just punishment? Is that commonly held to be good?"

"No," said I, "it is held to be the most miserable of all that can be imagined."

"Beware lest in following the common conception, we come to some truly inconceivable conclusion."

"What do you mean?"

"From what we have allowed," she said, "it results that the fortune of those who are in possession of virtue, or are gaining it, or advancing therein, is entirely good, whatever it be, while for those who remain in wickedness, their fortune is the worst."

"That is true, but who would dare confess it?"

"For this reason a wise man should never complain, whenever he is brought into strife with fortune; just as a brave man cannot properly be disgusted whenever the noise of battle is heard, since for both of them their very difficulty is their opportunity, for the brave man of increasing his glory, for the wise man of confirming and strengthening his wisdom. From this is virtue itself so named,[1] because it is so supported by its strength that it is not overcome by adversity. And you who were set in the advance of virtue have not come to this pass of being dissipated by delights, or enervated by pleasure; but you fight too bitterly against all fortune. Keep the middle path of strength and virtue, lest you be overwhelmed by misfortune or corrupted by pleasant fortune. All that falls short or goes too far ahead, has contempt for happiness, and gains not the reward for labour done. It rests in your own hands what shall be the nature of the fortune which you choose to form for yourself. For all fortune which seems difficult, either exercises virtue, or corrects or punishes vice.

"The avenging son of Atreus strove for full ten years before he expiated in the fall of Phrygian Troy the wrong done to his brother's marriage. The same Agamemnon must needs throw off his father's nature, and himself, an unwilling priest, thrust his knife into his unhappy daughter's throat, and buy the winds at the cost of blood, when he sought to fill the sails of the fleet of Greece. The King of Ithaca wept sore for his lost comrades whom the savage Polyphemus swallowed into his huge maw as he lay in his vast cave; but, when mad for his blinded eye, he paid back with rejoicings for the sad tears

[1] The Latin word "virtus" means by its derivation, manly strength.

he had drawn. Hercules became famous through hard labours. He tamed the haughty Centaurs, and from the fierce lion of Nemea took his spoil. With his sure arrows he smote the birds of Stymphalus; and from the watchful dragon took the apples of the Hesperides, filling his hand with their precious gold; and Cerberus he dragged along with threefold chain. The story tells how he conquered the fierce Diomede and set before his savage mares their master as their food. The Hydra's poison perished in his fire. He took the horn and so disgraced the brow of the river Achelous, who hid below his bank his head ashamed. On the sands of Libya he laid Antæus low; Cacus he slew to sate Evander's wrath. The bristling boar of Erymanthus flecked with his own foam the shoulders which were to bear the height of heaven; for in his last labour he bore with unbending neck the heavens, and so won again his place in heaven, the reward of his last work.

"Go forth then bravely whither leads the lofty path of high example. Why do ye sluggards turn your backs? When the earth is overcome, the stars are yours."

BOOK FIVE

Here she made an end and was for turning the course of her speaking to the handling and explaining of other subjects. Then said I: "Your encouragement is right and most worthy in truth of your name and weight. But I am learning by experience what you just now said of Providence; that the question is bound up in others. I would ask you whether you think that Chance exists at all, and what you think it is?"

Then she answered: "I am eager to fulfil my promised debt, and to shew you the path by which you may seek your home. But these things, though all-expedient for knowledge, are none the less rather apart from our path, and we must be careful lest you become wearied by our turnings aside, and so be not strong enough to complete the straight journey."

"Have no fear at all thereof," said I. "It will be restful to know these things in which I have so great a pleasure; and when every view of your reasoning has stood firm with unshaken credit, so let there be no doubt of what shall follow."

"I will do your pleasure," she made answer, and thus she began to speak:

(Philosophy discusses "chance.")

"If chance is defined as an outcome of random influence, produced by no sequence of causes, I am sure that there is no such thing as chance, and I consider that it is but an empty word, beyond shewing the meaning of the matter which we have in hand. For what place can be left for anything happening at random, so long as God controls everything in order? It is a true saying that nothing can come out of nothing. None of the old philosophers has denied that, though they did not apply it to the effective principle, but to the matter operated upon—that is to say, to nature; and this was the foundation upon which they built all their reasoning. If anything arises from no causes, it will appear to have risen out of nothing. But if this is impossible, then chance also cannot be anything of that sort, which is stated in the definition which we mentioned."

"Then is there nothing which can be justly called chance, nor anything 'by chance'?" I asked. "Or is there anything which common people know not, but which those words do suit?"

"My philosopher, Aristotle, defined it in his *Physics*[1] shortly and well-nigh truly."

"How?" I asked.

"Whenever anything is done with one intention, but something else, other than was intended, results from certain causes, that is called chance: as, for instance, if a man digs the ground for the sake of cultivating it, and finds a heap of buried gold. Such a thing is believed to have happened by chance, but it does not come from nothing, for it has its own causes, whose unforeseen and unexpected coincidence seem to have brought about a chance. For if the cultivator did not dig the ground, if the owner had not buried his money, the gold would not have been found. These are the causes of the chance piece of good fortune, which comes about from the causes which meet it, and move along with it, not from the intention of the actor. For neither the burier nor the tiller intended that the gold should be found; but, as I said, it was a coincidence, and it happened that the one dug up what the other buried. We may therefore define chance as an unexpected result from the coincidence of certain causes in matters where there was another purpose. The order of the universe, advancing with its inevitable sequences, brings about this coincidence of causes. This order itself emanates from its source, which is Providence, and disposes all things in their proper time and place.

"In the land where the Parthian, as he turns in flight, shoots his arrows into the pursuer's breast, from the rocks of the

[1] Aristotle, *Physics*, ii. 3.

crag of Achæmenia, the Tigris and Euphrates flow from out one source, but quickly with divided streams are separate. If they should come together and again be joined in a single course, all, that the two streams bear along, would flow in one together. Boats would meet boats, and trees meet trees torn up by the currents, and the mingled waters would together entwine their streams by chance; but their sloping beds restrain these chances vague, and the downward order of the falling torrent guides their courses. Thus does chance, which seems to rush onward without rein, bear the bit, and take its way by rule."

(*Philosophy asserts the existence of free will.*)

"I have listened to you," I said, "and agree that it is as you say. But in this close sequence of causes, is there any freedom for our judgment, or does this chain of fate bind the very feelings of our minds too?"

"There is free will," she answered. "Nor could there be any reasoning nature without freedom of judgment. For any being that can use its reason by nature, has a power of judgment by which it can without further aid decide each point, and so distinguish between objects to be desired and objects to be shunned. Each therefore seeks what it deems desirable, and flies from what it considers should be shunned. Wherefore all who have reason have also freedom of desiring and refusing in themselves. But I do not lay down that this is equal in all beings. Heavenly and divine beings have with them a judgment of great insight, an imperturbable will, and a power which can effect their desires. But human spirits must be more free when they keep themselves safe in the contemplation of the mind of God; but less free when they sink into bodies, and less still when they are bound by their earthly members. The last stage is mere slavery, when the spirit is given over to vices and has fallen away from the possession of its reason. For when the mind turns its eyes from the light of truth on high to lower darkness, soon they are dimmed by the clouds of ignorance, and become turbid through ruinous passions;

by yielding to these passions and consenting to them, men increase the slavery which they have brought upon themselves, and their true liberty is lost in captivity. But God, looking upon all out of the infinite, perceives the views of Providence, and disposes each as its destiny has already fated for it according to its merits: 'He looketh over all and heareth all.'[1]

"Homer with his honeyed lips sang of the bright sun's clear light; yet the sun cannot burst with his feeble rays the bowels of the earth or the depths of the sea. Not so with the Creator of this great sphere. No masses of earth can block His vision as He looks over all. Night's cloudy darkness cannot resist Him. With one glance of His intelligence He sees all that has been, that is, and that is to come. He alone can see all things, so truly He may be called the Sun."[2]

Then said I, "Again am I plunged in yet more doubt and difficulty."

(Boethius cannot reconcile God's foreknowledge with man's free will.)

"What are they," she asked, "though I have already my idea of what your trouble consists?"

"There seems to me," I said, "to be such incompatibility between the existence of God's universal foreknowledge and that of any freedom of judgment. For if God foresees all things and cannot in anything be mistaken, that, which His Providence sees will happen, must result. Wherefore if it knows beforehand not only men's deeds but even their designs and wishes, there will be no freedom of judgment. For there can neither be any deed done, nor wish formed, except such as the infallible Providence of God has foreseen. For if matters could ever so be turned that they resulted otherwise than was

---

[1] A phrase from Homer (*Iliad*, iii. 277, and *Odyssey*, xi. 109), where it is said of the sun.

[2] This sentence, besides referring to the application of Homer's words used above, contains also a play on words in the Latin, which can only be clumsily reproduced in English by some such words as "The sole power which can see all is justly to be called the solar."

foreseen of Providence, this foreknowledge would cease to be sure. But, rather than knowledge, it is opinion which is uncertain; and that, I deem, is not applicable to God. And, further, I cannot approve of an argument by which some men think that they can cut this knot; for they say that a result does not come to pass for the reason that Providence has foreseen it, but the opposite rather, namely, that because it is about to come to pass, therefore it cannot be hidden from God's Providence. In that way it seems to me that the argument must resolve itself into an argument on the other side. For in that case it is not necessary that that should happen which is foreseen, but that that which is about to happen should be foreseen; as though, indeed, our doubt was whether God's foreknowledge is the certain cause of future events, or the certainty of future events is the cause of Providence. But let our aim be to prove that, whatever be the shape which this series of causes takes, the fulfilment of God's foreknowledge is necessary, even if this knowledge may not seem to induce the necessity for the occurrence of future events. For instance, if a man sits down, it must be that the opinion, which conjectures that he is sitting, is true; but conversely, if the opinion concerning the man is true because he is sitting, he must be sitting down. There is therefore necessity in both cases: the man must be sitting, and the opinion must be true. But he does not sit because the opinion is true, but rather the opinion is true because his sitting down has preceded it. Thus, though the cause of the truth of the opinion proceeds from the other fact, yet there is a common necessity on both parts. In like manner we must reason of Providence and future events. For even though they are foreseen because they are about to happen, yet they do not happen because they are foreseen. None the less it is necessary that either what is about to happen should be foreseen of God, or that what has been foreseen should happen; and this alone is enough to destroy all free will.

"Yet how absurd it is that we should say that the result of

temporal affairs is the cause of eternal foreknowledge! And to think that God foresees future events because they are about to happen, is nothing else than to hold events of past time to be the cause of that highest Providence. Besides, just as, when I know a present fact, that fact must be so; so also when I know of something that will happen, that must come to pass. Thus it follows that the fulfilment of a foreknown event must be inevitable.

"Lastly, if any one believes that any matter is otherwise than the fact is, he not only has not knowledge, but his opinion is false also, and that is very far from the truth of knowledge. Wherefore, if any future event is such that its fulfilment is not sure or necessary, how can it possibly be known beforehand that it will occur? For just as absolute knowledge has no taint of falsity, so also that which is conceived by knowledge cannot be otherwise than as it is conceived. That is the reason why knowledge cannot lie, because each matter must be just as knowledge knows that it is. What then? How can God know beforehand these uncertain future events? For if He thinks inevitable the fulfilment of such things as may possibly not result, He is wrong; and that we may not believe, nor even utter, rightly. But if He perceives that they will result as they are in such a manner that He only knows that they may or may not occur, equally, how is this foreknowledge, this which knows nothing for sure, nothing absolutely? How is such a foreknowledge different from the absurd prophecy which Horace puts in the mouth of Tiresias: 'Whatever I shall say, will either come to pass, or it will not'?[1] How, too, would God's Providence be better than man's opinion, if, as men do, He only sees to be uncertain such things as have an uncertain result? But if there can be no uncertainty with God, the most sure source of all things, then the fulfilment of all that He has surely foreknown, is certain. Thus we are led to see that there is no freedom for the intentions or actions of men; for the mind of God, foreseeing all things without error

[1] Horace, *Satires,* II. v. 59.

or deception, binds all together and controls their results. And when we have once allowed this, it is plain how complete is the fall of all human actions in consequence. In vain are rewards or punishments set before good or bad, for there is no free or voluntary action of the mind to deserve them; and what we just now determined was most fair, will prove to be most unfair of all, namely to punish the dishonest or reward the honest, since their own will does not put them in the way of honesty or dishonesty, but the unfailing necessity of development constrains them. Wherefore neither virtues nor vices are anything, but there is rather an indiscriminate confusion of all deserts. And nothing could be more vicious than this; since the whole order of all comes from Providence, and nothing is left to human intention, it follows that our crimes, as well as our good deeds, must all be held due to the author of all good. Hence it is unreasonable to hope for or pray against aught. For what could any man hope for or pray against, if an undeviating chain links together all that we can desire? Thus will the only understanding between God and man, the right of prayer, be taken away. We suppose that at the price of our deservedly humbling ourselves before Him we may win a right to the inestimable reward of His divine grace: this is the only manner in which men can seem to deal with God, so to speak, and by virtue of prayer to join ourselves to that inaccessible light, before it is granted to us; but if we allow the inevitability of the future, and believe that we have no power, what means shall we have to join ourselves to the Lord of all, or how can we cling to Him? Wherefore, as you sang but a little while ago,[1] the human race must be cut off from its source and ever fall away.

"What cause of discord is it breaks the bonds of agreement here? What heavenly power has set such strife between two truths? Thus, though apart each brings no doubt, yet can they not be linked together. Comes there no discord between

[1] *Supra*, Book iv. Met. vi. p. 135.

these truths? Stand they for ever sure by one another? Yes,
'tis the mind, o'erwhelmed by the body's blindness, which
cannot see by the light of that dimmed brightness the finest
threads that bind the truth. But wherefore burns the spirit
with so strong desire to learn the hidden signs of truth? Knows
it the very object of its careful search? Then why seeks it to
learn anew what it already knows? If it knows it not, why
searches it in blindness? For who would desire aught un-
witting? Or who could seek after that which is unknown?
How should he find it, or recognise its form when found, if
he knows it not? And when the mind of man perceived the
mind of God, did it then know the whole and parts alike?
Now is the mind buried in the cloudy darkness of the body,
yet has not altogether forgotten its own self, and keeps the
whole though it has lost the parts. Whosoever, therefore, seeks
the truth, is not wholly in ignorance, nor yet has knowledge
wholly; for he knows not all, yet is not ignorant of all. He
takes thought for the whole which he keeps in memory, handling again what he saw on high, so that he may add to that
which he has kept, that which he has forgotten."

(Philosophy tries to shew how they may be reconciled.)

Then said she, "This is the old plaint concerning Providence which was so strongly urged by Cicero when treating
of Divination,[1] and you yourself have often and at length
questioned the same subject. But so far, none of you have
explained it with enough diligence or certainty. The cause of
this obscurity is that the working of human reason cannot
approach the directness of divine foreknowledge. If this could
be understood at all, there would be no doubt left. And this
especially will I try to make plain, if I can first explain your
difficulties.

"Tell me why you think abortive the reasoning of those
who solve the question thus; they argue that foreknowledge
cannot be held to be a cause for the necessity of future results,

[1] Cicero, *De Divinatione*, II.

and therefore free will is not in any way shackled by fore-knowledge.[1] Whence do you draw your proof of the necessity of future results if not from the fact that such things as are known beforehand cannot but come to pass? If, then (as you yourself admitted just now), foreknowledge brings no necessity to bear upon future events, how is it that the voluntary results of such events are bound to find a fixed end? Now for the sake of the argument, that you may turn your attention to what follows, let us state that there is no foreknowledge at all. Then are the events which are decided by free will, bound by any necessity, so far as this goes? Of course not. Secondly, let us state that foreknowledge exists, but brings no necessity to bear upon events; then, I think, the same free will will be left, intact and absolute. 'But,' you will say, 'though foreknowledge is no necessity for a result in the future, yet it is a sign that it will necessarily come to pass.' Thus, therefore, even if there had been no foreknowledge, it would be plain that future results were under necessity; for every sign can only shew what it is that it points out; it does not bring it to pass. Wherefore we must first prove that nothing happens but of necessity, in order that it may be plain that foreknowledge is a sign of this necessity. Otherwise, if there is no necessity, then foreknowledge will not be a sign of that which does not exist. Now it is allowed that proof rests upon firm reasoning, not upon signs or external arguments; it must be deduced from suitable and binding causes. How can it possibly be that things, which are foreseen as about to happen, should not occur? That would be as though we were to believe that events would not occur which Providence foreknows as about to occur, and as though we did not rather think this, that though they occur, yet they have had no necessity in their own natures which brought them about. We can see many actions developing before our eyes; just as chariot drivers see the development of their actions as they control and guide their chariots, and many

[1] Referring to Boethius's words on p. 104.

other things likewise. Does any necessity compel any of those things to occur as they do? Of course not. All art, craft, and intention would be in vain, if everything took place by compulsion. Therefore, if things have no necessity for coming to pass when they do, they cannot have any necessity to be about to come to pass before they do. Wherefore there are things whose results are entirely free from necessity. For I think not that there is any man who will say this, that things, which are done in the present, were not about to be done in the past, before they are done. Thus these foreknown events have their free results. Just as foreknowledge of present things brings no necessity to bear upon them as they come to pass, so also foreknowledge of future things brings no necessity to bear upon things which are to come.

"But you will say that there is no doubt of this too, whether there can be any foreknowledge of things which have not results bounden by necessity. For they do seem to lack harmony: and you think that if they are foreseen, the necessity follows; if there is no necessity, then they cannot be foreseen; nothing can be perceived certainly by knowledge, unless it be certain. But if things have uncertainty of result, but are foreseen as though certain, this is plainly the obscurity of opinion, and not the truth of knowledge. For you believe that to think aught other than it is, is the opposite of true knowledge. The cause of this error is that every man believes that all the subjects, that he knows, are known by their own force or nature alone, which are known; but it is quite the opposite. For every subject, that is known, is comprehended not according to its own force, but rather according to the nature of those who know it. Let me make this plain to you by a brief example: the roundness of a body may be known in one way by sight, in another way by touch. Sight can take in the whole body at once from a distance by judging its radii, while touch clings, as it were, to the outside of the sphere, and from close at hand perceives through the material parts the roundness of the body as it passes over the actual circumference. A man himself is differently comprehended by the senses, by imagination, by reason, and by intelligence. For the senses distinguish the form as set in the matter operated upon by the form; imagination distinguishes the appearance alone without the matter. Reason goes even further than imagination; by a general and universal contemplation it investigates the actual kind which is represented in individual specimens. Higher still is the view of the intelligence, which reaches above the sphere of the universal, and with the unsullied eye of the mind gazes upon that very form of the kind in its absolute simplicity. Herein the chief point for our consideration is this: the higher power of understanding includes the lower, but the lower never rises to the higher. For the senses are capable of understanding naught but the matter; imagination cannot look upon universal or natural kinds; reason cannot comprehend the absolute form; whereas the intelligence seems to look down from above and comprehend the form, and distinguishes all that lie below, but in such a way that it grasps the very form which could not be known to any other than itself. For it perceives and knows the general kind, as does reason; the appearance, as does the imagination; and the matter, as do the senses, but with one grasp of the mind it looks upon all with a clear conception of the whole. And reason too, as it views general kinds, does not make use of the imagination nor the senses, but yet does perceive the objects both of the imagination and of the senses. It is reason which thus defines a general kind according to its conception: Man, for instance, is an animal, biped and reasoning. This is a general notion of a natural kind, but no man denies that the subject can be approached by the imagination and by the senses, just because reason investigates it by a reasonable conception and not by the imagination or senses. Likewise, though imagination takes its beginning of seeing and forming appearances from the senses, yet without their aid it surveys each subject by an imaginative faculty of distinguishing, not by the distinguishing faculty of the senses.

"Do you see then, how in knowledge of all things, the subject uses its own standard of capability, and not those of the objects known? And this is but reasonable, for every judgment formed is an act of the person who judges, and therefore each man must of necessity perform his own action from his own capability and not the capability of any other.

"In days of old the Porch at Athens[1] gave us men, seeing dimly as in old age, who could believe that the feelings of the senses and the imagination were but impressions on the mind from bodies without them, just as the old custom was to impress with swift-running pens letters upon the surface of a waxen tablet which bore no marks before. But if the mind with its own force can bring forth naught by its own exertions; if it does but lie passive and subject to the marks of other bodies; if it reflects, as does, forsooth, a mirror, the vain reflections of other things; whence thrives there in the soul an all-seeing power of knowledge? What is the force that sees the single parts, or which distinguishes the facts it knows? What is the force that gathers up the parts it has distinguished, that takes its course in order due, now rises to mingle with the things on high, and now sinks down among the things below, and then to itself brings back itself, and, so examining, refutes the false with truth? This is a cause of greater power, of more effective force by far than that which only receives the impressions of material bodies. Yet does the passive reception come first, rousing and stirring all the strength of the mind in the living body. When the eyes are smitten with a light, or the ears are struck with a voice's sound, then is the spirit's energy aroused, and, thus moved, calls upon like forms, such as it holds within itself, fits them to signs without and mingles the forms of its imagination with those which it has stored within.

[1] Zeno, of Citium (342-270 B.C.), the founder of the Stoic school, taught in the Stoa Poekile, whence the name of the school. The following lines refer to their doctrine of presentations and impressions.

(*Human reasoning, being lower than divine intelligence, can at best
only strive to approach thereto.*)

"With regard to feeling the effects of bodies, natures which
are brought into contact from without may affect the organs
of the senses, and the body's passive affection may precede
the active energy of the spirit, and call forth to itself the
activity of the mind; if then, when the effects of bodies are
felt, the mind is not marked in any way by its passive reception thereof, but declares that reception subject to the body
of its own force, how much less do those subjects, which are
free from all affections of bodies, follow external objects in
their perceptions, and how much more do they make clear the
way for the action of their mind? By this argument many
different manners of understanding have fallen to widely different natures of things. For the senses are incapable of any
knowledge but their own, and they alone fall to those living
beings which are incapable of motion, as are sea shell-fish, and
other low forms of life which live by clinging to rocks; while
imagination is granted to animals with the power of motion,
who seem to be affected by some desire to seek or avoid certain
things. But reason belongs to the human race alone, just as
the true intelligence is God's alone. Wherefore that manner
of knowledge is better than others, for it can comprehend of
its own nature not only the subject peculiar to itself, but also
the subjects of the other kinds of knowledge. Suppose that
the senses and imagination thus oppose reasoning, saying,
'The universal natural kinds, which reason believes that it
can perceive, are nothing; for what is comprehensible to the
senses and the imagination cannot be universal: therefore
either the judgment of reason is true, and that which can be
perceived by the senses is nothing; or, since reason knows
well that there are many subjects comprehensible to the senses
and imagination, the conception of reason is vain, for it holds
to be universal what is an individual matter comprehensible
to the senses.' To this reason might answer, that 'it sees from
a general point of view what is comprehensible to the senses

and the imagination, but they cannot aspire to a knowledge of universals, since their manner of knowledge cannot go further than material or bodily appearances; and in the matter of knowledge it is better to trust to the stronger and more nearly perfect judgment.' If such a trial of argument occurred, should not we, who have within us the force of reasoning as well as the powers of the senses and imagination, approve of the cause of reason rather than that of the others? It is in like manner that human reason thinks that the divine intelligence cannot perceive the things of the future except as it conceives them itself. For you argue thus: 'If there are events which do not appear to have sure or necessary results, their results cannot be known for certain beforehand: therefore there can be no foreknowledge of these events; for if we believe that there is any foreknowledge thereof, there can exist nothing but such as is brought forth of necessity.' If therefore we, who have our share in possession of reason, could go further and possess the judgment of the mind of God, we should then think it most just that human reason should yield itself to the mind of God, just as we have determined that the senses and imagination ought to yield to reason.

"Let us therefore raise ourselves, if so be that we can, to that height of the loftiest intelligence. For there reason will see what it cannot of itself perceive, and that is to know how even such things as have uncertain results are perceived definitely and for certain by foreknowledge; and such foreknowledge will not be mere opinion, but rather the single and direct form of the highest knowledge unlimited by any finite bounds.

"In what different shapes do living beings move upon the earth! Some make flat their bodies, sweeping through the dust and using their strength to make therein a furrow without break; some flit here and there upon light wings which beat the breeze, and they float through vast tracks of air in their easy flight. 'Tis others' wont to plant their footsteps on the ground, and pass with their paces over green fields or under trees. Though all these thou seest move in different shapes, yet all have their faces downward along the ground, and this doth draw downward and dull their senses. Alone of all, the human race lifts up its head on high, and stands in easy balance with the body upright, and so looks down to spurn the earth. If thou art not too earthly by an evil folly, this pose is as a lesson. Thy glance is upward, and thou dost carry high thy head, and thus thy search is heavenward: then lead thy soul too upward, lest while the body is higher raised, the mind sink lower to the earth.

(Philosophy explains that God's divine intelligence can view all things from its eternal mind, while human reason can only see them from a temporal point of view.)

"Since then all that is known is apprehended, as we just now shewed, not according to its own nature but according to the nature of the knower, let us examine, so far as we lawfully may, the character of the divine nature, so that we may be able to learn what its knowledge is.

"The common opinion, according to all men living, is that God is eternal. Let us therefore consider what is eternity. For eternity will, I think, make clear to us at the same time the divine nature and knowledge.

"Eternity is the simultaneous and complete possession of infinite life. This will appear more clearly if we compare it with temporal things. All that lives under the conditions of time moves through the present from the past to the future; there is nothing set in time which can at one moment grasp the whole space of its lifetime. It cannot yet comprehend to-morrow; yesterday it has already lost. And in this life of to-day your life is no more than a changing, passing moment. And as Aristotle[1] said of the universe, so it is of all that is subject to time; though it never began to be, nor will ever cease, and its life is co-extensive with the infinity of time, yet it is not such as can be held to be eternal. For though it apprehends and grasps a space of infinite lifetime, it does not embrace the whole simultaneously; it has not yet experienced the

[1] Aristotle, *De Cœlo*, I.

future. What we should rightly call eternal is that which grasps and possesses wholly and simultaneously the fulness of unending life, which lacks naught of the future, and has lost naught of the fleeting past; and such an existence must be ever present in itself to control and aid itself, and also must keep present with itself the infinity of changing time. Therefore, people who hear that Plato thought that this universe had no beginning of time and will have no end, are not right in thinking that in this way the created world is co-eternal with its creator.[1] For to pass through unending life, the attribute which Plato ascribes to the universe is one thing; but it is another thing to grasp simultaneously the whole of unending life in the present; this is plainly a peculiar property of the mind of God.

"And further, God should not be regarded as older than His creations by any period of time, but rather by the peculiar property of His own single nature. For the infinite changing of temporal things tries to imitate the ever simultaneously present immutability of His life: it cannot succeed in imitating or equalling this, but sinks from immutability into change, and falls from the single directness of the present into an infinite space of future and past. And since this temporal state cannot possess its life completely and simultaneously, but it does in the same manner exist for ever without ceasing, it therefore seems to try in some degree to rival that which it cannot fulfil or represent, for it binds itself to some sort of present time out of this small and fleeting moment; but inasmuch as this temporal present bears a certain appearance of that abiding

---

[1] Boethius speaks of people who "hear that Plato thought, etc.," because this was the teaching of some of Plato's successors at the Academy. Plato himself thought otherwise, as may be seen in the *Timæus, e.g.* ch. xi. 38 B., "Time then has come into being along with the universe, that being generated together, together they may be dissolved, should a dissolution of them ever come to pass; and it was made after the pattern of the eternal nature that it might be as like to it as possible. For the pattern is existent for all eternity, but the copy has been, and is, and shall be, throughout all time continually." (Mr. Archer Hind's translation.)

present, it somehow makes those, to whom it comes, seem to be in truth what they imitate. But since this imitation could not be abiding, the unending march of time has swept it away, and thus we find that it has bound together, as it passes, a chain of life, which it could not by abiding embrace in its fulness. And thus if we would apply proper epithets to those subjects, we can say, following Plato, that God is eternal, but the universe is continual.

"Since then all judgment apprehends the subjects of its thought according to its own nature, and God has a condition of ever-present eternity, His knowledge, which passes over every change of time, embracing infinite lengths of past and future, views in its own direct comprehension everything as though it were taking place in the present. If you would weigh the foreknowledge by which God distinguishes all things, you will more rightly hold it to be a knowledge of a never-failing constancy in the present, than a foreknowledge of the future. Whence Providence is more rightly to be understood as a looking forth than a looking forward, because it is set far from low matters and looks forth upon all things as from a lofty mountain-top above all. Why then do you demand that all things occur by necessity, if divine light rests upon them, while men do not render necessary such things as they can see? Because you can see things of the present, does your sight therefore put upon them any necessity? Surely not. If one may not unworthily compare this present time with the divine, just as you can see things in this your temporal present, so God sees all things in His eternal present. Wherefore this divine foreknowledge does not change the nature or individual qualities of things: it sees things present in its understanding just as they will result some time in the future. It makes no confusion in its distinctions, and with one view of its mind it discerns all that shall come to pass whether of necessity or not. For instance, when you see at the same time a man walking on the earth and the sun rising in the heavens, you see each sight simultaneously, yet you distinguish between them, and decide that one is moving voluntarily, the other of necessity. In like manner the perception of God looks down upon all things without disturbing at all their nature, though they are present to Him but future under the conditions of time. Wherefore this foreknowledge is not opinion but knowledge resting upon truth, since He knows that a future event is, though He knows too that it will not occur of necessity. If you answer here that what God sees about to happen, cannot but happen, and that what cannot but happen is bound by necessity, you fasten me down to the word necessity, I will grant that we have a matter of most firm truth, but it is one to which scarce any man can approach unless he be a contemplator of the divine. For I shall answer that such a thing will occur of necessity, when it is viewed from the point of divine knowledge; but when it is examined in its own nature, it seems perfectly free and unrestrained. For there are two kinds of necessities; one is simple: for instance, a necessary fact, 'all men are mortal'; the other is conditional; for instance, if you know that a man is walking, he must be walking: for what each man knows cannot be otherwise than it is known to be; but the conditional one is by no means followed by this simple and direct necessity; for there is no necessity to compel a voluntary walker to proceed, though it is necessary that, if he walks, he should be proceeding. In the same way, if Providence sees an event in its present, that thing must be, though it has no necessity of its own nature. And God looks in His present upon those future things which come to pass through free will. Therefore if these things be looked at from the point of view of God's insight, they come to pass of necessity under the condition of divine knowledge; if, on the other hand, they are viewed by themselves, they do not lose the perfect freedom of their nature. Without doubt, then, all things that God foreknows do come to pass, but some of them proceed from free will; and though they result by coming into existence, yet they do not lose their own nature, because before they came to pass they could also not have come to pass.

" 'What then,' you may ask, 'is the difference in their not being bound by necessity, since they result under all circumstances as by necessity, on account of the condition of divine knowledge?' This is the difference, as I just now put forward: take the sun rising and a man walking; while these operations are occurring, they cannot but occur: but the one was bound to occur before it did; the other was not so bound. What God has in His present, does exist without doubt; but of such things some follow by necessity, others by their authors' wills. Wherefore I was justified in saying that if these things be regarded from the view of divine knowledge, they are necessary, but if they are viewed by themselves, they are perfectly free from all ties of necessity: just as when you refer all, that is clear to the senses, to the reason, it becomes general truth, but it remains particular if regarded by itself. 'But,' you will say, 'if it is in my power to change a purpose of mine, I will disregard Providence, since I may change what Providence foresees.' To which I answer, 'You can change your purpose, but since the truth of Providence knows in its present that you can do so, and whether you do so, and in what direction you may change it, therefore you cannot escape that divine foreknowledge: just as you cannot avoid the glance of a present eye, though you may by your free will turn yourself to all kinds of different actions.' 'What?' you will say, 'can I by my own action change divine knowledge, so that if I choose now one thing, now another, Providence too will seem to change its knowledge?' No; divine insight precedes all future things, turning them back and recalling them to the present time of its own peculiar knowledge. It does not change, as you may think, between this and that alternation of foreknowledge. It is constant in preceding and embracing by one glance all your changes. And God does not receive this ever-present grasp of all things and vision of the present at the occurrence of future events, but from His own peculiar directness. Whence also is that difficulty solved which you laid down a little while ago, that it was not worthy to say that our future events were the cause of God's knowledge. For this power of knowledge, ever in the present and embracing all things in its perception, does itself constrain all things, and owes naught to following events from which it has received naught. Thus, therefore, mortal men have their freedom of judgment intact. And since their wills are freed from all binding necessity, laws do not set rewards or punishments unjustly. God is ever the constant foreknowing overseer, and the ever-present eternity of His sight moves in harmony with the future nature of our actions, as it dispenses rewards to the good, and punishments to the bad. Hopes are not vainly put in God, nor prayers in vain offered: if these are right, they cannot but be answered. Turn therefore from vice: ensue virtue: raise your soul to upright hopes: send up on high your prayers from this earth. If you would be honest, great is the necessity enjoined upon your goodness, since all you do is done before the eyes of an all-seeing Judge."

THE IMITATION OF CHRIST

BY THOMAS À KEMPIS

CONTENTS

PART I

PART II

PART III

PART IV

THE IMITATION OF CHRIST

PART ONE

CHAPTER I

OF FOLLOWING OF CHRIST AND DESPISING OF ALL WORLDLY VANITIES

OUR Lord saith: he that followeth me goeth not in darkness
These are the words of Christ in the which we are admonished
to follow his life and his manners if we would be verily
illumined and be delivered from all manner of blindness
of heart

Wherefore let our sovereign study be—in the life of Jesu
Christ.

The teaching of Christ passeth the teaching of all saints and
holy men; and he that hath the spirit of Christ should
find there hidden manna.

But it happeneth that many feel but little desire of often hearing of the gospel; for they have not the spirit of Christ;

For whoever will understand the words of Christ plainly and
in their savour must study to conform all his life to his
life.

What availeth thee to dispute highly of the Trinity if thou
lack meekness and thereby thou displeasest the Trinity?

For high words make not a man holy and righteous, but it is
virtuous life that maketh man dear to God.

I desire rather to know compunction than its definition.

If thou knewest all the Bible without book and the sayings of
all the philosophers, what should that avail thee without
charity and grace?

All other things in the world, save only to love God and serve him, are vanity of vanities and all vanity.

This is sovereign wisdom by despising of the world for a man to draw him nearer to the realm of heaven: but for a man to seek perishing riches and to trust in them is vanity.

And it is vanity also to desire honour and for a man to lift himself on high

And it is vanity to follow the desires of the flesh and to desire the thing for which man must afterward grievously be punished

And it is vanity to desire a long life and to take no heed of a good life

And it is vanity for a man to take heed only to this present life and not to see before those things that are to come

And it is vanity to love the thing that passeth away with all manner of swiftness and not to hasten thither where joy abideth everlasting.

Have mind often of that proverb that the eye is not fulfilled with seeing nor the ear with hearing.

Study therefore to withdraw thy heart from love of things visible and turn thee to things invisible

For they that follow their senses spot their conscience and lose the grace of God.

CHAPTER II

OF MEEK KNOWING OF A MAN'S SELF

EVERY man naturally desireth to have knowledge: but knowledge without the grace and dread of God, what availeth it?

Certainly the meek plough man that serveth God is much better than the proud philosopher that, taking no heed of his own living, considereth the courses of the heavens.

He that knoweth himself well is vile in his own sight and hath no delight in man's praises.

If I knew all things that are in the world and be not in charity what should that help me before God who shall doom me according to my deeds?

Cease from over-great desire of knowledge, for therein shall be found great distraction and deceit.

They that are learned will gladly be seen and held wise and many things there be whose knowledge availeth the soul little or naught. And full unwise is he that more attendeth to other things than to the health of his soul.

Many words fill not the soul but a good life refresheth the mind and a pure conscience giveth a great confidence in God.

The more thou canst do and the better that thou canst do, the more grievously thou shalt be doomed unless thou live the more holily. Be not lift up therefore for any skill or any knowledge but rather dread for the knowledge that is given thee.

If it seemeth to thee that thou knowest many things and art understanding enough, yet are there many more things that thou knowest not.

Think not highly of thyself but rather acknowledge thine ignorance.

Why wilt thou prefer thyself before any other since many other are found better learned and more wise in the law of God than thou?

If thou wilt learn and know any thing profitably, love to be unknown and to be accounted as naught.

This is the highest and most profitable reading, the very knowing and despising of a man's self. For a man to account nothing of himself but evermore to think well and highly of other folks is sovereign wisdom and perfection.

If thou see any man sin openly or do grievous sins thou oughtest not to deem thyself better; for thou knowest not how long thou mayest abide in good.

All we be frail but thou shalt hold no man frailer than thyself.

CHAPTER III

OF THE TEACHING OF TRUTH

BLISSFUL is he whom truth herself teacheth not by figures or voices but as it is.

Our opinions and our feeling ofttimes deceive us and see but little.

What availeth great searching of dark and hidden things for the which we shall not be blamed in the judgment though we know them not?

A great unwisdom it is that we, setting at naught profitable and necessary things, give our utmost attention to curious and harmful things. We, having eyes, see not.

And why care we of general kinds and special kinds? (genera and species)

He to whom the word everlasting speaketh is sped and delivered from a multitude of opinions. Of one word came all things, and all things speak one word; that is the beginning that speaketh to us. No man without him understandeth or judgeth righteously.

He to whom all things are one and who draweth all things to one and seeth all things in one may be stable in heart and peaceably abide in God.

O God of truth make me one with thee in everlasting love.

Ofttimes it wearieth me to hear and read many things: in thee Lord is all that I will and desire.

All manner of teachers hold they their peace and all manner of creatures keep they their silence in thy sight: speak thou to me alone.

The more that a man is inwardly at one with thee alone the more things and the higher doth he understand, for he taketh his light of understanding from above.

A pure, simple and a stable spirit is not distracted with many works for he worketh all things to the honour of God and laboureth to be idle in himself from all manner of inquiry with his own knowledge.

What hindereth thee more and troubleth thee more than thine unmortified affection of heart?

A good and a devout man first disposeth his works inwardly which he proposeth to do outwardly. Nor do these works draw him to desires of vicious inclination but rather he boweth them to the judgment of right reason.

Who hath a stronger battle than he that useth force to overcome himself? and that should be our occupation, for a man to overcome himself and every day to be stronger than himself somewhat to do better.

All manner of perfection in this world hath a manner of imperfection annexed thereto and our speculation is not without darkness on some side.

Meek knowing of thyself is more acceptable to God than deep inquiry after knowing.

Knowledge or bare and simple knowing of things is not to be blamed, the which, in itself considered, is good and ordained of God: but a good conscience and a virtuous life is ever to be preferred.

And forasmuch as many people study more to have knowledge than to live well therefore ofttimes they err and bring forth little fruit or none.

O if men would give so great diligence to root out vices and to plant virtues as they do to move questions there would not be so much wickedness in the people nor so much laxity in cenobies (convents) and monasteries.

Certainly at the day of doom it shall not be asked of us what we have read but what we have done: nor what good we have said but how religiously we have lived.

Tell me now where are the lords and masters that thou knewest sometime while they lived and flourished in the schools? Now other men have their prebends and I wot not whether they once think upon them. In their lives they appeared somewhat and now almost no man speaketh of them. O Lord how soon passeth the glory of this world.

Would God that their life had been according to their knowledge for then they had well studied and well read.

How many be there that perish in this world by vain knowledge and little reck of the service of God. And for that they choose rather to be great than meek therefore they vanish away in their own thoughts.

Verily he is great that in himself is little and meek and setteth at naught all height of honour. Verily he is great that hath great charity. Verily he is prudent that deemeth all earthly things as stinking dung so that he may win Christ. And he is verily well learned that doth the will of God and forsaketh his own.

CHAPTER IV

OF PRUDENCE IN MAN'S WORKS

It is not fit to give credence to every word nor to every stirring (suggestion), but every thing is to be weighed according to God warily and in leisure.

Alas, evil of another man is rather believed than good; we are so weak.

But the perfect believe not lightly all things that men tell, for they know man's infirmity, ready to speak evil and sliding enough in words.

Hereto it belongeth also not to believe every man's words nor to tell other men that that we hear or lightly believe.

Have thy counsel with a wise man and a man of conscience and seek rather to be taught of thy better than to follow thine own inventions.

Good life maketh a man wise in God's sight and expert in many things.

The more meek that a man is and the more subject to God the more wise shall he be in all things,—and the more patient.

CHAPTER V

OF READING OF THE SCRIPTURES

TRUTH is to be sought in holy writings, not in eloquence. Every holy writing ought to be read with the same spirit wherewith it was made.

We ought in Scriptures rather to seek profitableness than highness of language.

We ought as gladly to read simple and devout books as high books and profound sentences.

Let not the authority of him that writeth whether he be of great name or little change thy thought, but let the love of pure truth draw thee to the love of God.

Ask not who said this but take heed what is said. Man passeth but the truth of our Lord abideth everlastingly.

God speaketh to us in diverse wise without acceptance of persons.

Our curiosity oft times in reading of the scriptures deceiveth us in that we search for curious thought where it is to be passed over simply and not curiously enquired.

If thou wilt draw profit in reading, read meekly simply and truly, not desiring to have a name of knowledge.

Ask gladly, and hear, holding thy peace.

And let not the parables of elder men displease thee for they are not brought forth without cause

CHAPTER VI

OF INORDINATE AFFECTIONS

WHENEVER a man coveteth anything inordinately anon, he is unrested in himself.

The proud man and covetous hath never rest: the poor man and meek in spirit is delighted in multitude of peace.

The man that is not perfectly dead in himself is soon tempted and soon overcome in small things and things of little price.

He that is feeble in spirit and yet in fleshly manner inclined to sensual things can not lightly withdraw himself wholly from earthly desires: wherefore ofttimes when he withdraweth a little he is sorry; and when any man withstandeth his will he disdaineth him.

And if he obtain that he desireth anon he is grieved in his conscience that he hath followed his own passion, the which helpeth nothing to the peace that he sought. Wherefore in withstanding of passions and not in serving them standeth very peace of heart.

Wherefore then is no peace in the heart of the fleshly man nor in him that is all given to outward things, but in the fervent spiritual man.

CHAPTER VII

OF FLEEING FROM VAIN HOPE TO ELATION

HE IS vain that putteth his hope in men or in creatures.

Be not ashamed to serve other men for the love of Jesu Christ and to be seen poor in this world. Stand not upon thyself but set thy trust in God. Do that in thee is and God shall be nigh to thy good will.

Trust not in thine own knowledge nor in the wiliness of any man living: but rather in the grace of God that helpeth meek folk and maketh low them that presume of themselves.

Rejoice thee not in riches if thou have any nor in friends if they be mighty: but in God that giveth all things and above all things desireth to give himself.

Lift not up thyself for greatness nor for beauty of body the which is corrupt and defouled with a little sickness.

Please not thyself for ability or for wit lest thou displease God of whom cometh all the good that thou hast naturally.

Account not thyself better than other lest peradventure thou be held worse in the sight of God that knoweth what is in man.

Be not proud of good works; for God's judgments are thiswise and man's otherwise; for ofttimes what pleaseth man displeaseth God.

If thou have any good things believe better things of others that thou may keep thy meekness.

It shall not annoy thee if thou set thee under all men: it might hinder thee much if thou set thyself afore other.

Continual peace is with the meek man but in the heart of the proud man is oft envy and indignation.

CHAPTER VIII

OF ESCHEWING OF TOO GREAT FAMILIARITY

Show not thy heart to every man but bring thy cause to him that is wise and dreadeth God.

Be rarely among young people and strange folks.

Blandish not rich men and appear not before great men: but accompany thyself with meek and simple men and treat of such things as belong to edification.

Be not familiar to any woman but generally commend all good women to God.

Desire to be familiar with God and with his angels and eschew knowledge of men. Charity is to be had towards all men but familiarity is not expedient.

It happeneth some times that a person unknown shineth by his bright fame whose presence offendeth and maketh dark the eyes of the beholders. We often hope to please others by our being and living together with them and often we begin to displease through ungodly manners found in us.

CHAPTER IX

OF OBEDIENCE AND SUBJECTION

IT IS a right great thing for a man to stand under obedience
and live under a prelate and not to be at his own liberty;
it is much more sure (safe) to stand in subjection than
in prelacy.

Many are under obedience more of necessity than of charity:
and they have pain and soon and lightly grutch (grumble)
and shall never get liberty of mind till they with all their
heart subdue themselves for God.

Run here and there, thou shalt never find quiet but in meek
subjection under a prelate; imagination and changing of
place have deceived many a one.

True is it that every man after his own wit is inclined most
to them that feel as he doth: but if God be among us it is
needful for us some times to forsake our own feelings for
the good of peace.

Who is so wise that may fully know all things? Wherefore
trust not too much in thine own feeling but desire gladly
to hear other men's feelings. If thy feeling be good and
thou, for God, leavest that and followest another man's
feeling thou shalt more profit thereby.

I have heard ofttimes that it is more sure (safe) to hear and
to take counsel than to give counsel.

It may well be that every man feel well (*i.e.*, have good
thoughts): but for a man no wise to agree with other men
when reason and the matter require it is token of pride
and obstinacy.

CHAPTER X

OF ESCHEWING SUPERFLUITY OF WORDS

ESCHEW thou noise and the press of men as much as thou mayest: for treating and talking of secular deeds though they

be brought forth with true and simple intention, hindereth much: for we be soon defiled and led into vanity.

I have wished myself ofttimes to have held my peace and not to have been among men; but why speak we and talk we together so gladly since seldom we come home without hurting of conscience?

Therefore we talk so oft together because by such speaking we seek comfort each from the other and to relieve the heart that is made weary with divers thoughts: and we speak much of such things as we love or desire or such things as are contrary to us: but, alas, ofttimes very vainly and unfruitfully. For such outward comfort is a great hindering of inward and heavenly consolation and therefore we ought to wake and to pray that our time pass not idly.

If it be lawful and expedient to speak, speak of such things as belong to edification. Evil use and the taking no heed of our ghostly (spiritual) increase and profiting doth much towards the evil keeping of our mouths. Nevertheless devout conference on spiritual things, and that where men of one soul and one spirit are fellowshipped together in God, helpeth greatly to spiritual profiting.

CHAPTER XI

OF PEACE TO BE GOTTEN AND ZEAL FOR PROFITING

WE SHOULD have much peace if we were not occupied with other men's deeds and sayings that belong not to our care. How may he long abide in peace that meddleth himself with other men's cares, that seeketh occasions outward and seldom gathereth himself within himself?

Blissful are the simple for they shall have much peace.

Why were some holy men sometime so perfect and so contemplative but that they studied to mortify themselves in all wise from earthly desires? And therefore they could take heed to themselves and cleave to God with all the inward of their hearts.

But we are occupied with our own passions and are busied overmuch in transitory things.

Also seldom it is that we overcome any vice perfectly: and we tend not every day to increase and therefore we abide cold and luke (lukewarm).

If we were perfectly dead to ourselves and not entangled too much with outward things then might we taste godly things and somewhat know of heavenly contemplation.

The whole and the greatest impediment is that we are not free from passions and concupiscences, nor do we force ourselves to enter in the way of holy men and saints.

Also when there cometh a little adversity we be anon thrown down and we turn us to seek man's comfort.

If we would force ourselves to stand in battle as mighty men we should see verily the help of our Lord come from heaven: for he is ready to help all them that fight for him and trust in his grace, and suffereth us to have occasions of fighting that we may have the victory.

If we put profiting of religion in outward observances alone our devotion shall soon have an end; but let us set the axe to the root that we, purged of our passions, may have a peaceable mind.

If every year we destroyed groundly (utterly) one vice we should soon be perfect men; but ofttimes we feel the contrary; for we find ourselves better and purer in the beginning of our conversion than after many years of our profession. Our fervour and our profiting ought to increase daily but now it seemeth a great thing if we may have but a part of our first fervour.

If we would in the beginning put (use) a little violence we should be able to do all things afterward with easiness and gladness.

It is grievous to leave things accustomed and it is more grievous for a man to do against his own will; but if thou overcome not small and light things when shalt thou overcome harder things?

Withstand thine inclination and unlearn evil custom lest little and little it bring thee to greater difficulty.

O if thou wouldst take heed how much peace thou shouldst get to thyself and how much gladness thou shouldst cause to other men in keeping thyself well, I suppose that thou wouldst be more busy about spiritual profiting.

CHAPTER XII

OF THE PROFIT OF ADVERSITY

It is good to us that we have some times grievances and contrarieties: for ofttimes they call a man into himself that he may know himself to be in an exile and that he may put not his trust in any earthly thing.

It is good that some time we suffer gainsaying and that men think of us evil and imperfectly; yea, though we do well and mean well.

Such things help ofttimes to meekness and defend us from vainglory: for then we seek better the inward witness, God, when we be little set by outwardly of men and little credence is given to us.

Therefore a man ought to firm (strengthen) himself in God so that he needeth not to seek any consolations outwardly.

When a man well disposed is troubled tempted or vexed with evil thoughts then he understandeth God to be more necessary unto him without whom he perceiveth that he may do no good thing; then he mourneth, then he waileth, and then he prayeth because of the miseries that he suffereth. Then also it wearieth him to live any longer: he desireth death that he may be dissolved and be with Christ.

Then also he perceiveth certainly that perfect surety and full peace may not be had in this world.

CHAPTER XIII

OF WITHSTANDING OF TEMPTATION

ALL the while we are in this world we may not be without
tribulation and temptation; as it is written in Job "Temptation is man's life on earth." And therefore every man
ought to be busy about his temptations and to wake
(watch) in prayers, that the enemy find no place to
deceive thee for he sleepeth never but goeth about seeking
whom he may devour.

There is no man so perfect nor so holy but that some time he
hath temptations and we may not fully lack them.

Nevertheless temptations are ofttimes right profitable to men,
though they be heavy and grievous; for in them a man is
meekened (humbled), purged and sharply taught.

All holy men have gone and profited by many tribulations
and temptations: and they that could not well suffer
temptation were made reprobate and they failed in their
way.

Neither is no order so holy nor no place so sure and secret but
there be temptations or adversities there.

There is no man all sure from temptations while he liveth; for
in ourselves is that whereof we be tempted since we are
born in concupiscence.

When one tribulation or temptation goeth another cometh
and ever shall we have somewhat to suffer for we have
lost the good of felicity.

Many men seek to overcome temptations only by fleeing of
them and they fall much more grievously into them. By
only fleeing we may not overcome, but by patience and
meekness we shall be stronger than all our enemies.

He that only outwardly declineth from temptation and taketh
it not up by the root shall little profit: but rather temptations shall come upon him again and he shall feel worse
and worse.

Thou shalt overcome them better little and little by patience
and long-suffering with the help of God than with hardness and thine own importunity.

In temptation ofttimes ask counsel.

Be not hard to him that is tempted, but give him comfort as
thou wouldest should be done to thee.

The beginning of all temptations is inconstancy of heart and
little trust in God; for as a ship without governance is
stirred hitherward and thitherward with the waves so a
man that is remiss and that holdeth not stedfastly his
purpose is diversely tempted.

Fire proveth gold and temptation proveth the righteous man.

Ofttimes we wot never what lieth in our power to do but
temptation openeth what we be.

Nevertheless we ought to watch principally about the beginning for then is the enemy soonest overcome if he be
not suffered to enter unto the door of the mind; but anon,
as he knocketh, meet him at entry.

First there cometh to mind a simple thought, after that a
strong imagination and then delectation of a shrewd
moving—and assenting.

So the wicked enemy while he is not withstood in the beginning
entereth in little and little till he be all in; and the longer
a man tarrieth in withstanding, the more feeble he waxeth
continually and his enemy against him is more mighty.

Some men have most grievous temptations in the beginning
of their conversion, some in the end: some in all their life
have no ease.

Many men are tempted full easily after the wisdom and equity
of the ordinance of God that peiseth (weigheth) the
states and merits of men and ordaineth all things to the
help of his chosen children.

Wherefore we ought not to despair when we be tempted but
the more fervently pray God that he vouchsafe to help
us in every tribulation; for he, as Saint Paul saith, shall
make in tribulation such profiting that we shall suffer it
and abide it.

Wherefore let us bow our souls under the mighty hand of God in every tribulation and temptation; for them that are meek in spirit he shall save and enhance.

In temptations and tribulations it is proved how much a man profiteth and *there* is most merit and virtue is best shown.

It is no great thing if a man be devout and fervent if he feel no heaviness but if he suffer patiently in time of adversity there is hope of great profiting.

Some men are preserved from great temptations and in small ones are daily overcome; that so, humbled, they may trust never in themselves in great things who are found feeble in so little things.

CHAPTER XIV

OF FLEEING RASH JUDGMENT

Turn thine eyes to thyself and be not a judge of other men's deeds.

In judging other men a man laboureth in vain, ofttimes erreth and lightly sinneth: but in judging and discussing a man's self ever he laboureth fruitfully.

As it lieth in our heart so for the most part we judge and lightly we lose our true judgment for our own likings.

If God were always the true intention of our desire we should not easily be troubled at the withstanding of our opinions; but ofttimes something is hidden within or cometh from without that draweth our judgment (aside).

Many privily seek their own advantage in things that they judge and yet they know it not.

It seemeth also to them that all is well when all things fall after their own rule and their own feelings; and if it fall otherwise than they desire then they are soon moved and sorry.

From diversity of opinions and of wits ofttimes come dissensions between friends and neighbours, between religious and devout people.

Old custom is hard to break and scarce any man will be led otherwise than seemeth good unto himself.

If thou lean more on thine own reason than on the humbling virtue of Jesu Christ it will be late before thou be a man illuminate; for God will have us perfectly subject unto him and by love brightened and burning will have us pass by the reason of all manner of men.

CHAPTER XV

OF WORKS DONE IN CHARITY

Evil is not to be done for nothing in this world nor for man's love. For the profit of him that is needy a good work may sometimes be left or else changed for the better: for in this manner the good work is not destroyed but changed.

Without charity the outward work availeth naught; but whatever is done of charity, be it never so simple nor so little, all is fruitful. For God weigheth more with how great charity a man doth a work than how great a work he doth.

He that loveth much doth much; and he doth much that doth a thing well.

He doth well that serveth more the common weal than his own weal.

Ofttimes it seemeth to be charity and it is carnality: for carnal inclination, one's own will, hope of reward, affection for profit are but seldom out of the way but ever ready.

He that hath very and perfect charity seeketh himself in nothing but only desireth the glory of God in all things and above all things. Also he hath envy to no man for he loveth no private or personal joy; nor he will not joy in himself but above all things he desireth to be made blissful in God. He ascribeth to no man any good thing but wholly referreth all things to God of whom they proceed originally in whom all saints rest finally.

O he that had verily that knowledge of charity would truly feel that all earthly things are full of vanity.

CHAPTER XVI

OF BEARING OTHER MEN'S INFIRMITIES AND FAULTS

Such things as a man may not amend in himself and in others he ought to suffer patiently till God ordain the contrary.

Think peradventure that it is better for thee to suffer such contrarieties for thy proving and thy patience; without which our merits are of little price. Nevertheless thou oughtest for such impediments to pray meekly to God that he vouchsafe to help thee that thou mayest suffer benignly.

If any such there be that be once or twice admonished and will not agree nor be counselled strive not with him but commit all to God that his will and his worship may be done and had in all his servants—he can well turn evil into good.

Study to be patient in suffering and bearing other men's faults and all manner infirmities: for thou hast in thee many things that must be suffered by other men. If thou canst not make thyself such as thou wouldest how canst thou have another at thy pleasure? Gladly we desire to make other men perfect but we will not amend our own fault; we will that other men be straightly corrected and we ourselves will not be corrected. Other men's large licence displeaseth us but we to ourselves will have nothing denied that we ask. We will have others restrained by statutes and we will suffer ourselves in no wise to be more restrained.

And thus it appeareth how seldom we weigh our neighbour as ourselves.

If all men were perfect what should we then have to suffer from other men for God's sake? Now therefore God hath ordained that we should learn each to bear others burdens. For there is no man without fault, no man without a burden, no man sufficient to himself, no man wise enough to himself but we must bear together, comfort together, help together, teach and admonish together.

What every man truly is is best shown by occasion of adversity: for occasions make not a man fail but they show what the man is.

CHAPTER XVII

OF THE RELIGIOUS LIFE

It BEHOVETH that thou learn to break thyself in many things if thou wilt accord and keep peace with others.

It is no little thing for a man to dwell in monasteries and congregations and there to live without quarrel and so truly to abide to his life's end. Blissful is he that liveth there well and graciously continueth.

If thou wilt stand rightly and wilt profit account thyself to be an exile and a pilgrim upon earth.

It behoveth thee to be a fool for Christ.

If thou wilt lead a religious life habit and tonsure avail little: but change of manners and whole mortification of the passions make a true religious man.

He that seeketh other than God to the health of his soul he shall find but tribulation and sorrow: nor may he long stand in peace unless he enforce himself to be least and subject to all.

Thou comest to serve and not to govern: know well that thou art called to suffer and to labour and not to be idle and tell tales.

Here are men proved as gold in the furnace: here may no man stand unless he will meeken (humble) himself with all his heart for God.

CHAPTER XVIII

OF THE EXAMPLES OF THE HOLY FATHERS

BEHOLD the living examples of the old fathers in the which shineth true perfection and thou shalt see how little it is and almost naught that we do. Alas, what is our life compared to them?

Holy men and the friends of God have served our Lord in hunger and in thirst, in cold and nakedness, in labour and weariness, in wakings and fastings, in prayers and holy meditations, in persecutions and many reproofs. O how many and how grievous tribulations apostles suffered, martyrs, confessors, virgins, and all Religious that would follow the steps of Christ: for they hated their souls, that is to say their bodily lives, that they might keep them into life everlasting.

O how strict a life lived the holy fathers in the desert; how long and how grievous temptations suffered they: how oft were they vexed by the enemy: how continual and how fervent prayers offered they to God: how sharp their abstinences; how great zeal and fervour had they to spiritual profiting: how great battle kept they about destruction of vices; how pure and right intention was theirs towards God.

By day they laboured and by night they gave themselves to prayer, though even in labouring they ceased not from inward prayer; every time they spent fruitfully, every hour given to thought of God seemed short and for the great sweetness of their contemplation sometimes the necessity of bodily food was forgotten.

They renounced all manner of riches, dignity, honours, friends and kin: they cared to have naught from the world, scarce they took what was necessary for life and were sorry to have to serve the body in its necessity. They were poor in earthly things but right rich in grace and virtues. Outwardly they were needy but inwardly they were refreshed with grace and ghostly comfort.

To the world they were aliens but to God they were familiar friends. To themselves they seemed as naught and despised by the world but in the eyes of God they seemed precious and chosen.

They stood in true meekness, they lived in simple obedience, they walked in charity and patience: and therefore every day they profited in spirit and gat great grace in the eyes of God.

They were given as an example to all Religious men and these ought to provoke us more to live and profit well than the great number of sluggish and lukewarm men to make us remiss and lax.

O how great was the fervour of religion in the beginning of its institution.

O how great devotion in praise, how great zeal for following virtue, how great discipline throve during that time: how great reverence and obedience under a rule flourished in them all.

Witness yet their steps that are left to show that they were truly holy men and perfect men who fighting so doughtily threw the world under foot.

Now is he accounted great that is not a breaker of the rule, that can suffer patiently what happeneth to him. O the sluggishness and the negligence of our time, that we so soon decline from our earlier fervour and are weary to live for very sluggishness and weariness.

Would God that the profiting of virtue sleep not utterly in thee that hast seen so many examples of devout men.

CHAPTER XIX

OF THE EXERCISES OF A GOOD RELIGIOUS MAN

THE life of a good Religious man ought to shine in all manner of virtue so that he be such inward as he appeareth to men outward. And rightly it ought to be much more inward than that which is seen outward. For God is our beholder whom chiefly we ought to worship wherever we be and go clean in his sight as angels.

Every day we ought to renew our purpose and stir ourselves to fervour as though we had been first converted and say "Help me, Lord God, in my good purpose and in thy service and grant me this day to begin perfectly; for naught it is that I have done unto this time."

According to our purpose so is the course of our profiting, and he that will profit well hath need of great diligence: for if he that purposeth seriously faileth ofttimes what shall hap to him that seldom or never purposeth anything seriously?

Nevertheless in divers manners it happeneth that men forsake their purpose; and though it appear to be slight yet it is not without some manner of hindering.

The purpose of righteous men hangeth rather in the grace of God than in man's own wisdom; in him they trust always in all things that they do.

For man purposeth and God disposeth; and man's way is not in man (to carry out).

If an accustomed exercise be sometimes left because of pity or for the profit of our neighbour it may soon be recovered again: but if it be lightly forsaken through heaviness of soul or negligence it is blameworthy and will be found hurtful.

Let us enforce ourselves as much as we can and yet we shall lightly fail in many things. But ever more somewhat certain is to be purposed and especially against those things that most hinder us.

Our outward and our inward exercises both ought to be searched and kept in order for both are expedient and helping to ghostly profit.

If thou may not continually gather thyself together, do it some time at least once a day, morning or evening.

In the morning purpose, in the eventide discuss the manner,

what thou hast been this day in word, work and thought:
for in these peradventure thou hast oft offended thy God
and thy neighbour.

Gird thee as a man against the Fiend's wickedness.

Refrain from gluttony and thou shalt the more easily restrain
all the inclination of the flesh.

Be never all idle, but either be reading or writing or praying
or thinking or something labouring for the common profit.

Bodily exercises are to be done discreetly; not to be taken
evenly and alike by all men.

Those things that are not common to all are not to be shown
outwardly, for private things are more safely exercised
in secret wise.

Nevertheless be ware that thou be not slow in common things
and more ready for private and singular exercises; but,
these that are due and enjoined being truly fulfilled, if
there be vacant time, yield thee to thyself as devotion
desireth.

All must not have one manner of exercise, but one this, another
that, as according.

Also diversity of exercises pleaseth, for some are more savoury
on festival days and some on common days; others we
need in time of temptation, others in time of peace and
quietness: others we must think when we are sorry and
others when we are glad in our Lord.

In principal feasts good exercises ought to be renewed and
the help of the saints more fervently to be sought.

From feast to feast we ought to purpose as though we should
at that time pass out of this world and go to the feast
everlasting.

Therefore we ought to array ourselves more busily in devout
works and live the more devoutly and keep every ob-
servance the more strictly as men that shall soon receive
the reward of our labour. And if it be delayed let us account ourselves as men not fully ready and unworthy to
come to so great a glory the which shall be revealed in us

in time ordained and let us study to make us ready to go out of the world.

"Blissful is that servant" saith Luke "whom our Lord when he cometh findeth waking; for I say to you verily he shall set him over all his goods."

CHAPTER XX

OF LOVE OF SILENCE AND TO BE ALONE

SEEK a convenient time to take heed to thyself and think ofttimes of the benefits of God.

Leave curious things and read such matters that rather give compunction than occupation.

If thou withdraw thyself from void speakings and idle circuits and from vanities and hearing of tidings thou shalt find time sufficient and convenient to have sweet meditations.

The great holy men where they might, fled men's fellowship and chose to live to God in secret places.

One said "as ofttimes as I was among men I came back a less man" that is to say less holy: this we find by experience when we talk any while.

It is easier for a man always to be still than not to exceed in words. It is easier for a man to abide privily at home than well to keep himself being away from home.

Wherefore whoever purposeth to come to inward and to spiritual things it behoveth him to decline from the company of people—with Jesu.

No man appeareth safely away from home but he that loveth gladly to abide at home.

No man speaketh safely but he that is glad to hold his peace.

No man is safe above but he that will gladly be beneath.

No man commandeth safely but he that hath learned to obey.

No man rejoiceth safely but he that hath the witness of a good conscience.

Nevertheless the safety of holy men was never without dread

of God; nor were they the less busy and meek in themselves though they had great virtues and grace.

The safety of shrews (wicked men) groweth from pride and presumption and in the end it turneth into deceit.

Promise thyself safety in this world never, though thou seem a good religious man or a devout hermit: Ofttimes they that are best in man's estimation fall most perilously for their trust in themselves.

Wherefore it is not profitable that they lack temptations utterly but they should ofttimes be attacked lest they be too secure and lest they be lift up by pride and lightly decline to outer consolations.

O he that never sought transitory gladness, he that never occupied him in the world, how good a conscience would he keep.

O he that would cut away all manner of vain business and would think all only on ghostly and godly things and set all his hope in God how great peace and quiet should he have.

There is no man worthy heavenly comfort unless he diligently exercise himself in holy compunction. If thou heartily be sorry enter into thy closet, exclude all worldly noise as it is written "Be ye sorry in your chambers"; thou shalt find there what outside thou shalt ofttimes lose.

The cell well continued waxeth sweet and the cell evil kept engendreth weariness. If in the beginning of thy conversion thou keep thy cell and dwell well therein it shall be to thee afterwards as a dear and well beloved friend and most pleasant solace.

In silence and quiet the devout soul profiteth and learneth the secrets of the scriptures: there he findeth the floods of tears wherewith every night he may wash and cleanse himself that he may be the more familiar to his creator the more he withdraweth him far from secular noise.

He that withdraweth himself from friends and known men, God shall come nigh unto him with his holy angels.

Better it is for a man to be hid and take care of himself than, taking no heed of himself, to work wonders.

It is commendable for a man of religion seldom to go out, to fly from being seen and not wish to see men; why wilt thou see what is not lawful for thee to have?

The world passeth and his concupiscence.

The desires of sensuality draw men to walk about; but when the hour is past what cometh thereof but grudging (murmuring) of conscience and dispersion of heart?

A glad going out ofttimes bringeth forth a sorrowful coming home and a glad watching over evening bringeth forth a sorry morning; so every fleshly joy entereth in pleasantly but in the end he biteth and slayeth.

What canst thou see elsewhere that thou canst not see here? Lo here heaven earth and all elements and of these all things are made.

What canst thou see elsewhere that may long abide under the sun? peradventure thou waitest to be filled; but thou shalt never come thereto.

If thou sawest all things that are present what were that but a vain sight? Lift up thine eyes to God on high and pray God for thy sins and negligence: leave vain things to the vain and take thou heed to the things that God commandeth thee.

Shut thy door upon thee and call to thee Jesu thy love: dwell with him in thy cell for thou shalt not find elsewhere so great peace.

If thou hadst not gone out nor heard no tidings thou wouldst the better have abided in peace; and since it delighteth thee sometimes to hear new tidings it behoveth, following this, that thou suffer turbation of heart.

CHAPTER XXI

OF COMPUNCTION OF HEART

IF THOU wilt any wise profit keep thee in the dread of God and be not in great liberty but refrain thy understanding under discipline and give not thyself to unseasonable gladness.

Give thyself to compunction of heart and thou shalt find devotion; compunction openeth many things which distraction of mind soon loseth.

Wonder it is that a man may at any time be glad that considereth his exile and so many perils of his soul. For through lightness of heart and negligence of our faults we feel not the sorrows and the harm done to our souls and ofttimes we laugh vainly when we should by reason rather weep.

There is no true liberty nor good mirth but in the dread of God with a good conscience; blissful is he that may put away every hindering distraction and bring himself to the unity of holy compunction: blissful is he that voideth from him all that may defoul or grieve his conscience.

Fight manly: custom is overcome with custom.

If thou canst leave men, they will well leave thee and suffer thee to do thine own deeds.

Draw not to thyself the matters of other men and implicate not thyself in causes of great men. Have thine eye first upon thyself and admonish thyself spiritually before all others whom thou lovest best.

If thou have not the favour of men be not sorry therefore: but let this be grievous to thee that thou hast (keepest) not thyself well and circumspectly as it beseemeth the servant of God and a devout religious man to live.

Ofttimes it is more profitable and more safe that a man have not many comforts in this life and specially after the flesh.

And that we have not or that we seldom feel godly consolations it is own our fault; for we seek not compunction, nor we put not away utterly vain and outward comforts.

Acknowledge thyself to be not worthy godly consolation but rather worthy much tribulation.

When a man is perfectly sorry then is all the world grievous and bitter to him.

A good man findeth sufficient matter of sorrowing and weeping; whether he consider himself or think on his neighbour he shall know that no man liveth here without tribulation; and the more strictly that he considereth himself so much more he sorroweth.

Matters of righteous sorrow and of inward compunction are our sins and our vices wherein we lie wrapped so that we may but seldom behold heavenly things.

If thou thoughtest ofter on death than thou dost of long life no doubt but thou wouldst more fervently amend thyself: or else if thou wouldst heartily behold the pains of hell and purgatory I believe that thou wouldst gladly suffer pain, labour and sorrow, dreading no manner of rigour: but because these go not to the heart and we yet love blandishings, therefore we remain cold and slow.

Ofttimes it is need (poverty) of spirit whereof the wretched body so easily complaineth: pray therefore meekly to our Lord that he give thee the spirit of compunction and say with the prophet "Feed me, Lord, with the bread of tears and give me drink of tears in measure."

CHAPTER XXII

OF CONSIDERATION OF MAN'S MISERY

WRETCHED thou art wherever thou be and whithersoever thou turn thee unless thou turn thee to God.

Why art thou troubled, that all things come not to thee as thou willest or desirest? who is he that hath all things

at his own will? neither I nor you, nor no man in earth;
there is no man in this world without some manner of
tribulation or anguish, though he be king or pope.

Then who is in the best case? forsooth he that may suffer
anything for God's sake.

Lord, now there are many weak folk that say "O how good
a life that man hath; how great, how rich, how mighty,
how high he is." But behold heavenly goods and thou
shalt see that all these temporal goods be as none but
that they be full uncertain, and more grieving than
easing; for they are never had without business and
dread.

It is man's felicity to have temporal goods in abundance but
mediocrity sufficeth him; verily it is a misery to live upon
earth: the more spiritual that a man will be the more
this present life appeareth bitter: for he feeleth better
and seeth more clearly the faults of man's corruption.

For to eat, to drink, to wake, to sleep, to rest, to labour, and
to be subject to the necessities of nature is very misery
and an affliction to a devout man that would fain be
loose and free from sin.

The inward man is full sore grieved with bodily necessities
in this world.

Wherefore the prophet prayeth devoutly that he may be free
from them saying "Lord, deliver me from my necessities."

But woe to them that know not their misery: but more woe
to them that love this misery and this corruptible life;
for there be some that so heartily clasp this wretched
life that though they may scarce have their necessities
with labour, yea and with begging, yet if they might
live here for ever, they would take no heed of the realm
of heaven.

O the mad men and out of true belief that live so deeply
in earthly things that they savour no heavenly things:
but these wretches yet in the end shall grievously feel
how nought it was and how vile that which they have
loved.

But the saints of God and all devout men and friends of Christ have not taken heed to that which pleaseth the flesh nor to them that have flourished in this world: but all their hope and all their intention hath been to things everlasting.

All their desire was borne up to things invisible and abiding lest by love of things visible they might be drawn to their lowest things.

Brother, lose not thy confidence in profiting by spiritual things: yet hast thou time and the hour; why wilt thou tarry thy purpose till to-morrow? Arise and begin anon and say "Now is the time of doing, now is the time of purging, now is the time of amending."

When thou art ill at ease then say "Now is the time of merit." Thou must go through fire and water ere thou come to refreshing.

Unless thou do force to thyself, thou shalt never overcome vice.

All the while that we bear this frail body we cannot be without sin, nor live without heaviness and sorrow.

We would gladly have quiet from all misery; but for as much as by sin we lost innocence, we lost also true blissfulness: therefore we must keep patience and abide the mercy of God till this wickedness go away and this mortality be swallowed up by life.

O how great is man's frailty that is prone and ready to vices; this day thou art shriven of thy sins and to-morrow thou dost like sins again. Now thou purposest to be ware and within two hours thou dost as though thou hadst never taken such purpose; wherefore we have great cause to humble ourselves and never to feel any great things of ourselves; for we be so frail and so unstable.

Also may soon be lost by negligence what is scarce gotten in great time by grace.

What shall happen to us in the end that are sluggish so early?

Woe be to us who thus wish to decline and rest as though

there were peace and safety, since there appeareth yet no step of true holiness in our conversation.

It were need that we should now be informed as young novices are in good manners, if peradventure there might be any hope of amendment to come or of more spiritual profiting.

CHAPTER XXIII

OF MEDITATION OF DEATH

THIS day a man is and to-morrow he appeareth not: full soon shall this be fulfilled in thee; look whether thou canst do otherwise.

And when man is out of sight soon he passeth out of mind.

O the dulness and the hardness of man's heart that only thinketh on things present and provideth not more for things to come. Thou shouldst have thyself so in every deed and in every thought as though thou shouldst die anon.

If thou hadst a good conscience thou wouldst not much dread death.

It is better to eschew sins than to flee death: if thou be not ready to-day, how shalt thou be ready to-morrow? The morrow is a day uncertain and how knowest thou that thou shalt live to-morrow?

What availeth it to live long when there is little amendment? A long life amendeth us not always but some times increaseth sin. Would God we had lived well in this world one day.

Many men count the years of their conversion but ofttimes little is the fruit of amendment. If it be dreadful to die peradventure it is more perilous to live long: blissful is he that hath the hour of his death ever before his eyes and that every day disposeth himself to die.

If thou have seen any man die think that thou thyself shalt go the same way.

When it is morning think thou shalt not come to the even; and when even cometh be not bold to promise thyself the morning.

Wherefore be ever ready and live so that death find thee never unready.

Many men die sudden and unadvised: for what hour we think not the Son of man shall come.

When that last hour cometh thou shalt begin to feel all otherwise of thy life that is past and thou shalt greatly sorrow that thou hast been so remiss and so negligent.

O how blessed is he that laboureth to be such in his life as he desireth to be found in his death.

These things shall give thee great trust in death—perfect contempt of the world, fervent desire to profit in virtues, love of discipline, labour in penance, promptitude in obedience, denying of oneself, bearing all manner of adversity for the love of Christ.

While thou art whole thou mayst do much good: but when thou art sick I wot not what thou mayst do: few there be that are amended by sickness even as they that go much on pilgrimage are but seldom the holier.

Delay not the health of thy soul through trust in friends or in neighbours; for men will forget sooner than thou thinkest: it is better now to make provision betimes and send before thee some good than to trust in other men's help.

If thou be not busy for thyself now, who shall be busy for thee in time to come?

Time now is right precious: but alas that thou spendest it no more profitably wherein thou canst deserve that whereby thou mayst live everlastingly.

Time shall come when thou shalt desire one day or one hour for thine amendment and thou wottest not whether thou shalt get it.

O my dear friend, from how great peril mayst thou make thyself free and from how great dread deliver thyself if thou be now always fearful and suspicious of death.

Study to live so now that thou may in the hour of death rather rejoice than dread: learn now to die to the world that thou mayst begin to live with Christ: learn now to despise all things that thou mayst then go freely to Christ. Chastise thy body by penance that thou mayst then have certain confidence.

And, thou fool, why thinkest thou shalt live long since thou art sure of no day?

How many are deceived and against all expectation drawn out of the body. How often hast thou heard men say "That man was slain with a sword, he drowned, he falling from high brake his neck, he in eating suddenly waxed stiff, he in playing met his end, another with fire, another with iron, another with pestilence, another slain among thieves."

And so the end of all is death and man's life passeth away suddenly as a shadow.

Who shall have mind on thee after death and who shall pray for thee?

Do, my dear brother, now what thou canst do for thou wottest not when thou shalt die and thou wottest not what shall come to thee after thy death.

While thou hast time gather riches immortal; think on nothing but thy soul's health; charge (care for) only those things that belong to thy soul.

Make thyself friends now worshipping holy saints and following their works that when thou failest in this life they may receive thee into everlasting tabernacles.

Keep thyself as a pilgrim and a guest upon the earth to whom belongeth nothing of worldly business.

Keep thy heart and rear it up to thy God for thou hast here none abiding city: thither direct prayers and daily mournings with tears that thy spirit after thy death may deserve blissfully to come to our Lord.

CHAPTER XXIV

OF THE JUDGMENT AND OF THE PAINS OF SINNERS

IN ALL things behold the end and how thou shalt stand before the righteous judge from whom is nothing hid. He is not pleased with gifts, he receiveth none excusations but that is righteous he shall judge.

O thou most wretched and unsavoury sinner what shalt thou answer God who knows all thy evils, thou that sometimes art afeard of the look of a man that is wroth?

Why dost thou not provide for thyself against the day of doom when no man shall be excused nor defended by another but every man's burden shall be enough for himself?

Now thy labour is fruitful, thy weeping acceptable, thy mourning is heard, thy sorrow is satisfactory and purgatory (purging). He hath a great and a wholesome purgatory that patiently receiveth wrongs, that sorroweth more for other men's malice than for his own wrongs, that gladly prayeth for his adversaries and heartily forgiveth his trespassers, that tarrieth not to ask forgiveness of others, that more easily forgiveth than is wroth, that doth violence to himself, that laboureth in all wise to hold his flesh under the spirit.

Better it is to cut away and purge thy sins and thy vices here than to reserve them to be purged in coming time.

Verily we deceive ourselves by inordinate love of our flesh.

What other thing shall that fire devour but only thy sins? The more that thou sparest thyself now and followest thy flesh the longer thou shalt be punished and the more matter for burning thou reservest.

In what thing a man hath sinned in those things a man shall be punished.

There slow men shall be pricked with burning pricks and gluttonous men shall be tormented with great hunger and great thirst, the lecherous men and lovers of their lusts shall be poured on with burning pitch and stinking brimstone.

And the envious shall howl for sorrow as mad hounds and there shall be no vice but he shall have his own proper torment.

There proud men shall be fulfilled with all manner of shame and confusion: and covetous men shall be straitened with most wretched need. There shall one hour be more grievous in pain than an hundred year here in laborous penance.

There is no rest, no consolation to damned folk; here some times men cease from labours and are solaced by their friends.

Be now busy and sorrowing for thy sins that thou mayst stand safe in the day of judgment with blissful men.

Then shall righteous men stand in great constancy against them that have anguished them and oppressed them; then shall he sit to judge that now subdueth himself meekly to the judgments of men; then shall the poor and the meek have great trust and the proud man shall dread on every side.

Then it shall appear that he was wise in this world who learned for Christ to be a fool and despised, then every tribulation suffered patiently for Christ shall please and all wickedness shall stop his mouth; then shall every devout man rejoice and every unreligious man sorrow.

Then shall the flesh that hath been in affliction rejoice much more than he that hath been nourished in delicates.

Then shall the vile coat shine bright and the subtle (woven) cloth shall be dark.

Then shall be more praised a poor cot than a golden palace.

Then shall constant patience more help than all the world's might.

Then shall meek obedience be higher exalted than all worldly wisdom.

Then shall a pure and good conscience gladden a man more than great philosophy.

Then shall contempt of riches weigh more than all the treasure of the earth.

Then shalt thou be more comforted by devout prayer than by delicate eating.

Then shalt thou rather rejoice for well kept silence than for long talking.

Then shall holy works more avail than many fair words.

Then shall straight life and hard penance more avail than all earthly delectation.

Learn now to suffer in a little that thus thou mayst be delivered from more grievous pains.

Prove here first what thou mayst suffer afterwards. If thou canst not suffer here so little things how shalt thou be able to suffer everlasting torments?

If now so little a passion maketh thee impatient, what shall hell do then?

Lo, verily, thou canst not have ij joys; to be delighted in this world and afterward to reign with Christ.

If thou hast lived until now in honours and in the lusts of the world, what could all that avail thee if it happened to thee to die in this moment?

All things therefore are vanity save to love God and to serve him alone. For he that loveth God with all his heart dreadeth neither death, nor torment, nor judgment, nor hell: for perfect love shall make a ready way to God and a sure coming.

He that yet delighteth to sin, it is no wonder that he dread death and the judgment.

Nevertheless it is good that, if love cannot revoke thee from sin, at least let dread do it: for he that putteth behind him the dread of God may not long stand in good but he shall soon run into the Fiend's snares.

CHAPTER XXV

OF THE FERVENT AMENDMENT OF ALL OF A MAN'S LIFE

BE WAKING and diligent in the service of God and think oft-times why thou camest here and forsookest the world: was it not that thou wouldest live to God and be a spiritual man?

Wherefore be fervent to profiting for thou shalt receive meed for thy labours and then shall there no more be dread nor sorrow in thy coasts.

Thou shalt labour now a little and thou shalt find great rest and everlasting gladness and if thou abide true and fervent in working without doubt God shall be true and rich in rewarding.

Thou oughtest to keep a good hope that thou shalt come to the victory; but it is not behoveful to make thyself sure lest thou wax sluggish or proud.

There was once a man in great heaviness ofttimes doubting between dread and hope; and on a time, encumbered with great sorrow, he fell down prostrate in his prayers before an altar in the church. This he thought in his mind "Would God I wist that I should persevere." And then he heard within himself an answer from God "What if thou wist, what wouldst thou do? Do now as thou wouldst do then and thou shalt be safe enow"; and anon he was comforted and committed himself to the will of God and the doubtful fluctuation ceased and he would no more search curiously of things that were to come but rather studied to inquire what was the well pleasing and perfect will of God wherewith to begin every good work and perform it.

"Trust in our Lord and do goodness," saith the Prophet "and dwell upon the earth and thou shalt be fed in the riches thereof."

One thing there is that letteth (hindereth) many men from

profiting and fervent amending—horror of difficulty and labour of striving or of fighting. They above all other profit in virtues that enforce themselves most manly to overcome the things that are most grievous and contrary to them: for there a man profiteth and most ample grace deserveth where he overcometh himself and mortifieth in spirit. But all have not alike much to overcome and mortify.

Nevertheless a diligent lover shall be more mighty to profit though he have more passions than he that is well mannered, being less fervent to virtue.

And ij things specially help to great amending: that is for a man to withdraw himself with violence from such things as nature is viciously inclined to and fervently to labour for the good that he most needeth.

Also study most to eschew and overcome those things that most fervently displease thee in other men.

Take thy profiting in every place, so that, if thou hear or see a good ensample, thou be fervent to follow it. If thou think of anything that is to be blamed, be ware that thou do it not. And if thou do it at any time, study soon to amend it. As thine eye considereth other folk, so other men note thee.

How sweet it is, how merry it is, to see fervent and devout brethren and well mannered and under discipline and how sorrowful and heavy it is to see brethren going inordinately, that practise not those things that they are called to; how noyous (hurtful) it is for a man to take none heed of the purpose of his calling and to bow his wit to such things as are not given him to do.

Have mind on the purpose that thou hast taken and ever put before thee the image of the crucifix. Thou mayest be well ashamed, beholding the life of our Lord Jesu Christ, that thou hast no more studied to conform thee thereto though thou have been long in the way of God. The religious man that attentively and devoutly exerciseth himself in the most holy life and passion of our Lord, he shall find abundantly all things that are needful and profitable to him nor shall he have no need to seek any better thing without Jesu.

O if Jesu Christ come into our heart how soon and how sufficiently we should be taught.

The negligent religious and the luke(warm) hath tribulation and on every side suffereth anguish: for he lacketh inward comfort and he is forbidden to seek any outward. The religious man that is without discipline is open to a grievous fall.

He that ever more seeketh those things that are most lax and most remiss shall ever be in anguish; for one thing or other shall evermore displease. How many religious men that are straightened under claustral discipline, live retired, eat poorly, are clothed boistrously (roughly), labour greatly, speak little, wake long, rise early, pray long, ofttimes read and keep them in all manner of discipline. Take heed of the Carthusians, the Cistercians, and monks and minchins (nuns) of diverse religious houses how they rise up every night to sing to our Lord; therefore it is foul that thou shouldst be sluggish in so holy a work, where so great multitude of religious folk begin to joy to God.

Would God we had naught else to do, but only to praise our Lord Jesu Christ with all our heart.

Would God thou needed never to eat nor drink nor sleep but ever praise God and to take heed to spiritual studies: but thou shouldst be more blissful than now when thou servest the flesh for any manner of need.

Would God that these necessities were not but that only spiritual refections existed for the soul the which alas we taste full seldom.

When a man is come to this that he seeketh his comfort of no creature then at first beginneth God to taste sweet to him perfectly. Then also he is well content of every chance, then he will not be glad for no great thing, nor sorry for no little thing, but putteth himself wholly and trustily in God that is to him all things in all things, to whom nothing perisheth nor dieth but all things live to him and serve him at his beckoning.

Have mind ever on the end and that time lost never cometh again.

Without business and diligence shalt thou never get virtue. If thou beginnest to be luke(warm) thou beginnest to be evil at ease. But if thou give thyself to fervour, thou shalt find great peace and thou shalt feel labour lighter for the grace of God and love of virtue. A fervent man and a diligent is ready to all things. There is more labour in withstanding vices and passions than to sweat in bodily labours.

He that escheweth not small defaults little and little shall slide in to greater.

Thou shalt ever joy at eventide if thou spend the day fruitfully.

Watch upon thyself, stir thyself, admonish thyself: and how ever it be with other, forget not thyself. So much thou shalt profit as thou doest violence to thyself.

Here endeth the first party of musica ecclesiastica. And now follow the chapters of the ij party.

PART TWO

CHAPTER I

OUR Lord saith that the kingdom of heaven is within you. Turn thyself to God with all thine heart and forsake this wretched world and thy soul shall find rest.

Learn to despise outward things and to turn thee to inward things and thou shalt see the kingdom come into thee; for the kingdom of God is peace and joy in the Holy Ghost the which is not given to wicked men.

Christ shall come to thee showing thee his consolation if thou make for him within thee a worthy dwelling place; all his glory and honour is within and there is his plesaunce.

His visitation is common and oft with an inward man; with *him* is his sweet talking, gracious consolation, much wonderful familiarity.

Eh, thou true soul, array thy soul for thy spouse that he may vouchsafe to come to thee and to dwell in thee: for thus he saith "whoso loveth me shall keep my word and to him we shall come and in him make our dwelling place." Wherefore give Christ place and as to all other hold them out.

When thou hast Christ thou art rich and it sufficeth thee; he shall be thy provisor thy true procurator in all things, so that thou shalt not need to trust in man. Men are soon changed and fail soon; Christ abideth for ever and standeth steadfastly unto the end.

Great trust is not to be put in a mortal and frail man though he be profitable and well beloved: nor great sorrow to be felt though sometimes he withstand thee and is contrary. They that are this day with thee to-morrow they may be contrary; and in contrary wise they be ofttimes turned as the wind.

Put all thy trust in God, let him be thy dread, let him be thy love; he shall answer for thee and do well and as is best.

Thou hast here no dwelling city and wherever thou be thou art as a stranger and a pilgrim: here gettest thou no rest, unless thou be inwardly one with Christ.

Why lookest thou about here, since this is not the place of thy resting? In heavenly things ought to be thine habitation and all earthly are to be considered as in a manner of passing; for all things pass and thou also with them. Look that thou cleave not to them lest thou be taken with them and perish.

Let thy thinking be on the high God and let thy prayer be lift up unto Christ without intermission. If thou canst not behold high celestial things, rest in the passion of Christ and dwell gladly in his holy wounds; for if thou flee devoutly to the wounds and the precious prints of Christ thou shall find great comfort in tribulation nor thou shalt not greatly care for man's despisings and thou shalt lightly bear backbiting words; for Christ was despised of men in this world and in his greatest need suffered reproofs, forsaken of his friends and of his known men.

Christ would suffer and be despised; and thou wilt have all men friends and benefactors?

Christ had adversaries and suffered shrewd speakers; and thou darest complain on any body?

How shall thy patience be crowned if there come no adversity? If thou wilt suffer no contrary, how shalt thou be the friend of Christ? Suffer for Christ and with Christ if thou wilt reign with Christ.

If thou hadst once perfectly entered in to the innerness of Jesu and hadst savoured a little of his burning love, thou wouldst have set naught by thine own profit or harm but rather thou wouldst rejoice of reproof done to thee; for the love of Jesu maketh a man set naught of himself.

A lover of Jesu and a very inward man and free from inordinate affections may freely turn himself to God and lift himself above himself in spirit and there rest joyously.

The man to whom all things taste as they be, not as they are said or thought to be he, is very wise and taught more by God than by men.

He that can go within and praise things without but little, he seeketh no place, nor abideth for no times to have devout exercises. The inward man soon gathereth himself together for he never poureth himself out wholly over outward things. Outward labour hindereth him not nor needful occupation of the day, but so as things come, so he giveth himself to them.

He that is well disposed and ordained within, he careth not for the wicked and wonderful conduct and bearing of men.

Just so much is a man hindered and distracted as things are drawn to him.

If it were well with thee and thou wert well purged all should turn for thee to good and profit.

Many things as yet trouble thee and displease thee, for thou art not yet dead to thyself nor parted from all earthly things: nothing so defouleth and entangleth man's heart as impure love in created things.

If thou forsake outward comfort thou shalt be able to behold heavenly things and ofttimes have jubilation within.

CHAPTER II

OF MEEK SUBMISSION

Set not much by this—who is against thee or with thee but so do and care that God be with thee.

In every thing that thou dost have a good conscience and God shall defend thee: for him that God will help no man's overthwartness shall be able to annoy.

If thou canst be still and suffer thou shalt see without any doubt the help of our Lord; he knoweth the time and manner of helping thee and therefore thou oughtest to reserve thyself for him.

To God it belongeth to help and to deliver from all confusion.

Ofttimes it availeth to the keeping of greater meekness that other men should know our faults and reprove them.

When a man humbleth himself for his faults then he appeaseth others lightly and easily maketh satisfaction to them that were displeased.

The meek man God defendeth and delivereth, the meek man he loveth and comforteth, to the meek man he bareth himself, to the meek man he granteth great grace and after his humbling he lifteth him in glory; to the meek man he sheweth his secrets and draweth him and calleth him sweetly.

The meek man receiving reproofs or wrong or confusion is in peace well enough, for he standeth in God and not in the world.

Account thyself never to have profited till thou feel thee lower than all others.

CHAPTER III

OF A GOOD PEACEABLE MAN

SET thyself first in peace and then shalt thou be able to set others at peace.

A peaceable man availeth more than a great learned man.

A passionate man turneth good into evil and soon believeth evil: a good peaceable man draweth all things to good.

He that is well in peace hath suspicion against no man; he that cannot be content but is moved, he is shaken with many suspicions; neither can he be in rest nor suffer others to be in rest. Ofttimes he saith that he should not say and leaveth that which were more expedient to do; he considereth what other men ought to do and taketh no heed to his own charge.

Have therefore first zeal to better thyself and then mayst
thou have zeal to thy neighbour.

Thou canst well excuse and colour thine own deeds but other
men's excuses thou wilt not receive. It were more
righteous first to accuse thyself and to excuse thy brother.

If thou wilt be borne, bear thou another.

See how far thou art yet from true charity and meekness the
which can not be wroth, nor have indignation with no
man but only with itself.

It is not a great thing for a man to be conversant with good
men and mild men: for that pleaseth all men naturally
and every man gladly hath peace with them that feel
as he doth; and such he loveth.

But for a man to live peaceably with hard and overthwart
men indisciplined and contrarious is a great grace and
a commendable and a manly deed.

There are some that keep themselves at peace and have peace
with others also; and there be some also that neither
have peace themselves nor suffer others to have peace;
to others they be grievous but most grievous to themselves. And there be some that keep their peace in themselves and study to reduce other men to peace.

Nevertheless all our peace in this wretched life is rather to
be set in meek suffering than in not feeling what goes
contrary.

He that can well suffer shall find most peace; he is an over-
comer of himself, lord of the world, the friend of Christ
and the heir of heaven.

CHAPTER IV

OF PURE AND SIMPLE INTENTION

A MAN is lift up from earthly things with ij wings—they are
simplicity and purity; simplicity ought to be in intention,
purity in affection: simplicity intendeth God, purity
taketh him and tasteth him.

There shall no good deed hinder thee if thou be free within from inordinate affection.

If thou intend not nor seek nothing else but the pleasing of God and the profit of thy neighbour thou shalt have inward liberty. If thine heart were right, then every creature should be to thee a mirror of life and a book of holy doctrine. There is no creature so little nor so vile but it represents the goodness of God.

If thou were inward, good and pure, then shouldest thou see all things without impediment and understand them.

A pure heart pierceth heaven and hell.

Such as every man is inwardly so he judgeth outwardly.

If there be any joy in this world the man of pure heart hath it; and if there be in any place tribulation and anguish an idle conscience knoweth it best.

Like as iron put in the fire loseth his rust and shall be made bright: so a man turning him wholly to God is freed and taken from sloth and changed into a new man.

When a man beginneth to wax luke(warm) then he dreadeth a little labour and receiveth gladly outward consolation: but when he beginneth perfectly to overcome himself and to go manly in the way of God then he setteth little by those things that before seemed to him right grievous.

CHAPTER V

OF CONSIDERATION OF ONESELF

WE OUGHT not to believe ourselves overmuch for ofttimes grace is lacking in us and understanding. Little light is in us and ofttimes we lose that by negligence. And also ofttimes we perceive not how blind we are within.

Ofttimes we do evil, and worse—we excuse it.

Ofttimes we be moved (to anger) and think that it is zeal.

We reprove small things in others and pass over our own faults that are greater.

We feel and weigh soon enough what we suffer from others: but how much others suffer from us, of this we take no heed.

He that would ponder well and truly his own faults he should find naught to judge in others grievously. An inward man before all other things taketh care of himself and he that diligently taketh heed of himself holdeth his peace of others. Thou shalt never be an inward and devout man unless thou keep silence of other men and specially behold thyself. If thou take heed only to God and to thyself what thou perceivest outside thee shall little move thee.

Where art thou when thou art not present to thyself? And when thou hast run over all things, taking no heed of thyself, what hast thou profited?

If thou wilt have peace and very unity thou must set all aside and only have thyself before thine eyes; and then thou shalt profit much if thou keep holiday and rest from every temporal care.

Thou shalt greatly fail if thou set great store by any temporal thing. Let nothing be great or high or acceptable to thee but purely God. All things deem as vain comfort that come from any creature—the soul that loveth God, let her despise all things but God alone.

God alone, everlasting and great, without any measure, fulfilling all things; he is the solace of man's soul and true gladness of heart.

CHAPTER VI

OF THE GLADNESS OF A GOOD CONSCIENCE

THE joy of a good man is the witness of a good conscience: have a good conscience and thou shalt ever have gladness. A good conscience may bear right many (very many) things and is right glad among adversities: an evil conscience is ever dreadful and out of quiet.

Thou shalt rest sweetly if thine heart reprehend thee not.

Be not glad but when thou hast done well.

Evil men have never true gladness nor never feel inward peace; for as our Lord saith there is no peace to wicked men; and if they say "we are in peace, there shall none evils come upon us" believe them not, for the wrath of God shall arise suddenly and their deeds shall be brought to naught and their thoughts shall perish.

For a man to rejoice in tribulation is not grievous to him who loves; for so to joy is to joy in the cross of Christ.

Short is the glory that is given and taken by men; and sorrow followeth ever the glory of the world.

The glory of good men is in their conscience and not in the mouths of men.

The gladness of righteous men is of God and in God: and their joy is of truth.

He that desireth everlasting and true glory setteth no care on that which is temporal: and he that seeketh not temporal glory but despiseth it from his heart he must needs love heavenly glory. He hath great tranquillity of heart that setteth nothing by praisings or blamings.

He whose conscience is clean, he will soon be content and pleased. Thou art not the holier though thou be praised nor the more vile though thou be blamed or dispraised.

What thou art, that thou art; that God knoweth thee to be and thou canst be said to be no greater.

If thou take heed what thou art within thou shalt not reck what men say of thee: man looketh on the visage and God on the heart; man considereth the deeds and God praiseth the thoughts.

For a man ever to do well and to hold (think) little of himself is token of a meek soul.

For a man not to wish to be comforted by any creature is a token of great purity and of inward trust.

He that seeketh no outward witness for himself, it appeareth openly that he hath committed himself all wholly to God:

for (as the apostle saith) he that commendeth himself is
not approved but only he whom God commendeth.

The state of the inner man is to walk with God and to be held
by no outward affection.

CHAPTER VII

OF THE LOVE OF JESU ABOVE ALL THINGS

BLISSFUL is he that understandeth what it is to love Jesu and
to despise himself for Jesu.

It behoveth thee to forsake all things for the loved one, for
Jesu would be loved alone above all things: the love of
a creature is failing and unstable; the love of Jesu is
true and persevering.

He that cleaveth to a creature shall fall with the sliding creature; he that clippeth (embraceth) Jesu shall be made
steadfast forever.

Love him and hold him fast as a friend which, when all goeth
away, shall not forsake thee nor shall not suffer thee to
perish at the end.

From all things thou must be departed some time whether
thou wilt or not. Hold thee with Jesu living and dying
and commit thee to his trust, who, all other failing, alone
may help thee.

Thy beloved is of such nature that he will admit no stranger,
but he alone will have thy heart and there sit as a king
on his own throne.

If thou couldest well free thee from every creature Jesu would
gladly dwell with thee.

Thou shalt find almost all lost whatever trust thou settest in
creatures: trust not nor lean not upon a windy reed:
for every flesh is grass and all his glory shall fall as the
flower of grass.

Thou shalt soon be deceived if thou look only to the outer
appearance of men. If thou seek thy solace and thy lucre
in others, thou shalt ofttimes find hindrances to thee.

If thou seek Jesu in all things, thou shalt find Jesu; and if thou seek thyself thou shalt find thyself but—to thine own harm.

A man hurteth himself more, if he seeketh not Jesu, than all the world and all his adversaries can hurt him.

CHAPTER VIII

OF THE FAMILIAR FRIENDSHIP OF JESU

When Jesu is nigh all goodness is nigh and nothing seemeth hard: but when Jesu is not nigh all things are hard.

When Jesu speaketh not within, the comfort is of little price; but if Jesu speak one word, there is found great comfort.

Did not Mary Mawdeleyn rise out of her place wherein she wept, anon as Martha said "Our master is nigh and calleth thee?"

Blissful is that man whom, when Jesu cometh, he calleth from tears to the joy of the spirit.

How dry and how hard thou art without Jesu; how unsavoury, how vain, if thou covet anything without Jesu; whether is it not more harm than if thou lost all the world?

What may the world avail thee without Jesu? to be without Jesu is a grievous hell and to be with Jesu is a sweet paradise.

If Jesu be with thee there may no enemy hurt thee.

He that findeth Jesu findeth a good treasure, yea, good above all good; and he that loseth Jesu he loseth over much and more than if he lost all that world.

It is a great craft for a man to be conversant with Jesu; and to know how to hold Jesu is a great prudence.

Be meek and peaceable and Jesu shall be with thee: be devout and restful and Jesu shall abide with thee; thou mayest soon chase out Jesu and lose his grace if thou wilt decline to outer things; and if thou chase out Jesu and lose him, to whom shalt thou flee? and what friend shalt thou seek? Without a friend thou canst not well live, and save Jesu be thy friend before all other, thou shalt be over sorry and over desolate: wherefore thou dost foolishly if thou trust or art glad in any other.

It is more to be chosen for a man to have all the world contrary to him than to have Jesu offended.

Among all therefore that are dear to thee, let Jesu be solely thy darling and thy special (friend).

Let all men be loved for Jesu and Jesu for himself.

Only Jesu Christ is singly to be loved, who only is found good and true before all other friends; for him and in him let both friends and enemies be dear to thee; and for all them he is to be prayed that they may know him and love him.

Desire never to be singularly praised or loved for that belongeth to God alone that hath none like him.

Nor desire not that any man be occupied in his mind about love of thee nor be not thou occupied about no other love: be pure and free within, without impediment or encumbrance of any creature.

Thou must be bare and bear to God a pure heart if thou wilt taste and see how sweet God is: and verily thereto shalt thou never come unless thou be prevented and nourished with his grace, that all things being voided and left, thou alone be united with him.

For when the grace of God cometh to a man then is he mighty to all things: and when it goeth away then shall he be poor and unmighty and as a man left only to scourgings and beatings and pains.

In these things be not thrown down, nor despair not: but stand simply at the will of God and suffer all things that come to thee praising our Lord Jesu Christ: for after winter cometh summer and after even cometh day and after tempest cometh clearness.

CHAPTER IX

OF LACKING OF ALL MANNER OF SOLACE

It is not grievous for a man to set no price as man's solace when God is nigh; but it is great, and right great, for a man to lack both God's solace and man's and for the honour of God gladly to suffer exile of heart and in nothing to seek himself and trust not to his own merit.

What great thing is it, when grace comes, that thou be glad and devout? for that hour is desirable to all men: he rideth easily and merrily whom the grace of God beareth

And what wonder that he feel no burden, who is borne of the almighty and led of the sovereign leader?

Gladly we take somewhat by way of solace and hard it is for a man to be drawn out of himself.

Saint Laurence overcame the world with his priest: for he despised all things delectable in the world and for the love of God suffered benignly the high priest Sextus whom he most loved to be taken away from him.

The love therefore of the creator overcame the love of man and he chose the well-willing of God before man's solace.

So learn thou to forsake for the love of God some dear friend that is necessary to thee, nor bear it heavily when thou art forsaken of thy friend knowing that at last we must all depart each from other.

It behoveth a man long time and mightily to strive with himself before a man shall be able perfectly to overcome himself and draw all his affection unto God.

When a man standeth upon himself he slideth lightly to man's consolations but the very true lover of Christ and studious follower of virtue slideth not to consolations nor seeketh such sensible sweetness but rather would suffer for Christ mighty trials and hard labours.

Wherefore, when spiritual consolation is given of God receive

it with great thanks and understand it to be the gift of
God and not thy merit.

Be not proud nor rejoice not too much nor presume not vainly:
but be the more meek for the gift and the more ware and
the more anxious in all thy deeds: for that hour shall
pass and temptation shall follow.

And when the consolation is taken away despair not anon but
with meekness and patience abide the heavenly visitation: for God is mighty enough to give thee greater consolation.

This is no new nor strange thing to them that are expert in
the way of God: for ofttimes in great saints and holy
prophets hath been this manner of alternation. Wherefore one, grace being present, said "I said in mine abundance I shall never be moved." And, when grace was
absent, he rehearsed what he felt, saying "Thou hast
turned away and I was troubled." Nevertheless among
these things he despised not but prayed God more
heartily saying, "Lord to thee shall I cry and I shall
pray to my God." And then he reported the fruit of his
prayer, confessing himself to be heard of God, saying
"Our Lord hath heard and hath pity on me and is made
my helper." But wherein? "Thou hast" he saith "turned
my sorrow into joy, and clothed me about with gladness."

If it were done then with great saints, we, feeble and poor,
ought not to despair, if some time we be in fervour and
some time in coldness; for the holy spirit goeth and
cometh after the well pleasing of his will. Wherefore Job
saith "Thou visitest him betimes or in the twilight and
suddenly thou provest him."

Upon what therefore shall I hope or in whom shall I trust
but in the great mercy of God and only in hope of
heavenly grace?

Whether good men be nigh thee or devout brethren or true
friends or holy books or fair treatises or sweet songs and
melodious hymns; all these help but little, savour but
little.

When I am forsaken of grace and left in my poverty then is there no better remedy than patience and denying of myself in the will of God.

I have found no man so religious or devout that feeleth not some time withdrawing of grace or diminution of fervour. There was never saint so highly ravished or illumined but that later or earlier he was tempted: for he is not high in the contemplation of God who is not tried for God in some tribulation: and tribulation going before is wont to be a token of consolation following; for to them that are proved in temptations is promised heavenly comfort.

"He that overcometh" saith our Lord "I shall give him to eat of the tree of life." Heavenly comfort is given that a man should be stronger to sustain adversities; temptation also followeth lest man be proud of the gift; the devil sleepeth never and the flesh is not dead.

Wherefore, cease not to array thee to battle: for both on the right hand and on the left are enemies that never cease.

CHAPTER X

OF THANKS FOR THE GRACE OF GOD

WHY seekest thou rest since thou art born to labour? Put thee to patience more than to consolations and to bear the cross more than to gladness.

What secular man is there that would not gladly have spiritual consolations and gladness if he might have it for ever? for spiritual consolations pass all the delights of the world and all fleshly pleasures.

For all the delights of the world, either they are vain or foul, but spiritual delights are jocund and honest, engendered of gentle virtues and infused into pure minds by God.

But no man may use these divine consolations at his own will; for the time of temptation ceaseth not for long.

False liberty and trust in self are much contrary to heavenly visitation.

God doth well in giving grace of consolation but man doth evil not giving all to God with thanks: and the gifts of God can not flow in on us, for we be ungrateful to the giver and we refund not again all to the original well.

Grace is ever due to him that thinketh worthily and that shall be taken away from the proud man which is wont to be given to meek men.

I wish not that consolation which shall take away from me compunction; nor do I desire that contemplation which shall bring me into elation: for not every high thing is holy, nor every sweet thing good, nor every desire pure, nor every dear thing acceptable to God.

I receive gladly that grace whereby I am found the more meek, the more anxious, and the more ready to forsake myself.

He that is taught with the gift of grace and learned (taught) with the beatings of its withdrawal dare ascribe nothing to himself but rather will acknowledge himself poor and naked.

Give to God that is his and ascribe to thyself that is thine: give God thanks for his grace and to thyself guilt and pain known to be due to thee for thy guilt.

Put thee ever at the lowest and the highest shall be given to thee: for the highest can not stand without the lowest.

The highest saints before God are lowest before themselves; and the more glorious that they be, the more meek they are in themselves.

They that are full of truth and heavenly glory are not desirous of vain glory.

They that are grounded and confirmed in God are not proud;

And they that ascribe all to God whatever good they receive they seek not glory each of the other but they wish the glory that is only of God; and they desire God to be praised in himself and in his saints above all things: and to that evermore they tend.

Be thankful therefore for a little thing and thou shalt be

worthy to take a greater: let also the least thing be to thee as the greatest and the least of price as a special gift.

If the dignity of the giver be considered there shall no gift appear little that is given of the high God: yea if he give pains and beatings it ought to be taken gladly: for all is done for our help, whatever he suffereth to come to us.

He that desireth to keep the grace of God let him be thankful for the grace given and patient when it is taken away: let him pray that it come again and be ware and meek that he lose it not.

CHAPTER XI

OF THE FEWNESS OF THE LOVERS OF THE CROSS OF CHRIST

JESU hath many lovers of the kingdom of heaven but few bearers of the cross; he hath many who desire consolations and few desiring tribulations: he findeth many fellows of the table and few of abstinence.

All desire to joy with him; but few will suffer any pain for him.

Many follow Jesu unto the breaking of the bread, but few unto the drinking of the cup of the passion.

Many worship his miracles but few follow the reproof of the Cross.

Many love Jesu when no adversity happeneth.

Many praise him and bless him while they take any consolations from him; but if Jesu hide himself and forsake them a little, they fall into a complaining or into over great dejection.

But they that love Jesu for Jesu, and not for any consolations, they bless him in every tribulation and anguish of heart as in the highest consolation; and if he would never give them consolation yet would they ever praise him and ever thank him.

O how mighty is the pure love of Jesu when it is mingled with no love of self nor profit of self.

Whether all they that always seek consolations are not to be called mercenaries and hired men?

Whether are they not proved lovers of themselves and not of Christ who think of their own lucre and profit? where is found one that will serve God freely?

Seldom shall there be any man found so spiritual that will be naked from all worldly things. And who shall find a man very poor in spirit and bare from every creature? his price is from the uttermost coasts.[1]

If a man give all his substance, it is as naught; and if he do great penance yet it is but little; and if he apprehend all manner of science yet is he far: and if he have great virtue and right fervent devotion, yet him lacketh much; but one thing is sovereignly necessary to him. What is that? that, all things forsaken, he forsake himself and go wholly out of himself and retain nothing of self-love.

When he hath done all things that he knoweth how to do let him feel himself to have done naught.

Let him not weigh as great all that may be esteemed great; but let him in truth pronounce himself an unprofitable servant, as the truth saith "when ye have done all things that are commanded to you say that we are unprofitable servants." For such a one may say with the prophet that "I am sole and poor" when he beginneth verily to be bare and poor in spirit.

Nevertheless no man is richer, no man is mightier, no man more free than he that can forsake himself and all things and put himself at the lowest.

[1] *i.e.* As a gem that is brought from far.

CHAPTER XII

OF THE KING'S HIGHWAY OF THE CROSS

THIS word "deny thyself and take thy cross and follow me" seemeth a hard word to many men: but much harder it shall be to hear this word "Go from me ye cursed people into the fire everlasting."

They that gladly hear and follow the word of the cross shall not dread the word of everlasting damnation.

This sign of the cross shall be in heaven when our Lord shall come to judgment.

Then all the servants of the cross that have conformed them to Christ in their life shall come nigh unto Christ the judge with great trust.

Why dreadest thou therefore to take the cross whereby men go to the kingdom?

In the cross is health, in the cross is life, in the cross is protection from enemies, in the cross is infusion of heavenly sweetness, in the cross is strength of mind, in the cross is joy of spirit, in the cross is the sum of virtue, in the cross is perfection of holiness: there is no health of soul nor hope of everlasting life, but in the cross. Take thy cross therefore and follow Jesu and thou shalt go into life everlasting.

He that bare his own cross is gone before and died for thee on the cross that thou shouldest bear thy cross and desire to die on the cross: and if thou be fellow in pain thou shalt be fellow in glory.

Lo, in the cross standeth all things and in dying lieth all: and there is none other way to life and to very inward peace but the way of the holy cross and of daily mortifying for if thou be dead with him thou shalt also live with him.

Walk therefore where thou wilt, seek wherever it pleaseth thee, and thou shalt find no higher way above nor surer way beneath than the way of the cross.

Dispose and ordain all things after thy will and thy seeming and thou shalt not find it anything but a duty to suffer somewhat either willingly or against thy will and thou shalt ever find the cross.

Thou shalt either suffer sorrow in thy body or tribulation of spirit in the soul.

Sometimes thou shalt be forsaken of God and sometimes thou shalt be stirred by thy neighbour and, what more is, sometimes thou shalt be grievous to thyself.

And yet it shall not lie in thy power to be eased or delivered with no remedy and with no solace; but, while God will, thou must needs suffer and bear.

God willeth that thou shalt learn to suffer tribulation without comfort, for thou shouldest subdue all things to him and be the meeker for tribulation.

No man so heartily feeleth the passion of Christ as he that suffereth like things.

The cross therefore is ever ready and over all things it abideth for thee: thou canst not flee it, wherever thou run; and wherever thou come, thou bearest thyself with thee, and ever thou shalt find thyself.

Turn thyself above, turn thyself below, turn thyself outward, turn thyself inward; and in all these thou shalt find the cross; and everywhere it is needful for thee to keep patience, if thou wilt have inward peace and deserve a crown everlasting.

If thou bear the cross gladly, it shall bear thee, and lead thee to a desirable end, where an end shall be of suffering— though it be not here.

If thou bear it against thy will thou makest for thyself an heavy burden and grievest thyself more and yet must thou needs sustain it.

If thou put away one cross doubtless thou shalt find another and peradventure a more grievous one.

Thinkest thou to escape what never mortal man might escape?

what saint in this world was without cross and tribulation? Not our Lord Jesu Christ was without sorrow of passion one hour in all his life. The evangelist saith "It behoved Christ to suffer and to rise from death and so to enter into his glory." And how seekest thou another way than the king's highway, the cross way? All Christ's life was a cross and a martyrdom: and thou seekest to thyself rest and joy.

Thou errest, thou goest out of the way if thou seek other thing to thee than tribulation, for all this mortal life is full of miseries and marked all about with crosses; and the higher that a man profiteth in spirit the higher crosses ofttimes he findeth: for the pain of his exile groweth more through love.

Nevertheless this man, thus pained, is not without some manner of comfort: for he feeleth great fruit grow to him through the suffrance of his cross; for while he gladly subdueth him thereto, all burden of tribulation is turned into trust of divine consolation; and the more that the flesh is thrown down by affliction, the more the spirit is strengthened by inward grace.

And ofttimes he is so greatly comforted and strengthened that for desire of tribulation and adversity, for love of conformity to the cross of Christ, he would not be without sorrow and tribulation; for the more acceptable he accounteth himself to God, the more and the greater are the pains that he must suffer for God.

This is not man's might but the grace of Christ that man doeth so great things in his frail flesh, that through fervour of spirit he can take upon him and love that thing which the flesh ever naturally fleeth and abhorreth.

It is not like man to bear the cross, to love the cross, to chastise the body, to bring it to thraldom, to flee honour, gladly to sustain reproofs and wrongs, to despise himself and to will to be despised, to suffer all manner of adversities with harms and to desire no manner of prosperity in this world.

If thou look to thyself, thou canst do no such thing of thyself; but, if thou trust in our Lord, strength shall be given to thee from heaven, and the world and the flesh shall be made subject to thy commandment: nor shalt thou dread thine enemy the devil, if thou be armed with faith and marked with the cross.

Put thee therefore forward as a good and true servant of Christ to bear manly the cross of thy Lord crucified for thee through love. Make thee ready to suffer many contrary things and diverse incommodities in this wretched life: for so he shall be with thee wherever thou be and so thou shalt find him wherever thou be hid.

It must be so: for there is no remedy of scaping from tribulation of evil men and sorrow—except that thou suffer.

Drink the chalice of our Lord lovingly if thou desire to be his friend and to have part with him. Consolations commit thou to God: let him do therewith as it pleaseth him.

Put thou thyself forward to suffer tribulations and account them as greatest consolations; for there are no passions of this time worthy to deserve the glory that is to come, yea, though thou mightest suffer all alone.

When thou comest to this, that tribulation is sweet to thee and is savoury to thee for Christ then deem it well with thee: for thou hast found paradise in earth.

As long as it is grievous to thee to suffer and thou seekest to flee it, so long shall it be evil with thee, and fleeing after thee, tribulation shall follow thee everywhere.

If thou puttest thee forward, as thou oughtest to do, to suffer and to die, it shall soon be better and thou shalt find peace.

Yea, if thou be ravished into the third heaven with Paul, thou art not yet sure to suffer no contrary thing: for Jesu said "I shall shew him how great things he must suffer for my name."

To suffer therefore remaineth to thee if thou wilt love and ever please him.

Would God that thou were worthy to suffer any thing for

the name of Jesu: how great glory should be to thee, how great exultation to all the saints of heaven, how great edification of thy neighbour; for all men commend patience, though few will suffer.

Thou shouldest gladly suffer for Christ since men suffer much more grievous things for the world.

Know for certain that thou must lead a dying life; and the more that a man dieth to himself, the more he beginneth to live to God: there is no man apt (fit) to take heavenly things unless he submit himself to bear adversities for Christ.

There is nothing more acceptable to God, nothing more wholesome to thee in this world than gladly to suffer for Christ: and if it lay in thy choice, thou shouldest rather desire to suffer contrary things for Christ than to be refreshed with many consolations: for thou wouldest be more like unto Christ and be more conformed to all saints.

For our merit and the profiting of our estate standeth not in sweetness and consolations but rather in suffering of grievous things and tribulations: for if there had been any thing more better or more profitable to man than to suffer, Christ would verily have shown it by word and example: but he exhorted all his disciples and all them that desired to follow him openly to bear the cross saying "Who that will come after me, let him deny himself and take his cross and follow me."

All things therefore being read over and searched, be this the final conclusion, that by many tribulations it behoveth us to enter into the kingdom of heaven.

Here end the admonitions drawing inward. And here follow the chapters of the third book that is of inward consolation.

PART THREE

CHAPTER I

I SHALL hear what our Lord Christ speaketh in me. Blissful
is that soul that heareth our Lord speaking in him and
taketh from his mouth the word of consolation. Blessed
be those ears that receive of God's rounding (whisper)
and take no heed of the rounding of this world. Plainly
those ears are blessed that take no heed to the outward
sounding voice but to the truth teaching inwardly.
Blessed be those eyes that are closed to earthly things
and attend to the inward things. Blessed are they that
pierce inward things and study to make themselves ready
by daily exercises more and more to take heavenly secrets. Blissful are they that desire to take heed to God
and cast themselves out from all impediments of the
world.

Take heed hereto, my soul, and close up the doors of thy
sensuality (senses) that thou mayst hear what thy Lord
God speaketh in thee. Thus saith thy well beloved, Thine
help am I, thy peace, and thy life: keep thee with me
and thou shalt find peace. Leave all transitory things
and seek everlasting. What are all temporal things but
deceivers and what avail all creatures if thou be forsaken
of thy creator? All other things therefore set aside, yield
thyself pleasant and true to thy creator that thou mayst
win very felicity.

CHAPTER II

THAT THE WORDS OF GOD ARE TO BE HEARD WITH MEEKNESS

SPEAK Lord for thy servant heareth. I am thy servant: give me understanding that I may know thy testimonies. Bow my heart to the words of thy mouth; let thy speech flow as sweet dew.

The children of Israel said on a time to Moses "Speak thou to us and we shall hear thee: let not our Lord speak lest we die."

Lord, Lord, not so; I pray not so, but rather with Samuel the prophet, meekly and affectionately I beseech thee "Speak thou, Lord, for thy servant heareth."

Let therefore Moses not speak to me, nor none of the prophets: but speak thou rather, Lord God, inspirer and illuminer of prophets; for thou alone without them mayst teach me perfectly: but they without thee shall nothing profit. They may sound words well but they give no spirit. They say passingly fair, but, if thou speak not, they set nothing afire. They take us to the letter, but thou openest the wit (meaning). They bring forth mysteries but thou makest open the understanding of the secrets. They tell out commandments but thou helpest us to perform them. They show the way but thou makest us strong to go. They work all without, but thou teachest and illuminest the hearts. They water from without, but thou givest increase. They cry with words, but to the hearing thou givest understanding. Let not therefore Moses speak to me but thou, my Lord God, everlasting truth: lest I die and be made unfruitful, lest I be only admonished outwardly and not set afire inwardly.

Therefore, lest the word heard and not done be to me my judgment, or the word known and not loved, or the word believed and not kept, speak thou, Lord, for thy servant heareth. Thou hast words of life everlasting; speak to me to some manner of comfort to my soul and to the amendment of my life; and to thee Lord be praise, glory, and everlasting honour.

CHAPTER III

THAT THE WORDS OF GOD ARE TO BE HEARD WITH MEEKNESS

Son, hear my words most sweet and passing the cunning of all the philosophers and all the wise men of this world. My words are spirit and life: they are not to be peised (weighed) with man's wits.

They be not to be turned to vain pleasure but to be heard in silence and to be taken with meekness and great desire.

And I said: Blissful is he whom thou hast learned and hast taught him of thy law that thou may make him a mitigation from evil days that the earth be not desolate.

I, saith our Lord, have taught the prophets from the beginning and until now I cease not to speak to all but many be hard and deaf to my voice, many more gladly hear the world than God: they follow more lightly the appetite of their flesh than the good pleasure of God.

The world promiseth temporal things and little things and is served with great greediness: and I promise most high things and everlasting and mortal men's hearts wax sluggish.

Who serveth and obeyeth me in all things as men serve the world and its lords? The sea said, "Be ashamed, Sidon"; and if thou ask the cause, hear why. For a little prebend men run a long way; but for everlasting life scarce the foot is once lift up from the earth.

A thing of little price is busily sought: other whiles men strive for one penny right shamefully; men dread not to weary themselves night and day for a vain thing, for a little promise. But, alas, for good incommutable, for need inestimable, for sovereign honour, for endless glory men will not suffer the least weariness.

Be ashamed therefore thou sluggish and complaining servant that they are more ready for perdition than thou for life; they joy more at vanity than thou at truth.

And lo, ofttimes they are defrauded of their hope: but my promise deceiveth no man; nor leaveth no man void that trusteth me.

That I have promised, I shall give: that I have said I shall fulfil, so that a man abide true in my love until the end.

I am rewarder of all good men and a mighty prover of all devout men. Write my words in thine heart and treat them diligently for in time of tribulation they shall be full necessary. That that thou knowest not when thou readest, thou shalt truly know in time of visitation.

I am wont in two manners to visit my chosen children that is to say with temptation and consolation.

And every day I read them two lessons: one in blaming their vices, another exhorting them to everlasting virtues.

He that heareth my words and despiseth them hath that shall doom (judge) him in the last day.

CHAPTER IV

A PRAYER TO ASK GRACE OF DEVOTION

MY LORD God all my goods thou art: and who am I that dare speak to thee? I am thy most poor servant, and an abject worm much poorer and more contemptible than I can or dare say. Nevertheless have mind that I am naught worth. Thou alone art good, righteous and holy: thou canst do all things: thou givest all things, thou fillest all things leaving void the sinner. Bring to mind thy pity and fulfil mine heart with thy grace for thou wilt not that thy work should be void. How may I suffer myself in this wretched life, unless thou comfort me with thy mercy and thy grace? Lord, turn not away thy face from me: prolong not thy visitation; withdraw not thy consolation, lest my soul be as earth without water to thee. Lord teach me to do thy will; teach me to live worthily and meekly for thee; for thou art my wisdom, thou knowest me truly and knewest me or ever the world were made and or ever I were born in the world.

CHAPTER V

THAT A MAN OUGHT TO LIVE BEFORE GOD IN TRUTH AND IN MEEKNESS

Son, go before me in truth, and in simplicity of heart seek me ever. He that goeth before me in truth shall be made sure from evil availings and truth shall deliver him from deceivers and from detractions of wicked men. If truth deliver thee thou shalt be verily free and thou shalt not reck of men's vain words.

Lord it is true that thou sayest: and, as thou sayest, so I beseech thee may it be with me. Let thy truth teach me, thy truth keep me and bring me to an healthful end.

Let her deliver me from all evil affection and inordinate loving and I shall go with thee in great liberty of heart.

Truth saith, I shall teach thee those things that are right and pleasant to me.

Think on thy sins with great displeasure and mourning and never account thyself anything for any good works. Verily a sinner thou art and encumbered and wrapped in many passions; of thyself ever thou drawest to naught; soon thou slidest, soon thou art overcome, soon thou art dissolved.

Thou hast nothing whereof thou mayst rejoice thee but many things thou hast whereof thou oughtest to set little by thyself; for thou are more sick than thou canst conceive.

Wherefore let nothing seem great to thee of all things that

thou doest, nothing precious, nothing wonderful; let nothing appear to thee worthy any reputation, for verily there is none other thing here laudable or desirable but that which is everlasting.

And above all things let everlasting truth please thee; let ever thy great vileness and unworthiness displease thee.

Dread nothing so much, blame nor flee nothing so much, as thy vices and thy sins the which ought to displease thee more than any worldly harm.

Some go not clearly before me but they be led with all manner of curiosity and arrogance, willing to know my secrets and to understand the high things of God, taking no heed of themselves and of their souls' health.

These folk, being displeased, ofttimes fall into great temptations for their pride and their curiosity.

Dread the judgments of God, be aghast of the wrath of him that is almighty.

Discuss not the works of the highest God: but search thy wickedness, in how many things thou hast trespassed and how many good deeds thou hast negligently left.

Some bear their devotion alone in their looks, some in images, some in outward signs and figures: some have me in mouth but little is there in the heart.

There be other that being illumined in the understanding and purged in affection, desire laboriously things everlasting, grieving to hear of earthly things: they serve the necessities of nature with great sorrow; and these feel what the spirit of truth speaketh in them for he teacheth them to love heavenly things, to set no price by the world and day and night to desire heaven.

CHAPTER VI

OF THE WONDERFUL EFFECT OF THE LOVE OF GOD

I BLESS thee, heavenly father, the father of my Lord Jesu
Christ for thou vouchest safe to have mind on me most
poor.

O father of mercies and God of all consolation I thank thee
that refreshest me with thy consolations, me that am
unworthy all manner of comfort.

I bless thee ever and glorify thee with thine only begotten
Son and the Holy Ghost the comforter into worlds of
worlds (for ever and ever).

Ah, my Lord God, my holy lover, when thou shalt come into
my heart all my inwards shall joy. Thou art my glory
and the exultation of mine heart; thou art mine hope
and my refuge in the day of my tribulation. But for that
I am feeble in love and imperfect in virtue, therefore I
have need to be comforted of thee.

Wherefore visit me Lord ofttimes and inform me with holy
discipline. Deliver me from mine evil passions, heal mine
heart from all inordinate affections; that I, inwardly
healed and well purged, may be apt to love, mighty to
suffer, stable to persevere.

Love is a great thing, a great good in every wise; it alone
maketh light every heavy thing and beareth evenly every
uneven thing: for it beareth burden without burden and
every bitter thing it maketh sweet and savoury.

The noble love of Jesu stirreth to do great things and ever
enticeth to desire more perfect things. Love will be above,
not retained with any low things. Love will be free and
alienate from all worldly affection lest his inward beholding be let (hindered) lest he be wrapped in and
encumbered by any temporal commodity or fall under
(disappear) by any incommodity.

There is nothing sweeter than love, nothing stronger, nothing higher, nothing broader, nothing more jocund, nothing fuller, nothing better in heaven nor in earth; for love is born of God nor it may not rest but in God above all creatures.

The lover flieth, runneth and is glad; he is free and is not holden. Love giveth all things for all things and it hath all things in all things; for it resteth above all things in one sovereign good of whom all good floweth and proceedeth. It looketh not to the gifts but turneth itself to the giver above all goods. Love ofttimes knows no measure but is fervent above all measure.

Love feeleth no burden, it accounteth no labour, it desireth more than it may attain, it complaineth never of impossibility, for it deemeth itself mighty to all things, and all things be lawful to it. It is valiant therefore to all things, it fulfilleth many things and bringeth them to effect where he that loveth not faileth and lieth still.

Love waketh; and, sleeping, it sleepeth not; love wearied is not weary, and love constrained is not constrained; it, afeard, is not troubled; but as a quick flame and a burning brand, he bursteth upwards and passeth surely (safe). He that loveth knoweth what this voice crieth. A great cry in the ears of God is that burning affection of soul that saith "My God, my love, thou art all mine and I thine."

Dilate me in love that I may learn to taste with the inward mouth of mine heart how sweet it is to love and in love to melt and to swim. Be I held with love going above myself for excellent fervour and astonishment. May I sing a song of love, may I follow thee my love into the height and let my soul fail in thy praise, jubilee-ing for love.

Let me love thee more than myself and myself only for thee and all in thee that verily love thee as the law of love commandeth shining out of thee.

Love is swift, pure, holy, jocund, merry, strong, patient, true, prudent, long-abiding, manly and never seeking himself. Where any man seeketh himself, there anon he falleth from love.

Love is circumspect, meek and right, not soft, not light, not intending to vain things, sober, chaste, stable, restful, kept in all wits (senses) devout to God and mankind.

Love is subject and obedient to prelates, vile and despicable to himself, trusting ever in God, yea when God savoureth him not, for without sorrow men live not in love.

He that is not ready to suffer all things and to stand at the will of his beloved, is not worthy to be called a lover. It behoveth the lover gladly to clip (grasp) to himself all manner hard things and bitter things for his beloved and not to bow (turn) from him for any contrary things that happen to fall.

CHAPTER VII

OF PROVING OF TRUE LOVE

Son, yet art thou not a mighty and a prudent lover.

Why, Lord?

For as much as for a little contrariousness thou failest in things begun, and over-greedily seekest consolation. A strong lover standeth in temptations nor will he believe the wily persuasions of the enemy. As I please him in prosperity, so I displease him not in adversity.

A prudent lover considereth not so much the gift of the lover as the love of the giver; he peiseth (weigheth) more the affection than the value and setteth all the gifts far beneath the beloved. The noble lover resteth not in the gift but in me above all gifts.

It is not therefore all lost, though some times thou feelest not so well of me and of my saints as thou wouldest. That good and sweet affection, that thou perceivest sometimes, is an effect of grace and a manner of foretaste of the heavenly country upon which it is not good to lean over-much, for it goeth and cometh.

For a man to fight against the evil moving of the soul and to despise the suggestions of the devil is a token of virtue and of great merit. Therefore let no strange fantasies brought in by any matter trouble thee; keep a mighty purpose and a right intention to God.

It is no illusion that some times thou art suddenly ravished in an excess and turnest anon again to the wonted japes (jests) of thine heart: for thou sufferest these unwillingly rather than doest them and as long as they displease thee, and thou wrestlest against them it is merit and no perdition.

Know well that the enemy laboureth in all wise to stay thy desire in good and to make thee void of all good exercise; from worshipping of saints, from minding of thy holy passion, from profitable thinking of thy saints, from keeping of thine heart, and from sad (settled) purpose of profiting in virtue; he putteth in many evil thoughts that he may cause in thee weariness and horror and may revoke thee from prayer and holy reading.

Meek confession displeaseth him, and, if he may, he will make thee to cease from holy communion. Believe him not nor take no hold of him though he ofttimes tend to thee gins of deceit. Impute it to himself when he soweth evil things and unclean. Say to him "Be ashamed, thou unclean spirit, and go away, wretch; thou art full unclean, that bringest such things to mine ears. Go hence, thou wicked deceiver, thou shalt have no part in me, but Jesu shall be with me as a mighty fighter and thou shalt stand confused. I had liever die and suffer all pain than con-sent to thee. Hold thy peace and be still; I will no more hear thee though thou labour to molest me never so oft. God is mine illumination and mine help, whom shall I dread? If battles be against me mine heart shall not be afeard. Our Lord is mine helper and my redemptor."

Fight as a good knight, and though sometime thou fall through frailty of flesh, resume strength more mighty than before, trusting on my more large grace and be well ware of vain complacency and pride; for thereby many men be led into error and some time they slide into a blindness incurable. Let it be to thee for a perpetual wariness and meekness—the falling of proud men presuming on themselves.

CHAPTER VIII

OF GRACE TO BE HID UNDER THE WORD OF MEEKNESS

Son, it is more profitable and more sure to thee to hide the grace of devotion and not to lift thyself on high, not to speak much thereof, nor much to peise (weigh) it, but rather to despise thyself and dread lest it be given to thee unworthy.

It is not good to cleave over-toughly to this affection that may so soon be turned into the contrary. Think, when in grace, how wretched and how needy thou wert wont to be, without grace.

Nor is there only spiritual profiting when thou feelest grace of consolation but also when thou bearest meekly and patiently the withdrawing thereof when it is denied; provided thou then be not slow from study of prayer nor let not slide away utterly other works that thou art wont to do, but as thou mayest after thine understanding gladly do that in thee is and for no dryness nor anxiety of mind be not negligent of thyself. For there be many to whom when it cometh not as they would anon they be impatient or slow.

Man's way is not ever in his own power but to God it belongs to give and to comfort when he will and as much as he will and to whom he will, as it pleaseth him—and no more.

Some indiscreetly for grace of devotion have destroyed themselves. For they do more than they can, peising (weighing) not the measure of their littleness but following more the affection of the heart than the judgment of reason. And for they presumed greater things than God was pleased with, therefore they soon lost grace. They were made needy and left as vile that had set their nest in heaven, that they, made so meek and poor, might learn not to fly on their own wings but to hope and trust under my feathers.

They that be yet new and inexpert in the way of God, unless they be governed by the counsel of discreet men, may soon be deceived and hurt. And if they will follow their own feeling rather than believe others that are experienced, the end will be perilous, if they will not be withdrawn from their own conceit. They that seem wise to themselves suffer but seldom to be governed by others.

Better is it to savour but a little with meekness and little understanding than to have great treasures of cunning with vain complacency.

Better is it for thee to have little than much whereof thou mayst be proud. He doth not discreetly that giveth himself all to gladness, forgetting his rather (earlier) poverty and the chaste dread of God, which dreadeth to lose grace that is offered. Nor doth he savour virtuously enough that in time of adversity or any heaviness holdeth himself over desperately and less trustingly thinketh or feeleth of me than it behoveth. For he that in time of peace will be over sure ofttimes in time of battle is found deject and fearful.

If thou couldst at all times abide meek and little in thyself and measure and rule thy spirit, then wouldest thou not fall so soon into peril and into offence.

It is good that, when the fervour of spirit is conceived, thou think what is to come, if the light goeth away; the which when it happeneth to fall (happen) think again that the light may come again the which I have withdrawn for a time to thy warnes (warning) and my glory. Such a proving is ofttimes more profitable than if thou haddest pleasant things at thine own will. For merits be not to be estimated if a man hath many visions and consolations or else be wise in the scriptures or be set in high degree: but if he be grounded in very meekness and fulfilled with divine charity, if he seek in all things purely and wholly the worship of God, if he account himself as naught and despise himself in truth and joy more to be despised and made low of others than to be worshipped, *there* is merit and matter of hope.

CHAPTER IX

OF VILE ESTIMATION OF ONESELF IN THE SIGHT OF GOD

I SHALL speak to my Lord though I be dust and ashes.

If I account myself more, lo thou standest against me and my wickedness beareth witness against me, I may not say nay.

But if I vilify myself and bring me to naught and fail from all manner of proper reputation (thought of myself) and make me dust as I am, thy grace shall be merciful to me and thy light nigh to my heart, and all manner of estimation, be it never so little, shall be drowned in the valley of my naughtiness and shall perish for ever.

There thou showest me myself what I am, what I was, and from whence I came: for I am naught and know not myself. If I be left to myself lo I am naught and all infirmity. If thou behold me suddenly anon I am made strong and am fulfilled with a new joy; and a wonderful thing is it that I am so suddenly lift up and so benignly clipped (embraced) of thee that with mine own weight am I ever borne down low. This thy love doth freely, going before me and helping me in so many needs and keeping me from grievous perils and delivering me, as I may truly say, from evils out of number.

In mis-loving I lost both thee and me and in seeking thee alone and in purely loving thee found both thee and me; and through love I brought myself more deeply to naught. For thou, most sweet, dost with me above all manner of merit and above that that I dare hope or pray.

Blessed be thou, my God, for though I be unworthy of all goods, yet thy noblesse and infinite goodness ceaseth not to do well, yea even to the unkind and the far-turned-away from thee.

Convert us Lord to thee that we may be meek, kind and devout, for thou art our help, our virtue, and our strength.

CHAPTER X

THAT ALL THINGS ARE TO BE REFERRED TO GOD AS TO THE LAST END

SON, I ought to be thy last and thy sovereign end if thou desire verily to be blissful; and through this intention shall thine affection be purged that is ofttimes evil bowed down to herself and to creatures. For if thou seek thyself in anything anon thou failest in thyself and waxest dry. Wherefore to me refer all things principally for I it am that have given all things.

Consider all things as welling from the highest and most sovereign good; and therefore they are to be reduced to me as to their original beginning. Of me little and great, poor and rich, draw quick water as from the well of life: and they that serve me willingly and gladly shall receive grace for (after) grace, but he that hath glory without me or is delighted in any private good shall never be stablished in very joy nor be delighted in heart but shall be let (hindered) in many wises (ways) and anguished.

Therefore thou oughtest to ascribe to thyself no manner of good nor attribute not virtue to any man but all to God without whom man hath naught. I gave all and I will have all again and with strictness I require thanks. This is truth whereby is chased away the vanity of glory.

And if heavenly grace and very charity enter in, there shall be no envy nor contraction of heart: private love shall not occupy it, for divine charity overcometh all things and dilateth all the might of the soul.

If thou savour aright thou shalt joy alone in me for there is no man good but God alone, that is to be praised above all things and to be blessed in all things.

CHAPTER XI

THAT, THE WORLD DESPISED, IT IS MERRY AND SWEET FOR TO SERVE GOD

Now Lord I shall speak again and keep no silence. I shall say in the ears of my God, my Lord, my King that is on high,

O Lord how great is the multitude of thy sweetness to them that dread thee. But what art thou to thy lovers? what to them that serve thee with all their hearts? Verily the sweetness of thy contemplation that thou grantest to thy lovers is unspeakable. Herein thou showest most the sweetness of thy charity, that, when I was not, thou madest me and when I erred from thee thou leddest me again that I should serve thee and thou commandest me to love thee.

O thou well of everlasting love, what shall I say of thee? How may I forget thee that vouchest safe to have mind on me? Yea after that I failed and perished thou hast been merciful with thy servant above all hope and hast showed grace and friendship above all merit.

What yield I thee again for this grace? It is not given to all that, all things forsaken, they renounce the world and take a religious life. Is that a great thing that I serve thee since every creature is bound to serve thee? It ought not to seem to me a great thing to serve thee; but rather

this appeareth to me great and wonderful, that thou
vouchsafe to receive as thy servant me so poor and so
unworthy and to one (unite) me to thy well beloved
servants.

Lo all things that I have and with the which I serve thee
are thine; nevertheless, in contrariwise thou servest me
rather than I thee. Lo, heaven and earth, that thou hast
made unto man's service are ready and every day do
that thou commandest them; and that is little; but,
over that, thou hast ordained also angels to man's min-
istry; but it passeth all—that thou thyself vouchest safe
to serve man and madest promise to give thyself to him.

What shall I give thee for all these thousand of goods? Would
God I might serve thee all the days of my life. Would
God at least I might suffice to do thee worthy service for
a day. Verily thou art worthy all manner of service, all
worship and everlasting praise. Verily thou art my Lord
and I thy poor servant, that am bound with all my might
to serve thee and never be weary of thy praise.

Thus I will and thus I desire and what lacketh me vouch
thou safe to fulfil. It is a great worship (honour) and a
great glory to serve thee and to set all things at no price
with (compared with) thee: for they that willingly subdue themselves to thy service shall have grace. And they
that for thy most holy love put away fleshly delectation
shall find the consolation of the Holy Ghost. They shall
get liberty of mind that enter into the straight life and
take no heed of no worldly care.

O the acceptable and the jocund service of God whereby a
man is verily made free and holy. O the holy state of religious servage, that maketh man even with angels,
pleasant to God, fearful to fiends and commendable to
all Christian men. O the service to be embraced and even
to be desired, whereby the highest and sovereign good
is deserved (won) and joy gotten that shall dwell without end.

CHAPTER XII

THAT THE DESIRES OF THE HEART MUST BE EXAMINED AND MODERED (MODERATED)

Son, yet thou must learn much thing the which thou hast not not learned as yet.

Lord, what are those?

That thou put thy desire wholly after my well-willing and that thou be not a lover of thyself but a desirous follower of my will. Desires ofttimes set thee on fire and hugely stir thee; but consider whether thou be moved more for my worship or for thine own profit. If I be at the root thou wilt be well content whatever I ordain; and if there be anything of thine own seeking that is hid privily, that it is that letteth (hindereth) and grieveth.

Be ware therefore that thou lean not too much upon any desire before conceived, me not counselled; lest it repent thee afterwards and that displease which first pleased and which thou heldest for the better. For not every affection that seemeth good is to be followed anon nor every contrary affection is to be fled at first.

It is expedient sometimes to use the bridle, yea in good studies and desires, lest by importunity thou fall into distraction of mind, lest thou engender slander in others through indiscipline or else lest thou be suddenly troubled and fall by withstanding of others. And thy flesh ought so long to be chastised and constrained to be subject in servage, till it learn to be ready for all things and to be content with few, and to delight in simple things and not grudge (grumble) against such things as are not convenient thereto.

CHAPTER XIII

OF THE LEARNING OF PATIENCE AND FIGHTING AGAINST CONCUPISCENCE

LORD, as I see, patience is right needful to me for many contrary things fall in this world. For, however I ordain for my peace, my life may not be without battle and sword.

So it is, son; but I will not that thou seek peace and lack temptations, and feel no contrariousness; but then deem to have found peace when thou art haunted in diverse temptations and proved in many contrary things. If thou say that thou canst not suffer many things how wilt thou then suffer the fire of purgatory?

Of two evils the less is ever to be chosen: wherefore that thou mayst escape torments that are to come study to suffer evenly for God present evils.

What—trowest thou that men of this world suffer naught or little? Nay thou shalt not find that, though thou seek most delicate men. But they have, thou sayest, many delectations and therefore they peise (weigh) little their tribulations. Be it so that they have what they will; but how long hopest thou it shall endure?

Lo they that are abundant in this world shall fail as the smoke and there shall be no more remembrance of the joys passed. And yet while they live they rest not in them without bitterness, weariness and dread; for ofttimes of the same thing whereof they conceive delectation they receive pain and sorrow. It falleth to them righteously that since they inordinately seek delectations and follow them they should not taste them fully without confusion. O how short, how inordinate, how false, how foul they all be.

Nevertheless for drunkenness and blindness they understand not but as dumb beasts run into death of soul for a little delectation of corruptible life. Wherefore, thou son, go not after thy concupiscence but turn away from thine own will. Delight thee in God and he shall give thee the petitions of thine heart.

Lo if thou wilt verily be delighted and more abundantly be comforted of me, lo, in contempt of all worldly and in cutting away of all lower delights shall be thy blessing and plenteous consolation shall be yielded to thee. And the more that thou withdrawest thyself from consolation of all creatures the sweeter and the mightier comforts thou shalt find in me. But first thou shalt not come to these without sorrow and labour of striving.

The old used custom (habit) will withstand thee but it shall be overcome by a better custom. The flesh will grudge (grumble); but it shall be refrained (bridled) with the fervour of spirit. The old serpent will stir thee and bring thee to bitterness; but with prayer he shall be driven away and with profitable labour his coming in shall be stopped.

CHAPTER XIV

OF OBEDIENCE OF A MEEK SUBJECT BY ENSAMPLE OF OUR LORD JESU

Son, he that laboureth to withdraw himself from obedience he withdraweth himself from grace; and he that seeketh to have private things loseth the common things.

He that freely and gladly subdueth not himself to his sovereign, it is a token that his flesh obeyeth him not perfectly yet but ofttimes kicketh against and grutcheth (grumbleth).

Learn therefore to obey thy sovereign swiftly if thou will that thy flesh shall obey thee; for the outer enemy is sooner overcome, if the inner be destroyed. There is not a more grievous nor a worse enemy of the soul than thou thyself, when not well according to the spirit.

It behoveth thee in all wise to take upon thee very despising of thyself if thou wilt prevail against flesh and blood. But for as much as thou lovest thyself inordinately therefore thou dreadest to resign thyself fully to the will of others. But what great thing is it if thou that art but ashes and naught subdue thyself to man for God.

Since I, almighty and highest, that made all things of naught, meekly made me subject to man for thee and was made meekest of all and lowest, thou shouldst overcome thy pride with my meekness.

Learn to obey, thou dust; learn to make thyself meek, thou earth and clay, and to bow thyself under the feet of all; learn to break thine own will and to put thee under subjection of all. Be wroth against thyself and suffer no volowing (swelling) pride to live in thee, but show thee so subject and so little that all men may go over thee and tread upon thee as upon mire of the street.

What hast thou, vain man, to complain of? Thou foul sinner. what hast thou to answer thy reprovers, thou that so ofttimes hast offended thy God and so ofttimes deserved hell? But mine eyes have spared thee for thy soul was precious in my sight; that thou shouldst know my love and be ever kind to (grateful for) my benefits and that thou shouldst give thyself continually to very subjection by meekness and bear patiently thine own despising.

CHAPTER XV

OF CONSIDERING THE PRIVY JUDGMENTS OF GOD AGAINST PRIDE

LORD, thou soundest thy dooms (judgments) upon me and shakest all my bones for dread and trembling and my soul is greatly afraid. I stand astonished and consider that heaven is not clean in thy sight. If thou foundest shrewdness (wickedness) in angels and sparedst them not what shall fall of me?

Stars fell from heaven, and I, dust, what presume I? They whose works seemed laudable fell to lowest things and they that ate bread of angels, I saw them delight in swines' draff (food).

Therefore Lord there is no surety if thou withdraw thine hand. There availeth no wisdom if thou leave thy governance. There helpeth no strength, if thou cease to keep. There is no chastity sure if thou defend it not. There availeth no keeping if thy holy watching be not nigh. If we be forsaken we be drowned and perish; if we be visited we are reared up and live. We be unstable but by thee be confirmed. We wax luke (warm) but by thee we be set afire.

O how meekly and abjectly it filleth me to feel of myself and how naught to set by is any good that I seem to have.

O how deeply I ought to submit myself under thy deep ground-less judgments, Lord, where I find myself nothing else but naught—and naught. O weight unmeasurable, O sea intransnatable (through which I cannot swim) when I find nothing of myself but all naught. Where is the lurk-ing hidels (secret boast) of glory, where is the trust con-ceived of virtue? All vain glory is swallowed up in the deepness of thy judgments upon me.

What is every flesh in thy beholding? Shall clay rejoice itself against him that maketh it? How may he be reared up (uplifted) in vain speech whose heart is subject to God in truth? all the world shall not rear up into pride him whom truth hath made subject to himself: nor shall he be moved by the mouths of all his praisers that stead-fasteth all his hope in God.

For they that speak in magnifying themselves, lo, are naught, and they shall fail with the sound of their words; but the truth of our Lord abideth for ever.

CHAPTER XVI

HOW A MAN SHALL STAND IN EVERYTHING
DESIRABLE

SON, say thou at all times, Lord if it please thee, be this thus. Lord if this be to thy worship (honour) be this done in thy name. Lord, if thou see it be expedient and prove it profitable to me, grant me to use it to thy worship: but if thou know that it be noyous (harmful) to me or not available to the health of my soul take such a desire from me: for not every desire cometh of the Holy Ghost, yea, though it seem to man right and good.

It is hard to deem truly whether a good spirit or an evil stir thee to desire this or that, or whether thou be moved of thine own spirit. Many in the end be deceived, but in the beginning seemed brought in (endued) with a good spirit. Wherefore with dread of God and meekness of heart is to be desired and asked whatever desirable thing that cometh to mind principally; for with proper resignation all things are to be committed to me saying, Lord thou knowest how it is best: be it thus or thus as thou wilt and when thou wilt; give what thou wilt, how much thou wilt and when thou wilt. Do with me as thou wilt and as it most pleaseth thee and as it is most to thy honour. Put me where thou wilt and do with me freely in all things. I am in thine hands: turn me and again turn me round about. Lo I am thy servant ready to all things: for I desire not to live to myself, but to thee, and that, would God, perfectly and worthily.

CHAPTER XVII

A PRAYER TO DO THE WILL OF GOD

Most benign Jesu, grant me thy grace, that it may be with
me and labour with me and abide with me to the end.
Grant me ever to do thy will and to desire that is most acceptable to thee and most dearly pleaseth thee. Thy will
be my will and may my will ever follow thy will and accord (agree) to it in all wise. Be there to me one willing
and one not willing with thee; and let me not will nor not
will but what thou wilt or wilt not. Grant me to die from
all things that are in this world, and for thee to love to
be despised and not known in this world. Grant me above
all things desired to rest in thee and to poise my soul
in thee. Thou art very peace of heart, thou art only rest:
without thee all things are hard and out of quiet. In this
peace that is in the one sovereign everlasting good may
I sleep and rest. Amen.

CHAPTER XVIII

THAT TRUE SOLACE IS TO BE SOUGHT IN
GOD ALONE

Whatever I may think or desire to my solace I abide it not
here but hereafter; so that if I alone had all the solaces
of the world and might use all the delights it is certain
that they may not endure.
Wherefore my soul thou mayest not fully be comforted nor
perfectly be refreshed but in God the consolation of
poor, and the undertaker (supporter) of meek, men.
Abide a little while, my soul; abide God's promise and
thou shalt have abundance of all goods in heaven.
If thou covet then present things over inordinately thou shalt

lose the everlasting heavenly things. Let temporal things be in use and everlasting things in desire. Thou mayest not be filled with no temporal good for thou wert not made to enjoy those.

Yea though thou hadst all goods that are made thou mayst not be blissful; but in God that made all things shall be thy bliss and thy felicity, not such as is seen and praised of foolish lovers of this world but such as good true Christian men abide and spiritual men foretaste whose conversation is in heaven.

Vain it is and short, all men's solace: but that is blissful solace and true that is perceived within from truth—the devout man beareth ever with him his comforter Jesu and saith to him, Be nigh to me Lord in every place and every time. Be this my consolation gladly to be willing to lack all man's solace. And if thy consolation fail thy will and just probation be to me as a sovereign solace; for thou shalt not perpetually be wroth nor thou shalt not threaten everlastingly.

CHAPTER XIX

THAT ALL BUSINESS IS TO BE SET IN GOD

My son, suffer me to do with thee what I will; I know what is most expedient to thee. Thou thinkest as a man, thou feelest in many things as man's affection persuadeth thee.

Lord, it is true that thou sayest. Thy business (care) is more for me than any care that I can bear (take) for myself. He standeth overcasually and like to fall that casteth not all his business into thee. So that my will be right and abide steadfast in thee do of me what pleaseth thee for it may not be but good whatever thou do of me.

If thou wilt that I be in darkness, blessed mayst thou be; and if thou wilt that I be in light, yet blessed mayst thou be. If thou vouch safe to comfort me, blessed mayst

thou be; and if thou wilt that I be troubled, be thou ever
alike blessed.

Son, so thou must stand, if thou desirest to go with me. Thou
oughtest to be as ready to suffer as to joy. As gladly thou
oughtest to be needy and poor as full and rich.

Lord I shall gladly suffer for thee whatever thou wilt shall
come upon me. I will indifferently receive of thy hand
good and evil, sweet and sour, glad and sorrowful, and for
all things that fall to me give thee thanks. Keep me from
all manner of sin and I shall not dread death nor hell.
While thou throw me not away for ever nor put me not out
of the book of life, it shall not annoy me, whatever tribulation come to me.

CHAPTER XX

THAT TEMPORAL MISERIES ARE TO BE SUFFERED BY THE ENSAMPLE OF CHRIST

Son, I came down from heaven for thy health: I took upon
me thy miseries, not of need, but for charity for thou
shouldst learn by patience to suffer temporal miseries not
grudgingly (grumbling). For from the hour of my birth
unto the day of my going out of this world on the cross
there lacked me never suffering of sorrows.

I had great lack of temporal goods. I heard many complaints
made of me, shames and reproofs I sustained benignly,
for benefits I received unkindness, for miracles blasphemies, for teachings reprehensions and blame.

Lord as thou wert patient in thy life, therein fulfilling the
commandment of thy father, it is worthy that I, most
wretched sinner, after thy will should sustain myself
patiently and that as long as thou wilt that I bear the
burden of this corruptible life.

For if this life be onerous and heavy yet by thy grace it is
full meritorious, and by thine ensample and the steps

of thy deeds, it is to the feeble and the sick the more tolerable and the more clear; and much more consolatory than it was sometime in the old Law, when the gate of heaven was yet closed and also the way more dark; for as much as so few at that time took any care to seek the realm of heaven. Neither good men that paid their debt by holy death might then enter into the realm of heaven (*i.e.* before Christ died).[1]

O how great thanks am I bound to yield to thee that hast vouch safed to show to me and to all Christian men the right way and the good way to thine everlasting realm.

Thy life is our way and by thine holy patience we go to thee that art our crown. If thou hadst not gone before and taught us the way who would have taken any care to have followed? Alas how many would have abode all afar and behind if they had not beheld thy clear ensample? Lo yet we wax luke(warm) hearing of so many signs and doctrines. What would fall (happen) if we had not so great a light to follow thee?

CHAPTER XXI

OF SUFFERING OF WRONGS AND WHO IS PROVED VERY PATIENT

WHAT is it that thou speakest, son? Cease thy complaining, considering my passion and the passion of other saints: for thou hast not yet withstood unto shedding of thy blood. Little it is that thou sufferest in comparison of them that suffered so great things, so mightily tempted, so grievously troubled, so manifoldly proved and tried.

It behoveth thee therefore to bring to mind other grievous pains that thou mayst the more mightily and more easily

---

[1] This is only one of the many passages in which the translator has missed the meaning of the Latin.

bear thy small pains. And if they seem not little to thee be ware lest thine impatience cause that. Nevertheless whether they be small, whether they be great, study to suffer all patiently.

The better that thou disposest thyself to suffer, the more wisely thou dost, and the more thou deservest: and the more easily thou shalt bear it, thy heart and thy use (custom) made ready thereto not sluggishly. And say not "I may not suffer this of such a man" nor "I ought not to suffer such things for he did me great harm and put things upon me that I never thought, but of another I will gladly suffer whatever I shall suffer."

Such a thought is full foolish which considereth not the virtue of patience nor of whom she is to be crowned, but taketh more heed of the persons and of the offences done to himself.

He is not very patient that will only suffer as much as he will: for the very patient taketh no heed whether he suffer of his prelate or of his peer or of his lover (friend); whether of a good man and an holy or whether he be tried by an overthwart (cross-grained) man and an unworthy; but, indifferently, whatever adversity and how oft it happeneth from any creature all that he taketh acceptably of the hand of God and accounteth that as a great gain: for nothing, be it never so little, so it be suffered for God, shall pass without merit. Wherefore be thou sped and ready for fighting if thou wilt have the victory. Without victory mayst thou not come to the crown of patience.

If thou wilt not suffer thou refusest to be crowned and if thou desire to be crowned fight manly, suffer patiently. Without labour men come not to rest nor without fighting men come not to victory.

Lord make possible by thy grace that which seemeth impossible by nature. Thou knowest, Lord, that I can suffer little and that I am soon thrown down with little adversity. Make Lord every trial of tribulation to me amiable and for thy name desirable: for to suffer and to be vexed for thee is full wholesome to my soul.

CHAPTER XXII

OF KNOWLEDGE OF OUR INFIRMITY AND OF MISERIES OF THIS LIFE

I SHALL acknowledge against myself my unrighteousness. I shall acknowledge to thee mine infirmity. Ofttimes a little thing throweth me down and maketh me sorry. I purpose to do mightily; but when a little temptation cometh, I am in great anguish. Otherwhiles, from things of little value riseth grievous temptation and while I ween myself somewhat sure, for I feel nothing (*i.e.* hurting me), I find myself ofttimes overcome through a light blast.

See therefore, Lord, my dejection and my frailty known to thee on every side. Have mercy on me (and snatch) me from the clay that I stick not therein nor abide dejected on every side. That it is which ofttimes rebuketh me before thee and confoundeth me that I am so sliding and so weak to withstand passions and though I fully not consent yet their vexation is grievous and heavy to me and it wearieth me so to live daily in strife.

And thereby is mine infirmity known to me that abominable fantasies come much lighter than they go away. Would God, thou most strong God of Israel, lover of true souls, that thou wouldst behold the labour and the sorrow of thy servant, and be assistant to him, to whatever things he goeth.

Strength me with heavenly might, lest the old man, the wretched flesh not yet fully subject to the spirit, have the better and the lordship, against which it behoveth to fight all the while men live in this life most wretched.

Alas, what a life is this where never lack tribulations and miseries where all things are full of gins and of enemies. For, one temptation or tribulation going away, another cometh; yea, sometime yet during the first conflict, other many come upon me unawares.

And how may a life be loved, having so many bitternesses, subject to so many miseries and mischances? how also is it called a life that engendereth so many deaths and pestilences and yet is loved and sought of many to have their delight therein.

The world is ofttimes reproved that it is false and vain and yet it is not lightly forsaken, for the lusts of the flesh have too great domination.

But some things draw men to love them, others to despise them. To love these draw, desire of the flesh, desire of eyes, and pride of life: but pains and miseries following bring forth hate of the world and weariness. But, alas, false delight overcometh the mind given to the world, and so she accounteth it a delight to be under the briars (*i.e.* pleasure) for the mind hath neither seen nor tasted the sweetness of God, nor the inward mirth of the soul.

But they that despise perfectly the world and study to live under holy discipline the sweetness of God that is promised to true lovers is not unknown to them and they see clearly how grievously the world erreth and how diversely it deceiveth.

CHAPTER XXIII

THAT MAN OUGHT TO REST IN GOD ABOVE ALL GIFTS

Above all goods and in all, my soul, thou shalt rest in our Lord ever for he is (the) everlasting rest of saints.

Grant me most loving and most sweet Jesu above every creature, above all health and all beauty, above all glory and worship, above all might and dignity, above all cunning and subtlety, above all riches and craft, above all gladness and exaltation, above all fame and praise, above all hope and promise, above all merit and desire, above all gifts that thou mayst give or pour on me, above all joy or jubilation that mind may take or feel; further more above angels and archangels, above all the knighthood of heaven, above all things visible and invisible, and above all things that thou, my God, art not; for thou my God, art best above all;

Thou alone art highest, thou alone most mighty, thou alone most sufficient and most full, thou alone most sweet and most solacious, thou alone most fair and most lovely, thou alone most noble and most glorious above all things; in whom all goods are together and are perfectly and ever have been and shall be.

And therefore it is little and insufficient whatever thou givest me beside thyself or revealest or promisest of thyself, thee not seen or gotten fully; for mine heart may not verily rest nor be fully and all wholly content, if it rest not in thee and ever pass thy gifts and every creature.

O my most sweet spouse Jesu Christ, most pure lover, lord of all manner of creatures who shall give me feathers of very liberty that I may flee and rest in thee? O when shall it be given to me fully that I may take heed and see how sweet thou art, my Lord God? when shall I at full gather myself in thee that for thy love I feel not myself but thee only above all feeling and all manner, in a manner not known to all.

Now ofttimes I mourn and bear my infelicity with sorrow: for in this valley of tears there come many evil things that ofttimes let (hinder) me trouble me sore and dark my mind and distract me and draw me and wrap me in that I may not have free coming to thee and that I may not enjoy these jocund embraces that are ready for holy spirits.

My sighing and my manifold sorrow on earth must move thee, O Jesu, the brightness of everlasting glory, comfort of the soul going in pilgrimage; before thee my mouth is without voice and my silence speaketh to thee. How long tarrieth my Lord ere he come?

Come to me, his poor servant, that he may make him glad; put (forth) his hand and deliver the wretch from all manner of anguish. Come, come; for without thee there shall be no blissful day nor hour; for thou art my gladness, and without thee my board is void.

I am a wretch and in a manner imprisoned and grievously afeared till thou refresh me with the light of thy presence and make me free and show me thy amiable visage. Let other men seek instead of thee what other things they like; for me—nothing pleaseth nor shall please but thou, my God, mine hope, and mine everlasting health.

I shall not hold my peace and I shall not cease to pray till thy grace turn again to me and thou speak within.

Lo, I am here; lo, I am come to thee, for thou calledst me inwardly; thy tears, the desire of thy soul, thine humiliation the contrition of thine heart they have bowed me and brought me to thee.

And I said—Lord I have called on thee inwardly and desired to have my joy in thee. I am ready to forsake all things for thee. Thou verily stirredst me first to seek thee. Wherefore, Lord, be thou blessed that hast done this goodness with thy servant after the multitude of thy mercy.

What hath thy servant more to say, Lord, before thee, but that he (should) meek himself greatly in thy sight having ever in mind his own wickedness and his vileness? for there is none like thee in all the innumerable things of heaven and earth.

Thy works are right good, thy judgments true, and by thy providence all things are governed. Praise therefore be to thee and glory, thou the wisdom of the father; my mouth, my soul and all things that are made, praise they thee and bless thee. Amen.

CHAPTER XXIV

OF RECORDING (REMEMBERING) THE MANIFOLD BENEFITS OF GOD

Lord open mine heart in thy law and teach me to go in thy precepts. Grant me to understand thy will and with great reverence and diligent consideration to remember thy benefits, both in general and special, that I may therefore worthily give thee thanks. But I know and acknowledge that I may not yield thee thanks for the least point. I am less than all thy goods given to me and when I think of thy noblesse, my spirit faileth for the greatness thereof.

All that we have in body and soul and all that we have outward or inward, naturally or supernaturally, all are thy benefits and commend thee as a benefactor holy and good of whom we have received all good things. And if one have taken more and another fewer, yet all are thine and without thee may not the least thing be had.

He that hath received greater may not rejoice him for his merit nor be lift up above other, nor despise the less; for he is more and better that less ascribeth to himself, and in thanking he is more meek and more devout. And he that weeneth himself to be more vile and deemeth himself more unworthy than all other, he is more apt (fit) to receive greater gifts. And he that taketh fewer, ought not to be sorry, nor bear indignation nor envy against the richer; but rather to take heed of thee and praise thy goodness sovereignly, that so plenteously, so freely, so gladly, granteth thy gifts without acceptance of persons.

All things came of thee and therefore thou art to be praised in all things. Thou knowest what is expedient to be given to everybody and why this hath more and this less; it is not for us to discern but for thee anenst (with) whom the merits of all are defined.

Wherefore, Lord God, I account it for a great benefit that I have not many things the praise and glory of which appear outwardly and according to man. So that a creature, the poverty and vileness of his person considered, should not conceive thereof heaviness, sorrow or dejection but rather consolation and great gladness; for thou God chosest in this world poor and meek (men) and despised of the world to (be) thy familiars and household men.

Witness hereof are thine apostles whom thou madest princes above all the earth. They were conversant (living) in the world without complaint, meek and simple, without all malice and guile, in so much that they joyed to suffer rebukes and wrongs for thy name and what the world abhorreth, that they embraced to them with great will (ingness).

Wherefore nothing ought so to make glad thy lover and the knower of thy benefits as thy will in him and the well-pleasing of thine everlasting disposition; with which only he ought to be content and comforted, so that he will be least as gladly as another will be most and as well pleased and content in the lower place as in the first and as gladly despicable and abject and of no fame as to be more worshipful and greater in the world than other. For thy will and the love of thy honour ought to pass all things and to comfort him more and please him more than all benefits given him or to be given him.

CHAPTER XXV

OF FOUR THINGS BRINGING GREAT PEACE

Son now shall I teach thee the way of peace and of very liberty.

Lord, do as thou sayest for that is agreeable to me to hear.

Study, son, rather to do the will of another than thine own. Choose evermore rather to have less than more. Seek ever the lower place and to be under all. Desire ever to pray that the will of God be all and wholly done. Lo, such a man entereth into the coasts of peace and quiet. Lord, this word of thine is greatly short but it containeth in itself much perfection. It is little in saying but full of wit and plenteous of fruit. And if this might be truly kept by me a light disturbance should not so soon spring up in me; and as ofttimes as I feel me unpleased and grieved I find that I have gone from this doctrine. But thou canst (do) all things and ever lovest the profiting of man's soul. Increase in me more grace that I may fulfil thy word and make perfect mine own health.

CHAPTER XXVI

AGAINST EVIL THOUGHTS

My LORD God be not eloyned (distant) from me: my God, behold mine health: for vain thoughts and dreads have risen against me, tormenting my soul. How shall I escape unhurt? how shall I break them? I shall go before thee, he saith, and I shall make low the glorious of the earth: I shall open the gate of the prison and I shall reveal to thee the inward of my secrets. Do, Lord, as thou speakest, and make to flee from thy visage all wicked thoughts. This is mine hope and my sole consolation to flee to thee in every tribulation, to trust to thee and inwardly to call upon thee and patiently to abide thy consolation.

CHAPTER XXVII

A PRAYER FOR ILLUMINATION OF MIND

CLARIFY me with thy clearness of everlasting light and bring out of the habitat of mine heart all manner of darkness

Restrain all evil wanderings and all mighty temptations. Fight for me mightily and bear (drive) out the wicked beasts, the perilous lusts, I mean; that peace be made in thy virtue and might and abundance of praise sound in the holy hall, that is in the pure conscience. Command winds and tempests, say to the sea Be in rest, and to the northern wind Blow not, and there shall be great tranquillity. Send out thy light and thy truth, that they may shine upon the earth; for I am idle earth and void, till thou illumine me. Pour out thy grace from above, wash my soul with that heavenly dew, minister waters of devotion to water the face of the earth, to bring forth good fruit and of the best. Lift up the mind that is pressed with the heavy burden of sin, and suspend all my desire to heavenly things; that the sweetness of thy felicity once tasted, it may not like me to think on earthly things. Tear me and deliver me from all passing comfort of creatures, for nothing created may fully quiet and comfort my appetite. Join me to thee with an undepartable bond of love, for thou alone sufficest to the lover and without thee all things are frivols (frivolous).

CHAPTER XXVIII

OF ESCHEWING CURIOUS INQUISITION OF ANOTHER MAN'S LIFE

Son, be not curious, nor be busy. What is this or that to thee? Follow thou me. What is it to thee whether a man be such and such or what this man doth or what he saith? Thou has no need to answer for others, but for thyself thou must yield accounts. Whereto wrappest thou and impliest (implicatest) thyself? Lo, I know all men and see all things that are done under heaven and know how it standeth with every man, what he thinketh, what he will, and to what end his intention draweth. Wherefore —to me all things are to be committed.

Keep thou thyself in good peace and let the stirrer stir as much as he will, whatever he doth or saith shall fall upon him for he may not deceive me. Take no heed of the shadow of a great name nor of the familiarity of many nor of private love of man; for all these engender distraction and great darkness of soul. I would gladly speak my word and show thee hid things if thou wouldst diligently observe my coming and open to me the door of thy heart.

Be ready, wake (watch) in prayer and in all things meek thyself.

CHAPTER XXIX

WHEREIN STANDETH PEACE OF HEART AND TRUE PROFITING

Son, I said, I leave peace to you, I give my peace to you; not as the world giveth so give I. All men desire but all men love not those things that long (belong) to true peace. My peace is with meek men and mild of heart: thy peace shall be in much patience. If thou hear me and follow my voice thou shalt live in great peace.

What shall I do therefore?

In everything take heed what thou dost and what thou sayest and dress (direct) all thine intention to please me alone, and out of me (outside me) covet nothing nor seek nothing. And also of other men's deeds deem nothing rashly nor meddle not nor imply (implicate) thee not with things that art not committed to thee and it shall be trouble to thee little or seldom. For a man never to feel trouble nor suffer no heaviness in body nor in soul, is not the state of this world but the state of everlasting quiet. Wherefore deem not to have found true peace if thou feel no grief, nor then all to be well if thou have no adversary;

nor (deem) thyself to be perfect if all things be after thy will. Nor then account thee great or specially beloved if thou be in great delight, devotion or sweetness for herein is not known a true lover of virtue nor in them profit and man's perfection stand.

Wherein then, Lord?

In offering thyself with all thine heart to the will of God, not asking those things that art thine neither in little, nor in much, nor in time nor in everlastingness. So that with one even cheer (face) thou abide in yielding of thanks—among pleasant things and contrarious, peising (weighing) all evenly.

If thou art so mighty and so long-abiding-in-hope that, all manner of inward consolation withdrawn, yet thou makest ready thine heart to suffer greater things and more, and dost not justify thyself as though thou oughtest not to suffer so great things but justifiest me in all my dispositions and praisest me as most holy; then thou goest in the true and right way of peace and thou mayst hope certainly to see my face in jubilation. And if thou wouldst come to full contempt of thyself, know that thou shalt then enjoy abundance of peace after the possibility of thy dwelling place.

CHAPTER XXX

OF THE EXCELLENCE OF A FREE MIND AND HOW IT IS RATHER GOTTEN BY PRAYER THAN BY READING

LORD, this is the work of a perfect man, never to release the soul from intention of holy things, and among many cares to go in a manner without care, not for sluggishness, but in a kind of right of a free mind in cleaving to no creature in inordinate affection.

I beseech thee, my most merciful God, preserve me from the cares of this world, that I be not too much implied (implicated); from many necessities of the body that I be not taken with pleasures; from all obstacles of the soul, that I be not broken and thrown down with heaviness. I say not only from such things as the vanity of the world coveteth with whole affection but also from these miseries that punishingly grieve the soul of thy servant with the common curse of mortality and tarry (hinder) it that it may not enter into liberty of spirit as oft as I would.

O my God, ineffable sweetness, turn into bitterness all fleshly comfort that draweth me away from love of everlasting things and wickedly draweth me to itself under colour of a present delightful good. My God let not flesh and blood overcome me, let not the world deceive me and his short glory, let not the fiend with his wiles supplant me. Give me strength to withstand, patience in suffering, constancy in persevering, give for all worldly consolations the most sweet unction of the Holy Ghost, and for fleshly love pour into me the love of thy name.

Lo, meat and drink, clothe and other things belonging to the body are onerous to a fervent spirit. Grant me to use such nourishings temperately, and not to be wrapped too much in desires. To cast all things away is not lawful, for nature must be sustained, but to seek superfluities and such things as most delight, holy law forbiddeth; for else the flesh would wanton against the spirit. In these things I pray that thine hand may govern me and teach me what is too much.

CHAPTER XXXI

THAT PRIVATE LOVE MOST TARRIETH A MAN FROM THE HIGHEST GOOD

Son, it behoveth thee to give all for all and for nothing of thine to be to thyself. Know well that love of thyself noyeth thee more than anything in the world. According to the love and affection that thou bearest, everything cleaveth to thee more or less. If thy love be pure, simple and ordinate thou shalt not be captive nor subject to earthly things. Covet not that thing that thou mayst not have; will not to have that thing that may let (hinder) thee and prive thee of thine inward liberty.

It is wonder that thou committest not thyself to me from the ground of thine heart with all things that thou mayst desire or have. Why art thou consumed with vain mourning? Why art thou made weary with superfluous cares? Stand at my well-pleasing and thou shalt suffer no hindering. If thou seek this or that or would be here or there for thine own profit and for thy more plesance thou shalt never be in quiet nor free from business: for in everything shall be some default and in every place shall be that that is contrary.

Therefore not everything gotten and multiplied from without helpeth but rather when it is set at naught and cut away by the root; which is not only understood of money and riches, but of ambition, of honour and desire of vain praise; the which all pass with the world.

The place wardeth but little if thou lack a fervent spirit; nor shall that peace long stand that is sought from without if the state of the heart be vacant of a right foundation; that is, unless thou stand in me thou mayst change but not do better. For, occasion once arisen and taken, thou shalt find that which thou fleddest and more thereto.

CHAPTER XXXII

A PRAYER FOR PURGATION OF HEART AND HEAVENLY WISDOM

CONFIRM me, God, by the grace of the Holy Ghost: and make virtue to be strengthened in the inner man, and make mine heart void from all unprofitable business;

not drawn with diverse desires of anything vile or precious but beholding all things as things passing— and me together with them. For there is nothing abiding under the sun where all things are vanity and affliction of spirit.

O how wise is he that thus considereth. Lord, give me heavenly wisdom that I may learn to seek thee and find thee above all things and above all things to savour thee and love thee and according to the order of wisdom to understand all other things as they be. Grant me prudently to decline the flatterer and patiently to suffer the adversary; for this is great wisdom not to be moved with every wind of words nor to give the ear to evil-blandishing mermaiden; and thus men go surely in the way begun.

CHAPTER XXXIII

AGAINST THE TONGUES OF DETRACTORS

Son, bear it not heavily, if some feel evil of thee and say that thou wouldst not gladly hear. Thou oughtest to feel of thyself worse things and to believe no man to be lower than thyself. If thou walk within, thou shalt not peise (weigh) flying words. It is no little prudence to keep silence in evil time and to turn inwardly to me and not to be troubled with man's judgment. Let not thy peace be in the mouths of men; whether they say well, whether they say evil, thou art not therefore another man. Where is very peace and very glory? Whether not in me? And he that coveteth not to please men nor dreadeth not to displease men, he shall rejoice in much peace. Of inordinate love and vain dread groweth all unrestfulness of heart and distraction of wits.

CHAPTER XXXIV

THAT IN TIME OF TRIBULATION GOD IS INWARDLY TO BE CALLED UPON AND TO BE BLESSED

LORD be thy name blessed for ever that wouldest this temptation to come upon me. I may not flee it. I pray thee help me and turn it to me into good. Lord now I am in tribulation and it is not well in mine heart, but I am greatly vexed with this present passion. And now, well beloved father, what shall I say? I am taken among anguishes. Save me in this hour. But therefore I come into this hour that thou shouldst be glorified when I shall be brought down low and by thee delivered. Please it thee, Lord, to deliver me, for I am poor and what shall I do and whither shall I go without thee?

Lord, give peace at this time; help me my Lord God and I shall not dread how much ever I be grieved. And now in this what shall I say? Lord, thy will be done and I have well deserved to be troubled and grieved. It is behoveful also that I suffer and, would God, patiently, till this tempest pass and better be.

Thine almighty hand is of power to take away this temptation from me, and to assuage his violence that I be not utterly overcome, as thou hast done ofttimes with me, my God, my mercy; and the harder that it is to me, the lighter it is to thee, this change of the right hand of the highest.

CHAPTER XXXV

OF ASKING OF GOD'S HELP AND TRUST IN RECOVERING GRACE

SON, I am the Lord comforting in the day of tribulation. Come to me when it is not well with thee. This it is that letteth (hindereth) most heavenly comfort for thou hast so late recourse to prayer, for before thou prayest me heartily thou seekest mean time many solaces and refreshest thee in outward things. And there-through it cometh that all availeth but little till thou take heed that I it am that deliver men trusting in me, nor without me is any availing, help, or profitable counsel or durable remedy.

But now taking again spirit after tempest wax strong in the light of my pity; for I am nigh, saith scripture, to restore all things, not only wholly, but abundantly and over-heaped. Whether is there anything hard to me or shall I be like a man that saith and doth not? Where is thy faith? stand steadfastly and perseveringly. Be of long hope and a strong man; consolation shall come to thee in time. Abide me and I shall come and cure thee.

It is a temptation that vexeth thee and a vain dread that feareth (frighteth) thee. What mattereth busy caring of things that are contingently to come, but to make thee have sorrow upon sorrow? Let the malice of the day suffice to it. Vain it is and unprofitable for a man to be troubled or rejoiced of things to come that peradventure shall never fall. But it is man's condition to be deluded with such imaginations and a sign of a soul as yet little, to be drawn so lightly at the suggestion of the enemy. For he taketh no heed whether he delude or deceive by true or by false, whether he throw down by loss of things present or dread of things to come.

Let not thine heart therefore be troubled nor dread such. Believe in me and have trust in my mercy. When thou weenest ofttimes that I am far from thee then am I next. When thou weenest thyself almost lost then ofttimes cometh greatest gain of merit.

It is not then all lost when the thing falleth into the contrary. Thou oughtest not to deem after the present feeling nor so to cleave to any heaviness where ever it come from and take her so as though hope of scaping were utterly taken away.

Ween not thyself to be all forsaken though I send thee some tribulation for a time or else withdraw desired consolation; for so men go to the realm of heaven. And without doubt it is more expedient to thee and to the remnant of my servants that ye be exercised with contrary things than if all things fell after your liking.

Lo, I know hid thoughts that it is greatly expedient for thine health that thou be left some time without savour lest thou be lift up in the succeeding of thy desire and please thyself in that thou art not. That I gave I may take away and restore it again when it pleaseth me. When I give it, it is mine; when I withdraw it, I take not thine, for mine is every good thing given and every perfect gift.

If I send thee any heaviness or any contrariousness, have no indignation thereof, nor let not thine heart fall, for lo, I may soon lift thee up again and change every heaviness into joy. Nevertheless I am righteous and commendable when I do so with thee.

If thou savour aright and behold truly, thou oughtest never for adversity to sorrow so deeply but rather to joy and give thanks, yea, to account this as for a singular joy that I paining thee with sorrows spare thee not.

"As the father loved me, so I love you" said I to my well beloved disciples whom I send not to temporal joys but to despites, not to idleness but to labours, not to rest but to bring forth much fruit in patience.

CHAPTER XXXVI

OF RECKING NEVER OF ALL CREATURES SO THE CREATOR MAY BE FOUND

Lord I need yet more grace if I shall come thither where no man nor other creature may let (hinder) me. For as long as any thing withholdeth me, I may not flee freely to thee. He desired to flee freely that said "Who shall give me feathers as a culver and I shall flee and rest?" What is more restful than a simple eye? and what is more free than he that desireth naught on earth?

It behoveth therefore to pass over every creature and to forsake oneself perfectly and to stand in ecstasy of mind and see thee creator of all to be nothing like his creatures. And unless a man be sped (freed) from all creatures he may never freely attend to godly things.

Therefore there are found but few contemplative men for few can fully sequester and depart themselves from perishing creatures. Therefore great grace is required thereto that may lift up the soul and ravish herself above herself. And save a man be lift up in spirit and delivered from all creatures and all wholly oned (united) to God, whatever he can (knoweth), whatever he have, it is of little weight.

He shall long be little and shall lie beneath that accounteth anything great but only one, that is without measure, everlasting good: and all save that is naught and for naught to be accounted. There is a great difference between him that is illumined with wisdom and a devout man and him that is lettered and studious in science called a clerk. That doctrine is much more noble that welleth from above of God's influence than that that is laboriously gotten by man's wit.

There are many desirers of contemplation; but they study not to practise the things that are required thereto. It is a great let (hindrance) that men abide in signs and sensible things and take little care of perfect mortification. I know not what it is nor what spirit we be led with nor what we mean, we that are called spiritual men, that we have so much labour and so much business about transitory things and vile things but of our inwards (inward things) we think full seldom, gathering our wits together.

Alas, anon after a little recollection we break out and we
weigh not our works with a strait examination. Where
our affections lie we take no heed and how impure all
our works are, this we bewail not. Every flesh had corrupt his way and therefore followed the great flood.
Wherefore when our inward affection is much corrupt it
must needs be that the following action, showing the lacking of inward strength, be corrupt also.

Of a pure heart proceedeth fruit of good life. Men seek how
much a man hath, but of how much good he doth no man
thinketh. It is inquired if he be mighty, rich, fair, able,
or a good writer, a good singer, a good labourer, but how
pure he be in spirit, how patient, how mild, how devout
and how inward, not many men speak. Nature beholdeth
the outward things of man, but grace turneth itself all
inward. Nature is ofttimes deceived, but grace trusteth
in God, that she be not deceived.

CHAPTER XXXVII

OF DENYING ONESELF AND FORSAKING OF ALL CUPIDITY

Son, thou mayst not have perfect liberty unless thou
deny thyself utterly. All lovers of themselves, covetous,
curious, wanderers about (are fettered), seeking ever
soft things and not those things that are of Jesu Christ
but ofttimes feigning and shaping what may not stand.
Hold a short and perfect saying—Leave all and thou
shalt find all; forsake coveting and thou shalt find rest.
Think this over in thy mind and when thou hast fulfilled
it thou shalt understand all things.

Lord this is not one day's work nor children's play; but, what
is more, in this short word is included all perfection of
Religious folk.

Son, thou oughtest not to be turned away nor anon to be all
thrown down when thou hearest the way of perfectness,

but rather to be provoked to higher things and at least to aspire thereto by desire. Would God it were so with thee and that thou wert come thereto, that thou wert no lover of thyself but stoodest purely at my beckoning and of him that I have put above thee as father. Then shouldst thou please me greatly and thy days should pass with great joy and in great peace. Thou hast many things yet to forsake the which unless thou resign them wholly to me, thou shalt not get that thou askest. Wherefore I make persuasion to thee to buy gold of me that thou mayst be made rich, that is, heavenly wisdom treading under foot all these low things.

Put behind (thee) all earthly wisdom and all thine own complacency. I have said to thee to buy vile things and of little price instead of things precious in man's reputation. For true and heavenly wisdom seemeth little and of no price and almost forgotten in this world, not thinking highly of itself nor seeking to be magnified on earth. Many preach with the mouth but in living they depart far therefrom. Nevertheless it is a precious margaret (pearl) and hid from many.

CHAPTER XXXVIII

OF UNSTABLENESS OF HEART AND OF INTENTION TO BE HAD TOWARDS GOD

Son, believe not thine own affection that now is for it shall soon be changed into another. As long as thou livest thou art subject to mutability, yea, though thou wilt not; so thou shalt be found now glad, now sorry, now pleased, now troubled, now devout, now indevout, now studious, now sluggish, now heavy, now light.

But above these changes standeth the wise man and well taught in spirit, taking no heed what he feels in himself, nor on which side the wind of unstableness bloweth, but that all the intention of his mind may profit to the due and best end. For so he may abide one and the same unshaken, with the simple eye of intention directed to me without ceasing among so many divers chances. For the more pure that the eye of intention is, the more steadfastly men go among divers storms.

But in many the eye of intention is darked, for anon they behold a delightful thing that appeareth and seldom is any found free from the venom of self-seeking. So the Jews sometime came into Bethany to Martha and Mary not for Jesu alone but for they would see Lazarus. Wherefore the eye of intention must be cleansed that it be simple and for the right and directed to me alone above all variant things that are between.

CHAPTER XXXIX

TO HIM THAT LOVETH, GOD SAVOURETH ABOVE ALL THINGS

Lo MY God and all. What would I more and what more blissful thing may I desire? O the savoury and the sweet word, to him that loveth the word of the father, not the world nor that that longeth to it.

Lo my God and all: To him that understandeth there is said enough and oft to rehearse it is jocund for the lover. Certainly, thou being present, all things are jocund and thou being absent all things are loth and weary. Thou makest in the heart tranquillity, great peace and solemn gladness.

Thou makest (man) to feel well of all and in all things to praise thee nor may there nothing long please without thee; but if anything is to be acceptable and savour well it behoveth that thy grace shall be nigh and make it savoury with the sauce of thy wisdom. To whom thou savourest, what shall not savour to him aright? and to whom thou savourest not, what thing may turn him to mirth?

But the worldly wise men fail in thy wisdom and they that savour the flesh; for there is much vanity and there is found death. But they that by despising of earthly things and mortification of the flesh follow thee be known verily to be wise men, for they are translate from vanity to verity and from the flesh to the spirit. To these men God savoureth; and whatever of good they find in creatures all that they refer to the praise of their maker. Unlike nevertheless, much unlike is the savour of the creator and of the creature, of everlastingness and of time, of light uncreate and light illuminate.

O thou light perpetual, passing all lights created, cast thou from above lightning, piercing all the inwards of my heart. Purify, make glad, quicken and clarify my spirit with its powers to cleave to thee in jubilant excess. O when shall that blessed and desirable hour come when thou wilt fill me with thy presence and thou shalt be all in all. As long as this is not given, there shall be no full joy.

Alas, yet liveth in me the old man; he is not all crucified, he is not perfectly all dead: yet he coveteth against the spirit and moveth inward battles and suffereth not the realm of the soul to be in quiet. But thou that hast lordship over the power of the sea and suagest the movings of his floods, arise and help me; bring to naught folks that will have battles. Knock them down in thy might and show thy greatness and be thy right hand glorified: for there is to me none other hope nor refuge but in thee, my Lord God.

CHAPTER XL

THAT THERE IS NO SURETY FROM TEMPTATION IN THIS LIFE

Son, thou art never sure in this life; but as long as thou livest, ever spiritual armour is necessary to thee. Thou dwellest among enemies, thou art impugned on the right hand and on the left hand. Wherefore if thou use not on every side the shield of patience thou shalt not be long without a wound.

Furthermore if thou set not thine heart fixed and firm in me with will to suffer for me thou shalt not be able to suffer this burning nor come to the victory of saints. It behoveth thee therefore to pass (by) all things manly and to use a mighty hand against things set against thee; for to the victor is given manna and to the coward is left much misery.

If thou seek rest in this world how shalt thou then come to rest everlasting? Set not thyself to (gain) great rest but to (gain) much patience. Seek very peace not in earth but in heaven; not in men nor in other creatures but in God alone.

For the love of God thou oughtest to suffer all things: labours and sorrows, temptations, vexations, anxieties, necessities, infirmities, wrongs, obloquy, reprehensions, humiliations, confusions, corrections, and despites. These things help to virtue, these prove the knight of Christ, these make the heavenly crown.

I shall give everlasting meed for a little labour and infinite glory for a transitory shame. Weenest thou to have at all times spiritual consolations at thy will? My saints had not so, but many heavinesses, diverse temptation and great desolations; but they bore themselves in all things patiently and trusted more to God than to themselves knowing that passions (sufferings) of this time are not worthy to deserve the glory that is to come.

Wilt thou have anon that that many men could scarce get after many tears and great labours? Abide the Lord, do manly and be comforted, and mistrust not nor go away, but constantly put forth both body and soul for the glory of God; and I shall give again most fully, I shall be with thee in every tribulation.

CHAPTER XLI

AGAINST MEN'S VAIN JUDGMENTS

Son, cast thine heart on to our Lord steadfastly and dread no
man's judgment where thy conscience declareth thee pure
and innocent. It is good and blissful for a man so to suffer;
nor shall that be grievous to him that is meek in heart,
trusting to God more than to himself.

Many men speak many things and to them little faith is to
be given. And to please all men is not possible; for though
Paul studied to please all men in our Lord and was made
all things to all men nevertheless he accounted it for the
least thing to be deemed (well) by man's sight. He did
enough for man's edification and health, as much as in
him was or he might do; but he could not let (hinder)
that sometimes he should be deemed (judged) and despised of others.

Therefore he committed all to God that knew all things and
defended himself with patience and meekness against
the mouths of wicked speakers and of them that think
vain things and lies and make boast at their own will.
Nevertheless other whiles he answered lest by his silence
occasion of offending might have been given to the feeble
in faith.

What art thou that dreadest so much of a mortal man that
this day is and to-morrow appeareth not? Dread God
and be not afeard of man's dreads. What may any man
do against thee with wrongs or with words? he noyeth
more himself than thee, whatever he be. Have thou God
ever before thine eyes and strive not with brawling
words.

And if thou for the time seemest to have the worse and
to suffer shame that thou hast not deserved, grudge
(grumble) not therefore, nor lose not thy crown by im-

patience but rather look up to me in heaven that am mighty to deliver from all confusion and wrong and to yield to every man after his works.

CHAPTER XLII

OF PURE RESIGNATION OF A MAN'S SELF

Son, forsake thyself and thou shalt find me. Stand without choice and without all manner of self and thou shalt win ever; for anon, as thou hast resigned thyself and not taken thyself again, then shall be thrown to thee more grace.

Lord, how oft shall I resign myself and wherein shall I forsake myself?

Ever and in every hour, as in little, so in great. I out-take (except) nothing but in all things I will find thee made bare: else, how canst thou be mine and I thine, unless thou be deprived outwardly and inwardly from all thine own will? The more swiftly that thou lost this the better it shall be with thee; and the more plainly and clearly it is done the more shalt thou please me and the more thou shalt win.

Some resign, but with some exception, for they trust not fully to God; wherefore they labour to provide for themselves. Some also first offer all but afterwards through a little temptation they go again to their own selves and therefore profit not in virtue. Then folk come not to true liberty of heart, nor to the grace of my jocund familiarity except with whole resignation and daily offering of themselves first being made, without which unity of fruition (pure enjoyment) standeth not, nor shall stand.

I have said to thee full oft, and yet I say again: Forsake thyself, resign of thyself and thou shalt enjoy great peace. Give all for all, seek nothing, ask nothing again;

stand purely and undoubtingly in me and thou shalt have me; thou shalt be free in heart and darkness shall not over go (overwhelm) thee. To this enforce thyself, this pray thou, this desire thou, that thou may be despoiled on all manner of self, and thou, bare, follow bare Jhesu (Jesus only) and die to thyself and live ever-lastingly to me. Then shall end all vain fantasies, wicked conturbations and superfluous cares; then also shall go away inordinate dread and inordinate love shall die.

CHAPTER XLIII

OF GOOD GOVERNANCE IN OUTWARD THINGS

Son, thou oughtest diligently to attend to this that in every place, every action or outward occupation thou be inwardly free and mighty in thyself and all things be under thee and thou not under them, that thou be lord and governor of thy deeds not servant, but rather exempt and a true Hebrew going in to the lot and liberty of the sons of God that stand upon these present goods and behold the everlasting that behold things transitory with the left eye and heavenly things with the right eye: whom temporal things draw not (them) to cleave to them but they rather draw such goods to serve God well with as they are ordained of God and instituted of the sovereign workman that leaveth nothing inordinate (unordered) in his creation.

Also if thou in every chance standest not in outward appearance nor with the fleshly eye turnest about to things seen or heard but anon in every cause thou enterest with Moses to ask counsel of our Lord, thou shalt hear oft-times God's answer and thou shalt come again instructed in things present and that are to come.

Moses at all times had recourse to the tabernacle for doubts and questions to be assoiled and fled to the help of prayer for relieving of perils and for mischiefs of men. So thou oughtest to fly into the secret place of thine heart beseeching inwardly the help of God. For Joshua and the children of Israel, as it is read, were deceived of the Gibeonites, for they asked no counsel first of our Lord but giving too much credence to sweet words were deluded with a false pity.

CHAPTER XLIV

THAT MAN BE NOT TOO BUSY IN WORLDLY BUSINESS

Son, at all times commit to me thy cause for I shall dispose it well in convenient time. Abide mine ordinance thou shalt feel profit thereof.

Lord, right gladly I commit to thee all things for little may my thinking profit. Would God that I cleaved not over much to chances that are to come that I might offer myself to thy well-pleasing without tarrying.

Son, ofttimes a man is sore moved about a thing that he desireth; but when he is come to it, he beginneth to feel otherwise; for affections are not abiding about one thing but they be shufted from one to another. It is not therefore a little thing, yea, it is not among least things for a man to forsake himself; true profit is denying of a man's self and a man so denied is full free and full sure. But the old enemy, adversary to all good, ceaseth not from temptation but day and night he lieth in a wait if he may bring headily (headlong) the unware man into the snare of deceit.

Work therefore and pray, saith our Lord, that ye enter not into temptation.

CHAPTER XLV

THAT A MAN HATH NO GOOD OF HIMSELF WHEREOF TO REJOICE

LORD what is man that thou hast mind on him or the son of man that thou visitest him? What deserved man that thou shouldst give him thy grace? Lord, why may I complain if thou forsake me or what can I righteously pretend against thee if thou do not that I ask? Certainly this may I think in truth and say: Lord, I am naught, I can naught, I have no good of myself but in all things I fail and ever tend to naught. And unless I be helpen (helped) of thee and inwardly informed I am made all luke (warm) and dissolute.

But thou Lord art ever one and abidest one everlastingly, ever God, righteous and holy, doing all things by wisdom. But I that am more prone to failing than to profit am not ever abiding in the same estate, for seven times change upon me. Nevertheless it is soon amended when it pleaseth thee to put to an helping hand; for thou alone without all man's succour mayst help and confirm me in such wise that my cheer (face) may no more be changed diversely but that in thee alone my heart may turn and be at rest.

Wherefore if I could well cast away all man's consolation either for getting of devotion or for necessity compelling me to seek thee—for there is no man that can comfort me —then might I worthily trust in thy grace and rejoice in the gift of new consolation.

Thanks be to thee whereof all cometh, as oft as it is well with me. For I am vanity and naught before thee, a man inconstant and sick; wherein therefore may I rejoice or why covet I to be held in reputation? Is it not of naught and a most vain thing? Verily vainglory is an evil pestilence and the greatest vanity, for it draweth away from true glory and despoileth (man) of heavenly grace. For while a man pleaseth himself, he displeaseth thee; and while he gapeth after man's praises he is deprived of true virtues.

For true glory and holy exultation is to rejoice in thee and not in oneself, to joy in thy name and not in man's own virtue, and to delight in no creature save for thee. Praised be therefore thy name, not mine; magnified be thy work and not mine; blessed be thine holy name, but to me be nothing given of man's praises.

Thou art my glory, thou art the exultation of my heart. In thee shall I rejoice and joy all day, for myself not at all, save in my infirmities. Let the Jews seek glory each of the other, I shall seek that that is of God alone, for all man's glory, all temporal worship (honour), all worldly height, compared to thine everlasting glory is vanity and folly. O my truth and my mercy, my God, blessed trinity, to thee alone be praise and honour virtue and glory through worlds infinite. Amen.

CHAPTER XLVI

OF CONTEMPT OF ALL HONOUR

Son, if thou see other men honoured take no such thing to thyself but rather be despised and made low. Lift up thine heart to me in heaven and men's despising on earth shall not make thee sorry.

Lord, we be in blindness and some are deceived of vanity. Lord, if I behold me aright there was never wrong done to me by no creature; wherefore of right I have nothing to complain of against thee. Forasmuch as I have oft and grievously offended thee, rightly is every creature armed against me.

To me therefore is due confusion and despite but to thee praise honour and glory. And unless I make myself ready to this that I will gladly be despised of every creature and forsaken and utterly seem naught I may not be inwardly peaced (at peace) and stablished, nor spiritually be illumined nor fully oned (united) to thee.

CHAPTER XLVII

THAT PEACE IS NOT TO BE SET (PUT) IN MEN

Son, if thou set (put) thy peace in any person for thine own feeling and living together (with them) thou shalt be unstable and unpeaced (not at peace). But if thou have recourse to the truth living and abiding, the friend that goeth from thee or dieth from thee shall not make thee sorry. In me ought to stand the love of the friend and whoever seemeth good to thee and dear in this life is to be beloved—for me.

Without me friendship is not worth and may not endure: and the love is not very true or pure that I couple not. Thou oughtest to be so dead from such affections of men beloved, as in thee is; thou shouldest will to be without man's fellowship. The further that a man goeth from all earthly solace, the more he nigheth unto God. Also the more profoundly that a man goeth down into himself and waxeth vile to himself the higher he styeth (climbeth) up to God.

He that ascribeth any good to himself, he letteth (hindreth) the coming of the grace of God into him, for the grace of the Holy Ghost seeketh ever the meek heart. If thou couldest perfectly make thyself naught and void (empty) thyself from all love of creatures then should I well into thee with great grace. When thou lookest to creatures thine affection is withdrawn from the creator.

Learn in all things to overcome thyself for thy creator and thou shalt then be able to attain to the knowledge of God. How little ever it be that is beheld and loved inordinately, it tarrieth (keepeth men) from the highest love and draweth (them) into wickedness.

CHAPTER XLVIII

AGAINST VAIN AND SECULAR KNOWLEDGE

Son, let not the fair and the subtle sayings of men move thee for the realm of God is not in word but in virtue. Take heed to my words the which set hearts afire and illuminate minds, bring in compunction and manifold consolations. Read never anything for thee to seem better taught or wiser. Study for mortification of sins and vices for that shall avail thee more than the knowledge of many hard questions. When thou hast read and known many things, it behoveth ever to have recourse to one principal thing.

I am he that teacheth man cunning and I grant to meek men more clear understanding than may be taught of man. He to whom I speak shall soon be wise for he shall greatly profit in spirit. Woe to them that inquire many curious things of men but of the way to serve me care but little. Time shall come when there shall appear the Master of masters, Christ Jesu, to hear the lesson of all angels, that is to search the consciences of all men: and then shall Jerusalem be searched with lanterns and then shall be open the hidils (secrets) of darkness and then shall arguments of tongues be at peace.

I it am that in a point lift up the meek soul so that he shall take (understand) my reasons of everlasting truth more than though he had studied ten years in schools. So I teach without noise of words, without confusion of opinions, without desire of honour, without fighting of arguments.

I it am that teach to despise earthly things, to be weary of things present, to seek heavenly things, to savour things everlasting, to flee honours, to suffer slanders, to put all whole trust in me and covet nothing outside me and above all things to love me burningly.

A certain man in loving me entirely learned godly things and spake marvels; he profited more in forsaking all things than in studying of subtleties. But to some I speak common things, to some special, to some I appear surely in signs and figures, and to some I reveal mysteries in a great light.

There is one voice of the books but it informeth (men) not alike: for I am the teacher of truth within, searcher of the heart, understander of the thoughts, promoter of the works, dealing to every man as I deem worthy.

CHAPTER XLIX

OF NOT ATTRACTING OUTWARD THINGS TO A MAN

Son, in many things suppose thyself as dead upon the earth and one to whom all the world is crucified; and many things thou must pass over with a deaf ear and think rather on those things that belong unto thy peace. It is more profitable to turn away thine eye from things that displease and to leave to every man his own feeling than to strive with contentious words. If thou stand well with God and behold his judgment thou shalt bear it the more easily if thou be overcome.

O Lord whither are we come? Lo, temporal harm is sorrowed for, men labour and run for little getting and spiritual harm is forgotten and scarcely and late cometh to mind again. That that availeth little or naught is taken heed to and that that is sovereignly necessary is negligently passed over; for man floweth out all to outer things and unless he turn again soon, gladly he lieth and resteth in outer things.

CHAPTER L

THAT IT IS NOT RIGHT TO BELIEVE ALL MEN AND OF LIGHT LAPSE OF WORDS

LORD, give me help out of tribulation for man's help is vain. How oft have I not found faith and trust where I weened to have had it; how oft also have I found it where I least presumed. Vain therefore is trust of man but the help of righteous men is in thee, God. Blessed be thou, Lord my God, in all things that fall to us. We be sick and unstable, soon changed and soon deceived.

Who is he that so warily and so circumspectly may keep himself in all things but that some time he shall come into some deceit and some perplexity? But he that trusteth in thee Lord and seeketh thee with a simple heart, slideth not so lightly. And if he fall into any tribulation or be wrapped in any perplexity he shall soon be delivered thereof by thee or comforted by thee for thou shalt not forsake them that trust in thee to the end.

Seldom is found a trusty friend that is persevering (lasting) in all the necessities of his friend. So, Lord, in all things thou art most trusty and among all there is not such another. O how well knew that holy soul that said "My mind is settled in God and grounded in Christ." If it was so with me, dread of man should not so trouble me, nor the darts of words should not move me.

Who may see before and be ware of all things? If things foreseen ofttimes hurt what then do things unforeseen but hurt grievously? But why did I not foresee better for myself, wretch that I am? Also why believed I so lightly other men? But we are men and we are none other than frail men though we be deemed and called of other men as angels.

Whom shall I believe, Lord, whom but thee that art truth that deceivest not nor canst be deceived? And, on the other side, every man is a liar, sick, unstable and sliding and specially in words. So that scarce may be believed anon that that soundeth well and righteously in a man's ear.

How prudently warnedst thou men to be ware of men and that a man's familiar friends are his enemies and that it is not good to believe those who say "Lo there" and "lo here." I am taught, and would God (it led) to greater wariness and less folly in me.

"Be ware," said one, "be ware: keep to thyself that I say" and whiles I kept silence and weened it to be hid, he could not keep counsel of that he asked to be kept hid but anon discovered both me and him and went his way. From such fables and unwary men Lord defend me that I fall not into their hands nor do no such things.

Give to my mouth a true word and a stable and a false wily tongue put far from me. O how good and how peaceable a thing it is for a man not to speak of other men, nor indifferently to believe all things nor lightly to speak a thing forth; to reveal himself to few, yea evermore to be sought (looked on) as a beholder of the heart, and not to be borne about with every wind of words but to desire all things inwardly and outwardly after the good pleasure of thy will.

How sure a thing it is for the keeping of heavenly grace to flee from and not to desire such things that should give matter for minding outwardly: but with all manner of business (care) to follow the things that make for amendment of life and fervour of spirit. O how many have been hurt by virtue known and praised and how wholesomely hath grace, kept under silence, availed men in this frail life that is all temptation and knighthood (service).

CHAPTER LI

OF TRUST TO BE HAD IN GOD AGAINST EVIL WORDS

Son, stand steadfastly and trust in me: for what are words but words? they flee through the air but they hurt not a stone. If thou be guilty think that thou art going gladly to amend thyself. If thou know thyself guilty in nothing, think that thou wilt suffer all gladly for God. It is little enough that thou now and then shouldst suffer words who canst not yet suffer strong beatings.

And why takest thou so small things to heart, except that thou art fleshly and takest more heed to man than behoveth thee? And because thou dreadest to be despised thou wilt not be reproved for thine excesses and seekest the shadows of excuses. But behold thyself better and thou shalt know that yet the world liveth in thee and vain love of pleasing men.

But all the while that thou fleest (shunnest) to be rebuked and confounded for thy faults it appeareth verily that thou art not very meek, nor the world dead to thee, nor thou crucified to the world. But hear my word and thou shalt not charge (care for) ten thousand words of men. Lo if all things were said against thee that would maliciously be feigned against thee how should they annoy thee if thou wouldst suffer them utterly to pass and wouldest no more set by them than a straw? Whether may they take one hair out from thee?

But he that hath no heart within and hath not God before his eyes is soon moved with a word of blame. But he that trusteth in me and coveteth not to stand by his own judgment shall be without dread of man. Lo I am judge and knower of all secrets; I know how all things are done, I know the wrong-doer and the sufferer. Out from me went this word and by my sufferance this hath happened that the thoughts of many hearts might be revealed.

I shall judge the guilty and the innocent; but with a privy judgment, for I would prove both. Man's wits often fail and deceive but my judgment is true; wherefore it shall stand and shall not be subverted. It is hid ofttimes and is open to few in all things—but it never erreth and it may not err, though to the eye of unwise men it appeareth not righteous; wherefore in every judgment recourse ought to be had to me and (men ought) not to lean to their own decision. For the righteous man shall not be sorry whatever come to him from God; yea, though anything unrighteously be brought forth against him, he shall not much charge (care for) it; nor he shall not vainly rejoice if he be reasonably excused by others for he thinketh that I search the heart and the reins and that I judge not after the face and after man's appearance; for ofttimes in mine eyes that is found culpable which to the judgment of man seemeth laudable.

Lord God, righteous judge, mighty and patient, thou knowest man's frailty and man's shrewdness (perversity): be my strength and all my trust for my conscience sufficeth not for me. Thou knowest that I know not: and therefore I ought in every blame and reproof to meek myself and suffer mildly.

Merciful Lord, forgive me as oft as I have not done so; and give me grace of more large sufferance, for thy copious mercy is better to me for getting of indulgence than my fancied righteousness for the defence of my secret conscience. And though I find no guilt in my conscience yet in that may I not justify myself; for in thy sight no man living can be justified.

CHAPTER LII

THAT ALL GRIEVOUS THINGS ARE TO BE SUFFERED FOR THE LIFE TO COME

Son, let not the labours that thou hast taken upon thee for me make thee weary nor tribulations throw thee all down; but let my promise in every adventure strength thee and comfort thee. I am sufficient to reward above all manner and all measure. Thou shalt not labour long nor shalt ever be grieved with sorrows. Abide a little while and thou shalt see a swift end of all evils.

One hour shall come when all labour shall cease and all noise; little it is and short, all that passeth with time. Do that thou dost, labour truly in my vineyard; I shall be thy reward. Write, read, sing, mourn, keep silence, pray, suffer contrariousness manly; for everlasting life is worth all these and much more and much greater battles.

Peace shall come in one day known to our Lord, and of that time shall there be neither day nor night but light perpetual, infinite brightness, sovereign peace and sicker (sure) rest. Thou shalt not say then, Who shall deliver me from the body of this death, nor thou shalt not cry, Wo me for my dwelling here is overlong tarried; for death shall be thrown down headlong and health shall be without fauting (blemish), none anxiety, blissful pleasure, sweet company and pleasant to behold.

O if thou hadst seen the perpetual crowns of saints in heaven and in how much glory they joy now that sometimes in this world were deemed contemptible and as folk unworthy to live, forsooth thou wouldst meek (humble) thyself unto the earth and wouldst rather be subject under all than to be above one; nor thou wouldst desire the merry days of this world but rather thou wouldst joy to suffer tribulation for God and wouldst take it as for a great gain to be accounted for naught among men.

O if these things tasted well to thee and entered into thine heart how durst thou once complain? Whether all laborious things ought not to be suffered for everlasting life? It is no little thing to win or to lose the kingdom of God. Lift up therefore thy visage unto heaven. Lo, I and all my saints with me which that in this world have had great battle, now they joy, now they be comforted, now they be sure, now they rest and in that end shall abide with me in the kingdom of my father.

CHAPTER LIII

OF THE DAY OF ETERNITY AND THE ANGUISH OF THIS LIFE

O THE most blissful dwelling place of that high city. O the most clear day of eternity which no night maketh dark but sovereign truth ever beshineth it; the day ever glad, ever sure and never changing state into the contrary. O would God that that day had once shined and all these temporal things had taken an end. And this day shineth to saints in a perpetual bright clearness but to pilgrims all afar and by a mirror.

The citizens of heaven know how joyous is that day; the exiled sons of Eve wail, so sorrowful is this day. The days of this time are little and evil, full of sorrow and anguish; when man is defouled with many sins, tied with many passions, strained with many dreads, distant with many cares, distract with many curiosities, wrapped in many vanities, surrounded with many errors, broken with many labours, grieved with many temptations, made soft and weak with delights, tormented with need and poverty.

O when shall there be an end of all these evils? when shall I be delivered from the wretched thraldom of vices? when shall I, Lord, have mind on thee alone? when shall I at full be glad in thee? when shall I be without any impediment in true liberty, without grievance of soul or body. When shall there be sad (settled) peace, peace undisturbed and sure, peace within and without, peace firm on every side?

Good Jesu, when shall I stand to see thee? when shall I behold the glory of thy kingdom? when wilt thou be to me all in all? When shall I be with thee in thy kingdom that thou hast ordained to thy well beloved from everlasting? I am left poor and exile in the land of enemies where are daily battles and greatest misfortunes. Comfort mine exile, assuage my sorrow, for to thee suspireth all my desire; for all that the world offereth me as solace is to me an heavy burden.

I desire to enjoy thee inwardly but I cannot take thee. I desire to cleave to heavenly things but fleshly things and unmortified passions depress me. I will in my mind be above all things, but in despite of myself I am constrained to be beneath. So I unhappy man fight with myself and am made grievous to myself while the spirit seeketh what is above and the flesh what is beneath. O what I suffer within while I think on heavenly things in my mind; the company of fleshly things cometh against me when I pray.

My God, be not far from me, decline not from thy servant in wrath. Lighten out in shining and waste them, send out thine arrows and thou shalt spill them and all the fantasies of the enemy shall be borne down. Gather together all my wits to thee, make me to forget all worldly things and grant me soon to cast away and despise all fantasies of vices.

Thou, truth eternal, succour me that no vanity may move me. Come heavenly sweetness and make to flee from thy visage all manner of impurity. Forgive me also and mercifully forget as ofttimes as in my prayer I think on any other thing than thee. I acknowledge truly that I am wont to behave me there full distractedly and many times

I am not there where I stand or sit bodily but rather I am there where I am borne with my thoughts. Where my thought is, there am I; and where my thought is there I love. That thing cometh soon to mind that naturally pleaseth or delighteth through use. Wherefore thou, truth, saidest openly "Where is thy treasure there is thine heart."

If I love heaven I am glad to think on heavenly things. If I love the world, I joy in the world's felicity and sorrow in the world's adversity. If I love the flesh I imagine ofttimes on such things as belong to the flesh. If I love the spirit, I have a delight to think on spiritual things. Whatever things that I love of them gladly I speak and hear and the images of such I bear to mine house.

But blissful is that man that, for the Lord, giveth all creatures licence to go their way, that doth violence to nature, that crucifieth the lusts of the flesh with the fervour of the spirit, that with a clear conscience he may offer to thee a pure prayer and be worthy to be present with the quire (choir) of angels, all earthly things excluded within and without.

CHAPTER LIV

OF DESIRE OF EVERLASTING LIFE AND HOW GREAT THINGS ARE PROMISED TO FIGHTERS

Son, when thou feelest the desire of everlasting bliss to be poured into thee from above, and thou desirest to go out of the tabernacle of the body, that thou mayst behold my clearness without shadow of changeableness, open thine heart and receive this holy inspiration with all manner of desire. Yield to the sovereign bounty most large thanks that doth with thee so worthily, visiteth mercifully, exciteth ardently, lifteth up mightily, lest thou with thine own weight slide down to earthly things.

For thou takest not this with thine own thought or thine own power but only by worthiness of the most high grace and of God's beholding thee that thou mayst profit the more in virtues and greater meekness and make thee ready for battles that are to come and cleave to me with all thine affection and that thou mayst study to serve me with a fervent will.

Son, ofttimes the fire burneth but without flame and smoke it styeth (riseth) never up. So the desires of some men are lift up to heavenly things and nevertheless they are not free from the temptation of fleshly affections; and therefore they do not in all wise purely for the service of God in that they ask so desirously of God. And such is ofttime the desire that thou hast said should be so importunate, for that is not pure and perfect that is done for one's own profit.

Ask that thing that is not to thee delightful nor profitable but that that is to me acceptable and honourable; for if thou judge righteously thou oughtest to put mine ordinance before thy desire and prefer and follow it afore all things. For I have heard thy desire and thy manifold mournings.

Now thou wouldst be in the liberty of the glory of the sons of God; now the house everlasting delighteth thee and the heavenly country full of joy; but yet this hour is not come; there is yet another time, time of battle, time of labour and of proving. Thou desirest to be fulfilled with the most sovereign good; but thou canst not follow that now.

"I am" saith our Lord "abide me, till the kingdom of God come." As yet thou art to be proved on earth and to be exercised in many things. Consolation shall be given thee now and then but copious fulfilling is not granted. Be thou comforted therefore and be strong as well in doing as in suffering things contrary to nature.

It behoveth thee to be clothed in a new man and to be changed into another. It behoveth thee to do ofttimes that thou wouldest not do, and to forsake that thou wouldest do. That that pleaseth others shall cause profit, but that that pleaseth thyself shall not profit; what other men say shall be heard, what thou sayest shall be accounted as naught.

Other men shall ask and take: thou shalt ask and not get. Others shall be great in men's mouths; of thee men shall hold their peace. To others this or that shall be committed; thou shalt be judged in nothing profitable. Wherefore kind (nature) shall some time be sorry and suffer great battle if thou in silence hear these things. In these and in many other like things the true servant of God is wont to be proved, how he may deny and break himself.

There is scarce any such thing which thou needest think of as to see and suffer such things as are contrary to thy will, specially when thou art commanded to do such things as seem to thee disconvenient and least profitable. And for thou darest not withstand the higher power set above thee under our Lord therefore it seemeth to thee hard to go at another man's beckoning and to leave all thine own feeling.

But, son, peisie (weigh) the fruit and the swift end of all these labours and the meed, great without measure; and then shalt thou have no grievance thereat but a mighty comfort of patience. For this little will that thou forsakest freely thou shalt ever have thine own will in heaven. There thou shalt find whatever thou wilt and all that thou canst desire; there shall be plenty of all good without dread of losing or foregoing. There thy will, ever being one with me, shall never covet strange things nor private.

There shall no man withstand thee, there shall no man complain on thee, no man shall let (hinder) thee, no man shall contrary thee, but all things desired shall be present together and shall refresh all thy desire and shall fill it to the highest. There shall I give glory and honour for shame and reproof, a pall of praise for mourning and instead of the lowest place a seat in the kingdom for ever. There shall appear the fruit of obedience, there the labour of penance and meek subjection shall be crowned gloriously. Wherefore bow down thyself meekly under the hands of all and take no heed who said this or who commanded this; but take care of this above all whether prelate or one less than thou or one even with thee ask any thing of thee or move (apply) any thing to thee, that thou take all as good and study to fulfil it with a pure will.

Let one seek this, another that; let one rejoice in this and one in that; let one be praised a thousand thousand times; but joy thou neither in this nor in that, but in contempt of thyself and in my well pleasing and honour. This is ever to be desired of thee but both by life and death let God be ever glorified in thee.

CHAPTER LV

THAT THE DESOLATE MAN OUGHT TO OFFER HIMSELF INTO THE HANDS OF GOD

LORD God, holy father, blessed mayst thou be now and everlastingly, for as thou wilt so it is done and that thou dost is good. Glad must thy servant be in thee and not in himself nor in any other thing, for thou alone art true gladness, thou art mine hope and my crown, thou art my joy and my honour. What hath thy servant but what he hath taken of thee and that without merit of his own? All things are thine that thou hast given and that thou hast made.

I am poor and in labour from my youth up and my soul is ofttimes sorry unto tears and some times it is troubled towards itself for encumbrance of passions. I desire the joy of peace; the peace of thy sons I ask that are fed of thee in the light of consolation. If thou give peace, if thou pour on me holy joy, the soul of thy servant shall be full of and devout in thy praise.

But if thou withdraw thyself as thou art wont to do full oft, he may not run the way of thy commandments; but rather his knees are bound to knock his breast; for it is not with him as it was yesterday and the other day when thy lantern shined upon his head and he was defended under the shadow of thy wings from temptations falling upon him. Righteous father and ever to be praised, the hour is come that thy servant may be proved. Lovely father, it is worthy that this hour thy servant should suffer somewhat for thee. Father perpetually to be honoured, let thy servant live inwardly (the inner life) ever before thee whom thou knowest from the beginning to be such that he should for a little time fall outwardly (in the outer life).

For a little time let him be set little by, be meeked (humbled) and fail afore men, let him be broken with passions and languors, that he may rise again with thee in the morrow tide of a new light and be made bright in heavenly things. Holy father, thou hast so ordained and willed and that is done that thou hast commanded, for this is thy grace to thy friend in this world to suffer and to be troubled for thy love, how oft and at whose hand soever thou sufferest it to be done.

Without thy counsel and thy prudence and without cause is nothing done on earth. Good is it for me, Lord, that thou hast meeked (humbled) me, that I may learn thy laws and cast away elation of heart and presumption. It is profitable to me that shame and confusion have covered my face that I may require thee to be my comfort rather than men. I have learned hereby to dread thine inscrutable judgments that painest (punishest) the righteous man with the wicked, but not without righteousness and equity.

Lord I thank thee that thou hast not spared my evils (sins) but that thou hast bruised me with beatings, putting sorrows into me and sending anguish unto me within and without. There is none that may comfort me of all that are under heaven but thou my Lord God the heavenly leech of souls that smitest and healest, that leadest to the lowest places and bringest from thence again. Thy discipline is upon me and thy rod she shall teach me.

Lo, well beloved father, I am in thine hands. I incline me under the rod of thy correction, smite my back and my neck so that I may bow my crookedness to thy will. Make me a meek disciple, as thou art wont to do, that I may go entirely at thy beckoning. To thee I commit me and all mine, to correct; for it is better to be chastised here than in time coming. Thou knowest all things and every thing and nothing in man's conscience is hid from thee. Thou knowest things to come ere they be done, nor is there need that man teach thee or admonish thee of those things that are done on earth.

Thou knowest what is expedient for my profit and how much tribulation is needed to purge the rust of my vices. Do with me thy desired will and despise not my sinful life— to none better known nor clearer than to thee alone. Grant me, Lord, to know all that is to be known and to love all that is to be loved and to praise all that sovereignly pleaseth thee; to have in reputation that that appeareth precious to thee and to blame that is foul in thine eyes.

Suffer me not to judge after the sight of the outward eyes, nor give sentence after the hearing of ears of unlearned men, but to discern in a true judgment both of things visible and spiritual and above all things ever to inquire after the will of thy pleasure. Men's wits are ofttimes deceived in judging; as lovers of this world are ofttimes blinded in loving only things visible.

What is a man the better therefore that he is accounted greater of man? The deceivable beguileth the deceivable, the vain the vain, the blind the blind, the sick the sick whiles he lifteth him up, and truly confoundeth him more whiles he vainly praiseth him. For what any man is in thine eyes, Lord, so much he is and no more, as saith meek Francis.

CHAPTER LVI

THAT MAN MUST GIVE HIMSELF TO LOW WORKS WHEN HIGH WORKS FAIL

SON, thou mayst not always stand in the most fervent desire of virtue, nor abide stedfastly in the highest degree of contemplation; but thou hast need now and then because of original corruption to descend to lower things and bear the burden of this corruptible life against thy will and with weariness. As long as thou bearest a mortal body thou shalt find heaviness and grievance of heart. It behoveth thee therefore ofttimes in the flesh to wail under the burdens of the flesh inasmuch as thou mayst not without ceasing cleave to spiritual studies and divine contemplation.

Then it is speedful to thee to draw thyself to meek and outward works and to take recreation in good active occupations abiding my coming and the high visitation with a stedfast trust and to suffer patiently thine exile and dryness of soul till thou be visited anew and delivered from all anxieties; for I shall make thee to forget thy labours and enjoy inward quiet: I shall open before thee the meadows of the scriptures that thou with a heart may run the way of my commandments: and then thou shalt say "the sufferings of this time are not worthy to the glory that shall be revealed in us."

CHAPTER LVII

THAT MAN SHOULD ACCOUNT HIMSELF WORTHY OF NO CONSOLATION

LORD I am not worthy of any consolation nor of any spiritual visitation, and therefore thou dost righteously with me when thou forsakest me, needy and desolate. For if I could pour out tears like the sea, yet were I not worthy of thy consolation. Wherefore I am nothing more worthy than to be scourged and punished for I have ofttimes offended thee and forsaken thee greatly in many things. Wherefore, true reason peised (being weighed) I am not worthy the least consolation.

But thou gracious and merciful Lord that wilt not that thy works should perish and wilt show the riches of thy goodness in the vessels of mercy above all our merit, vouchsafe to comfort thy servant above all man's measure; for thy consolations are not as man's talkings or what have I done, Lord, that thou shouldst give me any heavenly consolation? I have no remembrance of any good that I have done but the very truth is that I have been ever ready and prone to vices and slow to amendment the which I can not deny. If I would say otherwise thou wouldst stand against me and there would no man defend me.

What have I deserved for my sins but hell and everlasting fire? I acknowledge in truth that I am worthy of all manner of scorning and despite nor it sitteth (suiteth) me not to be numbered among thy devout servants. And though I bear not this easily nevertheless for truth's sake I shall against myself reprove my sins that I may the more easily get thy mercy. What shall I say, a guilty man and full of all confusion? I have no words to speak but only this word: I have sinned, Lord, I have sinned: have mercy on me, forgive me. Suffer me a little while that I may wail my sorrow or ever I go to the dark land covered with the darkness of death.

What requirest thou most of the guilty and the wretched sinner but that he be converted and meek (humble) himself for his sins? In true contrition and meekness of heart is brought forth hope of forgiveness, the troubled conscience is reconciled, grace lost is repaired, man is defended from wrath that is to come and God and the meek soul meet in a holy kiss. Contrition for sin is to the Lord an acceptable sacrifice, smelling much sweeter than any sweet incense. This is also that acceptable ointment that thou wouldst should be poured upon thy most holy feet; for thou hast never despised the contrite and the meeked (humbled) heart. There is the place of refuge from the visage of the wrath of the enemy; there is amended and washen away all that is contract and defouled elsewhere.

CHAPTER LVIII

THAT GRACE IS NOT PART OF THEM THAT FOLLOW EARTHLY THINGS

Son, my grace is precious, suffereth not itself to be mingled with strange things nor earthly consolations. Wherefore it behoveth thee to cast away impediments to grace if thou wilt to receive the inpouring thereof. Ask for thyself a secret place, love to dwell alone with thyself, seek confabulation of none other; but rather put out to God a devout prayer that thou mayst have a devout mind and a pure conscience. Deem all the world as naught; put the vacation to (readiness for) God before all other things for thou canst not both take heed to me and delight thee in things transitory.

It behoveth thee to be eloyned (distant) from known and dear friends and keep thy mind private from all temporal solace. So beseecheth the blessed apostle Peter that all true Christian men should hold themselves in this world as strangers and pilgrims. O how great confidence shall be to the man that shall die whom affection for no earthly thing withholdeth in this world. But thus to have the heart departed from all things, a sick and a weak soul cannot understand it nor doth the beastly (natural) man know the liberty of the inward man.

Nevertheless if one would be very spiritual, it behoveth him to renounce both them that be afar and them that are nigh and of none so much to be ware as of himself. If thou overcome thyself perfectly thou shalt the more lightly put under foot all other things. It is perfect victory for a man to overcome himself. If any keep himself so under that sensuality obeys reason and reason me in all things he shall be a true victor of himself and lord of the world.

If thou desire to stie (step) up to the height of perfection thou must begin manly and set the axe to the root that thou mayst root up and destroy all inordinate affection to thyself and to all private and material good. On this vice that a man loveth himself too inordinately hangs every thing almost that is groundly (utterly) to be overcome; the which evil overcome and put under forthwith there shall be great peace and tranquillity.

But few there are that labour perfectly to die to themselves and do not fully stretch themselves beyond themselves; therefore they remain implicated and encumbered in themselves that they may not be lift up in spirit above themselves. Whoso that desireth freely to walk with me if behoveth him that he mortify all his shrewd (evil) and inordinate affections and that he cleave to no creature lustfully with any private love.

CHAPTER LIX

OF DIVERSE MOVINGS OF NATURE AND OF GRACE

Son, attend diligently to the movings of nature and of grace, for they are full contrary and subtly moved and they can scarce be perceived except it be by a spiritual man and a man inwardly illumined. All folk desire that is good and in their words and in their deeds they put forward some manner of good; wherefore many are deceived under colour of good.

Nature is wily and draweth many men and holdeth them as in a snare and deceiveth them and hath herself ever as an end, seeking none other. But grace goeth simply and declineth from all that seemeth evil, pretending no falseness or deceits and doth all things purely for God in whom finally she resteth. Nature dieth against his will, he will not be thrown down nor overcome nor be under nor willingly come under yoke; but grace laboureth and studieth to mortification of itself, she withstandeth sensuality, she seeketh to be made subject, she desireth to be overcome, she will not use her own liberty but she loveth to be under discipline, she coveteth to have lordship over nobody but to live, to stand and to be only under God, ready, for God, to be meekly inclined and bowed to every creature of mankind.

Nature laboureth for his own profit and taketh heed what lucre may come to himself alone, but grace considereth not what is profitable and advantageous to one but to many. Nature receiveth gladly honour and reverence; but grace giveth all worship and glory freely to God. Nature dreadeth shame and despite; but grace rejoiceth to suffer for the name of Jesu. Nature loveth idleness and bodily rest, but grace cannot be void or idle, but gladly taketh upon her labour and travail. Nature seeketh to have curious things and fair things and loatheth all vile things and gross things, but grace delighteth in simple things and low things and despiseth no asperity nor refuseth to be clothed in old clothes. Nature beholdeth temporal things and joyeth of earthly winnings and sorroweth for worldly harms and is moved soon to wrath with a little word of wrong; but grace attendeth everlasting things nor cleaveth not to temporal things nor is troubled with the loss of them, nor is not angered with sharp words for she setteth all her joy and her treasure in heaven where nothing perisheth.

Nature is covetous and more gladly taketh than giveth, he loveth his own and private goods; but grace is full of pity, she is common, she escheweth singular (private) things and is content with few and deemeth it more blissful to give than to take. Nature inclineth to creatures, to his own flesh, to vanities, to discourses and running about; but grace draweth to God and to virtues, renounceth creatures, fleeth the world, hateth the fleshly desires, restraineth wanderings about and is ashamed to appear in open places. Nature gladly receiveth outward comforts; but grace delighteth in the sovereign good above all things visible. Nature doth all things for his own gain and for his own profit and can do nothing freely; and if he do any benefit he will wait (expect) to have as good or better, or praise, or favour, and desireth that his deeds and his gifts should be praised and much set by. But grace seeketh no temporal things, nor seeketh none other meed but God whom solely she desireth for her reward; nor desireth she no more of temporal things than as may be helping to her to get everlasting things.

Nature rejoiceth of many friends and allies and joyeth of noble places and of great birth, laugheth upon might and power, blandisheth rich folk, and hath plesance in such as are like to himself; but grace loveth her enemies; she is not proud of multitude of friends nor accounteth place nor birth unless there be the more virtue there; she favoureth more the poor than the rich; she hath more companion in the innocent than in the mighty, she joyeth with the true man, not with the false man, and ever exhorteth to good, to seek more grace and to be like the Son of God in virtues. Nature complaineth soon of faults and of grievance but grace stedfastly beareth poverty and need. Nature reflecteth all things to himself and for himself he striveth and argueth: but grace reduceth all things to God of whom they well out groundly and originally; she ascribeth nothing that is good to herself nor presumeth nothing proudly, nor striveth not, nor preferreth not her sentence (opinion) before others, but in every feeling and in every understanding submitteth herself to the everlasting wisdom and to God's examination.

Nature coveteth to know secrets and to hear new things; he will appear outwardly and by feeling have experience of many things; he desireth to be known and to do such things of which praise and wonder may arise. But grace taketh no heed to perceive new things and curious, for all this groweth of corruption, since there is nothing new and durable upon the earth. Grace also teacheth to restrain the wits, to eschew vain plesance and ostentation, meekly to hide such things as are commendable and wonderful and in every thing and every science to seek out the fruit of profit and God's praise and his honour. Grace desireth neither herself nor her works to be preached openly, but desireth God to be blest in his gifts that granteth all things of his pure largesse.

This grace is a light supernatural and a special gift of God and a proper sign of the chosen children of God and the earnest of everlasting health; for God lifteth up man from earthly things to love heavenly things and of him that is fleshly he maketh (a) spiritual (man). Wherefore the more that nature is holden under and overcome, the more grace is poured in and the inward man is every day renewed according to the image of God with new visitations.

CHAPTER LX

OF CORRUPTION OF NATURE AND OF THE MIGHT OF GRACE

My Lord God that hast made me to thine image and likeness, grant me this grace that thou hast shown to be so great and so needful to man's health that I may overcome my most wicked nature that draweth me to sins and to perdition. For I feel in my flesh the law of sin contrarying the law of my mind and leading me as a caitiff to obey sensuality in many things; nor may I withstand his passion unless thy most holy grace passed into mine hearth be assistant to me. Needful it is to have thy grace yea and thy great grace that nature may be overcome that is ever ready to evil, of young age and youth. For nature (having) slidden and (being) vitiated by the first man Adam through sin, the pain of that spot hath come down to all men so that nature that was well and evenly made by thee is now set for (fixed in) vice and infirmity of corrupt nature, inasmuch as its movement left and abandoned to himself draweth ever to evil and to low things and that little good strength that is left is as but a little sparkle hid in ashen. This is natural reason surrounded on every side with darkness having yet judgment of good and evil and distance of (distinction between) true and false, though it be unable to fulfil that it approveth nor useth it now full light of truth or holiness of affections.

Therefore it is, my God, that after the inward man I delight me in thy law knowing thy commandment to be good and just and holy, proving also all sins and all evil to be fled, but in my flesh I serve the law of sin while I obey sensuality more than reason. Herethrough it is that to will good cometh to me, but to do it in deed I find not in me. Wherefore ofttimes I purpose many good things but for that thy grace lacketh (faileth) that should help mine infirmity, through a light resistance 1 turn back and fail. Herethrough it happeneth that though I know the way of perfection and that I see clearly what I ought to do yet I am so pressed with the weight of mine own corruption that I may not arise to more perfection.

O Lord how most necessary is grace to begin good, to profit in good and to be perfected in good. For without it I may do nothing but in thee I am mighty in all things, grace strengthening me. O that true heavenly grace, without which properly there are no merits nor no gifts of nature to be peised. Lord, without grace, as compared with thee they be of no value, neither crafts nor riches nor beauty nor strength nor wit nor eloquence. For gifts of nature are common to the good and to the evil but the proper gift of the chosen children is grace or charity wherewith he that is nobled shall be worthy everlasting life. This grace is so eminent and so excellent that neither the gift of prophecy nor working of miracles nor speculation, be it never so high, is of any estimation without her; yea, neither faith nor hope nor other virtues are acceptable to thee without grace and charity.

O thou most blissful grace, that makest the poor in spirit rich in virtue and the meek in heart rich in many goods. Come, descend unto me, fulfil me betimes with thy consolation lest my soul fail for weariness and dryness of mind. Lord I beseech thee that I may find grace in thine eyes; for thy grace sufficeth me, other things that nature desireth not being counted. If I be tempted and vexed with many tribulations I shall not dread while thy grace is with me. She is my strength, she giveth me counsel and help. She is more mighty than all enemies, she is wiser than all the wise. She is mistress of truth, teacher of discipline, light of the heart, the solace of pressure (trouble), thrower down and driver away of sorrow, taker away of dread, nourisher of devotion and bringer forth of tears. What am I without her, but a dry tree and an unprofitable stock? Wherefore, Lord, let thy grace ever more go afore me and follow me and make me to be continually and busily given to good works by our Lord Jesu Christ, thy Son.

CHAPTER LXI

THAT WE OUGHT TO DENY OURSELVES AND FOLLOW CHRIST BY THE CROSS

Son, as much as thou canst go out from thyself. As for a man to covet nothing outward maketh inward peace so for a man inwardly to forsake himself joineth and uniteth him to God. I will that thou learn perfect abnegation of thyself to my will without contradiction and complaining. Follow me: I am the way, truth and life. Without a way men go not, without truth men know not, without life men live not.

I am the way that thou shalt follow, I am the truth that thou shalt believe, and the life that thou shalt hope (for). I am the way undefouled, the truth infallible, the life interminable. I am the most even way, most sovereign truth, true life increate and life blissful. If thou dwell in my way thou shalt know truth and truth shall deliver thee and thou shalt have everlasting life.

If thou wilt live keep the commandments. If thou wilt know truth believe me. If thou will be perfect sell all things. If thou wilt be my disciple deny thyself. If thou wilt have the life that is to come despise this that is present. If thou wilt be enhanced in heaven, meek (humble) thyself in the world. If thou wilt reign with me, bear my cross; for only the servants of the cross find the way of bliss and of everlasting light.

Lord Jesu, for thy way was strait and despised of the world, grant me to follow thee with the world's despising: for the servant is no greater than his lord nor the disciple above his master. Let thy servant be exercised in thy life for there is mine health and very holiness. Whatever

I hear or read besides that, it refresheth not nor delighteth not fully.

Son, for thou hast read and knowest all these things thou art blissful if thou do them. He that hath my commandments and keepeth them he it is that loveth me and I shall love him and show myself to him and shall make him an heir in the kingdom of my father.

Lord Jesu as thou hast said and promised so be it to me and so may I deserve. I have taken from thy hand the cross and so shall I bear it to my death as thou hast laid it upon me. Verily the cross is the life of a good monk and the leader to paradise. (When) it is begun it is not lawful to go backward nor is it behoveful to forsake it. Have done, brother, go we together; Jesu shall be with us. For Jesu we have taken this cross for Jesu persevere we in the cross. He shall be our help that is our leader and our predecessor.

Lo our king goeth before us and shall fight for us. Let us follow manly, let no man dread terrors; be we ready to die bravely in battle; let us put no spot on our glory in fleeing from the cross.

CHAPTER LXII

THAT A MAN (MUST) NOT BE THROWN DOWN TOO MUCH IF HE FALL IN ANY FAULTS

Son, patience and meekness in adversity pleaseth me more than much jubilation and devotion in prosperity. Why doth a little thing said or done against thee make thee sorry? It is no new thing: it is not the first, nor shall not be the last, if thou live long. Thou art manly enough all the while no contrary cometh against thee. Thou canst counsel well and labour (prove) other men with wise words; but when a sudden tribulation cometh to thy gate, thou failest both in counsel and in strength.

Take heed to thy frailty whereof thou hast experience in many small objects and contrarinesses, nevertheless when these are all done for thine health and when they and such other happen, purpose as well as thou canst in thine heart that if they touch thee they throw thee not down nor long encumber thee; and at least suffer patiently if thou canst not suffer joyfully. And if thou canst not bear it gladly and feelest in thyself a loathing, restrain thyself and let nothing inordinate pass thy mouth that might be to the small and to the feeble an occasion of falling. The moving that would out (disturbance) shall soon rest and, grace returning again, the inward sorrow shall soon be made sweet.

Yet I live, saith our Lord, ready to help thee and comfort thee more than I am wont so that thou trust in me and inwardly and devoutly pray to me. Be mighty in soul and gird thee and make thee ready to more sufferance. It is not done idly if thou perceive thyself ofttimes troubled or grievously tempted. Thou art a man and not God, thou art flesh and no angel; how canst thou abide ever in one state of virtue, since that the first angel in heaven lacked and the first man in paradise.

I am it that reareth to health them that mourn and bring to my Godhead them that know their own infirmity.

Lord, blessed be thy word sweet to my mouth above the honey and the honeycomb. What should I do in so great tribulation and in mine anguish unless thou comfortedst me with thy holy words? If at the last I may come to the port of health what reck I what things and how great things I suffer? Grant me a good end, grant me a gracious going out of this world; have mind on me, my God and direct me in the right way to thy kingdom. Amen.

CHAPTER LXIII

HIGH THINGS AND PRIVY JUDGMENTS OF GOD MUST NOT
BE SEARCHED

Son, be ware that thou dispute not of high matters and of the privy judgments of God, why this (one) is forsaken and another is taken up to so great grace; why this (one) is greatly pained and he is so excellently lift up. These things pass all man's faculty nor is there reason nor disputation that sufficeth to search God's judgment.

Wherefore when the enemy bringeth such things to mind or else curious men ask thee, answer and say with David: Lord thou art just and thy judgment is righteous; the judgments of God are true and justified in themselves. My judgments are to be dreaded and not to be searched; for they be incomprehensible to man's understanding.

Inquire nor dispute not of the merits of saints who is holier than another or who is greater in the kingdom of heaven. Such things ofttimes engender strifes and unprofitable contentions and nourish pride and vainglory whereof grow envies and dissensions while this (man) is about proudly to prefer one saint and another, another. For a man to will to search and to know such things bringeth forth not fruit but rather displeaseth saints; for I am no God of dissension but of peace, which peace standeth more in true meekness than in selfish exaltation.

Some with a manner of zeal of love are drawn with more affection to these saints or to those saints but that affection is more of man than it is godly. I it am that made all saints and granted (them) grace. I gave glory: I know the merits of every (one); I presented them with blessings of sweetness; I predestinated them before the world; I chose them out of the world; they chose not me before; I called them by grace; I drew them by mercy; I led them by divers temptations; I poured into them great consolations; I gave perseverance; I crowned their patience.

I know the first and the last, I call them all with an inestimable love. I am to be praised in all my saints. I am to be blessed above all things and to be honoured in every one of them whom I have so graciously magnified and predestined without any merits going before. He therefore that despiseth one of my least, honoureth not the great; for I made both the great and the small. And he that doth hindering to any of my saints doth derogation to me and to all other in the kingdom of saints.

All are one by the bond of charity; they feel the same, and all one; they will the same and they all love in one. And yet what is most high of all, they love me more than themselves, and drawn out of their own love go all and wholly into love of me in whom they rest rejoicing. There is nothing that can turn them away or throw them down since they being full of everlasting truth burn in an unquenchable fire of charity.

Wherefore let fleshly and beastly (natural) men cease to dispute of the state of saints that can only love their own and private joys. They put away and add according to their own inclination not as it pleaseth the everlasting truth; in many there is ignorance and specially in those that but little illumined can seldom love anybody with perfect spiritual love. They be greatly drawn with natural affection and men's friendship to these and to those; and as they behave them in these lower things so they imagine in heavenly things.

But there is a distance incomparable between those things that imperfect men think and those that men illumined by high revelation behold. Be ware therefore son that thou treat not curiously of such things as pass thy cunning but rather tend and labour to this that thou mayst be found though it be the least in the kingdom of heaven. And if a man knew what saint were holier or greater than another in the kingdom of heaven what should that knowing avail unless a man by the same knowledge meeked (humbled) himself before me and arose to greater praise of my name?

They are much more acceptable to God that think on the greatness of their sins and of the littleness of their virtues and how far they be from the perfection of saints than they that dispute of the greatness and of the littleness of saints. Better it is to pray to saints with devout prayer and tears and to desire their glorious suffrages with a meek soul than to search their secrets with vain inquiry.

They be well content and in the best manner content if men could be content and could restrain their vain speeches. They rejoice not in their own merits, they ascribe to themselves no goodness but all to me; for I gave them all things of mine infinite charity. They are fulfilled with so great love of the Godhead and such overflowing joy that nothing faileth them of glory, nothing faileth them of bliss. All saints the higher that they are in glory the more meek they be and the nearer to me. Therefore it is written that they laid their crowns before God and fell down prostrate before the Lamb and worshipped him for ever and ever.

Many ask who is greatest in the kingdom of heaven that know not whether they shall be worthy to be accounted among the least. This is a great thing for a man to be the least in heaven where all be great and all are called the sons of God and so they shall be. When the disciples asked who was greatest in the kingdom of heaven they had this answer: Unless ye be converted and made as small children ye shall not enter into the kingdom of heaven; who ever therefore meeketh (humbleth) him as this little child he is the greatest in the kingdom of heaven.

Woe to them that disdain to meek (humble) themselves willingly as small children for the low gate of the kingdom of heaven shall not admit them to enter in. Woe also to rich men that have their consolations here; for, poor men

entering into the kingdom of heaven, they shall stand
without, wailing. Joy, ye meek folk, and be glad ye poor;
for yours is the kingdom of God so that ye go in truth.

CHAPTER LXIV

THAT ALL HOPE AND TRUST IS TO BE FIXED ONLY IN GOD

LORD what is the trust that I have in this life or what is my
greatest solace of all things appearing under heaven?
Whether not thou my Lord of whose mercy is no number? Where was it well with me without thee or when
might it be evil, thou being present? I had liever be poor
for thee than rich without thee. I choose rather to be a
pilgrim with thee in earth than to have heaven without
thee. Where thou art there is heaven: and where thou
are not there is death and hell. Thou art my desire and
therefore after thee it is needful to mourn, to cry and to
pray. I may fully trust in none that may help me in
opportune necessities but only in thee my God.

Thou art mine hope, thou art my trust, thou my comfort and
most faithful in all things. All other ask and seek their
own advantages; thou pretendest only mine health and
my profit and turnest all things to me into good. Yea
though thou lay me out to divers temptations and adversities, all that thou ordainest to my profit, that art
wont to prove thy chosen children in thousands of manners. In the which proving thou oughtest no less to be
loved and praised than if thou fulfilledst me with heavenly consolations.

In thee therefore my Lord God I put all mine hope and all
my refuge. In thee therefore I set all my tribulation and
my anguish for I find all infirm and unstable whatever
I behold outside thee. For many friends shall not avail
nor many helpers shall not be able nor many wise coun-
sellors give profitable counsel nor books of doctors give

comfort nor precious substance of good deliver nor any secret or merry place make sure if thou be not assistant helping, comforting, informing and keeping. For all things that seem to be for the getting of peace and felicity, thou being absent, are not worth nor in truth give anything belonging to true felicity.

Thou therefore art the end of all good, the height of life, the depth of scriptures; and to hope in thee above all is the most mighty solace of thy servants. To thee are mine eyes dressed (directed), my God, father of mercies. Bless and sanctify my soul with an heavenly blessing, that it may be thy holy habitation and the seat of thine everlasting glory: and that nothing be found in the temple of thy dignity that may offend the eyes of thy majesty.

Look upon me according to the greatness of thy goodness and the multitude of thy pities and hear the prayer of thy poor servant being in exile all afar in the region of the shadow of death. Defend and keep the soul of thy little servant among so many perils of this corruptible life, and, thy grace going with him, direct him by the way of peace to the country of everlasting clearness. Amen.

PART FOUR

Here beginneth the fourth book of the following Jesu Christ and of the contemning of the world. Imprinted at the commandment of the most excellent Princess Margaret mother unto our sovereign lord King Henry the VII Countess of Rychemount and Derby, and by the same Princess it was translated out of French into English in form and manner ensuing, the year of our Lord God MDiiii.

PROLOGUS

COME to me, saith our merciful Lord, all that labour and be charged and I shall give unto you refection. And the bread that I shall give unto you shall be my flesh for the life of the world. Take and eat it for it is my body that for you shall be given in sacrifice. Do ye this in remembrance of me. For whoso eateth my flesh and drinketh my blood he shall dwell in me and I in him. These words that I have said unto you be life and spirit of health.

CHAPTER I

O MY Lord Jesu Christ, eternal truth, these words before said
be thy words, albeit they have not been said in one time
nor written in one place yet for that they be thy words
I ought faithfully and agreeably to understand them.

They be thy words and thou hast proffered them; and they be
now mine for thou hast said them for my health. I will
gladly receive them from thy mouth to the end that they
may be better sown and planted in my heart. Thy words
of so great pity, full of love and sweetness, greatly excite
me; but Lord my proper sins fear and draw back my
conscience, not pure enough to receive so great a mystery.

The sweetness of thy words incite and provoke me; but the
multitude of my sins charge and sore grieve me.

Thou commandest that I shall come unto thee faithfully if
I will have part with thee to the end that I may receive
the nourishment of immortality if I desire to obtain the
joy and life eternal.

Thou sayest, Lord, "Come ye to me all that labour and be
charged and I shall refresh you."

O how sweet and amiable a word is that in the ear of a sinner
that thou, my Lord and God, listest of thy benign grace
to bid me that am so poor and have so much need to the
communion of thy precious body. O good Lord, what am
I to presume to desire thee whom the heaven and earth
may not comprehend: and thou sayest "Come ye all to
me." What is this condescension and amiable bidding?

How shall I dare come unto thee, I who feel not that I have
done any manner of good?

How shall I entertain thee in my house, I who so often have offended before thy glorious and right benign face?

The angels and archangels honour thee: the holy and just creatures dread thee and thou sayest, good Lord, "yet come ye all unto me." Lord, who should believe this thing to be true, if thyself did not say it?

And who is he that durst approach thereunto if thou didst not command it?

Noah, that just man, laboured for an hundred year to make the ark to the end that he might be saved with a few of his people. How may I prepare me then in an hour to receive thee with due reverence composer and creator of the world?

Moses, thy great familiar and special friend, made the ark of timber not corruptible which he covered with right pure gold and put in it the tables of the Law; and I, a corrupt creature how shall I now dare receive thee that are the maker of the Law and giver of grace and life unto all creatures?

The righteous Solomon, King of Israel, edified a rich temple to the praising and worshipping of thy name by the space of vii year and for viii days hallowed the feast of the dedication of the same: he offered a thousand victims to pacify thy goodness with and put the ark of the Covenant in the place made ready for the same with the sound of clarions and trumpets.

How dare I then, cursed and right poor among other creatures, receive thee into my house, I who scarce can know that I have well passed and employed one hour of time nor to my knowledge that I have devoutly passed one half hour.

O blessed Jesu, how many there have been before me that have studied to do anything that might please thee; alas, how little a thing is it that I do albeit the time is short. And yet when I dispose myself to receive thy holy communion I am but loosely gathered together and full coldly purged from all distractions of mind; and certainly no thoughts unprofitable ought to come into the holy presence of thy deity.

Also I ought not to occupy me with any creature for I shall not receive an angel but the Lord of angels into the secret of my heart.

For there is a great difference between the ark of the Covenant with his relics and the right pure and precious body with this virtues not failing but evermore enduring; and between the sacrifice of the prefigurative Law that was to come and the true victim thy precious body that is the accomplishment of all the old sacrifice.

Wherefore then should not I be more inflamed in thy venerable presence and with more solicitude prepare myself to receive the sacred and holy gifts and benefits of thee, inasmuch as the holy ancient patriarchs and prophets, kings and princes, with all the people, have showed so great affection towards thine honour and divine service in time past.

The right devout King David inclined to the ark of God with all his strength acknowledging and remembering the benefits done unto his fathers: he made organs of divers manners, and he composed psalms and instituted that they should be sung and he himself sang them with gladness and often times with the harp of the Holy Ghost. This king was inspired with the grace of God for he taught the people of Israel to praise God with all their hearts, blessing, honouring and preaching daily his holy name.

If so great devotion and remembrance was done with divine service and praise before the ark of his testament how great reverence and devotion ought we then to have in the presence of the sacrament and in the assumption of the right excellent body of our Lord Jesu Christ.

Also all Christian people use for to run to divers places for to visit the relics of saints and marvel to hear the marvellous deeds and works of them. They behold the great edifices or buildings of temples and kin the sacrificed bones of saints wrapped in cloth of silk and gold and thou my Lord God, saint of all saints, creator of all things, Lord of all angels, thou art present on this altar here before me.

Oftentimes the curiosity of men and the novelties of things not yet seen be of little fruit and less to be set by; principally where there is so light recourse to them and great wavering without any contrition; but, my God, thou art all present in this blessed sacrament of the altar, very God and man, Jesu Christ, in whom the fruit eternal of health aboundeth and is perceived at all times when thou art worthily received.

And to this not any lightness of sensual curiosity draweth us but firm faith, devout hope and pure charity.

O God invisible, creator of all the world, how marvellously dost thou with us, how faithfully dost thou with them that do purpose to receive thyself in this blessed sacrament.

Certainly it surmounteth all understanding and draweth especially the hearts of devout people to devotion and embraceth their affection; for thy true and faithful friends that dispose all their life to amend themselves receive often great grace of devotion and virtue from that most worthy sacrament.

O marvellous hid grace which all manner of faithful Christian people of our Lord Jesu Christ only know; but the infidels and subjects unto sin may thereof have no experience.

In that sacrament the spiritual graces be confirmed and the virtue that was lost in the soul is repaired and beauty, by sin wasted, is recovered.

Sometimes this grace is so great that often with the plenitude of devotion not only the mind but also the feeble body feels its might and strength augmented; wherefore it behoveth us to have sorrow and pity for our sloth and negligence that we are not drawn with so great desire and affection to receive our Lord Jesu Christ in whom is all hope and the merit of them that ought to be saved:

for he is our health and redemption and the consolation of travellers and the eternal fruition of saints.

Also we ought to have sorrow that so many understand, savour and reverence so little this holy sacrament which rejoiceth heaven and keepeth all the world.

Alas for this blindness and hardness of men's hearts that will not consider so singular and also so inestimable a gift as is given unto us but it falleth into inadvertence by daily and accustomable usage.

For if the sacrifice of this holy sacrament were done openly but in one place and but by one priest in all the world with how great desire, think ye, the people would go to that place and to that priest to hear the godly mysteries done by him; but now be made many priests and in many places this holy sacrament is offered to the end that the grace and love of God to man may the more appear forasmuch as this holy communion is spread throughout the world.

Thanks be unto thee, good pastor eternal, that hast vouchsafed to refresh and feed us poor banished creatures with thy right precious body and blood and also by the words of thine own mouth hast desired us to receive this holy mystery saying "Come ye all unto me that be charged and I will refresh you."

CHAPTER II

HOW THE GREAT CHARITY AND BOUNTY OF GOD IS SHEWED UNTO MAN IN THE HOLY SACRAMENT

O MY God, I come unto Thee putting my confidence in Thy mercy and bounty; I sigh and come unto my Saviour; I, hungry and thirsty, unto the fountain of life; poor and needy unto the King of heaven; the servant unto his Lord, the creature unto his maker, a person desolate unto his piteous comforter.

But wherefore is this that thou comest thus unto me? who am I that thou wilt give thus thine own self to me? How dare I so simple and poor a sinner be bold to appear before thee and how can it please thee to come unto such a wretch?

Thou knowest thy servant and well understandest that nothing is good in him why thou shouldst do this grace unto me.

Then do I confess my unworthiness and acknowledge thy bounty and praise thy pity and give unto thee thanks for thy so much great charity; and thou doest this for thyself, good Lord, and not for my merit, to the end that thy bounty may the more be known unto me.

Thy charity is more largely verified and thy meekness commended more perfectly since it thus pleaseth thee and also thou hast commanded it to be done; this thy pleasure contenteth me and, with my will, my wickedness shall not resist against thee.

O sweet and benign Jesu how great reverence and thanksgiving with perpetual praise be due unto thee, my good Lord, Jesu Christ, that by thy pleasure and will I may receive thy blessed body whose worthiness no man is found able to declare or express.

But what shall I think of this communion when I shall come unto thee my Lord God, which I cannot duly honour, and yet I desire devoutly to receive thee.

What may I think better and more profitable for me than to humble myself wholly before thee and to praise thine infinite bounty above all things.

I praise thee my Lord God everlasting and dispraise myself and submit me unto the deepness of my wretchedness. O my God thou art saint of all saints and I the filth of all sinners, yet thou inclinest thyself unto me that am not worthy to behold thee.

Alas my sweet creator that so meekly comest unto me and willest to be with me and desirest me unto thy dinner and givest unto me the meat of heaven and the bread of angels which is bread of life and no less thing than thyself which didst descend from heaven and give life unto the world; let us see here what great love proceedeth from thee and what gentleness doth shine upon us.

How great yieldings of thanks and love be due unto thee from us sinners. O how profitable and how healthful was thy counsel when thou didst institute and ordain this gracious gift. O how sweet and joyous is that feast wherein thou hast given unto us the feeding of thy precious body.

O good Lord how marvellous be thy operations and how mighty is thy virtue and thy truth unable to be told. Thou hast said and all things were done and all that thou hast commanded hath taken effect.

A marvellous thing to be believed and far above the understanding of man that thou, my Lord God, very God and man, art wholly contained under a little likeness of bread and wine and thou art wholly received without consuming him that so receiveth thee.

Thou, Lord of all, that hast no need of any manner of thing yet thou hast willed to inhabit within us by this thy holy sacrament. Lord, keep my heart and my body undefiled to the end that with a pure and joyous conscience I may often receive to my everlasting health these holy mysteries which be instituted and ordained chiefly unto thine honour and perpetual remembrance.

O my soul, rejoice thee and give thanks unto thy God for his noble gift and singular comfort that it will please him here in this vale of tears thus to comfort thee. For as oftentimes as thou rememberest this mystery and receivest this blessed body of our Lord, so often thou receivest the work of thy redemption and art made partner of all the merits of our Lord Jesu Christ. For his charity is never minished and the greatness of his mercy is never consumed; wherefore thou oughtest to dispose thee alway with a new revolving of thy thought and oughtest to consider this great mystery of thy health by attentive raising of thy soul.

And this work ought to be unto thee as greatly new and joyous when thou receivest it as if that same day our Lord had first descended into the womb of the Virgin Mary to be made man; or as if he that day had suffered death for the health of man upon the cross.

CHAPTER III

WHAT GREAT PROFIT IT IS OFTEN TO RECEIVE THE BODY OF OUR LORD JESU CHRIST

Lord I come unto Thee to the end that wealth may come unto me of Thy gift and that I may joy at the holy feast that Thou hast made ready unto me, poor wretch, by thy sweet benignity in the which my Saviour is all that I may or ought to desire: for Thou art my health, my redemption, my strength, honour and joy.

Alas my Lord God make thy daily servant joyous. For my Lord Jesu I have raised my soul unto thee and now desire devoutly and reverently to receive thee into my house to the end that I may deserve with Zacchaeus to be blessed of thee and to be accompted among the children of Abraham.

My soul desireth thy body, my heart desireth to be united only with thee. Give thyself unto me good Lord and then I am sufficed, for without thee no consolation nor comfort is good; without thee I may not be and without thy visitation I may not live; wherefore it behoveth me oftentimes to come and approach to thy high presence to receive thee for the remedy of my health to the intent I fail not in the way of this mortal life if I am defrauded of thy spiritual nourishing.

Also my right merciful Lord Jesu when thou hast preached unto the people and healed them of divers sickness thou hast said "I will not leave them fasting and without any refection lest peradventure they might fail in their way."

Do with me then, good Lord, in that manner since thou hast left this holy sacrament for the comfort of all faithful people; for thou art the sweet refection of the souls of them that have worthily received and eaten thee and they shall be partners and also inheritors of the eternal joy.

Certain it is unto me necessary who so often sins and so soon cools and at every hour fails to come unto the end that by continual orisons and confessions and by the receiving of thy holy body I may purify and renew the heat of my refection. For peradventure in abstaining too long to receive thee, I may leave, forget and run from my good purpose.

For the wit of man and woman from their childhood be inclined unto all evil, and also if that this divine and godly medicine help us not, innocent we fall unto worse. Then this holy communion draweth men from evil and comforteth them again in goodness for I am many times very negligent and very often cooled when that I commune or worship my God. What should I then do if I took not that medicine and asked of him grace and help?

And albeit I am not alway well disposed to receive thy creature yet shall I put me unto pain to receive those sacred mysteries in time convenient so that I may be made partner of so great grace. For it is one of the most principal and greatest consolations unto faithful souls all the time they shall make their pilgrimage in this mortal body and to the intent we may have the more mind of thy benefits.

My Lord God I shall more often receive thee, my loving Lord, with a devout thought. O marvellous gentleness of thine unspeakable pity towards us that thou, Lord God, creator and giver of life unto all spirits, hath willed to come to one so poor a soul with thy deity and humanity and hath granted to my poor lean and dry soul to be made fat

with thy grace and thy holy unction of thy sweet spirit.
O happy thought and well happy soul that deserveth devoutly
to receive his God his Lord and creator and in that
receiving to be fulfilled with joy and spiritual gladness.

O what great Lord receivest thou. O what and how great an
host entertainest thou into thy lodging, how joyous a
fellow takest thou into thy house, how faithful a friend
thou admittest unto thee, and how good noble and sweet
a spouse embracest thou which ought to be beloved and
desired above all things.

O right sweet beloved Lord, the heaven and earth and all the
ornaments of them hold silence in the presence of thy
face. For what praise, honour and beauty they have it is
of thy mercy and largeness and cannot be like unto the
honour and beauty of thy holy name and of thy wisdom,
whereof there is no number neither end.

CHAPTER IV

HOW MANY ADVANTAGES BE GIVEN UNTO THEM THAT DEVOUTLY RECEIVE THIS HOLY SACRAMENT

My Lord God I humbly beseech thee to prevent me thy
servant in the blessings of thy sweet meekness, so that
I may deserve to come worthily and devoutly to the holy
sacrament most to be magnified. Stir my heart and loose
it from the dull heaviness of my mortal body. Visit me
with the messenger of health and give me to taste thy
sweetness spiritual which is hid fully in the sacrament
as in a fountain of all sweetness. Illumine mine eyes to
behold this great mystery and strongly confirm me to
believe the faith undoubtable; for it is thy work and
not the power of man; it is thy holy ordinance and not
(done) by man's device. For there is no man found able
of himself to conceive and understand these holy mysteries which pass the subtlety of angels.

Then how may I poor unworthy sinner which am but earth and ashes search and conceive so high and holy secrecy? Lord I come unto thee in simpleness of heart and in firm faith and by thy commandment and with meek hope and reverence. And truly I believe that thou art here present in this holy sacrament, very God and man.

And thou wilt I shall receive thee and join me unto thee by charity: wherefore I humbly pray and require that it may please thee to give unto me thy special grace so that I may be all relented and flow over with thy love in such wise that I shall not desire any other consolation.

For this high worthy sacrament is the health of soul and body. It is the medicine of all spiritual sickness, in the which my sins be healed, passions be refrained, temptations be overcome and minished, more great graces be given, the virtue begun increased, faith is established, hope is made strong and fortified, charity is burning and spread abroad.

O my God the defender of my soul and the repairer of the weakness of man and the sender of all inward comfort, thou hast given and daily givest unto thy well beloved friends in this holy sacrament devoutly receiving it many advantages. For thou infusest into their souls great comfort against divers tribulations and from the depth of their own overthrowing thou arisest them to the hope of thy divine help. And with a new grace thou inwardly renewest and lightenest them in such wise that though they feel before the receiving of the sacrament heavy and dull and overthrown and without affection and moisture, of devotion after that they have been fed with this heavenly meat and drink they have found themselves changed with a marvellous joy: which things thou dost unto thy chosen people by dispensation of thy pure bounty so that they may truly know by open experience that they have nor may have nothing of themselves; and what grace or goodness they have, it cometh of thee.

For of themselves they be cold, hard and undevout but of

thee they be made fervent, joyous and devout: for who is he that cometh meekly unto the fountain of sweetness and shall not bring some little quantity of sweetness therefrom?

I shall alway put my mouth unto the hole of the heavenly pipe of that fountain so that I may at the least take a little drop to satisfy my thirst, so that I be not all dry; and though I may not be heavenly inflamed as the cherubim and seraphim yet will I enforce me to devotion and prepare my heart meekly to receive this holy loving sacrament and shall desire to be embraced with a little flame of that goodly love.

O good Jesu, holy and right piteous saviour, whatsoever virtue or goodness faileth in me I benignly beseech thee graciously of thy pity to supply it by thy great mercy. Thou that hast called all faithful creatures in saying unto them: Come ye all unto me that labour and be charged and I shall refresh you.

But alas, good Lord, I poor sinner labour in the sweat of my visage and am tormented with sorrow of heart. I am charged with sins and travailed with temptations, entricked and oppressed with many evil passions. And, Lord, there is none that may deliver me or make me safe but thou, my only God and saviour, to whom I commit me and all my causes to the end thou keep me and lead me to the life eternal.

Receive me unto the praise of thy name that hast made ready unto me thy precious body and blood for meat and drink. My Lord God and saviour grant unto me by thy great bounty that in customable (accustomed) receiving of thy holy mystery the affection and desire of my devotion may be increased.

CHAPTER V

OF THE DIGNITY OF THE SACRAMENT OF THE ALTAR AND OF THE ORDER OF PRIESTHOOD

IF THOU hadst the purity of angels and the holiness of Saint John Baptist, thou shouldst not be worthy to receive or treat of that holy sacrament: for that is not due to the merits of men that a man should consecrate and treat of the sacrament of this blessed body of Jesu Christ and take in meat the bread of angels.

O the great mystery and the marvellous dignity of priests unto whom is given that that is not granted unto the angels. For the priests only, duly ordered in the church of Christ, have power to do and to consecrate the holy body of Jesu Christ. Certainly the priest is the minister of God using the word of God by the commandment and ordinance of God.

But God is the principal and invisible worker to whom be submitted all creatures to be ordered after his will and all to obey his commandment. Then thou oughtest more to believe in almighty God and in that right excellent sacrament than in thine own will or any other visible token: And therefore to this holy work thou oughtest to come with great dread and reverence.

Take good heed then and see from whom this mystery is given unto thee and that is by the putting to of the hands of the Bishop thou art admitted unto that high room. Behold now thou art made a priest and consecrated to do this holy mystery. See then that faithfully and devoutly and in due time thou offer thy sacrifices unto God and show thyself irreprovable and without fault.

Thou hast not loosed thy charge (lightened thy burden) of living but hast bound thee with a more strait bond of discipline and art holden to a more great perfection of holiness. Also the priest ought to be adorned with all virtues and to give to all their example of good and holy life.

His conversation ought not to be with common people or the ways of common men but with the angels in heaven or with the perfect men in the earth. The priest clothed with holy vestments occupieth the room of our Lord Jesu Christ to the end that he may right humbly pray unto God for himself and also for all others. For he hath both before him and behind him the very sign of the cross that he may continually remember the passion of our Lord Jesu Christ. Before him he beareth the cross to the end that he may diligently behold the traces and the example of our Lord Jesu Christ and that he may fervently study to follow them. Behind him also he is signed with the cross to the intent he should suffer for the honour of God all adversities and injuries done unto him of other. Before him he beareth the cross for that he should bewail properly his sins; and behind him likewise to sorrow with great compassion for the sins of others and to know himself that he is a man between God and the sinner: And that he should depart not from orison and from that holy oblation till he deserves to purchase the grace of God. When the priest saith mass he honoureth God, he giveth joy unto the angels, he edifieth the church, he helpeth the loving people, he giveth rest to them that be passed and maketh himself partner of all good works.

CHAPTER VI

AN INWARD REMEMBRANCE AND EXERCISE THAT A MAN OUGHT
TO HAVE AFORE THE RECEIVING OF THE BODY OF OUR
LORD JESU CHRIST

LORD when I think of thy worthiness and of my great filthiness I tremble strongly and am confounded in myself. For if I receive thee not I flee the eternal life and if I unworthily receive thee I run into thy wrath. What shall I then do, my good Lord, my helper, protector, comforter, and right sure counsellor in all mine infirmities and necessities? Teach me good Lord thy right way, and purpose unto me some exercise fit to the receiving of this holy mystery. For it is necessary unto me and greatly profitable to know how devoutly and reverently I ought to prepare my heart to receive this holy sacrament or to make so goodly sacrifice.

CHAPTER VII

THE REMEMBERING OF HIS OWN CONSCIENCE WITH PURPOSE OF AMENDMENT

THE priest above all things ought to desire with sovereign reverence and profound meekness of heart, full and firm faith, humble hope and piteous (pious) intent to the honour of God to celebrate, take and receive this worthy sacrament, to examine diligently and make clear and open the conscience by true contrition and make confession as far as he hath power, so that thou know nothing that grieves thee or bites thy said conscience or lets (hinders) thee freely to come unto the same daily.

To have displeasure of all thy sins in general and for thine excesses and sins thou oughtest to have sighing and sorrow more special. And if the time suffer it confess unto God in secret of thy heart the miseries of all thy passions, weep and have sorrow that thou art yet so carnal and worldly and so ill mortified from thy passions, so full of motions and lusts, so ill composed and ordered in thy outward wits, so often applied unto vain fantasies, so much inclined unto outward things, so negligent in the inward spiritual things, so ready to laughter and to all dissolution, so hard to weep and to compunction, so ready to follow the loose manner and the pleasures of the flesh, so slow and dull to the fervour of virtue, so curious to behold and to hear new fair things, so negligent and loath to learn and desire things that be meek and abject, so covetous to receive and possess many goods, and so scarce (sparing) to give them and glad to hold and retain them, so evil advised in speaking and so incontinent to be still, so unordered in manners, so importune in thy deeds, so greedy and so quick in thy meat, so deaf unto the word of God, so ready to rest, so unhasty to labour, so waking to fables, so sleepy to holy vigils, so negligent unto the service of God, so speedy to the end thereof, so wavering to take heed, so cold in devotion in the time of the mass, so dry in receiving of the sacrament, so soon withdrawn, so seldom well gathered unto thyself, so suddenly moved unto wrath, so easily stirred to the displeasure of others, so hasty to judge, so rough in reproving, so joyous in prosperity, so weak in adversity, so often purposing many good things and bringing little to effect.

These and other thy defaults with sorrow and great displeasure of thine own frailty must be confessed and sorrowfully be wept. Set thee then with full purpose always to amend thyself and to perfect thee from better unto better; and, after, offer thyself with plain resignation and entire will to the honour of my name a perpetual sacrifice within the altar of thine heart.

Then, thy soul and body commit faithfully unto me, that thou so may deserve worthily to come and offer thy sacrifice to God and to receive the sacrament of my body healthfully. For no oblation is more worthy and no satisfaction can be so great for to deface the sins of man as to offer himself to God purely and entirely with the oblation of the holy body of Christ Jesu in the mass and the holy communion.

And they who ever shall do as much as lieth in them and have true repentance of their offences past, as oft as they shall come unto me, they shall recover pardon and grace.

I am Life and will not the death of a sinner, but rather will that he return and live again. And then will I no more remember his sins and trespass but all shall be forgiven and pardoned unto him.

CHAPTER VIII

OF THE OBLATION OF JESU CHRIST ON THE CROSS; OF THE PROPER RESIGNATION THAT MAN SHOULD MAKE OF HIMSELF

O MAN, as I did offer myself and my free-will unto God my father, my hands spread on the cross, and my body naked for thy sins; insomuch that nothing remained in me, but all passed in sacrifice to appease His wrath, in like wise thou oughtest to offer unto me willingly thyself in pure oblation daily in the mass with all thine affections and strengths, as profoundly and fervently as thou mayest.

What ask I of thee more but that thou study to resign thyself unto me entirely? What thing so ever thou givest me else I care not for.

For I demand not thy gifts but only thyself.

As nothing should suffice thee without me, likewise nothing may please me what soever thou shalt give if thou offer not thyself to me.

Offer thee then, give thee wholly unto me: and that oblation shall be acceptable.

Behold I did offer myself wholly unto my father for thee, and for thee I did give all my body and blood, to the end that I should be all wholly thine, and thou mine also.

But and if thou rest in thyself and present thee not with good will unto me then there is no full oblation neither entire perfect union between us; for the free oblation of thyself into the hands of almighty God ought to go before all thy works, if thou wouldst obtain liberty and grace.

And the lack of this is the cause that so few folk be illumined and have inward liberty, for they cannot renounce themselves.

My sentence is firm and stable, that none may be my disciple,
without he renounceth all that he hath.

Then if thou desire to be my disciple offer thyself unto me
with all thine affection.

CHAPTER IX

THAT WE OUGHT TO OFFER UNTO GOD ALL THAT WE HAVE; AND TO PRAY FOR ALL PEOPLE

LORD, all things that be in heaven and in earth be thine, and
my willing desire is to offer me unto thee perpetually in
oblation, so that I may be thine everlastingly.

And this day, good Lord, I offer unto thee myself perpetually
for ever more to be thy servant with my heart and soul
fully to continue. I beseech thee receive this holy oblation
of me that am unworthy to offer me unto thy precious
body in the presence of angels assisting invisible, to the
end that it may be to the health of one and all thy people.
Lord I also offer unto thee all my sins which I have committed before thee and thy holy angels since the first day
I began or in any wise might sin unto this present day.
And I beseech thee to inflame me with the burning fire of
charity and to deface and put away all the conditions of
my sins. Cleanse my conscience from all sin and restore
it unto thy grace which by sin I have lost. And perfectly
pardon me of all mine offences that I may receive perfectly the sweet kiss of peace. What can I do more for
my sins but meekly confess them with sorrowful weeping
and incessantly praying to thee of thy piteous mercy?

I beseech thee Lord exalt me and be ready unto me when I
am before thee. O my good Lord greatly all my sins displease me and by thy grace I will never begin them
again; but ever shall have sorrow for them as long as I
shall live and shall be ready to do penance and make
satisfaction to the best of my little power. Wherefore now

good Lord pardon me of my great and abominable sins and for the honour of thy holy name save my soul which thou hast dearly bought with thy most precious blood. And I commit me good Lord unto thy great mercy and resign me wholly unto thy hands. Do with me Lord after thy bounty and not after my malice and iniquity.

Also I offer unto thee all my deeds that I have done albeit they be full few and imperfect that thou mayst sanctify and amend them as they be agreeable and acceptable unto thee. And always good Lord draw me from better to better and conduct and lead me slothful and unworthy sinner unto a good and lawful end.

In like wise I offer unto thee the desires of all devout persons, the necessities of my kinsfolk and friends and of all them that have done me good or be dear unto me and all other for thy love, and they that have desired or required me to make sacrifice for their friends, living or past the world, so that they may feel help, Consolation, Defence, and Preservation from all perils, and deliverance of pains by thy grace so that they may yield unto thee joy and gladness with magnifying and praise for their deliverance.

I offer unto thee also prayer and holy oblations for all them specially that have caused unto me heaviness, hurt, or any manner of damage; and likewise for them that I have troubled, grieved, vexed or slandered in words or deeds, knowingly or ignorantly, to the end, blessed Lord, that we all may be pardoned of our offences done the one against the other. And good Lord Jesu take from our heart all suspicion, wrath and indignation, and all that may break or let (hinder) charity, or diminish us from thine eternal love.

O Lord, have pity; blessed Jesu, have pity; and give thy mercy unto all them that ask it and thy grace unto them that have need. And make us so worthy to have thy grace that we may go unto the life eternal. Amen.

CHAPTER X

THAT THE HOLY SACRAMENT OUGHT NOT LIGHTLY TO BE FORBORNE

IT BEHOVETH thee often to return unto the fountain of grace, mercy, bounty, pity and purity that thou mayst be cleansed from thy vices and passions, so that thou mayst be made more strong and waking against all temptations and subtle crafts of the fiend.

For thine enemy knowing the great fruit and remedy in receiving of this holy sacrament, striveth, by all manner of occasions that he may, to draw thee unto him again and hindereth the faithful and devout people when any dispose them to the receiving of this holy communion.

The enemy, Satan, putteth to them the most grievous temptations that he may. Also, it is written in the history of Job, this evil spirit cometh among the children of God to the end that by his cursed custom he perturbeth, perplexeth and maketh them fearful, diminishing their affection and impugning them of their faith, so that peradventure they leave their good purpose in respect of that holy body which they at that time come for to receive.

But we should take no thought nor fear of the crafty wiles of that false enemy that be so foul and horrible, but all such fantasies we should cast again at the head of that wicked spirit.

It is a poor mischievous spirit, that so letteth (hindereth) and mocketh us; and for any assaults or commotions that he exciteth, this holy sacrament ought not to be left.

Also oftentimes too great solicitude for devotion hindereth us, and sometimes seriousness about the confession to be made. But do after the counsel of the wise and take away this anxiety and stryple (scruple): for it hindereth the grace of God and destroyeth devotion.

And leave not the holy receiving of Jesu Christ for little tribulation, dejection or faint heart; but with good will go to the confessor, and pardon all other that have offended thee; and if thou have offended any other, meekly ask forgiveness. And then dread not but God will pardon *thee*.

What profiteth it long to tarry from confession or to defer the receiving of thy blessed saviour? First purge thee and cast out the venom and then haste thee to take the remedy, and thou shalt feel the much better than if thou hadst deferred it.

For if thou this day leave the holy receiving for coldness of devotion and feebleness of mind, peradventure to-morrow thou shalt find thyself more slack, and withdraw so long that thou shalt find thyself much worse and more unable.

Then as soon as thou mayst take away this feebleness of mind and the spice (species) of sloth; for to be always only in anguish and heaviness for thy sin, passing the time in tribulation and because of daily obstacles and imperfections to withdraw thee from these divine mysteries without turning unto the pitiful merit of our saviour Christ Jesu, this profiteth thee not.

But the long tarrying to receive thy saviour annoyeth thee greatly and maketh thee slow and shall bring daily unto thee a greater slothfulness.

But, alas for sorrow, some cold and desolate persons gladly seek reasons for tarrying from confession and from the receiving of this holy sacrament; because they covet many delays lest they shall be bound to give themselves to a stricter manner in the ordering of their life.

Alas how little charity and how slender devotion have they that put away so easily the receiving of this holy sacrament.

O how happy be they and agreeable unto almighty God who lead so holy a life that they keep their conscience in clean and pure fear, so that they may daily dispose themselves and make them ready and with great affection desire to receive that holy sacrament at all times, if it were lawful.

Nevertheless sometimes by meekness to abstain or for other lawful causes that may hinder reverence, this is to be praised.

But if sloth or negligence keep him back he ought to endeavour himself as far as in him is, and our Lord shall be present to his desire and will specially behold his good will; but when he is lawfully hindered and have a good will and pious mind to receive his maker, he shall not fail to have the fruit of that blessed sacrament.

For every person with perfect devotion may every day receive that holy sacrament spiritually to his health and without prohibition; and in certain times and days established he ought to receive the body of his saviour with effectual reverence sacramentally; and to seek and do it more to the praise and honour of God almighty than to his own consolation.

For as often as he spiritually is communed and refreshed invisibly so often he remembreth devoutly the mystery of the incarnation of Christ and his painful passion and is kindled in love of him; he that otherwise prepareth not himself except at the time of a great feast or else when compelled by custom he shall oftentimes be full unready.

Blessed is he that offers himself unto almighty God as oft as he doth the mass or else receives this honourable sacrament.

And in doing this mystery, tarry not nor be too hasty but keep the common manner with such as thou livest among. Thou oughtest not to do so that the hearers thereof take grief or irksomeness but keep the common way after the ordinances of the holy fathers. And rather conform thee to the profit of others than to thine own devotion or private pleasure.

CHAPTER XI

HOW THE BLESSED BODY OF OUR LORD JESU CHRIST IS
GREATLY NECESSARY FOR THE HEALTH OF MAN'S SOUL

O RIGHT sweet Jesu how great consolation and sweetness is
it to a devout soul to eat with thee at thy dinner where
none other meat is given but thyself which art the only
lover and oughtest to be desired above all desires of man's
heart: and how sweet a thing should it be in thy presence from the bottom of the heart to send out tears, to
dew and wash thy precious feet with the piteous Mag-
dalen. But where is that devotion or the plenteous effu-
sion of holy tears?

Certainly in beholding thee with thy holy angels all my heart
ought to burn and weep with joy: for I have verily thee
present, though thou be hid under a strange likeness, for
mine eyes may not suffer to behold thee in thy proper
and godly clearness: nor might all the world abide to
behold the clearness of thy joy and majesty.

Wherefore, good Lord, thou helpest my weakness in that it
pleaseth thee to cover thyself under the form of that holy
sacrament.

I verily worship thee whom the angels worship in heaven, but
in me it is as yet but in faith and the angels worship thee
there in thine own likeness without coverture.

I must be content with true faith and so walk till the day
come of eternal clearness when the shadow of figures shall
vanish; for when that perfect day shall come the usage
of this holy sacrament shall cease.

For they that be blessed in heavenly joy shall have no need
of any sacramental medicine: for they shall joy without end in the presence of God, seeing him in his glory
face to face and shall be transformed from clearness unto
clearness with the Godhead incomprehensible: they shall

taste the son of God made man as he was from the beginning and shall be everlastingly.

I then remembering me of the great marvels and solace though it be spiritual, it is to me grievous when I remember those marvels. For all things that I hear or see in this world I count as nothing so long as I see not my Lord God in his glory.

Lord God, thou art my witness that nothing can give me comfort nor no creature may give me rest but thou my Lord God whom I desire eternally to behold.

But that is a thing to me not possible while that I am in this mortal life; wherefore it behoveth me with great patience to order myself and meekly to submit me unto thee in all my desires.

Good Lord, the saints that now joy with thee in the kingdom of heaven abode the coming of the joy with great faith and patience as long as they lived.

I believe the same that they did believe, and hope as they have hoped, and trust by the means of thy grace to come thither as they now be.

In the meanwhile I shall in good and fast faith be comforted by examples of holy saints. Also I have full virtuous and holy books for the consolation and mirror of my life and also above all these things thy sacred body for my singular refuge and remedy. I feel that two things be unto me right necessary without which this miserable life should be unto me inportable. For as long as I shall be holden in this present body I confess me to have need of two things, that is to know (say) of meat and light.

But therefore thou hast given unto me which am poor and sick thy holy body to the refreshing of my soul and body, and also thou hast put before my faith the light of thy holy word; and without these two things I may not well live spiritually; for thy word, my Lord and God, is the light of my soul and the holy sacrament is the bread of my life.

These two things so necessary may also be called the tables

set on either side in the treasury of holy church; the one table is of the holy altar having this lovely bread, that is to say, the precious body of Jesu Christ; the other is the law of God containing the holy doctrine and showing the right faith and surely guiding me unto the inward sacrifice where are the holy jewels called Sancta Sanctorum (Holy of Holies).

I yield unto thee thanks Lord Jesu Christ which art the very clearness of eternal light for this table of holy doctrine which thou hast ministered unto us by thy servants, prophets, apostles and other doctors; and I yield unto thee thanks again, creator and redeemer of mankind, which hast declared thy great charity unto all the world and hast prepared this royal supper in the which thou hast not purposed to be eaten the figurative lamb but thy most holy body and precious blood rejoicing all thy creatures by that sacred banquet and sweetly fulfilling them with that healthful chalice, wherein be hid all the delights and joys of Paradise; and the holy angels be fed with us with sweetness very plenteous.

O how great and honourable is the office of priests to whom is given power to consecrate by divine words, to bless with their lips, to hold with their hands, receive with their mouths and to minister unto other the Lord and God of all majesty. O how clean ought to be the hands, how pure the mouth, how holy the body and how undefiled the heart of a priest unto whom so often entereth the author of all purity.

Certainly from the mouth of a priest ought no word to proceed but that which is honest and profitable, that so often receiveth sacrament of the holy body of Jesu Christ; his eyes ought to be simple and shamefast that so customably behold the holy body; the hands pure to lift up unto heaven which handle the creator of heaven and earth. For specially for a priest it is said in the law, Be ye holy for I your Lord God am holy. O God omnipotent thy grace be helping unto us that we which have taken the office of priesthood may reverently and devoutly serve thee with all purity and good conscience and if we may not live in so great innocency of life as we ought to do, give us grace at the least that we may weep and sorrow for the evils that we have committed and done, so that in spiritual meekness and purpose of good will we may from henceforth strongly serve thee with fervent courage.

CHAPTER XII

WITH HOW GREAT DILIGENCE HE OUGHT TO PREPARE HIMSELF THAT SHOULD RECEIVE THE SACRAMENT OF CHRIST

OUR Lord saith: I the lover of purity and the liberal giver of all holiness, I search the pure clean heart and there will I rest. Make ready then for me thine heart and I shall be with thee then as I was with my disciples at Easter (the Passover).

I shall come and dwell with thee if thou wilt, but then it behoveth thee to purify and cleanse the habitation of thine heart from all sins, leave all bruit (sound) and noise of the world with all thy vices, and inclose and shut thee in thy chamber, as doth a solitary bird under the evesings (eaves) of a house, and remember all the excuses and all thy defaults committed; remember them with all thy soul and with bitterness of heart.

For a good friend will make ready for his well beloved friend a good and a pleasant place to dwell in and in doing that it is well known with what good affection he receiveth his said friend.

It is for truth that thou oughtest to understand that thou canst not give satisfaction by any merit or labour of thyself, not and if thou diddest labour with the best of thy power by a whole year, though thou haddest none other thing to do.

But thou shalt understand that by my power only and grace it is permitted and granted unto thee to come to my table and that if a poor man were called unto the table of a rich lord and the poor man had none other thing to give again for the benefit of that rich man but sweetly and meekly to thank him, he would do it.

So oughtest thou to do diligently as much as is in thee and not by custom or necessity, but with all dread, reverence and affection thou oughtest to take the blessed body of our Lord God since that it pleaseth him to come unto thee.

Certainly I am he that calleth thee and I have commanded it so to be done and I shall supply that which faileth in thee; wherefore come and receive me and when in doing that I give unto thee grace of devotion, yield thou thanks unto me thy God, not thinking that thou art worthy thereof of thyself but that I have had mercy on thee.

And if thou have not that grace when thou wouldest but feel thyself dry and unlusty, yet continue thine orison with sorrowful weeping and smite at my door without ceasing unto the time that thou mayst receive a little crumb or drop of healthful grace and know of a truth thou hast much need of me and I have none of thee.

Thou comest not to sanctify me but I am he that shall sanctify thee and make thee better to the end that thou mayst be united with me to receive new grace and to purpose amendment.

Be not willing to defer my grace but with all diligence prepare thine heart to receive within thee thy loving Lord. And not only prepare thee before thy communion, but also maintain and keep thee after the receiving of thy said holy sacrament in that same devotion in as much as thou mayst: for thou oughtest to have no less diligence than thou hadst afore.

For the good and diligent keeping of thy soul after the receiving of the blessed sacrament is a good preparation to obtain greater grace. And they that do not so, show themselves greatly evil-disposed when they abandon themselves so soon and so largely to outward solace and inward pleasures.

Wherefore keep thee from great bruit (sound) and speaking and abide in the secret graces and fruits of thy God, for thou hast him that all the world may not take away; and I am he to whom thou oughtest to give thyself in such manner that from henceforth thou live no more in thyself but in me only.

CHAPTER XIII

HOW THE DEVOUT SOUL OUGHT EFFECTUALLY WITH ALL HIS HEART TO BE UNITED UNTO JESU CHRIST

O LORD who shall grant me that I may find thee alone and that I may open to thee all my heart and joy with thee as my poor soul desireth and that here there be no creature to behold me but thou alone to speak to me and I to thee, good Lord, as of custom one friend speaketh to another secretly.

This I desire and pray thee, Lord Jesu, that I may be fully united unto thee and withdraw my heart from all other created things, that I may the sooner learn the eternal and heavenly things by means of the receiving of this holy sacrament.

Alas, my good Lord, when shall I be united and gathered all wholly in thee and utterly forget myself? Thou art in me and I with thee and thus assembled make us dwell together I pray thee.

Truly thou art my chosen and beloved Lord and it hath pleased thy benign grace to be inhabited in my soul all the days of my life. Thou art my peacemaker in whom is sovereign peace and true rest; without thee there is nothing but labour, sorrow and infinite misery.

Thou my God are closed and hid and thy counsel is not shared by evil folks: but thy familiar speaking is with the meek and simple folks.

O Lord, how good, benign and sweet is thy spirit which, that thou mayst show unto the sons and children thy sweetness, hast vouched safe to refresh them again and gives to them refection of thy right sweet bread descended from heaven.

Certainly there is none other so great a nation, lacking Christ's faith, that hath their gods so near unto them as thou art, our God and Lord, to all thy faithful Christian people to whom thou givest thy blessed body to eat for their daily comfort and to raise their hearts to high celestial things. O what other folks be there so noble as the Christian people or what creature is there so strongly beloved under heaven as is the devout soul in whom God entereth and giveth feeding with his own glorious flesh and blood.

O grace inestimable and marvellous worthiness. O love without measure singularly shewed unto man. But what shall I yield unto God? and wherewith shall I recompense this so great grace and charity? Truly there is nothing I may give more agreeable to his mercy than to join my heart perfectly unto him.

And when my soul shall be perfectly united with him, then shall all my inward parts rejoice and then my Lord will say unto me, If thou wilt be with me I will be with thee. And I shall answer him, Blessed Lord I beseech thee dwell with me, for all the desire of my heart is to be with thee inseparable without departing.

CHAPTER XIV

OF THE BURNING DESIRE THAT SOME CREATURES HAVE TO THE BLESSED BODY OF OUR LORD JESU CHRIST

O LORD, how great is the multitude of thy sweetness which thou hast hid for them that dread thee. When I remember me of many devout persons that have come to this thy holy sacrament with so great fervent affection and devotion I am then many times in myself confused and have great shame that I go unto the altar and table of that holy communion so rudely, with so cold devotion and am so dry without affection of heart.

I am abashed that I am not all wholly inflamed in thy presence and so strongly drawn and established as many good devout persons have been, which by the great desire of this holy sacrament and sensible love of heart might not contain nor withhold them from weeping, but effectually with mouth, heart and body come unto that good Lord as to the living fountain of all bounty and may not attain to fulfil their hunger unless they take thy holy body which they so desirously and spiritually may receive.

O true and benign faith of them that prevably (truly) show the proof of thy holy presence; to them is verily known their God in the breaking of bread which burneth and broileth so strongly the heart of them in the love of Jesu Christ: certainly such affection, devotion and vehement burning love is far from me.

O good sweet and benign Jesu be unto me piteous and ready to give and grant to thy poor beggar sometimes to feel a little of that hearty love and affection in the receiving of thy holy body to the end that my faith may be more firm and my hope more perfect in thy bounty; and my charity sometime so perfectly inflamed that I may experiently have the heavenly manna that never may fail: I know certainly the might of thy mercy may lend me thy grace so much desired and visit me burningly with a burning spirit when the day of thy good pleasure shall come. And though I be not inflamed with so great a desire of thy special devout things yet have I desire by thy grace to be inflamed with that burning love, praying the good Lord that I may be made partner with all such thy fervent lovers and that I may be numbered in their devout company. Amen.

CHAPTER XV

HOW MEEKLY THOU OUGHTEST TO BESEECH THE GRACE OF DEVOTION AND TO RENOUNCE THYSELF

IT BEHOVETH thee instantly to seek the grace of devotion and to ask incessantly, to abide it patiently and faithfully, joyously to receive it and meekly to conserve it, and with that studiously to remit unto God the time and the manner of his sovereign visitation unto the time his pleasure be to come unto thee: and principally thou oughtest to meek (humble) thee when thou feelest but little devotion within thee: and for all that thou oughtest not to let thyself to fall or sorrow too much inordinately: for full often our blessed Lord in a short moment giveth thee which before he hath long time denied: also sometime he giveth at the end of prayers that he did defer at the beginning of the same.

If alway grace were so soon given that a man might have it at his will or wish, it should not be easily borne of a weak and imperfect soul. And therefore in good hope and meek patience the grace of devotion ought to be abided (waited for) and thou oughtest to impute it unto thyself and to thy sins when it is not given unto thee or when it is secretly taken away from thee. Some time a little thing it is that may let (hinder) or hide thy grace if that may be called little that letteth (hindreth) so great avail (good).

But be it little or great if thou take that same away and
perfectly overcome it thou shalt obtain that thou desirest
as soon as thou with all thy heart hast given thyself to
God. And therefore seek not this nor that at thy pleasure
but put the whole in the hand of God and thou shalt
certainly find thyself right with him and in great peace
of soul; for there is nothing that ought to be so savoury
and pleasant as is the pleasure and divine will of God.

Then whosoever lifteth up his intent unto God with a simple
perfect heart and so voideth and maketh him naked of all
disordinate love or pleasure to any created things in all
the world he is most meet to receive the gift of devotion;
for our Lord gave his blessing there where he found the
vessels clean and void; and the more perfectly that any
renounce, mortify, despise and contemn themselves and
all the low things, the sooner grace shall enter and copi-
ously abound so that he shall feel his heart lift up as
though it were set in freedom and then he shall see his
heart largely abound and marvellously joy within himself, for that the hand of God shall be over him and he
shall submit him perpetually into his holy hands.

And so shall the man be blessed that seeketh God with all
his heart and his soul shall not be taken in vain works:
but such an one certainly in the receiving the holy body
of Jesu Christ meriteth and deserveth the grace of divine
union with God. For he beholdeth not only his own devotion and consolation but the great honour and glory
of God.

CHAPTER XVI

HOW WE OUGHT TO SHOW OUR NECESSITIES UNTO JESU CHRIST AND ASK OF HIM BENIGN GRACE

O RIGHT sweet and most beloved Lord whom I now desire
to receive, thou, good Lord, knowest the sickness of
soul and necessity that I suffer, in what evils and vices

I sleeping am put, how often grieved, tempted, troubled and dissolute. I come unto thee, Lord, to have consolation and comfort. I speak to thee Lord; thou knowest all my secret and inward thoughts which be manifest and open unto thee. It is thou only that perfectly mayst help me, for thou knowest what unto me is necessary and of what goods above all other I have most need.

Albeit I am poor in virtue, alas, yet, merciful Lord, behold me here before thee poor and naked, demanding piteously thy sweet grace and mercy. And give thy poor beggar that dieth for hunger some of thy heavenly refection and chafe my cold heart with the burning flame of thy love. Illumine me that am blinded and cannot see with the clearness of thy presence; take away from my thought all the earthly and inward things and turn them into, and make me think them, foul and bitter and grievous and contrary unto me.

And that I may take pleasure in the things that may please thee; and all earthly created things may I have in oblivion and turn my heart towards thee in heaven. And let me not waver nor err upon earth but be thou only my sweetness and consolation, my meat and drink, my love and all my joy; so that my will be changed, inflamed, and burn all towards thee; so that I may be made a spirit and inwardly united unto thee by grace and burning love.

And suffer me not, blessed saviour, to depart from thee fasting and dry with hunger and thirst, but do with me mercifully as often thou hast marvellously done with thy holy servants.

What marvel it is to me that I am not all inflamed in thee seeing that thou art the burning fire always illumining and lightening the understanding of thy creatures.

CHAPTER XVII

OF THE BURNING LOVE AND GREAT AFFECTION THAT WE
SHOULD HAVE TO RECEIVE OUR SAVIOUR CHRIST JESU

O Lord God, in sovereign devotion, burning love and all
fervent affection of heart I desire as many other holy and
devout persons have desired to receive, who have been
greatly pleasant by the holiness of their life and by great
devotion.

O my God and eternal love and my eternal felicity I by right
great desire wish to receive thee as worthily and as
reverently as ever did any of thy holy servants. Albeit
that I am not worthy to have so great feelings of devotion, yet offer I unto thee the affections of my heart as
truly as though I had all the burning and flaming desires
that they had.

Also I give and offer unto thee in sovereign reverence and
veneration all that a good debonair heart may contain.
And I will not nor do I covet to reserve anything to myself but I offer and make sacrifice unto thee with free
and perfect will of myself with all my goods.

Lord God, my creator and redeemer, this day I desire to
receive thee with such affection, reverence, praise,
honour, worthiness and love and with such faith hope
and purity as thy right holy mother and glorious Virgin
Mary who conceived thee, when she answered meekly
and devoutly unto the angel that showed unto her the
holy mystery of the incarnation of thee, the son of God,
"See here the handmaid of God; so be it done as thou
hast said."

And the right excellent precursor St. John Baptist that with
great joy sprang in thy presence by inspiration of the
Holy Ghost, then being in the womb of his mother; and
afterward beholding thee Jesu walking meekly among
men, he greatly humbling himself to the same with a

devout mind said: "The friend of the spouse standeth and hearkneth and with comfort rejoiceth for to hear the voice of the spouse." So I wish to be inflamed with great and holy desire and with all my heart present me unto thee.

And I give and offer unto thee for me all the jubilations of devout hearts with burning affections, the excessive thoughts, the high and spiritual illuminations and the heavenly visions with all the virtues and praises, as well celebrated as those which shall be celebrated, of all the creatures of heaven and earth; to the end that thou, Lord, be worthily praised and be perpetually glorified of all creatures; beseeching thee, Lord, to receive my prayers and my desire for thine infinite benediction and praises without end which rightly be due unto thee according to the great abundance and multitude of thine inestimable magnificence. And so my desire is to yield unto thee at all hours and all moments of time; and so I desire and beseech all the heavenly spirits with all faithful Christian creatures to yield unto thee praises with effectual prayers.

All the universal people praise thee. All generations and kinds magnify thy holy and sweet name in great joy and burning devotion, and I pray that they who celebrate that right high and holy sacrament and receive it in plain faith and great reverence and devotion may merit well towards thee and find grace and mercy.

And for me, wretched sinner, I meekly beseech thee, when I shall have a taste of that sweet union and devotion so much wished and desired that I may be fulfilled and fed so marvellously at that heavenly and holy table that at my departing from thence, thou, good Lord, wilt have me, poor sinner, in thy piteous remembrance.

CHAPTER XVIII

THAT A MAN SHOULD NOT BE TOO CURIOUS AN INQUISITOR
OF THAT HOLY SACRAMENT, BUT A MEEK FOLLOWER
OF CHRIST JESU IN SUBMITTING HIS REASON AND
FEELING TO THE HOLY FAITH

IT BEHOVES thee to keep thee from too curious inquisition of
the right deep sacrament if thou wilt not be confounded
in thine own fault and drowned in the depth of opinions.
For he that will inquire of the high majesty of God, he
shall anon be oppressed and thrust down from the glory
of the same. God may open more than man may understand.

The devout and meek inquiry of truth is always ready to be
instructed and taught; and if thou study to go by the
holy and entire sentences of holy fathers, it is not re-
provable but well to be praised. And that simpleness is
well to be praised which leaveth the ways of difficulties
and questions and goeth by the plain and firm path of
the commandments of God. Many have lost their devotion in seeking so busily high unspeakable things.

It is enough to demand of thee fast faith, pure and clean life,
and not the high and subtle profound mysteries of God;
for if thou canst not comprehend and understand that
which is within thee, how canst thou then understand
things that be above thee?

Submit thee then meekly unto God and all thy understanding
to the faith of holy church; and the light of true science
shall be given unto thee such as shall be to thee most
necessary and profitable.

Some be greatly tempted with the faith of that holy sacrament but that is not to be reputed (set down) unto them
but rather unto that cursed enemy the fiend.

And therefore care not nor dispute not in thy thoughts nor
answer not to the doubts that the enemy of hell bringeth

before thee; but firmly trust in the words of God and believe in saints and holy prophets and then shall that cursed enemy soon fly from thee. It is often profitable that the servants of God suffer and sustain such assaults; for the enemy tempteth not the miscreants and unfaithful people, nor also the great sinners that he surely holdeth and possesseth; but he tempteth, travaileth and tormenteth in divers manners the good faithful and Christian creatures.

And therefore keep thee always with meek true faith and doubt thee not but come unto this holy sacrament with long reverence, and that thou canst not understand commit unto almighty God for he shall not deceive thee but he shall be deceived that too much trusteth in himself.

God walked with the simple people and showed himself openly unto the meek; he gave understanding unto them that were poor in spirit, and hid his grace and secrets from them that were proud, high and curious.

For the human reason may lightly err and be deceived but the true faith may never deceive nor fail. All reason and natural inquiry ought to follow the true faith without further reasoning. Fast faith and true love surmounteth all curious inquiry principally in this matter and marvellously openeth to an understanding in secret manner of this holy and right excellent sacrament.

O eternal God and without measure of height and bounty, which hast made the infinite great and wonderful things in the heaven and earth, none is sufficient to inquire into, understand or find the secrets of thy so marvellous works; and therefore they be called inestimable for man's reason neither may nor can comprehend thy works; to whom Lord God almighty be given laud and praise, without end. Amen.

Thus endeth the fourth book following
Jesu Christ and the contemning
of the world.

RELIGIO MEDICI

BY SIR THOMAS BROWNE

TO THE READER

CERTAINLY that man were greedy of Life, who should desire to live when all the world were at an end; and he must needs be very impatient, who would repine at death in the society of all things that suffer under it. Had not almost every man suffered by the Press, or were not the tyranny thereof become universal, I had not wanted reason for complaint: but in times wherein I have lived to behold the highest perversion of that excellent invention, the name of his Majesty defamed, the Honour of Parliament depraved, the Writings of both depravedly, anticipatively, counterfeitly imprinted; complaints may seem ridiculous in private persons; and men of my condition may be as incapable of affronts, as hopeless of their reparations. And truely, had not the duty I owe unto the importunity of friends, and the allegiance I must ever acknowledge unto truth, prevailed with me, the inactivity of my disposition might have made these sufferings continual, and time, that brings other things to light, should have satisfied me in the remedy of its oblivion. But because things evidently false are not onely printed, but many things of truth most falsely set forth, in this latter I could not but think my self engaged: for, though we have no power to redress the former, yet in the other the reparation being within our selves, I have at present represented unto the world a full and intended Copy of that Piece, which was most imperfectly and surreptitiously published before.

This, I confess, about seven years past, with some others of affinity thereto, for my private exercise and satisfaction, I had at leisurable hours composed; which being communicated unto one, it became common unto many, and was by Transcription successively corrupted, untill it arrived in a most depraved Copy at the Press. He that shall peruse that work, and shall take notice of sundry particularities and personal expressions therein, will easily discern the intention was not publick; and, being a private Exercise directed to my self, what is delivered therein, was rather a memorial unto *me*, than an Example or Rule unto any other; and therefore, if there be any singularity therein correspondent unto the private conceptions of any man, it doth not advantage them; or if dissentaneous thereunto, it no way overthrows them. It was penned in such a place, and with such disadvantage, that, (I protest), from the first setting of pen unto paper, I had not the assistance of any good Book whereby to promote my invention or relieve my memory; and therefore there might be many real lapses therein, which others might take notice of, and more than I suspected my self. It was set down many years past, and was the sense of my conceptions at that time, not an immutable Law unto my advancing judgement at all times; and therefore there might be many things therein plausible unto my passed apprehension, which are not agreeable unto my present self. There are many things delivered Rhetorically, many expressions therein meerly Tropical, and as they best illustrate my intention; and therefore also there are many things to be taken in a soft and flexible sense, and not to be called unto the rigid test of Reason. Lastly, all that is contained therein is in submission unto maturer discernments; and, as I have declared, shall no further father them than the best and learned judgments shall authorize them: under favour of which considerations I have made its secrecy publick, and committed the truth thereof to every Ingenious Reader.

THO. BROWNE.

RELIGIO MEDICI

THE FIRST PART

FOR my Religion, though there be several Circumstances that
might perswade the World I have none at all, (as the general
scandal of my Profession, the natural course of my Studies,
the indifferency of my Behaviour and Discourse in matters of
Religion, neither violently Defending one, nor with that
common ardour and contention Opposing another); yet, in
despight hereof, I dare without usurpation assume the honourable Stile of a Christian. Not that I meerly owe this Title
to the Font, my Education, or the clime wherein I was born,
(as being bred up either to confirm those Principles my Parents instilled into my unwary Understanding, or by a general
consent proceed in the Religion of my Country); but having
in my riper years and confirmed Judgment seen and examined
all, I find my self obliged by the Principles of Grace, and the
Law of mine own Reason, to embrace no other Name but this.
Neither doth herein my zeal so far make me forget the general
Charity I owe unto Humanity, as rather to hate than pity
Turks, Infidels, and (what is worse), Jews; rather contenting
my self to enjoy that happy Stile, than maligning those who
refuse so glorious a Title.

But, because the Name of a Christian is become too general to express our Faith, (there being a Geography of Religions as well as Lands, and every Clime distinguished not
only by their Laws and Limits, but circumscribed by their
Doctrines and Rules of Faith); to be particular, I am of that
Reformed new-cast Religion, wherein I dislike nothing but
the Name; of the same belief our Saviour taught, the Apostles
disseminated, the Fathers authorized, and the Martyrs confirmed; but by the sinister ends of Princes, the ambition and

avarice of Prelates, and the fatal corruption of times, so decayed, impaired, and fallen from its native Beauty, that it required the careful and charitable hands of these times to restore it to its primitive Integrity. Now the accidental occasion whereupon, the slender means whereby, the low and abject condition of the Person by whom so good a work was set on foot, which in our Adversaries beget contempt and scorn, fills me with wonder, and is the very same Objection the insolent Pagans first cast at CHRIST and His Disciples.

Yet have I not so shaken hands with those desperate Resolutions, (who had rather venture at large their decayed bottom, than bring her in to be new trimm'd in the Dock; who had rather promiscuously retain all, than abridge any, and obstinately be what they are, than what they have been), as to stand in Diameter and Swords point with them. We have reformed from them, not against them; for (omitting those Improperations and Terms of Scurrility betwixt us, which only difference our Affections, and not our Cause), there is between us one common Name and Appelation, one Faith and necessary body of Principles common to us both; and therefore I am not scrupulous to converse and live with them, to enter their Churches in defect of ours, and either pray with them, or for them. I could never perceive any rational Consequence from those many Texts which prohibit the Children of Israel to pollute themselves with the Temples of the Heathens; we being all Christians, and not divided by such detested impieties as might prophane our Prayers, or the place wherein we make them; or that a resolved Conscience may not adore her Creator any where, especially in places devoted to His Service; where, if *their* Devotions offend Him, mine may please Him; if theirs prophane it, mine may hallow it. Holy-water and Crucifix (dangerous to the common people), deceive not my judgment, nor abuse my devotion at all. I am, I confess, naturally inclined to that which misguided Zeal terms *Superstition*. My common conversation I do acknowledge austere, my behaviour full of rigour, sometimes not without morosity; yet at my Devotion I love to use the civility of my knee, my hat, and hand, with all those outward and sensible motions which may express or promote my invisible Devotion. I should violate my own arm rather than a Church; nor willingly deface the name of Saint or Martyr. At the sight of a Cross or Crucifix I can dispense with my hat, but scarce with the thought or memory of my Saviour. I cannot laugh at, but rather pity, the fruitless journeys of Pilgrims, or contemn the miserable condition of Fryars; for, though misplaced in Circumstances, there is something in it of Devotion. I could never hear the Ave-Mary Bell without an elevation; or think it a sufficient warrant, because *they* erred in one circumstance, for me to err in all, that is, in silence and dumb contempt. Whilst, therefore, they directed their Devotions to *Her*, I offered mine to GOD, and rectified the Errors of their Prayers by rightly ordering mine own. At a solemn Procession I have wept abundantly, while my consorts, blind with opposition and prejudice, have fallen into an excess of scorn and laughter. There are, questionless, both in Greek, Roman, and African Churches, Solemnities and Ceremonies, whereof the wiser Zeals do make a Christian use, and stand condemned by us, not as evil in themselves, but as allurements and baits of superstition to those vulgar heads that look asquint on the face of Truth, and those unstable Judgments that cannot consist in the narrow point and centre of Virtue without a reel or stagger to the Circumference.

As there were many Reformers, so likewise many Reformations; every Country proceeding in a particular way and method, according as their national Interest, together with their Constitution and Clime, inclined them; some angrily, and with extremity; others calmly, and with mediocrity; not rending, but easily dividing the community, and leaving an honest possibility of a reconciliation; which though peaceable Spirits do desire, and may conceive that revolution of time and the mercies of GOD may effect, yet that judgment that shall consider the present antipathies between the two extreams, their contrarieties in condition, affection, and opinion,

may with the same hopes expect an union in the Poles of
Heaven.

But (to difference my self nearer, and draw into a lesser Circle), there is no Church whose every part so squares unto my
Conscience; whose Articles, Constitutions, and Customs seems
so consonant unto reason, and as it were framed to my particular Devotion, as this whereof I hold my Belief, the Church
of England; to whose Faith I am a sworn Subject, and therefore in a double Obligation subscribe unto her Articles, and
endeavour to observe her Constitutions. Whatsoever is beyond, as points indifferent, I observe according to the rules
of my private reason, or the humour and fashion of my
Devotion; neither believing this, because Luther affirmed it,
or disproving that, because Calvin hath disavouched it. I
condemn not all things in the Council of Trent, nor approve
all in the Synod of Dort. In brief, where the Scripture is silent,
the Church is my Text; where that speaks, 'tis but my Comment: where there is a joynt silence of both, I borrow not the
rules of my Religion from Rome or Geneva, but the dictates
of my own reason. It is an unjust scandal of our adversaries,
and a gross errour in our selves, to compute the Nativity of
our Religion from Henry the Eighth, who, though he rejected
the Pope, refus'd not the faith of Rome, and effected no more
than what his own Predecessors desired and assayed in Ages
past, and was conceived the State of Venice would have at-
tempted in our days. It is as uncharitable a point in *us* to
fall upon those popular scurrilities and opprobrious scoffs of
the Bishop of Rome, to whom, as a temporal Prince, we owe
the duty of good language. I confess there is cause of passion
between us: by his sentence I stand excommunicated; *Heretick*
is the best language he affords me; yet can no ear witness I
ever returned him the name of *Antichrist, Man of Sin,* or
Whore of Babylon. It is the method of Charity to suffer without reaction: those usual Satyrs and invectives of the Pulpit
may perchance produce a good effect on the vulgar, whose ears
are opener to Rhetorick than Logick; yet do they in no wise
confirm the faith of wiser Believers, who know that a good

cause needs not to be patron'd by passion, but can sustain it self upon a temperate dispute.

I could never divide my self from any man upon the difference of an opinion, or be angry with his judgment for not agreeing with me in that from which perhaps within a few days I should dissent my self. I have no Genius to disputes in Religion, and have often thought it wisdom to decline them, especially upon a disadvantage, or when the cause of Truth might suffer in the weekness of my patronage. Where we desire to be informed, 'tis good to contest with men above our selves; but to confirm and establish our opinions, 'tis best to argue with judgments below our own, that the frequent spoils and Victories over their reasons may settle in ourselves an esteem and confirmed Opinion of our own. Every man is not a proper Champion for Truth, nor fit to take up the Gauntlet in the cause of Verity: many, from the ignorance of these Maximes, and an inconsiderate Zeal unto Truth, have too rashly charged the troops of Error, and remain as Trophies unto the enemies of Truth. A man may be in as just possession of Truth as of a City, and yet be forced to surrender; 'tis therefore far better to enjoy her with peace, than to hazzard her on a battle. If, therefore, there rise any doubts in my way, I do forget them, or at least defer them till my better settled judgement and more manly reason be able to resolve them; for I perceive every man's own reason in his best Œdipus, and will, upon a reasonable truce, find a way to loose those bonds wherewith the subtleties of error have enchained our more flexible and tender judgements. In Philosophy, where Truth seems double-fac'd, there is no man more Paradoxical than my self: but in Divinity I love to keep the Road; and, though not in an implicite, yet an humble faith, follow the great wheel of the Church, by which I move, not reserving any proper Poles or motion from the Epicycle of my own brain. By this means I leave no gap for Heresies, Schismes, or Errors, of which at present I hope I shall not injure Truth to say I have no taint or tincture. I must confess my greener studies have been polluted with two or three; not any begotten in the latter

Centuries, but old and obsolete, such as could never have been revived, but by such extravagant and irregular heads as mine: for indeed Heresies perish not with their Authors, but, like the river Arethusa, though they lose their currents in one place, they rise up again in another. One General Council is not able to extirpate one single Heresie: it may be cancell'd for the present; but revolution of time, and the like aspects from Heaven, will restore it, when it will flourish till it be condemned again. For as though there were a Metempsuchosis, and the soul of one man passed into another, Opinions do find, after certain Revolutions, men and minds like those that first begat them. To see our selves again, we need not look for Plato's year: every man is not only himself; there hath been many Diogenes, and as many Timons, though but few of that name: men are liv'd over again, the world is now as it was in Ages past; there was none then, but there hath been some one since that parallels him, and is, as it were, his revived self.

Now the first of mine was that of the Arabians, That the Souls of men perished with their Bodies, but should yet be raised again at the last day. Not that I did absolutely conceive a mortality of the Soul; but if that were, (which Faith, not Philosophy, hath yet throughly disproved), and that both entred the grave together, yet I held the same conceit thereof that we all do of the body, that it should rise again. Surely it is but the merits of our unworthy Natures, if we sleep in darkness until the last Alarum. A serious reflex upon my own unworthiness did make me backward from challenging this prerogative of my Soul: so that I might enjoy my Saviour at the last, I could with patience be nothing almost unto Eternity.

The second was that of Origen, That GOD would not persist in His vengeance for ever, but after a definite time of His wrath, He would release the damned Souls from torture. Which error I fell into upon a serious contemplation of the great Attribute of GOD, His Mercy; and did a little cherish it in my self, because I found therein no malice, and a ready weight to sway me from the other extream of despair, where-unto Melancholy and Contemplative Natures are too easily disposed.

A third there is, which I did never positively maintain or practise, but have often wished it had been consonant to Truth, and not offensive to my Religion, and that is, the Prayer for the Dead; whereunto I was inclin'd from some charitable inducements, whereby I could scarce contain my Prayers for a friend at the ringing of a Bell, or behold his Corps without an Orison for his Soul. 'Twas a good way, methought, to be remembred by posterity, and far more noble than an History.

These opinions I never maintained with pertinacy, or en-deavoured to enveagle any mans belief unto mine, nor so much as ever revealed or disputed them with my dearest friends; by which means I neither propagated them in others, nor confirmed them in my self; but suffering them to flame upon their own substance, without addition of new fuel, they went out insensibly of themselves. Therefore these Opinions, though condemned by lawful Councels, were not Heresies in me, but bare Errors, and single Lapses of my understanding, without a joynt depravity of my will. Those have not onely depraved understandings, but diseased affections, which can-not enjoy a singularity without an Heresie, or be the Author of an Opinion without they be of a Sect also. This was the villany of the first Schism of Lucifer, who was not content to err alone, but drew into his Faction many Legions of Spirits; and upon this experience he tempted only Eve, as well under-standing the Communicable nature of Sin, and that to deceive but one, was tacitely and upon consequence to delude them both.

That Heresies should arise, we have the Prophesie of CHRIST; but that old ones should be abolished, we hold no prediction. That there must be Heresies, is true, not only in our Church, but also in any other: even in doctrines heretical, there will be super-heresies; and Arians not only divided from their Church, but also among themselves. For heads that are disposed unto Schism and complexionally propense to innovation, are naturally indisposed for a community, nor will be ever confined unto the order or œconomy of one body; and, therefore, when they separate from others, they knit but loosely among themselves; nor contented with a general breach or dichotomy with their Church do subdivide and mince themselves almost into Atoms. 'Tis true, that men of singular parts and humours have not been free from singular opinions and conceits in all Ages; retaining something, not only beside the opinion of his own Church or any other, but also any particular Author; which, notwithstanding, a sober Judgment may do without offence or heresie; for there is yet, after all the Decrees of Councils and the niceties of the Schools, many things untouch'd, unimagin'd, wherein the liberty of an honest reason may play and expatiate with security, and far without the circle of an Heresie.

As for those wingy Mysteries in Divinity, and airy subtleties in Religion, which have unhing'd the brains of better heads, they never stretched the *Pia Mater* of mine. Methinks there be not impossibilities enough in Religion for an active faith; the deepest Mysteries ours contains have not only been illustrated, but maintained, by Syllogism and the rule of Reason. I love to lose my self in a mystery, to pursue my Reason to an *O altitudo!* 'Tis my solitary recreation to pose my apprehension with those involved Ænigmas and riddles of the Trinity, with Incarnation, and Resurrection. I can answer all the Objections of Satan and my rebellious reason with that odd resolution I learned of Tertullian, *Certum est, quia impossibile est*. I desire to exercise my faith in the difficultest point; for to credit ordinary and visible objects is not faith, but perswasion. Some believe the better for seeing Christ's Sepulchre; and, when they have seen the Red Sea, doubt not of the Miracle. Now, contrarily, I bless my self and am thankful that I lived not in the days of Miracles, that I never saw Christ nor His Disciples. I would not have been one of those Israelites that pass'd the Red Sea, nor one of Christ's patients on whom He wrought His wonders; then had my faith been thrust upon me, nor should I enjoy that greater blessing pronounced to all that believe and saw not. 'Tis an easie and necessary belief, to credit what our eye and sense hath examined. I believe He was dead, and buried, and rose again; and desire to see Him in His glory, rather than to contemplate Him in His Cenotaphe or Sepulchre. Nor is this much to believe; as we have reason, we owe this faith unto History: *they* only had the advantage of a bold and noble Faith, who lived before His coming, who upon obscure prophesies and mystical Types could raise a belief, and expect apparent impossibilities.

'Tis true, there is an edge in all firm belief, and with an easie Metaphor we may say, the *Sword* of Faith; but in these obscurities I rather use it in the adjunct the Apostle gives it, a *Buckler;* under which I conceive a wary combatant may lye invulnerable. Since I was of understanding to know we knew nothing, my reason hath been more pliable to the will of Faith; I am now content to understand a mystery without a rigid definition, in an easie and Platonick description. That allegorical description of Hermes pleaseth me beyond all the Metaphysical definitions of Divines. Where I cannot satisfy my reason, I love to humour my fancy: I had as live you tell me that *anima est angelus hominis, est Corpus* DEI, as *Entelechia;—Lux est umbra* DEI, as *actus perspicui.* Where there is an obscurity too deep for our Reason, 'tis good to sit down with a description, periphrasis, or adumbration; for by acquainting our Reason how unable it is to display the visible and obvious effects of Nature, it becomes more humble and submissive unto the subtleties of Faith; and thus I teach my haggard and unreclaimed Reason to stoop unto the lure of Faith. I believe there was already a tree whose fruit our unhappy Parents tasted, though, in the same Chapter when GOD forbids it, 'tis positively said, the plants of the field were not yet grown, *for* GOD *had not caus'd it to rain upon the earth.* I believe that the Serpent, (if we shall literally understand it), from his proper form and figure, made his motion on his belly before the curse. I find the tryal of the Pucellage and virginity of Women, which GOD ordained the Jews, is very fallible. Experience and History informs me, that not onely many particular Women, but likewise whole Nations, have escaped the curse of Childbirth, which GOD seems to pronounce upon the whole Sex. Yet do I believe that all this is true, which indeed my Reason would perswade me to be false; and this I think is no vulgar part of Faith, to believe a thing not only above but contrary to Reason, and against the Arguments of our proper Senses.

In my solitary and retired imagination

> (*neque enim cum porticus aut me*
> *Lectulus accepit, desum mihi,*)

I remember I am not alone, and therefore forget not to contemplate Him and His Attributes Who is ever with me, especially those two mighty ones, His Wisdom and Eternity. With the one I recreate, with the other I confound, my understanding; for who can speak of Eternity without a solœcism, or think thereof without an Extasie? Time we may comprehend; 'tis but five days elder then our selves, and hath the same Horoscope with the World; but to retire so far back as to apprehend a beginning, to give such an infinite start forwards as to conceive an end, in an essence that we affirm hath neither the one nor the other, it puts my Reason to St. Paul's Sanctuary. My Philosophy dares not say the Angels can do it. GOD hath not made a Creature that can comprehend Him; 'tis a privilege of His own nature. I AM THAT I AM, was His own definition unto Moses; and 'twas a short one, to confound mortality, that durst question GOD, or ask Him what He was. Indeed, He onely is; all others have and shall be. But in Eternity there is no distinction of Tenses; and therefore that terrible term *Predestination*, which hath troubled so many weak heads to conceive, and the wisest to explain, is in respect to GOD no prescious determination of our Estates to come, but a definitive blast of His Will already fulfilled, and at the instant that He first decreed it; for to His Eternity, which is indivisible and all together, the last

Trump is already sounded, the reprobates in the flame, and the blessed in Abraham's bosome. St. Peter speaks modestly, when he saith, *a thousand years to* GOD *are but as one day;* for, to speak like a Philosopher, those continued instances of time which flow into a thousand years, make not to Him one moment: what to us is to come, to His Eternity is present, His whole duration being but one permanent point, without Succession, Parts, Flux, or Division.

There is no Attribute that adds more difficulty to the mystery of the Trinity, where, though in a relative way of Father and Son, we must deny a priority. I wonder how Aristotle could conceive the World eternal, or how he could make good two Eternities. His similitude of a Triangle comprehended in a square doth somewhat illustrate the Trinity of our Souls, and that the Triple Unity of GOD; for there is in us not three, but a Trinity of Souls; because there is in us, if not three distinct Souls, yet differing faculties, that can and do subsist apart in different Subjects, and yet in us are so united as to make but one Soul and substance. If one Soul were so perfect as to inform three distinct Bodies, that were a petty Trinity: conceive the distinct number of three, not divided nor separated by the intellect, but actually comprehended in its Unity, and that is a perfect Trinity. I have often admired the mystical way of Pythagoras, and the secret Magick of numbers. *Beware of Philosophy*, is a precept not to be received in too large a sense; for in this Mass of Nature there is a set of things that carry in their Front (though not in Capital Letters, yet in Stenography and short Characters), something of Divinity, which to wiser Reasons serve as Luminaries in the Abyss of Knowledge, and to judicious beliefs as Scales and Roundles to mount the Pinacles and highest pieces of Divinity. The severe Schools shall never laugh me out of the Philosophy of Hermes, that this visible World is but a Picture of the invisible, wherein, as in a Pourtraict, things are not truely, but in equivocal shapes, and as they counterfeit some more real substance in that invisible fabrick.

That other Attribute wherewith I recreate my devotion,

is His Wisdom, in which I am happy; and for the contemplation of this only, do not repent me that I was bred in the way of Study: the advantage I have of the vulgar, with the content and happiness I conceive therein, is an ample recompence for all my endeavours, in what part of knowledge soever. Wisdom is His most beauteous Attribute; no man can attain unto it, yet Solomon pleased GOD when he desired it. He is wise, because He knows all things; and He knoweth all things, because He made them all: but His greatest knowledge is in comprehending *that* He made not, that is, Himself. And this is also the greatest knowledge in man. For this do I honour my own profession, and embrace the Counsel even of the Devil himself: had he read such a Lecture in Paradise as he did at Delphos, we had better known our selves, nor had we stood in fear to know *him*. I know He is wise in all, wonderful in what we conceive, but far more in what we comprehend not; for we behold Him but asquint, upon reflex or shadow; our understanding is dimmer than Moses Eye; we are ignorant of the back-parts or lower side of His Divinity; therefore to prie into the maze of His Counsels is not only folly in man, but presumption even in Angels. Like us, they are His Servants, not His Senators; He holds no Counsel, but that mystical one of the Trinity, wherein, though there be three Persons, there is but one mind that decrees without contradiction. Nor needs He any: His actions are not begot with deliberation, His Wisdom naturally knows what's best; His intellect stands ready fraught with the superlative and purest Ideas of goodness; consultation and election, which are two motions in us, make but one in Him, His actions springing from His power at the first touch of His will. These are Contemplations metaphysical: my humble speculations have another Method, and are content to trace and discover those expressions He hath left in His Creatures, and the obvious effects of Nature. There is no danger to profound these mysteries, no *sanctum sanctorum* in Philosophy. The World was made to be inhabited by Beasts, but studied and contemplated by Man: 'tis the Debt of our Reason we owe unto

GOD, and the homage we pay for not being Beasts. Without this, the World is still as though it had not been, or as it was before the sixth day, when as yet there was not a Creature that could conceive or say there was a World. The Wisdom of GOD receives small honour from those vulgar Heads that rudely stare about, and with a gross rusticity admire His works: those highly magnifie Him, whose judicious inquiry into His Acts, and deliberate research into His Creatures, return the duty of a devout and learned admiration. Therefore,

> Search while thou wilt, and let thy Reason go,
> To ransome Truth, even to th' Abyss below;
> Rally the scattered Causes; and that line,
> Which Nature twists, be able to untwine.
> It is thy Makers will, for unto none
> But unto Reason can He e'er be known.
> The Devils do know Thee, but those damnèd Meteors
> Build not Thy Glory, but confound Thy Creatures.
> Teach my indeavours so Thy works to read,
> That learning them in Thee, I may proceed.
> Give Thou my reason that instructive flight,
> Whose weary wings may on Thy hands still light.
> Teach me to soar aloft, yet ever so
> When neer the Sun, to stoop again below.
> Thus shall my humble Feathers safely hover,
> And, though near Earth, more than the Heavens discover.
> And then at last, when homeward I shall drive,
> Rich with the Spoils of Nature, to my Hive,
> There will I sit like that industrious Flie,
> Buzzing Thy praises, which shall never die,
> Till Death abrupts them, and succeeding Glory
> Bid me go on in a more lasting story.

And this is almost all wherein an humble Creature may endeavour to requite and some way to retribute unto his Creator: for if *not he that saith, "Lord, Lord," but he that doth the will of his Father, shall be saved;* certainly our wills must be our performances, and our intents make out our Actions; otherwise our pious labours shall find anxiety in our Graves, and our best endeavours not hope, but fear, a resurrection.

There is but one first cause, and four second causes of all things. Some are without efficient, as God; others without matter, as Angels; some without form, as the first matter: but every Essence, created or uncreated, hath its final cause, and some positive end both of its Essence and Operation. This is the cause I grope after in the works of Nature; on this hangs the Providence of God. To raise so beauteous a structure as the World and the Creatures thereof, was but His Art; but their sundry and divided operations, with their predestinated ends, are from the Treasure of His Wisdom. In the causes, nature, and affections of the Eclipses of the Sun and Moon, there is most excellent speculation; but to profound farther, and to contemplate a reason why His Providence hath so disposed and ordered their motions in that vast circle as to conjoyn and obscure each other, is a sweeter piece of Reason, and a diviner point of Philosophy. Therefore sometimes, and in some things, there appears to me as much Divinity in Galen his books *De Usu Partium*, as in Suarez Metaphysicks. Had Aristotle been as curious in the enquiry of this cause as he was of the other, he had not left behind him an imperfect piece of Philosophy, but an absolute tract of Divinity.

Natura nihil agit frustra, is the only indisputed Axiome in Philosophy. There are no Grotesques in Nature; not anything framed to fill up empty Cantons, and unnecessary spaces. In the most imperfect Creatures, and such as were not preserved in the Ark, but, having their Seeds and Principles in the womb of Nature, are everywhere, where the power of the Sun is, in these is the Wisdom of His hand discovered. Out of this rank Solomon chose the object of his admiration. Indeed, what Reason may not go to School to the wisdom of Bees, Ants, and Spiders? what wise hand teacheth *them* to do what Reason cannot teach *us?* Ruder heads stand amazed at those prodigious pieces of Nature, Whales, Elephants, Dromidaries and Camels; these, I confess, are the Colossus and majestick pieces of her hand: but in these narrow Engines there is more curious Mathematicks; and the civility of these little Citizens more neatly sets forth the Wisdom of their Maker. Who admires not Regio-Montanus his Fly beyond his Eagle, or wonders not more at the operation of two Souls in those little Bodies, than but one in the Trunk of a Cedar? I could never content my contemplation with those general pieces of wonder, the Flux and Reflux of the Sea, the increase of Nile, the conversion of the Needle to the North; and have studied to match and parallel those in the more obvious and neglected pieces of Nature, which without further travel I can do in the Cosmography of myself. We carry with us the wonders we seek without us: there is all Africa and her prodigies in us; we are that bold and adventurous piece of Nature, which he that studies wisely learns in a compendium what others labour at in a divided piece and endless volume.

Thus there are two Books from whence I collect my Divinity; besides that written one of GOD, another of His servant Nature, that universal and publick Manuscript, that lies expans'd unto the Eyes of all: those that never saw him in the one, have discover'd Him in the other. This was the Scripture and Theology of the Heathens: the natural motion of the Sun made *them* more admire Him than its supernatural station did the Children of Israel; the ordinary effects of Nature wrought more admiration in *them* than in the other all His Miracles. Surely the Heathens knew better how to joyn and read these mystical Letters than we Christians, who cast a more careless Eye on these common Hieroglyphicks, and disdain to suck Divinity from the flowers of Nature. Nor do I so forget GOD as to adore the name of Nature; which I define not, with the Schools, to be the principle of motion and rest, but that streight and regular line, that settled and constant course the Wisdom of GOD hath ordained the actions of His creatures, according to their several kinds. To make a revolution every day is the Nature of the Sun, because of that necessary course which GOD hath ordained it, from which it cannot swerve but by a faculty from that voice which first did give it motion. Now this course of Nature GOD seldome alters or perverts, but, like an excellent Artist, hath so contrived His work, that with the self same instrument, without a new creation, He may effect His obscurest designs. Thus He sweetneth the Water with a Wood, preserveth the Creatures in the Ark, which the blast of His mouth might have as easily created; for GOD is like a skilful Geometrician, who, when more easily and with one stroak of his Compass he might describe or divide a right line, had yet rather do this in a circle or longer way, according to the constituted and fore-laid principles of his Art. Yet this rule of His He doth sometimes pervert, to acquaint the World with His Prerogative, lest the arrogancy of our reason should question His power, and conclude He could not. And thus I call the effects of Nature the works of GOD, Whose hand and instrument she only is; and therefore to ascribe His actions unto her, is to devolve the honour of the principal agent upon the instrument; which if with reason we may do, then let our hammers rise up and boast they have built our houses, and our pens receive the honour of our writings. I hold there is a general beauty in the works of GOD, and therefore no deformity in any kind or species of creature whatsoever. I cannot tell by what Logick we call a Toad, a Bear, or an Elephant ugly; they being created in those outward shapes and figures which best express the actions of their inward forms, and having past that general Visitation of GOD, Who saw that all that He had made was good, that is, conformable to His Will, which abhors deformity, and is the rule of order and beauty. There is no deformity but in Monstrosity; wherein, notwithstanding, there is a kind of Beauty; Nature so ingeniously contriving the irregular parts, as they become sometimes more remarkable than the principal Fabrick. To speak yet more narrowly, there was never any thing ugly or mis-shapen, but the Chaos; wherein, notwithstanding, (to speak strictly), there was no deformity, because no form; nor was it yet impregnant by the voice of GOD. Now Nature is not at variance with Art, nor Art with Nature, they being both servants of His Providence. Art is the perfection of Nature. Were the World now as it was the sixth day, there were yet a Chaos. Nature hath made one World, and Art another. In brief, all things are artificial; for Nature is the Art of GOD.

* This is the ordinary and open way of His Providence, which Art and Industry have in a good part discovered; whose effects we may foretel without an Oracle: to foreshew these, is not Prophesie, but Prognostication. There is another way, full of Meanders and Labyrinths, whereof the Devil and Spirits have no exact Ephemerides; and that is a more particular and obscure method of His Providence, directing the operations of individuals and single Essences: this we call *Fortune,* that serpentine and crooked line, whereby He draws those actions His Wisdom intends, in a more unknown and secret way. This cryptick and involved method of His Providence have I ever admired; nor can I relate the History of my life, the occurrences of my days, the escapes of dangers, and hits of chance, with a *Bezo las Manos* to Fortune, or a bare *Gramercy* to my good Stars. Abraham might have thought the Ram in the thicket came thither by accident; humane reason would have said that meer chance conveyed Moses in the Ark to the sight of Pharaoh's Daughter: what a Labyrinth is there in the story of Joseph, able to convert a Stoick! Surely there are in every man's Life certain rubs, doublings, and wrenches, which pass a while under the effects of chance, but at the last, well examined, prove the meer hand of GOD. 'Twas not dumb chance, that, to discover the Fougade or Powder-plot, contrived a miscarriage in the Letter. I like the Victory of '88 the better for that one occurrence, which our enemies imputed to our dishonour and the partiality of Fortune, to wit, the tempests and contrariety of Winds. King Philip did not detract from the Nation, when he said, *he sent his Armado to fight with men, and not to combate with the Winds.* Where there is a manifest disproportion between the powers and forces of two several agents, upon a Maxime of reason we may promise the victory to the Superior; but when unexpected accidents slip in, and unthought of occurrences intervene, these must proceed from a power that owes no obedience to those Axioms; where, as in the writing upon the wall, we may behold the hand, but see not the spring that moves it. The success of that petty Province of Holland (of which the Grand Seignour proudly said, *if they should trouble him as they did the Spaniard, he would send his men with shovels and pick-axes, and throw it into the Sea*), I cannot altogether ascribe to the ingenuity and industry of the people, but the mercy of GOD, that hath disposed them to such a thriving Genius; and to the will of His Providence, that disposeth her favour to each Country in their pre-ordinate season. All cannot be happy at once; for, because the glory of one State depends upon the ruine of another, there is a revolution and vicissitude of their greatness, and must obey the swing of that wheel, not moved by Intelligences, but by the hand of GOD, whereby all Estates arise to their *Zenith* and Vertical points according to their predestinated periods. For the lives, not only of men, but of Commonwealths, and the whole World, run not upon an *Helix* that still enlargeth, but on a Circle, where, arriving to their Meridian, they decline in obscurity, and fall under the Horizon again.

These must not therefore be named the effects of Fortune, but in a relative way, and as we term the works of Nature. It was the ignorance of man's reason that begat this very name, and by a careless term miscalled the Providence of GOD; for there is no liberty for causes to operate in a loose and straggling way; nor any effect whatsoever, but hath its warrant from some universal or superiour Cause. 'Tis not a ridiculous devotion to say a prayer before a game at Tables; for even in *sortilegies* and matters of greatest uncertainty, there is a setled and pre-ordered course of effects. It is we that are blind, not Fortune: because our Eye is too dim to discover the mystery of her effects, we foolishly paint her blind, and hoodwink the Providence of the Almighty. I cannot justifie that contemptible Proverb, *That fools only are Fortunate,* or that insolent Paradox, *That a wise man is out of the reach of Fortune;* much less those approbrious epithets of Poets, *Whore, Bawd,* and *Strumpet.* 'Tis, I confess, the common fate of men of singular gifts of mind to be destitute of those of Fortune, which doth not any way deject the Spirit of wiser judgements, who thoroughly understand the justice of this proceeding; and being inriched with higher donatives, cast a more careless eye on these vulgar parts of felicity. It is a most unjust ambition to desire to engross the mercies of the Almighty, not to be content with the goods of mind, without a possession of those of body or Fortune; and it is an error worse than heresie, to adore these complemental and circumstantial pieces of felicity, and undervalue those perfections and essential points of happiness wherein we resemble our Maker. To wiser desires it is satisfaction enough to deserve, though not to enjoy, the favours of Fortune: let Providence provide for Fools. 'Tis not partiality, but equity in GOD, Who deals with us but as our natural Parents: those that are able of Body and Mind He leaves to their deserts; to those of weaker merits He imparts a larger portion, and pieces out the defect of one by the excess of the other. Thus have we no just quarrel with Nature for leaving us naked; or to envy the Horns, Hoofs, Skins, and Furs of other Creatures, being provided with Reason, that can supply them all. We need not labour with so many Arguments to confute Judicial Astrology; for, if there be a truth therein, it doth not injure Divinity. If to be born under *Mercury* disposeth us to be witty, under *Jupiter* to be wealthy; I do not owe a Knee unto these, but unto that merciful Hand that hath ordered my indifferent and uncertain nativity unto such benevolous Aspects. Those that hold that all things are governed by Fortune, had not erred, had they not persisted there. The Romans, that erected a Temple to Fortune, acknowledged therein, though in a blinder way, somewhat of Divinity; for, in a wise supputation, all things begin and end in the Almighty. There is a nearer way to Heaven than Homer's Chain;

an easie Logic may conjoyn Heaven and Earth in one Argument, and with less than a *Sorites* resolve all things into GOD. For though we christen effects by their most sensible and nearest Causes, yet is GOD the true and infallible Cause of all; whose concourse, though it be general, yet doth it subdivide itself into the particular Actions of every thing, and is that Spirit, by which each singular Essence not only subsists, but performs its operation.

The bad construction and perverse comment on these pair of second Causes, or visible hands of GOD, have perverted the Devotion of many unto Atheism; who, forgetting the honest Advisoes of Faith, have listened unto the conspiracy of Passion and Reason. I have therefore always endeavoured to compose those Feuds and angry Dissentions between Affection, Faith, and Reason; for there is in our Soul a kind of Triumvirate, or triple Government of three Competitors, which distract the Peace of this our Commonwealth, not less than did that other the State of Rome.

As Reason is a Rebel unto Faith, so Passion unto Reason: as the propositions of Faith seem absurd unto Reason, so the Theorems of Reason unto Passion, and both unto Reason. Yet a moderate and peaceable discretion may so state and order the matter, that they may be all Kings, and yet make but one Monarchy, every one exercising his Soveraignty and Prerogative in a due time and place, according to the restraint and limit of circumstance. There is, as in Philosophy, so in Divinity, sturdy doubts and boisterous Objections, wherewith the unhappiness of our knowledge too nearly acquainteth us. More of these no man hath known than myself, which I confess I conquered, not in a martial posture, but on my Knees. For our endeavours are not only to combat with doubts, but always to dispute with the Devil. The villany of that Spirit takes a hint of Infidelity from our Studies, and, by demonstrating a naturality in one way, makes us mistrust a miracle in another. Thus, having perused the *Archidoxis* and read the secret Sympathies of things, he would disswade my belief from the miracle of the Brazen Serpent, make me conceit that Image worked by Sympathy, and was but an Ægyptian trick to cure their Diseases without a miracle. Again, having seen some experiments of *Bitumen*, and having read far more of *Naphtha*, he whispered to my curiosity the fire of the Altar might be natural; and bid me mistrust a miracle in Elias, when he entrenched the Altar round with Water; for that inflamable substance yields not easily unto Water, but flames in the Arms of its Antagonist. And thus would he inveagle my belief to think the combustion of Sodom might be natural, and that there was an Asphaltick and Bituminous nature in that Lake before the Fire of Gomorrah. I know that *Manna* is now plentifully gathered in Calabria; and Josephus tells me, in his days it was as plentiful in Arabia; the Devil therefore made the *quære, Where was then the miracle in the days of Moses? the Israelites saw but that in his time, the Natives of those Countries behold in ours*. Thus the Devil played at Chess with me, and yielding a Pawn, thought to gain a Queen of me, taking advantage of my honest endeavours; and whilst I laboured to raise the structure of my Reason, he strived to undermine the edifice of my Faith.

Neither had these or any other ever such advantage of me, as to incline me to any point of Infidelity or desperate positions of Atheism; for I have been these many years of opinion there was never any. Those that held Religion was the difference of Man from Beasts, have spoken probably, and proceed upon a principle as inductive as the other. That doctrine of Epicurus, that denied the Providence of GOD, was no Atheism, but a magnificent and high strained conceit of His Majesty, which he deemed too sublime to mind the trivial Actions of those inferiour Creatures. That *fatal Necessity* of the Stoicks is nothing but the immutable Law of His Will. Those that heretofore denied the Divinity of the HOLY GHOST, have been condemned but as Hereticks; and those that now deny our Saviour, (though more than Hereticks), are not so much as Atheists; for, though they deny two persons in the Trinity, they hold, as we do, there is but one GOD.

That Villain and Secretary of Hell, that composed that

miscreant piece *Of the Three Impostors,* though divided from all Religions, and was neither Jew, Turk, nor Christian, was not a positive Atheist. I confess every Country hath its Machiavel, every Age its Lucian, whereof common Heads must not hear, nor more advanced Judgments too rashly venture on: it is the Rhetorick of Satan, and may pervert a loose or prejudicate belief.

I confess I have perused them all, and can discover nothing that may startle a discreet belief; yet are there heads carried off with the Wind and breath of such motives. I remember a Doctor in Physick, of Italy, who could not perfectly believe the immortality of the Soul, because Galen seemed to make a doubt thereof. With another I was familiarly acquainted in France, a Divine, and a man of singular parts, that on the same point was so plunged and gravelled with three lines of Seneca, that all our Antidotes, drawn from both Scripture and Philosophy, could not expel the poyson of his errour. There are a set of Heads, that can credit the relations of Mariners, yet question the Testimonies of St. Paul; and peremptorily maintain the traditions of Ælian or Pliny, yet in Histories of Scripture raise Queries and Objections, believing no more than they can parallel in humane Authors. I confess there are in Scripture Stories that do exceed the Fables of Poets, and to a captious Reader sound like *Garagantua* or *Bevis*. Search all the Legends of times past, and the fabulous conceits of these present, and 'twill be hard to find one that deserves to carry the Buckler unto Sampson; yet is all this of an easie possibility, if we conceive a Divine concourse, or an influence but from the little Finger of the Almighty. It is impossible that either in the discourse of man, or in the infallible Voice of God, to the weakness of our apprehensions, there should not appear irregularities, contradictions, and antinomies: my self could shew a Catalogue of doubts, never yet imagined nor questioned, as I know, which are not resolved at the first hearing; not fantastick Queries or Objections of Air; for I cannot hear of Atoms in Divinity. I can read the History of the Pigeon that was sent out of the Ark, and returned no more, yet not question how she found out her Mate that was left behind: that Lazarus was raised from the dead, yet not demand where in the interim his Soul awaited; or raise a Lawcase, whether his Heir might lawfully detain his inheritance bequeathed unto him by his death, and he, though restored to life, have no Plea or Title unto his former possessions. Whether Eve was framed out of the left side of Adam, I dispute not; because I stand not yet assured which is the right side of a man, or whether there be any such distinction in Nature: that she was edified out of the Rib of Adam I believe, yet raise no question who shall arise with that Rib at the Resurrection. Whether Adam was an Hermaphrodite, as the Rabbins contend upon the Letter of the Text, because it is contrary to reason, there should be an Hermaphrodite before there was a Woman, or a composition of two Natures before there was a second composed. Likewise, whether the World was created in Autumn, Summer, or the Spring, because it was created in them all; for whatsoever Sign the Sun possesseth, those four Seasons are actually existent. It is the nature of this Luminary to distinguish the several Seasons of the year, all which it makes at one time in the whole Earth, and successive in any part thereof. There are a bundle of curiosities, not only in Philosophy, but in Divinity, proposed and discussed by men of most supposed abilities, which indeed are not worthy our vacant hours, much less our serious Studies: Pieces only fit to be placed in *Pantagruel's* Library, or bound up with Tartaretus *De modo Cacandi*.

These are niceties that become not those that peruse so serious a Mystery. There are others more generally questioned and called to the Bar, yet methinks of an easie and possible truth.

'Tis ridiculous to put off or drown the general Flood of Noah in that particular inundation of Deucalion. That there was a Deluge once, seems not to me so great a Miracle, as that there is not one always. How all the kinds of Creatures, not only in their own bulks, but with a competency of food and sustenance, might be preserved in one Ark, and within the extent of three hundred Cubits, to a reason that rightly examines it, will appear very feasible. There is another secret, not contained in the Scripture, which is more hard to comprehend, and put the honest Father to the refuge of a Miracle; and that is, not only how the distinct pieces of the World, and divided Islands, should be first planted by men, but inhabited by Tigers, Panthers, and Bears. How America abounded with Beasts of prey and noxious Animals, yet contained not in it that necessary Creature, a Horse, is very strange. By what passage those, not only Birds, but dangerous and unwelcome Beasts, came over; how there be Creatures there, which are not found in this Triple Continent; (all which must needs be strange unto us, that hold but one Ark, and that the Creatures began their progress from the Mountains of Ararat): they who, to salve this, would make the Deluge particular, proceed upon a principle that I can no way grant; not only upon the negative of Holy Scriptures, but of mine own Reason, whereby I can make it probable, that the world was as well peopled in the time of Noah as in ours; and fifteen hundred years to people the World, as full a time for them, as four thousand years since have been to us.

There are other assertions and common Tenents drawn from Scripture, and generally believed as Scripture, whereunto, notwithstanding, I would never betray the liberty of my Reason. 'Tis a Postulate to me, that Methusalem was the longest liv'd of all the Children of Adam; and no man will be able to prove it, when, from the process of the Text, I can manifest it may be otherwise. That Judas perished by hanging himself, there is no certainty in Scripture: though in one place it seems to affirm it, and by a doubtful word hath given occasion to translate it; yet in another place, in a more punctual description, it makes it improbable, and seems to overthrow it. That our Fathers, after the Flood, erected the Tower of Babel to preserve themselves against a second Deluge, is generally opinioned and believed; yet is there another intention of theirs expressed in Scripture: besides, it is improbable from the circumstance of the place, that is, a plain in the Land of Shinar.

These are no points of Faith, and therefore may admit a free dispute.

There are yet others, and those familiarly concluded from the text, wherein (under favour), I see no consequence. The Church of Rome confidently proves the opinion of Tutelary Angels from that Answer, when Peter knockt at the Door, *'Tis not he, but his Angel;* that is, (might some say), his *Messenger,* or some body from him; for so the Original signifies, and is as likely to be the doubtful Families meaning. This exposition I once suggested to a young Divine, that answered upon this point; to which I remember the Franciscan Opponent replyed no more, but *That it was a new, and no authentick interpretation.*

These are but the conclusions and fallible discourses of man upon the Word of GOD, for such I do believe the Holy Scriptures: yet, were it of man, I could not chuse but say, it was the singularest and superlative piece that hath been extant since the Creation. Were I a Pagan, I should not refrain the Lecture of it; and cannot but commend the judgment of Ptolomy, that thought not his Library compleat without it. The Alcoran of the Turks (I speak without prejudice), is an ill composed Piece, containing in it vain and ridiculous Errors in Philosophy, impossibilities, fictions, and vanities beyond laughter, maintained by evident and open Sophisms, the Policy of Ignorance, deposition of Universities, and banishment of Learning, that hath gotten Foot by Arms and violence: this without a blow hath disseminated it self through the whole Earth. It is not unremarkable what Philo first observed, that the Law of Moses continued two thousand years without the least alteration; whereas, we see the Laws of other Commonweals do alter with occasions; and even those that pretended their original from some Divinity, to have vanished without trace or memory. I believe, besides Zoroaster, there were divers that writ before Moses, who, notwithstanding, have suffered the common fate of time. Mens Works have an age like themselves; and though they out-live their Authors, yet have they a stint and period to their duration: this only is a work too hard for the teeth of time, and cannot perish but in the general Flames, when all things shall confess their Ashes.

I have heard some with deep sighs lament the lost lines of Cicero; others with as many groans deplore the combustion of the Library of Alexandria: for my own part, I think there be too many in the World, and could with patience behold the urn and ashes of the Vatican, could I, with a few others, recover the perished leaves of Solomon. I would not omit a Copy of Enoch's Pillars, had they many nearer Authors than Josephus, or did not relish somewhat of the Fable. Some men have written more than others have spoken; Pineda quotes more Authors in one work, than are necessary in a whole World. Of those three great inventions in Germany, there are two which are not without their incommodities, and 'tis disputable whether they exceed not their use and commodities. 'Tis not a melancholy *Utinam* of my own, but the desires of better heads, that there were a general Synod; not to unite the incompatible difference of Religion, but for the benefit of learning, to reduce it as it lay at first, in a few and solid Authors; and to condemn to the fire those swarms and millions of Rhapsodies, begotten only to distract and abuse the weaker judgements of Scholars, and to maintain the trade and mystery of Typographers.

I cannot but wonder with what exception the Samaritans could confine their belief to the Pentateuch, or five Books of Moses. I am ashamed at the Rabbinical Interpretation of the Jews upon the Old Testament, as much as their defection from the New: and truly it is beyond wonder, how that contemptible and degenerate issue of Jacob, once so devoted to Ethnick Superstition, and so easily seduced to the Idolatry of their Neighbours, should now in such an obstinate and peremptory belief adhere unto their own Doctrine, expect impossibilities, and, in the face and eye of the Church, persist without the least hope of Conversion. This is a vice in *them,* that were a vertue in *us;* for obstinacy in a bad Cause is but constancy in a good. And herein I must accuse those of my own Religion, for there is not any of such a fugitive Faith, such an unstable belief, as a Christian; none that do so oft transform themselves, not unto several shapes of Christianity and of the same Species, but unto more unnatural and contrary Forms of Jew and Mahometan; that, from the name of *Saviour,* can condescend to the bare term of *Prophet;* and, from an old belief that He is come, fall to a new expectation of His coming. It is the promise of CHRIST to make us all one Flock; but how and when this Union shall be, is as obscure to me as the last day. Of those four Members of Religion we hold a slender proportion. There are, I confess, some new additions, yet small to those which accrew to our Adversaries, and those only drawn from the revolt of Pagans, men but of negative Impieties, and such as deny CHRIST, but because they never heard of Him. But the Religion of the Jew is expressly against the Christian, and the Mahometan against both. For the Turk, in the bulk he now stands, he is beyond all hope of conversion; if he fall asunder, there may be conceived hopes, but not without strong improbabilities. The Jew is obstinate in all fortune; the persecution of fifteen hundred years hath but confirmed them in their Errour: they have already endured whatsoever may be inflicted, and have suffered in a bad cause, even to the condemnation of their enemies. Persecution is a bad and indirect way to plant Religion: it hath been the unhappy method of angry Devotions, not only to confirm honest Religion, but wicked Heresies, and extravagant Opinions. It was the first stone and Basis of our Faith; none can more justly boast of Persecutions, and glory in the number and valour of Martyrs. For, to speak properly, those are true and almost only examples of fortitude: those that are fetch'd from the field, or drawn from the actions of the Camp, are not oft-times so truely precedents of valour as audacity, and at the best attain but to some bastard piece of fortitude. If we shall strictly examine the circumstances and requisites which Aristotle requires to true and perfect valour, we shall find the name only in his Master, Alexander, and as little in that Roman Worthy, Julius Cæsar; and if any in that easie and active way have done so nobly as to deserve that name, yet in the passive and more terrible piece these have surpassed, and in a more heroical way may claim the honour of that Title. 'Tis not in the power of every honest Faith to proceed thus far, or pass to Heaven through the flames. Every one hath it not in that full measure, nor in so audacious and resolute a temper, as to endure those terrible tests and trials; who, notwithstanding, in a peaceable way, do truely adore their Saviour, and have (no doubt), a Faith acceptable in the eyes of GOD.

Now, as all that dye in the War are not termed *Souldiers;* so neither can I properly term all those that suffer in matters of Religion, *Martyrs.* The Council of Constance condemns John Huss for an Heretick; the Stories of his own Party stile him a Martyr: he must needs offend the Divinity of both, that says he was neither the one nor the other. There are many (questionless), canonized on earth, that shall never be Saints in Heaven; and have their names in Histories and Martyrologies, who in the eyes of GOD are not so perfect Martyrs as was that wise Heathen, Socrates, that suffered on a fundamental point of Religion, the Unity of GOD. I have often pitied the miserable Bishop that suffered in the cause of Antipodes; yet cannot chuse but accuse *him* of as much madness, for exposing his living on such a trifle, as those of ignorance and folly, that condemned him. I think my conscience will not give me the lye, if I say there are not many extant that in a noble way fear the face of death less than myself; yet, from the moral duty I owe to the Commandment of GOD, and the natural respects that I tender unto the conservation of my essence and being, I would not perish upon a Ceremony, Politick points, or indifferency: nor is my belief of that untractible temper, as not to bow at their obstacles, or connive at matters wherein there are not manifest impieties. The leaven, therefore, and ferment of all, not only civil but Religious actions, is Wisdom; without which, to commit ourselves to the flames is Homicide, and (I fear), but to pass through one fire into another.

That Miracles are ceased, I can neither prove, nor absolutely deny, much less define the time and period of their cessation. That they survived CHRIST, is manifest upon the Record of Scripture; that they outlived the Apostles also, and were revived at the Conversion of Nations many years after, we cannot deny, if we shall not question those Writers whose testimonies we do not controvert in points that make for our own opinions. Therefore that may have some truth in it that is reported by the Jesuites of their Miracles in the Indies; I could wish it were true, or had any other testimony than their own Pens. *They* may easily believe those Miracles abroad, who daily conceive a greater at home, the transmutation of those visible elements into the Body and Blood of our Saviour. For the conversion of Water into Wine, which He wrought in Cana, or, what the Devil would have had Him done in the Wilderness, of Stones into Bread, compared to this, will scarce deserve the name of a Miracle: though indeed, to speak properly, there is not one Miracle greater than another, they being the extraordinary effects of the Hand of GOD, to which all things are of an equal facility; and to create the World, as easie as one single Creature. For this is also a Miracle, not onely to produce effects against or above Nature, but before Nature; and to create Nature, as great a Miracle as to contradict or transcend her. We do too narrowly define the Power of GOD, restraining it to our capacities. I hold that GOD can do all things; how He should work contradictions, I do not understand, yet dare not therefore deny. I cannot see why the Angel of GOD should question Esdras to recal the time past, if it were beyond His own power; or that GOD should pose mortality in that which He was not able to perform Himself. I will not say GOD cannot, but He will not, perform many things, which we plainly affirm He cannot. This, I am sure, is the mannerliest proposition, wherein, notwithstanding, I hold no Paradox; for, strictly, His power is the same with His will, and they both, with all the rest, do make but one GOD.

Therefore that Miracles have been, I do believe; that they may yet be wrought by the living, I do not deny; but have no confidence in those which are fathered on the dead. And this hath ever made me suspect the efficacy of reliques, to examine the bones, question the habits and appurtenances of Saints, and even of CHRIST Himself. I cannot conceive why the Cross that Helena found, and whereon CHRIST Himself dyed, should have power to restore others unto life. I excuse not Constantine from a fall off his Horse, or a mischief from his enemies, upon the wearing those nails on his bridle, which our Saviour bore upon the Cross in His Hands. I compute among your *Piæ fraudes,* nor many degrees before consecrated Swords and Roses, that which Baldwyn, King of Jerusalem, returned the Genovese for their cost and pains in his War, to wit, the ashes of John the Baptist. Those that hold the sanctity of their Souls doth leave behind a tincture and sacred faculty on their bodies, speak naturally of Miracles, and do not salve the doubt. Now one reason I tender so little Devotion unto Reliques, is, I think, the slender and doubtful respect I have always held unto Antiquities. For that indeed which I admire, is far before Antiquity, that is, Eternity; and that is, GOD Himself; Who, though He be styled *the Ancient of Days,* cannot receive the adjunct of Antiquity; Who was before the World, and shall be after it, yet is not older than it; for in His years there is no Climacter; His duration is Eternity, and far more venerable than Antiquity.

But above all things I wonder how the curiosity of wiser heads could pass that great and indisputable Miracle, the cessation of Oracles; and in what swoun their Reasons lay, to content themselves and sit down with such a far-fetch'd and ridiculous reason as Plutarch alleadgeth for it. The Jews, that can believe the supernatural Solstice of the Sun in the days of Joshua, have yet the impudence to deny the Eclipse, which every Pagan confessed, at His death: but for this, it is evident beyond all contradiction, the Devil himself confessed it. Certainly it is not a warrantable curiosity, to examine the verity of Scripture by the concordance of humane history, or seek to confirm the Chronicle of Hester or Daniel, by the authority of Megasthenes or Herodotus. I confess, I

have had an unhappy curiosity this way, till I laughed my
self out of it with a piece of Justine, where he delivers that the
Children of Israel for being scabbed were banished out of
Egypt. And truely since I have understood the occurrences
of the World, and know in what counterfeit shapes and deceitful vizards times present represent on the stage things past,
I do believe them little more then things to come. Some have
been of my opinion, and endeavoured to write the History of
their own lives; wherein Moses hath outgone them all, and
left not onely the story of his life, but (as some will have it),
of his death also.

It is a riddle to me, how this story of Oracles hath not
worm'd out of the World that doubtful conceit of Spirits and
Witches; how so many learned heads should so far forget
their Metaphysicks, and destroy the ladder and scale of crea
tures, as to question the existence of Spirits. For my part, I
have ever believed and do now know, that there are Witches:
they that doubt of these, do not onely deny *them*, but Spirits;
and are obliquely and upon consequence a sort not of Infidels,
but Atheists. Those that to confute their incredulity desire
to see apparitions, shall questionless never behold any, nor
have the power to be so much as Witches; the Devil hath them
already in a heresie as capital as Witchcraft; and to appeal
to them, were but to convert them. Of all the delusions where·
with he deceives mortality, there is not any that puzzleth me
more than the Legerdemain of Changelings. I do not credit
those transformations of reasonable creatures into beasts, or
that the Devil hath a power to transpeciate a man into a
Horse, who tempted CHRIST (as a trial of His Divinity), to
convert but stones into bread. I could believe that Spirits use
with man the act of carnality, and that in both sexes; I conceive they may assume, steal, or contrive a body, wherein
there may be action enough to content decrepit lust, or passion
to satisfie more active veneries; yet, in both, without a possibility of generation: and therefore that opinion that Antichrist should be born of the Tribe of Dan by conjunction with
the Devil, is ridiculous, and a conceit fitter for a Rabbin than

a Christian. I hold that the Devil doth really possess some men, the spirit of Melancholly others, the spirit of Delusion others; that, as the Devil is concealed and denyed by some, so GOD and good Angels are pretended by others, whereof the late defection of the Maid of Germany hath left a pregnant example.

Again, I believe that all that use sorceries, incantations, and spells, are not Witches, or, as we term them, *Magicians*. I conceive there is a traditional Magick, not learned immediately from the Devil, but at second hand from his Scholars, who, having once the secret betrayed, are able, and do emperically practise without his advice, they both proceeding upon the principles of Nature; where actives, aptly conjoyned to disposed passives, will under any Master produce their effects. Thus I think at first a great part of Philosophy was Witchcraft; which, being afterward derived to one another, proved but Philosophy, and was indeed no more but the honest effects of Nature: what, invented by us, is Philosophy, learned from him, is Magick. We do surely owe the discovery of many secrets to the discovery of good and bad Angels. I could never pass that sentence of Paracelsus without an asterisk or annotation; *Ascendens constellatum multa revelat quærentibus magnalia naturæ,* (i.e. *opera* DEI). I do think that many mysteries ascribed to our own inventions have been the courteous revelations of Spirits; (for those noble essences in Heaven bear a friendly regard unto their fellow Natures on Earth); and therefore believe that those many prodigies and ominous prognosticks, which fore-run the ruines of States, Princes, and private persons, are the charitable premonitions of good Angels, which more careless enquiries term but the effects of chance and nature.

Now, besides these particular and divided Spirits, there may be (for ought I know), an universal and common Spirit to the whole World. It was the opinion of Plato, and it is yet of the Hermetical Philosophers. If there be a common nature that unites and tyes the scattered and divided individuals into one species, why may there not be one that unites them all? However, I am sure there is a common Spirit that plays within us, yet makes no part of us; and that is, the Spirit of GOD, the fire and scintillation of that noble and mighty Essence, which is the life and radical heat of Spirits, and those essences that know not the vertue of the Sun; a fire quite contrary to the fire of Hell. This is that gentle heat that brooded on the waters, and in six days hatched the World; this is that irradiation that dispels the mists of Hell, the clouds of horrour, fear, sorrow, despair; and preserves the region of the mind in serenity. Whosoever feels not the warm gale and gentle ventilation of this Spirit, though I feel his pulse, I dare not say he lives: for truely, without this, to me there is no heat under the Tropick; nor any light, though I dwelt in the body of the Sun.

> As, when the labouring Sun hath wrought his track
> Up to the top of lofty Cancers back,
> The ycie Ocean cracks, the frozen pole
> Thaws with the heat of the Celestial coale;
> So, when Thy absent beams begin t' impart
> Again a Solstice on my frozen heart,
> My winter's ov'r, my drooping spirits sing,
> And every part revives into a Spring.
> But if Thy quickning beams a while decline,
> And with their light bless not this Orb of mine,
> A chilly frost surpriseth every member,
> And in the midst of June I feel December.
> O how this earthly temper both debase
> The noble Soul, in this her humble place;
> Whose wingy nature ever doth aspire
> To reach that place whence first it took its fire.
> These flames I feel, which in my heart do dwell,
> Are not Thy beams, but take their fire from Hell
> O quench them all, and let Thy Light divine
> Be as the Sun to this poor Orb of mine;
> And to Thy sacred Spirit convert those fires,
> Whose earthly fumes choak my devout aspires.

Therefore for Spirits, I am so far from denying their existence, that I could easily believe, that not onely whole Countries, but particular persons, have their Tutelary and Guardian Angels. It is not a new opinion of the Church of Rome, but an old one of Pythagoras and Plato; there is no heresie in it; and if not manifestly defin'd in Scripture, yet is it an opinion of a good and wholesome use in the course and actions of a mans life, and would serve as an Hypothesis to salve many doubts, whereof common Philosophy affordeth no solution. Now, if you demand my opinion and Metaphysicks of their natures, I confess them very shallow; most of them in a negative way, like that of GOD; or in a comparative, between ourselves and fellow-creatures; for there is in this Universe a Stair, or manifest Scale of creatures, rising not disorderly, or in confusion, but with a comely method and proportion. Between creatures of meer existence, and things of life, there is a large disproportion of nature; between plants, and animals or creatures of sense, a wider difference; between them and Man, a far greater: and if the proportion hold one, between Man and Angels there should be yet a greater. We do not comprehend their natures, who retain the first definition of Porphyry, and distinguish them from our selves by immortality; for before his Fall, 'tis thought, Man also was Immortal; yet must we needs affirm that he had a different essence from the Angels. Having therefore no certain knowledge of their Natures, 'tis no bad method of the Schools, whatsoever perfection we find obscurely in our selves, in a more compleat and absolute way to ascribe unto them. I believe they have an extemporary knowledge, and upon the first motion of their reason do what we cannot without study or deliberation; that they know things by their forms, and define by specifical difference what we describe by accidents and properties; and therefore probabilities to us may be demonstrations unto them: that they have knowledge not onely of the specifical, but numerical forms of individuals, and understand by what reserved difference each single Hypostasis (besides the relation to its species), becomes its numerical self: that, as the Soul hath a power to move the body it informs, so there's a faculty to move any, though inform none: ours upon restraint of time, place, and distance; but that invisible hand that conveyed Habakkuk to the Lyons Den, or Philip to Azotus, infringeth this rule, and hath a secret conveyance, wherewith mortality is not acquainted. If they have that intuitive knowledge, whereby as in reflexion they behold the thoughts of one another, I cannot peremptorily deny but they know a great part of ours. They that, to refute the Invocation of Saints, have denied that they have any knowledge of our affairs below, have proceeded too far, and must pardon my opinion, till I can thoroughly answer that piece of Scripture, *At the conversion of a sinner the Angels in Heaven rejoyce.* I cannot, with those in that great Father, securely interpret the work of the first day, *Fiat lux,* to the creation of Angels; though I confess, there is not any creature that hath so neer a glympse of their nature as light in the Sun and Elements. We stile it a bare accident; but, where it subsists alone, 'tis a spiritual Substance, and may be an Angel: in brief, conceive light invisible, and that is a Spirit.

These are certainly the Magisterial and masterpieces of the Creator, the Flower, or (as we may say), the best part of nothing; actually existing, what we are but in hopes and probability. We are onely that amphibious piece between a corporal and spiritual Essence, that middle form that links those two together, and makes good the Method of God and Nature, that jumps not from extreams, but unites the incompatible distances by some middle and participating natures. That we are the breath and similitude of God, it is indisputable, and upon record of Holy Scripture; but to call ourselves a Microcosm, or little World, I thought it only a pleasant trope of Rhetorick, till my neer judgement and second thoughts told me there was a real truth therein. For first we are a rude mass, and in the rank of creatures which onely are, and have a dull kind of being, not yet priviledged with life, or preferred to sense or reason; next we live the life of Plants, the life of Animals, the life of Men, and at last the

life of Spirits, running on in one mysterious nature those five
kinds of existences, which comprehend the creatures, not
onely of the World, but of the Universe. Thus is Man that
great and true *Amphibium,* whose nature is disposed to live,
not onely like other creatures in divers elements, but in divided and distinguished worlds: for though there be but one
to sense, there are two to reason, the one visible, the other
invisible; whereof Moses seems to have left description, and
of the other so obscurely, that some parts thereof are yet in
controversie. And truely, for the first chapters of Genesis, I
must confess a great deal of obscurity; though Divines have
to the power of humane reason endeavoured to make all go
in a literal meaning, yet those allegorical interpretations are
also probable, and perhaps the mystical method of Moses bred
up in the Hieroglyphical Schools of the Egyptians.

Now for that immaterial world, methinks we need not
wander so far as beyond the first moveable; for even in this
material Fabrick the Spirits walk as freely exempt from the
affection of time, place, and motion, as beyond the extreamest
circumference. Do but extract from the corpulency of bodies,
or resolve things beyond their first matter, and you discover
the habitation of Angels, which if I call the ubiquitary and
omnipresent Essence of GOD, I hope I shall not offend Divinity: for before the Creation of the World GOD was really
all things. For the Angels He created no new World, or de-
terminate mansion, and therefore they are everywhere where
is His Essence, and do live at a distance even in Himself.
That GOD made all things for Man, is in some sense true, yet
not so far as to subordinate the Creation of those purer Creatures unto ours, though as *ministring Spirits* they do, and are
willing to fulfil the will of GOD in these lower and sublunary
affairs of Man. GOD made all things for Himself, and it is
impossible He should make them for any other end than His
own Glory; it is all He can receive, and all that is without
Himself. For, honour being an external adjunct, and in the
honourer rather than in the person honoured, it was necessary to make a Creature, from whom He might receive this

homage; and that is, in the other world, Angels, in this, Man; which when we neglect, we forget the very end of our Creation, and may justly provoke GOD, not onely to repent that He hath made the World, but that He hath sworn He would not destroy it. That there is but one World, is a conclusion of Faith: Aristotle with all his Philosophy hath not been able to prove it, and as weakly that the World was eternal. That dispute much troubled the Pen of the ancient Philosophers, but Moses decided that question, and all is salved with the new term of a *Creation,* that is, a production of something out of nothing. And what is that? whatsoever is opposite to something; or more exactly, that which is truely contrary unto GOD: for He onely is, all others have an existence with dependency, and are something but by a distinction. And herein is Divinity conformant unto Philosophy, and generation not onely founded on contrarieties, but also creation; GOD, being all things, is contrary unto nothing, out of which were made all things, and so nothing became something, and Omneity informed Nullity into an Essence.

The whole Creation is a Mystery, and particularly that of Man. At the blast of His mouth were the rest of the Creatures made, and at His bare word they started out of nothing: but in the frame of Man (as the Text describes it), He played the sensible operator, and seemed not so much to create, as make him. When He had separated the materials of other creatures, there consequently resulted a form and soul; but, having raised the walls of Man, He was driven to a second and harder creation of a substance like Himself, an incorruptible and immortal Soul. For these two affections we have the Philosophy and opinion of the Heathens, the flat affirmative of Plato, and not a negative from Aristotle. There is another scruple cast in by Divinity concerning its production, much disputed in the Germane auditories, and with that indifferency and equality of arguments, as leave the controversie undetermined. I am not of Paracelsus mind, that boldly delivers a receipt to make a man without conjunction; yet cannot but wonder at the multitude of heads that do deny traduction, having no other argument to confirm their belief then that Rhetorical sentence and *Antimetathesis* of Augustine, *Creando infunditur, infundendo creatur*. Either opinion will consist well enough with Religion: yet I should rather incline to this, did not one objection haunt me, (not wrung from speculations and subtilties, but from common sense and observation; not pickt from the leaves of any Author, but bred amongst the weeds and tares of mine own brain); and this is a conclusion from the equivocal and monstrous productions in the conjunction of Man with Beast: for if the Soul of man be not transmitted and transfused in the seed of the Parents, why are not those productions meerly beasts, but have also an impression and tincture of reason in as high a measure as it can evidence it self in those improper Organs? Nor, truely, can I peremptorily deny that the Soul, in this her sublunary estate, is wholly and in all acceptions inorganical; but that for the performance of her ordinary actions there is required not onely a symmetry and proper disposition of Organs, but a Crasis and temper correspondent to its operations: yet is not this mass of flesh and visible structure the instrument and proper corps of the Soul, but rather of Sense, and that the hand of Reason. In our study of Anatomy there is a mass of mysterious Philosophy, and such as reduced the very Heathens to Divinity: yet, amongst all those rare discoveries and curious pieces I find in the Fabrick of Man, I do not so much content myself, as in that I find not, there is no Organ or Instrument for the rational Soul; for in the brain, which we term the seat of Reason, there is not any thing of moment more than I can discover in the crany of a beast: and this is a sensible and no inconsiderable argument of the inorganity of the Soul, at least in that sense we usually so receive it. Thus we are men, and we know not how: there is something in us that can be without us, and will be after us; though it is strange that it hath no history what it was before us, nor cannot tell how it entred in us.

Now, for these walls of flesh, wherein the Soul doth seem to be immured before the Resurrection, it is nothing but an elemental composition, and a Fabrick that must fall to ashes. *All flesh is grass,* is not onely metaphorically, but literally, true; for all those creatures we behold are but the herbs of the field, digested into flesh in them, or more remotely carnified in our selves. Nay further, we are what we all abhor, *Anthropophagi* and Cannibals, devourers not onely of men, but of our selves; and that not in an allegory, but a positive truth; for all this mass of flesh which we behold, came in at our mouths; this frame we look upon, hath been upon our trenchers; in brief, we have devour'd our selves. I cannot believe the wisdom of Pythagoras did ever positively, and in a literal sense, affirm his Metempsychosis, or impossible transmigration of the Souls of men into beasts. Of all Metamorphoses or transmigrations, I believe only one, that is of Lots wife; for that of Nebuchodonosor proceeded not so far: in all others I conceive there is no further verity than is contained in their implicite sense and morality. I believe that the whole frame of a beast doth perish, and is left in the same state after death as before it was materialled unto life: that the Souls of men know neither contrary nor corruption; that they subsist beyond the body, and outlive death by the priviledge of their proper natures, and without a Miracle; that the Souls of the faithful, as they leave Earth, take possession of Heaven: that those apparitions and ghosts of departed persons are not the wandring souls of men, but the unquiet walks of Devils, prompting and suggesting us unto mischief, blood, and villainy; instilling and stealing into our hearts that the blessed Spirits are not at rest in their graves, but wander sollicitous of the affairs of the World. But that those phantasms appear often, and do frequent Cœmeteries, Charnel-houses, and Churches, it is because those are the dormitories of the dead, where the Devil, like an insolent Champion, beholds with pride the spoils and Trophies of his Victory over Adam.

This is that dismal conquest we all deplore, that makes us so often cry, *O Adam, quid fecisti?* I thank GOD I have not those strait ligaments, or narrow obligations to the World, as to dote on life, or be convulst and tremble at the name of death. Not that I am insensible of the dread and horrour thereof; or by raking into the bowels of the deceased, continual sight of Anatomies, Skeletons, or Cadaverous reliques, like Vespilloes, or Grave-makers, I am become stupid, or have forgot the apprehension of Mortality; but that, marshalling all the horrours, and contemplating the extremities thereof, I find not anything therein able to daunt the courage of a man, much less a well-resolved Christian; and therefore am not angry at the errour of our first Parents, or unwilling to bear a part of this common fate, and like the best of them to dye, that is, to cease to breathe, to take a farewel of the elements, to be a kind of nothing for a moment, to be within one instant of a Spirit. When I take a full view and circle of my self without this reasonable moderator, and equal piece of Justice, Death, I do conceive my self the miserablest person extant. Were there not another life that I hope for, all the vanities of this World should not intreat a moments breath from me: could the Devil work my belief to imagine I could never dye, I would not outlive that very thought. I have so abject a conceit of this common way of existence, this retaining to the Sun and Elements, I cannot think this is to be a Man, or to live according to the dignity of humanity. In exspectation of a better, I can with patience embrace this life, yet in my best meditations do often defie death; I honour any man that contemns it, nor can I highly love any that is afraid of it: this makes me naturally love a Souldier, and honour those tattered and contemptible Regiments that will die at the command of a Sergeant. For a Pagan there may be some motives to be in love with life; but for a Christian to be amazed at death, I see not how he can escape this Dilemma, that he is too sensible of this life, or hopeless of the life to come.

Some Divines count Adam thirty years old at his Creation, because they suppose him created in the perfect age and stature of man. And surely we are all out of the computation of our age, and every man in some months elder than he be-

thinks him; for we live, move, have a being, and are subject
to the actions of the elements, and the malice of diseases, in
that other World, the truest Microcosm, the Womb of our
Mother. For besides that general and common existence we
are conceived to hold in our Chaos, and whilst we sleep within
the bosome of our causes, we enjoy a being and life in three
distinct worlds, wherein we receive most manifest graduations.
In that obscure World and Womb of our Mother, our time
is short, computed by the Moon, yet longer than the days of
many creatures that behold the Sun; our selves being not yet
without life, sense, and reason; though for the manifestation
of its actions, it awaits the opportunity of objects, and seems
to live there but in its root and soul of vegetation. Entring
afterwards upon the scene of the World, we arise up and become another creature, performing the reasonable actions of
man, and obscurely manifesting that part of Divinity in us;
but not in complement and perfection, till we have once more
cast our secondine, that is, this slough of flesh, and are delivered into the last World, that is, that ineffable place of
Paul, that proper *ubi* of Spirits. The smattering I have of the
Philosophers Stone (which is something more then the perfect
exaltation of gold), hath taught me a great deal of Divinity,
and instructed my belief, how that immortal spirit and incorruptible substance of my Soul may lye obscure, and sleep a
while within this house of flesh. Those strange and mystical
transmigrations that I have observed in Silkworms, turned
my Philosophy into Divinity. There is in these works of nature, which seem to puzzle reason, something Divine, and hath
more in it than the eye of a common spectator doth discover.

I am naturally bashful; nor hath conversation, age, or
travel, been able to effront or enharden me; yet I have one
part of modesty which I have seldom discovered in another,
that is, (to speak truely), I am not so much afraid of death,
as ashamed thereof. 'Tis the very disgrace and ignominy of
our natures, that in a moment can so disfigure us, that our
nearest friends, Wife, and Children, stand afraid and start
at us: the Birds and Beasts of the field, that before in a natural

fear obeyed us, forgetting all allegiance, begin to prey upon us. This very conceit hath in a tempest disposed and left me willing to be swallowed up in the abyss of waters, wherein I had perished unseen, unpityed, without wondering eyes, tears of pity, Lectures of mortality, and none had said,

Quantum mutatus ab illo!

Not that I am ashamed of the Anatomy of my parts, or can accuse Nature for playing the bungler in any part of me, or my own vitious life for contracting any shameful disease upon me, whereby I might not call my self as wholesome a morsel for the worms as any.

Some, upon the courage of a fruitful issue, wherein, as in the truest Chronicle, they seem to outlive themselves, can with greater patience away with death. This conceit and counterfeit subsisting in our progenies seems to me a meer fallacy, unworthy the desires of a man that can but conceive a thought of the next World; who, in a nobler ambition, should desire to live in his substance in Heaven, rather than his name and shadow in the earth. And therefore at my death I mean to take a total adieu of the World, not caring for a Monument, History, or Epitaph, not so much as the bare memory of my name to be found any where but in the universal Register of GOD. I am not yet so Cynical as to approve the Testament of Diogenes; nor do I altogether allow that *Rodomontado* of Lucan,

——*Cælo tegitur, qui non habet urnam.*

He that unburied lies wants not his Herse,
For unto him a Tomb's the Universe.

but commend in my calmer judgement those ingenuous intentions that desire to sleep by the urns of their Fathers, and strive to go the neatest way unto corruption. I do not envy the temper of Crows and Daws, nor the numerous and weary days of our Fathers before the Flood. If there be any truth in Astrology, I may outlive a Jubilee: as yet I have not seen one revolution of Saturn, nor hath my pulse beat thirty years; and yet, excepting one, have seen the Ashes and left under ground all the Kings of Europe; have been contemporary to three Emperours, four Grand Signiours, and as many Popes. Methinks I have outlived my self, and begin to be weary of the Sun; I have shaken hands with delight, in my warm blood and Canicular days, I perceive I do anticipate the vices of age; the World to me is but a dream or mock-show, and we all therein but Pantalones and Anticks, to my severer contemplations.

It is not, I confess, an unlawful Prayer to desire to surpass the days of our Saviour, or wish to outlive that age wherein He thought fittest to dye; yet if (as Divinity affirms), there shall be no gray hairs in Heaven, but all shall rise in the perfect state of men, we do but outlive those perfections in this World, to be recalled unto them by a greater Miracle in the next, and run on here but to be retrograde hereafter. Were there any hopes to outlive vice, or a point to be superannuated from sin, it were worthy our knees to implore the days of Methuselah. But age doth not rectify, but incurvate our natures, turning bad dispositions into worser habits, and (like diseases), brings on incurable vices; for every day as we grow weaker in age, we grow stronger in sin, and the number of our days doth but make our sins innumerable. The same vice committed at sixteen, is not the same, though it agree in all other circumstances, at forty, but swells and doubles from the circumstance of our ages; wherein, besides the constant and inexcusable habit of transgressing, the maturity of our judgment cuts off pretence unto excuse or pardon. Every sin, the oftner it is committed, the more it acquireth in the quality of evil; as it succeeds in time, so it proceeds in degrees of badness; for as they proceed they ever multiply, and, like figures in Arithmetick, the last stands for more than all that went before it. And though I think no man can live well once, but he that could live twice, yet for my own part I would not live over my hours past, or begin again the thread of my days: not upon Cicero's ground, because I have lived them well, but for fear I should live them worse. I find my growing Judgment daily instruct me how to be better, but my untamed affections and confirmed vitiosity makes me daily do worse. I find in my confirmed age the same sins I discovered in my youth; I committed many then, because I was a Child; and because I commit them still, I am yet an infant. Therefore I perceive a man may be twice a Child, before the days of dotage; and stand in need of Æsons Bath before threescore.

And truly there goes a great deal of providence to produce a mans life unto threescore: there is more required than an able temper for those years; though the radical humour contain in it sufficient oyl for seventy, yet I perceive in some it gives no light past thirty: men assign not all the causes of long life, that write whole Books thereof. They that found themselves on the radical balsome, or vital sulphur of the parts, determine not why Abel lived not so long as Adam. There is therefore a secret glome or bottome of our days: 'twas His wisdom to determine them, but His perpetual and waking providence that fulfils and accomplisheth them; wherein the spirits, ourselves, and all the creatures of GOD in a secret and disputed way do execute His will. Let *them* not therefore complain of immaturity that die about thirty; they fall but like the whole World, whose solid and well-composed substance must not expect the duration and period of its constitution: when all things are completed in it, its age is accomplished; and the last and general fever may as naturally destroy it before six thousand, as me before forty. There is therefore some other hand that twines the thread of life than that of Nature: we are not onely ignorant in Antipathies and occult qualities; our ends are as obscure as our beginnings; the line of our days is drawn by night, and the various effects therein by a pensil that is invisible; wherein though we confess our ignorance, I am sure we do not err if we say it is the hand of GOD.

I am much taken with two verses of Lucan, since I have

been able not onely, as we do at School, to construe, but understand:

> *Victurosque Dei celant, ut vivere durent,*
> *Felix esse mori.*

> We're all deluded, vainly searching ways
> To make us happy by the length of days;
> For cunningly to make's protract this breath,
> The Gods conceal the happiness of Death.

There be many excellent strains in that Poet, wherewith his Stoical Genius hath liberally supplied him; and truely there are singular pieces in the Philosophy of Zeno, and doctrine of the Stoicks, which I perceive, delivered in a Pulpit, pass for current Divinity: yet herein are they in extreams, that can allow a man to be his own Assassine, and so highly extol the end and suicide of Cato. This is indeed not to fear death, but yet to be afraid of life. It is a brave act of valour to contemn death; but where life is more terrible than death, it is then the truest valour to dare to live. And herein Religion hath taught us a noble example; for all the valiant acts of Curtius, Scevola, or Codrus, do not parallel or match that one of Job; and sure there is no torture to the rack of a disease, nor any Ponyards in death it self like those in the way or prologue to it.

> *Emori nolo, sed me esse mortuum nihil curo.*

> I would not die, but care not to be dead.

Were I of Cæsar's Religion, I should be of his desires, and wish rather to go off at one blow, then to be sawed in pieces by the grating torture of a disease. Men that look no farther than their outsides, think health an appurtenance unto life, and quarrel with their constitutions for being sick; but I, that have examined the parts of man, and know upon what tender filaments that Fabrick hangs, do wonder that we are not always so; and, considering the thousand doors that lead to death, do thank my GOD that we can die but once. 'Tis not onely the mischief of diseases, and the villany of poysons, that make an end of us; we vainly accuse the fury of Guns, and the new inventions of death; it is in the power of every hand to destroy us, and we are beholding unto every one we meet, he doth not kill us. There is therefore but one comfort left, that, though it be in the power of the weakest arm to take away life, it is not in the strongest to deprive us of death: GOD would not exempt Himself from that, the misery of immortality in the flesh, He undertook not that was immortal. Certainly there is no happiness within this circle of flesh, nor is it in the Opticks of these eyes to behold felicity. The first day of our Jubilee is Death; the Devil hath therefore failed of his desires: we are happier with death than we should have been without it: there is no misery but in himself, where there is no end of misery; and so indeed, in his own sense, the Stoick is in the right. He forgets that he can dye who complains of misery; we are in the power of no calamity while death is in our own.

Now, besides this literal and positive kind of death, there are others whereof Divines make mention, and those, I think, not meerly Metaphorical, as mortification, dying unto sin and the World. Therefore, I say, every man hath a double Horoscope, one of his humanity, his birth; another of his Christianity, his baptism; and from this do I compute or calculate my Nativity, not reckoning those *Horæ combustæ* and odd days, or esteeming my self any thing, before I was my Saviours, and inrolled in the Register of CHRIST. Whosoever enjoys not this life, I count him but an apparition, though he wear about him the sensible affections of flesh. In these moral acceptions, the way to be immortal is to dye daily: nor can I think I have the true Theory of death, when I contemplate a skull, or behold a Skeleton, with those vulgar imaginations it casts upon us; I have therefore enlarged that common *Memento mori,* into a more Christian memorandum, *Memento quatuor Novissima,* those four inevitable points of us all, Death, Judgement, Heaven, and Hell. Neither did the contemplations of the Heathens rest in their graves, without a further thought of Rhadamanth, or some judicial proceeding after death, though in another way, and upon suggestion of their natural reasons. I cannot but marvail from what Sibyl or Oracle they stole the Prophesie of the Worlds destruction by fire, or whence Lucan learned to say,

> *Communis mundo superest rogus, ossibus astra*
> *Misturus.*

> There yet remains to th' World one common Fire,
> Wherein our bones with stars shall make one Pyre.

I believe the World grows near its end, yet is neither old nor decayed, nor shall ever perish upon the ruines of its own Principles. As the work of Creation was above Nature, so is its adversary, annihilation; without which the World hath not its end, but its mutation. Now what force should be able to consume it thus far, without the breath of GOD, which is the truest consuming flame, my Philosophy cannot inform me. Some believe there went not a minute to the Worlds creation, nor shall there go to its destruction; those six days, so punctually described, make not to them one moment, but rather seem to manifest the method and Idea of the great work of the intellect of GOD, than the manner how He proceeded in its operation. I cannot dream that there should be at the last day any such Judicial proceeding, or calling to the Bar, as indeed the Scripture seems to imply, and the literal Commentators do conceive: for unspeakable mysteries in the Scriptures are often delivered in a vulgar and illustrative way; and, being written unto man, are delivered, not as they truely are, but as they may be understood; wherein, notwithstanding, the different interpretations according to different capacities may stand firm with our devotion, nor be any way prejudicial to each single edification.

Now to determine the day and year of this inevitable time, is not onely convincible and statute-madness, but also manifest impiety. How shall we interpret Elias six thousand years, or imagine the secret communicated to a Rabbi, which GOD hath denyed unto His Angels? It had been an excellent Quære to have posed the Devil of Delphos, and must needs have forced him to some strange amphibology. It hath not onely mocked the predictions of sundry Astrologers in Ages past, but the prophesies of many melancholy heads in these present; who, neither understanding reasonably things past or present, pretend a knowledge of things to come; heads ordained onely to manifest the incredible effects of melancholy, and to fulfil old prophecies rather than be the authors of new. *In those days there shall come Wars and rumours of Wars,* to me seems no prophecy, but a constant truth, in all times verified since it was pronounced. *There shall be signs in the Moon and Stars;* how comes He then *like a Thief in the night,* when He gives an item of His coming? That common sign drawn from the revelation of Antichrist, is as obscure as any: in our common compute He hath been come these many years: but for my own part, (to speak freely), I am half of opinion that Antichrist is the Philosopher's stone in Divinity, for the discovery and invention whereof, though there be prescribed rules and probable inductions, yet hath hardly any man attained the perfect discovery thereof. That general opinion that the World grows near its end, hath possessed all ages past as nearly as ours. I am afraid that the Souls that now depart, cannot escape that lingring expostulation of the Saints under the Altar, *Quousque,* DOMINE? *How long,* O LORD? and groan in the expectation of that great Jubilee.

This is the day that must make good that great attribute of GOD, His Justice; that must reconcile those unanswerable doubts that torment the wisest understandings; and reduce those seeming inequalities and respective distributions in this world, to an equality and recompensive Justice in the next. This is that one day, that shall include and comprehend all that went before it; wherein, as in the last scene, all the Actors must enter, to compleat and make up the Catastrophe of this great piece. This is the day whose memory hath onely power to make us honest in the dark, and to be vertuous without a witness.

Ipsa sui pretium virtus sibi,

that Vertue is her own reward, is but a cold principle, and not able to maintain our variable resolutions in a constant and settled way of goodness. I have practised that honest artifice of Seneca, and in my retired and solitary imaginations, to detain me from the foulness of vice, have fancied to my self the presence of my dear and worthiest friends, before whom I should lose my head, rather than be vitious: yet herein I found that there was nought but moral honesty, and this was not to be vertuous for His sake Who must reward us at the last. I have tryed if I could reach that great resolution of his, to be honest without a thought of Heaven or Hell: and indeed I found, upon a natural inclination and inbred loyalty unto virtue, that I could serve her without a livery; yet not in that resolved and venerable way, but that the frailty of my nature, upon an easie temptation, might be induced to forget her. The life, therefore, and spirit of all our actions is the resurrection, and a stable apprehension that our ashes shall enjoy the fruit of our pious endeavours: without this, all Religion is a Fallacy, and those impieties of Lucian, Euripides, and Julian, are no blasphemies, but subtle verities, and Atheists have been the onely Philosophers.

How shall the dead arise, is no question of my Faith; to believe only possibilities, is not Faith, but meer Philosophy. Many things are true in Divinity, which are neither inducible by reason, nor confirmable by sense; and many things in Philosophy confirmable by sense, yet not inducible by reason. Thus it is impossible by any solid or demonstrative reasons to perswade a man to believe the conversion of the Needle to the North; though this be possible, and true, and easily credible, upon a single experiment unto the sense. I believe that our estranged and divided ashes shall unite again; that our separated dust, after so many Pilgrimages and transformations into the parts of Minerals, Plants, Animals, Elements, shall at the Voice of GOD return into their primitive shapes, and joyn again to make up their primary and predestinate forms. As at the Creation there was a separation of that confused mass into its species; so at the destruction thereof there shall be a separation into its distinct individuals. As at the Creation of the World, all the distinct species that we behold lay involved in one mass, till the fruitful Voice of GOD separated this united multitude into its several species; so at the last day, when those corrupted reliques shall be scattered in the Wilderness of forms, and seem to have forgot their proper habits, GOD by a powerful Voice shall command them back into their proper shapes, and call them out by their single individuals. Then shall appear the fertility of Adam, and the magick of that sperm that hath dilated into so many millions. I have often beheld as a miracle, that artificial resurrection and revivification of Mercury, how being mortified into a thousand shapes, it assumes again its own, and returns into its numerical self. Let us speak naturally and like Philosophers, the forms of alterable bodies in these sensible corruptions perish not; nor, as we imagine, wholly quit their mansions, but retire and contract themselves into their secret and unaccessible parts, where they may best protect themselves from the action of their Antagonist. A plant or vegetable consumed to ashes to a contemplative and school-Philosopher seems utterly destroyed, and the form to have taken his leave for ever; but to a sensible Artist the forms are not perished, but withdrawn into their incombustible part, where they lie secure from the action of that devouring element. This is made good by experience, which can from the Ashes of a Plant revive the plant, and from its cinders recall it into its stalk and leaves again. What the Art of man can do in these inferiour pieces, what blasphemy is it to affirm the finger of GOD cannot do in these more perfect and sensible structures! This is that mystical Philosophy, from whence no true Scholar becomes an Atheist, but from the visible effects of nature grows up a real Divine, and beholds not in a dream, as Ezekiel, but in an ocular and visible object, the types of his resurrection.

Now, the necessary Mansions of our restored selves are those two contrary and incomparable places we call *Heaven* and *Hell*. To define them, or strictly to determine what and where these are, surpasseth my Divinity. That elegant Apostle, which seemed to have a glimpse of Heaven, hath left but a negative description thereof; *which neither eye hath seen, nor ear hath heard, nor can enter into the heart of man:* he was translated out of himself to behold it; but, being returned into himself, could not express it. St. John's description by Emerals, Chrysolites, and precious Stones, is too weak to express the material Heaven we behold. Briefly therefore, where the Soul hath the full measure and complement of happiness; where the boundless appetite of that spirit remains compleatly satisfied, that it can neither desire addition nor alteration; that, I think, is truly Heaven: and this can onely be in the injoyment of that essence, whose infinite goodness is able to terminate the desires of it self, and the unsatiable wishes of ours: wherever GOD will thus manifest Himself, there is Heaven, though within the circle of this sensible world. Thus the Soul of man may be in Heaven any where, even within the limits of his own proper body; and when it ceaseth to live in the body, it may remain in its own soul, that is, its Creator: and thus we may say that St. Paul, *whether in the body, or out of the body,* was yet in Heaven. To place it in the Empyreal, or beyond the tenth sphear, is to forget the world's destruction; for, when this sensible world shall be destroyed, all shall then be here as it is now there, an Empyreal Heaven, a *quasi* vacuity; when to ask where Heaven is, is to demand where the presence of GOD is, or where we have the glory of that happy vision. Moses, that was bred up in all the learning of the Egyptians, committed a gross absurdity in Philosophy, when with these eyes of flesh he desired to see GOD, and petitioned his Maker, that is, Truth it self, to a contradiction. Those that imagine Heaven and Hell neighbours, and conceive a vicinity between those two extreams, upon consequence of the Parable, where Dives discoursed with Lazarus in Abraham's bosome, do too grosly conceive of those glorified creatures, whose eyes shall easily out-see the Sun, and behold without a perspective the extreamest distances: for if there shall be in our glorified eyes, the faculty of sight and reception of objects, I could think the visible species there to be in as unlimitable a way as now the intellectual. I grant that two bodies placed beyond the tenth sphear, or in a vacuity, according to Aristotle's Philosophy, could not behold each other, because there wants a body or Medium to hand and transport the visible rays of the object unto the sense; but when there shall be a general defect of either Medium to convey, or light to prepare and dispose that Medium, and yet a perfect vision, we must suspend the rules of our Philosophy, and make all good by a more absolute piece of opticks.

I cannot tell how to say that fire is the essence of Hell: I know not what to make of Purgatory, or conceive a flame that can either prey upon, or purifie the substance of a Soul. Those flames of sulphur mention'd in the Scriptures, I take not to be understood of this present Hell, but of that to come, where fire shall make up the complement of our tortures, and have a body or subject wherein to manifest its tyranny. Some, who have had the honour to be textuary in Divinity, are of opinion it shall be the same specifical fire with ours. This is hard to conceive; yet can I make good how even that may prey upon our bodies, and yet not consume us: for in this material World there are bodies that persist invincible in the powerfullest flames: and though by the action of fire they fall into ignition and liquation, yet will they never suffer a destruction. I would gladly know how Moses with an actual fire calcined or burnt the Golden Calf unto powder: for that mystical metal of Gold, whose solary and celestial nature I admire, exposed unto the violence of fire, grows onely hot, and liquifies, but consumeth not; so, when the consumable and volatile pieces of our bodies shall be refined into a more impregnable and fixed temper like Gold, though they suffer from the action of flames, they shall never perish, but lye immortal in the arms of fire. And surely, if this frame must suffer onely by the action of this element, there will many bodies escape; and not onely Heaven, but

Earth will not be at an end, but rather a beginning. For at present it is not earth, but a composition of fire, water, earth, and air; but at that time, spoiled of these ingredients, it shall appear in a substance more like it self, its ashes. Philosophers that opinioned the worlds destruction by fire, did never dream of annihilation, which is beyond the power of sublunary causes; for the last and proper action of that element is but vitrification, or a reduction of a body into glass; and therefore some of our Chymicks facetiously affirm, that at the last fire all shall be christallized and reverberated into glass, which is the utmost action of that element. Nor need we fear this term, *annihilation,* or wonder that GOD will destroy the works of his Creation; for man subsisting, who is, and will then truely appear, a Microcosm, the world cannot be said to be destroyed. For the eyes of GOD, and perhaps also of our glorified selves, shall as really behold and contemplate the World in its Epi-tome or contracted essence, as now it doth at large and in its dilated substance. In the seed of a Plant to the eyes of GOD, and to the understanding of man, there exists, though in an invisible way, the perfect leaves, flowers, and fruit thereof; for things that are *in posse* to the sense, are actually existent to the understanding. Thus GOD beholds all things, Who con-templates as fully His works in their Epitome, as in their full volume; and beheld as amply the whole world in that little compendium of the sixth day, as in the scattered and dilated pieces of those five before.

Men commonly set forth the torments of Hell by fire, and the extremity of corporal afflictions, and describe Hell in the same method that Mahomet doth Heaven. This indeed makes a noise, and drums in popular ears: but if this be the terrible piece thereof, it is not worthy to stand in diameter with Heaven, whose happiness consists in that part that is best able to com-prehend it, that immortal essence, that translated divinity and colony of GOD, the Soul. Surely, though we place Hell under Earth, the Devil's walk and purlue is about it: men speak too popularly who place it in those flaming mountains, which to grosser apprehensions represent Hell. The heart of man is the place Devils dwell in: I feel sometimes a Hell within my self; Lucifer keeps his Court in my breast, Legion is revived in me. There are as many Hells, as Anaxagoris conceited worlds. There was more than one Hell in Magdalene, when there were seven Devils, for every Devil is an Hell unto himself; he holds enough of torture in his own *ubi,* and needs not the misery of circumference to afflict him: and thus a distracted Conscience here, is a shadow or introduction unto Hell hereafter. Who can but pity the merciful intention of those hands that do destroy themselves? the Devil, were it in his power, would do the like; which being impossible, his miseries are endless, and he suffers most in that attribute wherein he is impassible, his immortality.

I thank GOD, and with joy I mention it, I was never afraid of Hell, nor never grew pale at the description of that place. I have so fixed my contemplations on Heaven, that I have almost forgot the Idea of Hell, and am afraid rather to lose the Joys of the one, than endure the misery of the other: to be deprived of them is a perfect Hell, and needs, methinks, no addition to compleat our afflictions. That terrible term hath never detained me from sin, nor do I owe any good action to the name thereof. I fear GOD, yet am not afraid of Him: His Mercies make me ashamed of my sins, before His Judgements afraid thereof. These are the forced and secondary method of His wisdom, which He useth but as the last remedy, and upon provocation; a course rather to deter the wicked, than incite the virtuous to His worship. I can hardly think there was ever any scared into Heaven; they go the fairest way to Heaven that would serve GOD without a Hell; other Mercenaries, that crouch into Him in fear of Hell, though they term themselves the servants, are indeed but the slaves, of the Almighty.

And to be true, and speak my soul, when I survey the occurrences of my life, and call into account the Finger of GOD, I can perceive nothing but an abyss and mass of mercies, either in general to mankind, or in particular to my self. And (whether out of the prejudice of my affection, or an inverting and partial conceit of His mercies, I know not; but) those which others term crosses, afflictions, judgements, misfortunes, to me, who inquire farther into them then their visible effects, they both appear, and in event have ever proved, the secret and dissembled favours of His affection. It is a singular piece of Wisdom to apprehend truly, and without passion, the Works of GOD, and so well to distinguish His Justice from His Mercy, as not to miscall those noble Attributes: yet it is likewise an honest piece of Logick, so to dispute and argue the proceedings of GOD, as to distinguish even His judgements into mercies. For GOD is merciful unto all, because better to the worst than the best deserve; and to say He punisheth none in this World, though it be a Paradox, is no absurdity. To one that hath committed Murther, if the Judge should only ordain a Fine, it were a madness to call this a punishment, and to repine at the sentence, rather than admire the clemency of the Judge. Thus, our offences being mortal, and deserving not only Death, but Damnation, if the goodness of GOD be content to traverse and pass them over with a loss, misfortune, or disease, what frensie were it to term this a punishment rather than an extremity of mercy, and to groan under the rod of His Judgements, rather than admire the Scepter of His Mercies! Therefore to adore, honour, and admire Him, is a debt of gratitude due from the obligation of our nature, states, and conditions; and with these thoughts, He that knows them best, will not deny that I adore Him. That I obtain Heaven, and the bliss thereof, is accidental, and not the intended work of my devotion; it being a felicity I can neither think to deserve, nor scarce in modesty to expect. For these two ends of us all, either as rewards or punishments, are mercifully ordained and disproportionably disposed unto our actions; the one being so far beyond our deserts, the other so infinitely below our demerits.

There is no Salvation to those that believe not in CHRIST, that is, say some, since His Nativity, and, as Divinity affirmeth, before also; which makes me much apprehend the ends of those honest Worthies and Philosophers which dyed before His Incarnation. It is hard to place those Souls in Hell, whose worthy lives do teach us Virtue on Earth; methinks, amongst those many subdivisions of Hell, there might have been one Limbo left for these. What a strange vision will it be to see their Poetical fictions converted into Verities, and their imagined and fancied Furies into real Devils! How strange to them will sound the History of Adam, when they shall suffer for him they never heard of! when they who derive their genealogy from the Gods, shall know they are the unhappy issue of sinful man! It is an insolent part of reason, to controvert the Works of GOD, or question the Justice of His proceedings. Could Humility teach others, as it hath instructed me, to contemplate the infinite and incomprehensible distance betwixt the Creator and the Creature; or did we seriously perpend that one simile of St. Paul, *Shall the Vessel say to the Potter, "Why hast thou made me thus?"* it would prevent these arrogant disputes of reason; nor would we argue the definitive sentence of GOD, either to Heaven or Hell. Men that live according to the right rule and law of reason, live but in their own kind, as beasts do in theirs; who justly obey the prescript of their natures, and therefore cannot reasonably demand a reward of their actions, as onely obeying the natural dictates of their reason. It will, therefore, and must at last appear, that all salvation is through CHRIST; which verity, I fear, these great examples of virtue must confirm, and make it good how the perfectest actions of earth have no title or claim unto Heaven.

Nor truely do I think the lives of these, or of any other, were ever correspondent, or in all points conformable, unto their doctrines. It is evident that Aristotle transgressed the rule of his own Ethicks. The Stoicks that condemn passion, and command a man to laugh at Phalaris his Bull, could not endure without a groan a fit of the Stone or Colick. The Scepticks that affirmed they knew nothing, even in that opinion confute themselves, and thought they knew more than all the World beside. Diogenes I hold to be the most vain-glorious man of his time, and more ambitious in refusing all Honours, than Alexander in rejecting none. Vice and the Devil put a

Fallacy upon our Reasons, and, provoking us too hastily to run from it, entangle and profound us deeper in it. The Duke of Venice, that weds himself unto the Sea by a Ring of Gold, I will not argue of prodigality, because it is a solemnity of good use and consequence in the State: but the Philosopher that threw his money into the Sea to avoid Avarice, was a notorious prodigal. There is no road or ready way to virtue: it is not an easie point of art to disentangle our selves from this riddle, or web of Sin. To perfect virtue, as to Religion, there is required a *Panoplia*, or compleat armour; that, whilst we lye at close ward against one Vice, we lye not open to the venny of another. And indeed wiser discretions that have the thred of reason to conduct them, offend without pardon; whereas under-heads may stumble without dishonour. There go so many circumstances to piece up one good action, that it is a lesson to be good, and we are forced to be virtuous by the book. Again, the Practice of men holds not an equal pace, yea, and often runs counter to their Theory: we naturally know what is good, but naturally pursue what is evil: the Rhetorick wherewith I perswade another, cannot perswade my self. There is a depraved appetite in us, that will with patience hear the learned instructions of Reason, but yet perform no farther than agrees to its own irregular humour. In brief, we all are monsters, that is, a composition of Man and Beast, wherein we must endeavour to be as the Poets fancy that wise man Chiron, that is, to have the Region of Man above that of Beast, and Sense to sit but at the feet of Reason. Lastly, I do desire with GOD that all, but yet affirm with men that few, shall know Salvation; that the bridge is narrow, the passage strait, unto life: yet those who do confine the Church of GOD, either to particular Nations, Churches, or Families, have made it far narrower than our Saviour ever meant it.

The vulgarity of those judgements that wrap the Church of GOD in Strabo's *cloak*, and restrain it unto Europe, seem to me as bad Geographers as Alexander, who thought he had Conquer'd all the World, when he had not subdued the half of any part thereof. For we cannot deny the Church of GOD

both in Asia and Africa, if we do not forget the Peregrinations
of the Apostles, the deaths of the Martyrs, the Sessions of
many and (even in our reformed judgement) lawful Councils,
held in those parts in the minority and nonage of ours. Nor
must a few differences, more remarkable in the eyes of man
than perhaps in the judgement of GOD, excommunicate from
Heaven one another; much less those Christians who are in a
manner all Martyrs, maintaining their Faith in the noble way
of persecution, and serving GOD in the Fire, whereas we
honour him but in the Sunshine. 'Tis true we all hold there is
a number of Elect, and many to be saved; yet, take our
Opinions together, and from the confusion thereof there will
be no such thing as salvation, nor shall any one be saved. For
first, the Church of Rome condemneth us, we likewise them;
the Subreformists and Sectaries sentence the Doctrine of our
Church as damnable; the Atomist, or Familist, reprobates all
these; and all these, them again. Thus, whilst the Mercies of
GOD do promise us Heaven, our conceits and opinions exclude
us from that place. There must be, therefore, more than one
St. Peter: particular Churches and Sects usurp the gates of
Heaven, and turn the key against each other; and thus we go
to Heaven against each others wills, conceits, and opinions,
and, with as much uncharity as ignorance, do err, I fear, in
points not only of our own, but one anothers salvation.

I believe many are saved, who to man seem reprobated;
and many are reprobated, who, in the opinion and sentence
of man, stand elected. There will appear at the Last day
strange and unexpected examples both of His Justice and His
Mercy; and therefore to define either, is folly in man, and
insolency even in the Devils. Those acute and subtil spirits,
in all their sagacity, can hardly divine who shall be saved;
which if they could Prognostick, their labour were at an end,
nor need they compass the earth *seeking whom they may devour*. Those who, upon a rigid application of the Law, sentence
Solomon unto damnation, condemn not onely him, but themselves, and the whole World: for, by the Letter and written
Word of GOD, we are without exception in the state of Death;

but there is a prerogative of God, and an arbitrary pleasure above the Letter of His own Law, by which alone we can pretend unto Salvation, and through which Solomon might be as easily saved as those who condemn him.

The number of those who pretend unto Salvation, and those infinite swarms who think to pass through the eye of this Needle, have much amazed me. That name and compellation of *little Flock*, doth not comfort, but deject, my Devotion; especially when I reflect upon mine own unworthiness, wherein, according to my humble apprehensions, I am below them all. I believe there shall never be an Anarchy in Heaven; but, as there are Hierarchies amongst the Angels, so shall there be degrees of priority amongst the Saints. Yet is it (I protest), beyond my ambition to aspire unto the first ranks; my desires onely are (and I shall be happy therein), to be but the last man, and bring up the Rere in Heaven.

Again, I am confident and fully perswaded, yet dare not take my oath, of my Salvation. I am as it were sure, and do believe without all doubt, that there is such a City as Constantinople; yet for me to take my Oath thereon were a kind of Perjury, because I hold no infallible warrant from my own sense to confirm me in the certainty thereof. And truly, though many pretend an absolute certainty of their Salvation, yet, when an humble Soul shall contemplate her own unworthiness, she shall meet with many doubts, and suddenly find how little we stand in need of the Precept of St. Paul, *Work out your salvation with fear and trembling*. That which is the cause of my Election, I hold to be the cause of my Salvation, which was the mercy and beneplacit of God, before I was, or the foundation of the World. *Before Abraham was, I am*, is the saying of Christ; yet is it true in some sense, if I say it of my self; for I was not onely before my self, but Adam, that is, in the Idea of God, and the decree of that Synod held from all Eternity. And in this sense, I say, the World was before the Creation, and at an end before it had a beginning; and thus was I dead before I was alive: though my grave be England, my dying place was Paradise: and Eve miscarried of me before she conceiv'd of Cain.

Insolent zeals, that do decry good Works and rely onely upon Faith, take not away merit: for, depending upon the efficacy of their Faith, they enforce the condition of God, and in a more sophistical way do seem to challenge Heaven. It was decreed by God, that only those that lapt in the water like Dogs, should have the honour to destroy the Midianites; yet could none of those justly challenge, or imagine he deserved, that honour thereupon. I do not deny but that true Faith, and such as God requires, is not onely a mark or token, but also a means, of our Salvation; but where to find this, is as obscure to me as my last end. And if our Saviour could object unto His own Disciples and Favourites, a Faith, that, to the quantity of a grain of Mustard-seed, is able to remove Mountains; surely, that which we boast of, is not any thing, or at the most, but a remove from nothing. This is the Tenor of my belief; wherein though there be many things singular, and to the humour of my irregular self, yet, if they square not with maturer Judgements, I disclaim them, and do no further father them, than the learned and best judgements shall authorize them.

THE SECOND PART

Now for that other Virtue of Charity, without which Faith is a meer notion, and of no existence, I have ever endeavoured to nourish the merciful disposition and humane inclination I borrowed from my Parents, and regulate it to the written and prescribed Laws of Charity. And if I hold the true Anatomy of my self, I am delineated and naturally framed to such a piece of virtue; for I am of a constitution so general, that it consorts and sympathiseth with all things. I have no antipathy, or rather Idiosyncrasie, in dyet, humour, air, any thing. I wonder not at the French for their dishes of Frogs, Snails and Toadstools, nor at the Jews for Locusts and Grasshoppers; but being amongst them, make them my common Viands, and I find they agree with my Stomach as well as theirs. I could digest a Salad gathered in a Church-yard, as well as in a Garden. I cannot start at the presence of a Serpent, Scorpion, Lizard, or Salamander: at the sight of a Toad or Viper, I find in me no desire to take up a stone to destroy them. I feel not in my self those common Antipathies that I can discover in others: those National repugnances do not touch me, nor do I behold with prejudice the French, Italian, Spaniard, or Dutch: but where I find their actions in balance with my Countrymen's, I honour, love, and embrace them in the same degree. I was born in the eighth Climate, but seem for to be framed and constellated unto all. I am no Plant that will not prosper out of a Garden. All places, all airs, make unto me one Countrey; I am in England every where, and under any Meridian. I have been shipwrackt, yet am not enemy with the Sea or Winds; I can study, play, or sleep in a Tempest. In brief, I am averse from nothing: my Conscience would give me the lye if I should say I absolutely detest or hate any essence but the Devil; or so at least abhor any thing, but that we might come to composition. If there be any among those common objects of hatred I do contemn and laugh at, it is that great enemy of Reason, Virtue and Religion, the Multitude: that numerous piece of monstrosity, which, taken asunder, seem men, and the reasonable creatures of GOD; but, confused together, make but one great beast, and a monstrosity more prodigious than Hydra. It is no breach of Charity to call these *Fools;* it is the style all holy Writers have afforded them, set down by Solomon in Canonical Scripture, and a point of our Faith to believe so. Neither in the name of *Multitude* do I onely include the base and minor sort of people; there is a rabble even amongst the Gentry, a sort of Plebeian heads, whose fancy moves with the same wheel as these; men in the same Level with Mechanicks, though their fortunes do somewhat guild their infirmities, and their purses compound for their follies. But as, in casting account, three or four men together come short in account of one man placed by himself below them; so neither are a troop of these ignorant *Doradoes* of that true esteem and value, as many a forlorn person, whose condition doth place him below their feet. Let us speak like Politicians: there is a Nobility without Heraldry, a natural dignity, whereby one man is ranked with another, another filed before him, according to the quality of his Desert, and preheminence of his good parts. Though the corruption of these times and the byas of present practice wheel another way, thus it was in the first and primitive Commonwealths, and is yet in the integrity and Cradle of well-order'd Polities, till corruption getteth ground; ruder desires labouring after that which wiser considerations contemn, every one having a liberty to amass and heap up riches, and they a licence or faculty to do or purchase any thing.

This general and indifferent temper of mine doth more neerly dispose me to this noble virtue. It is a happiness to be born and framed unto virtue, and to grow up from the seeds of nature, rather than the inoculation and forced graffs of education: yet if we are directed only by our particular Natures, and regulate our inclinations by no higher rule than that of our reasons, we are but Moralists; Divinity will still call us

Heathens. Therefore this great work of charity must have other motives, ends, and impulsions. I give no alms only to satisfie the hunger of my Brother, but to fulfil and accomplish the Will and Command of my GOD: I draw not my purse for his sake that demands it, but His That enjoyned it: I relieve no man upon the Rhetorick of his miseries, nor to content mine own commiserating disposition; for this is still but moral charity, and an act that oweth more to passion than reason. He that relieves another upon the bare suggestion and bowels of pity, doth not this, so much for his sake as for his own; for by compassion we make others misery our own, and so, by relieving them, we relieve our selves also. It is as erroneous a conceit to redress other Mens misfortunes upon the common considerations of merciful natures, that it may be one day our own case; for this is a sinister and politick kind of charity, whereby we seem to bespeak the pities of men in the like occasions. And truly I have observed that those professed Eleemosynaries, though in a croud or multitude, do yet direct and place their petitions on a few and selected persons: there is surely a Physiognomy, which those experienced and Master Mendicants observe, whereby they instantly discover a merciful aspect, and will single out a face wherein they spy the signatures and marks of Mercy. For there are mystically in our faces certain Characters which carry in them the motto of our Souls, wherein he that cannot read A. B. C. may read our natures. I hold moreover that there is a Phytognomy, or Physiognomy, not only of Men, but of Plants and Vegetables; and in every one of them some outward figures which hang as signs or bushes of their inward forms. The Finger of GOD hath left an Inscription upon all His works, not graphical or composed of Letters, but of their several forms, constitutions, parts, and operations, which, aptly joyned together, do make one word that doth express their natures. By these Letters GOD calls the Stars by their names; and by this Alphabet Adam assigned to every creature a name peculiar to its Nature. Now there are, besides these Characters in our Faces, certain mystical figures in our Hands, which I dare not call

meer dashes, strokes *à la volée,* or at random, because delineated by a Pencil that never works in vain; and hereof I take
more particular notice, because I carry that in mine own
hand which I could never read of nor discover in another.
Aristotle, I confess, in his acute and singular Book of *Physiognomy,* hath made no mention of Chiromancy; yet I believe
the Egyptians, who were neerer addicted to those abstruse
and mystical sciences, had a knowledge therein, to which
those vagabond and counterfeit Egyptians did after pretend,
and perhaps retained a few corrupted principles, which sometimes might verifie their prognosticks.

It is the common wonder of all men, how among so many
millions of faces, there should be none alike: now contrary,
I wonder as much how there should be any. He that shall
consider how many thousand several words have been care-
lesly and without study composed out of twenty-four Letters;
withal, how many hundred lines there are to be drawn in the
Fabrick of one Man, shall easily find that this variety is necessary; and it will be very hard that they shall so concur as to
make one portract like another. Let a Painter carelessly limb
out a million of Faces, and you shall find them all different;
yea, let him have his Copy before him, yet after all his art
there will remain a sensible distinction; for the pattern or
example of every thing is the perfectest in that kind, whereof
we still come short, though we transcend or go beyond it,
because herein it is wide, and agrees not in all points unto
the copy. Nor doth the similitude of Creatures disparage the
variety of Nature, nor any way confound the Works of GOD.
For even in things alike there is diversity; and those that do
seem to accord do manifestly disagree. And thus is man like
GOD; for in the same things that we resemble Him, we are
utterly different from Him. There was never anything so like
another as in all points to concur: there will ever some reserved difference slip in, to prevent the identity; without
which, two several things would not be alike, but the same,
which is impossible.

But to return from Philosophy to Charity: I hold not so

narrow a conceit of this virtue, as to conceive that to give Alms is onely to be Charitable, or think a piece of Liberality can comprehend the Total of Charity. Divinity hath wisely divided the act thereof into many branches, and hath taught us in this narrow way many paths unto goodness; as many ways as we may do good, so many ways we may be charitable. There are infirmities not onely of Body, but of Soul, and Fortunes, which do require the merciful hand of our abilities. I cannot contemn a man for ignorance, but behold him with as much pity as I do Lazarus. It is no greater Charity to cloath his body, than apparel the nakedness of his Soul. It is an honourable object to see the reasons of other men wear our Liveries, and their borrowed understandings do homage to the bounty of ours: it is the cheapest way of beneficence, and, like the natural charity of the Sun, illuminates another without obscuring itself. To be reserved and caitiff in this part of goodness, is the sordidest piece of covetousness, and more contemptible than pecuniary Avarice. To this (as calling my self a Scholar), I am obliged by the duty of my condition: I make not therefore my head a grave, but a treasure, of knowledge; I intend no Monopoly, but a community, in learning; I study not for my own sake only, but for theirs that study not for themselves. I envy no man that knows more than my self, but pity them that know less. I instruct no man as an exercise of my knowledge, or with an intent rather to nourish and keep it alive in mine own head then beget and propagate it in his: and in the midst of all my endeavours there is but one thought that dejects me, that my acquired parts must perish with my self, nor can be Legacied among my honoured Friends. I cannot fall out or contemn a man for an errour, or conceive why a difference in Opinion should divide an affection; for Controversies, Disputes, and Argumentations, both in Philosophy and in Divinity, if they meet with discreet and peaceable natures, do not infringe the Laws of Charity. In all disputes, so much as there is of passion, so much as there is of nothing to the purpose; for then Reason, like a bad Hound, spends upon a false Scent, and forsakes the question first started. And this is one reason why Controversies are never determined; for, though they be amply proposed, they are scarce at all handled, they do so swell with unnecessary Digressions; and the Parenthesis on the party is often as large as the main discourse upon the subject. The Foundations of Religion are already established, and the Principles of Salvation subscribed unto by all: there remains not many controversies worth a Passion; and yet never any disputed without, not only in Divinity, but in inferiour Arts. What a βατραχομυομαχία and hot skirmish is betwixt S. and T. in Lucian! How do Grammarians hack and slash for the Genitive case in *Jupiter!* How do they break their own pates to salve that of Priscian!

Si foret in terris, rideret Democritus.

Yea, even amongst wiser militants, how many wounds have been given, and credits slain, for the poor victory of an opinion, or beggarly conquest of a distinction! Scholars are men of Peace, they bear no Arms, but their tongues are sharper than Actius his razor; their Pens carry farther, and give a louder report than Thunder: I had rather stand the shock of a Basilisco, than the fury of a merciless Pen. It is not meer Zeal to Learning, or Devotion to the Muses, that wiser Princes Patron the Arts, and carry an indulgent aspect unto Scholars; but a desire to have their names eternized by the memory of their writings, and a fear of the revengeful Pen of succeeding ages; for these are the men, that, when they have played their parts, and had their *exits,* must step out and give the moral of their Scenes, and deliver unto Posterity an Inventory of their Virtues and Vices. And surely there goes a great deal of Conscience to the compiling of an History: there is no reproach to the scandal of a Story; it is such an authentick kind of falshood that with authority belies our good names to all Nations and Posterity.

There is another offence unto Charity, which no Author hath ever written of, and few take notice of; and that's the reproach, not of whole professions, mysteries, and conditions, but of whole Nations, wherein by opprobious Epithets we miscall each other, and by an uncharitable Logick, from a disposition in a few, conclude a habit in all.

> *Le mutin Anglois, et le bravache Escossois,*
> *Et le fol François,*
> *Le poultron Romain, le larron de Gascongne,*
> *L'Espagnol superbe, et l'Aleman yvrongne.*

St. Paul, that calls the Cretion *lyars,* doth it but indirectly, and upon quotation of their own Poet. It is as bloody a thought in one way, as Nero's was in another; for by a word we wound a thousand, and at one blow assassine the honour of a Nation. It is as compleat a piece of madness to miscal and rave against the times, or think to recal men to reason by a fit of passion. Democritus, that thought to laugh the times into goodness, seems to me as deeply Hypochondriack as Heraclitus, that bewailed them. It moves not my spleen to behold the multitude in their proper humours, that is, in their fits of folly and madness; as well understanding that wisdom is not prophan'd unto the World, and 'tis the priviledge of a few to be Virtuous. They that endeavour to abolish Vice, destroy also Virtue; for contraries, though they destroy one another, are yet the life of one another. Thus Virtue (abolish vice), is an Idea. Again, the community of sin doth not disparage goodness; for when Vice gains upon the major part, Virtue, in whom it remains, becomes more excellent; and being lost in some, multiplies its goodness in others which remain untouched and persist intire in the general inundation. I can therefore behold Vice without a Satyr, content only with an admonition, or instructive reprehension; for Noble Natures, and such as are capable of goodness, are railed into vice, that might as easily be admonished into virtue; and we should all be so far the Orators of goodness, as to protect her from the power of Vice, and maintain the cause of injured truth. No man can justly censure or condemn another, because indeed no man truly knows another. This I perceive in my self; for I am in the dark to all the world, and my nearest friends behold me but in a

cloud. Those that know me but superficially, think less of
me than I do of myself; those of my neer acquaintance think
more; GOD, Who truly knows me, knows that I am nothing;
for He only beholds me and all the world, Who looks not on
us through a derived ray, or a trajection of a sensible species,
but beholds the substance without the helps of accidents, and
the forms of things as we their operations. Further, no man
can judge another, because no man knows himself: for we
censure others but as they disagree from that humour which
we fancy laudable in our selves, and commend others but for
that wherein they seem to quadrate and consent with us. So
that, in conclusion, all is but that we all condemn, Self-love.
'Tis the general complaint of these times, and perhaps of
those past, that charity grows cold; which I perceive most
verified in those which most do manifest the fires and flames
of zeal; for it is a virtue that best agrees with coldest natures,
and such as are complexioned for humility. But how shall we
expect Charity towards others, when we are uncharitable to
our selves? *Charity begins at home,* is the voice of the World;
yet is every man his greatest enemy, and, as it were, his own
Executioner. *Non occides,* is the Commandment of GOD, yet
scarce observed by any man; for I perceive every man is his
own *Atropos,* and lends a hand to cut the thred of his own days.
Cain was not therefore the first Murtherer, but Adam, who
brought in death; whereof he beheld the practice and example
in his own son Abel, and saw that verified in the experience
of another, which faith could not perswade him in the Theory
of himself.

There is, I think, no man that apprehends his own miseries
less than my self, and no man that so neerly apprehends anothers. I could lose an arm without a tear, and with few
groans, methinks, be quartered into pieces; yet can I weep
most seriously at a Play, and receive with true passion the
counterfeit grief of those known and professed Impostures.
It is a barbarous part of inhumanity to add unto any afflicted
parties misery, or indeavour to multiply in any man a passion
whose single nature is already above his patience. This was

the greatest affliction of Job, and those oblique expostulations of his Friends a deeper injury than the down-right blows of the Devil. It is not the tears of our own eyes only, but of our friends also, that do exhaust the current of our sorrows; which, falling into many streams, runs more peaceably, and is contented with a narrower channel. It is an act within the power of charity, to translate a passion out of one breast into another, and to divide a sorrow almost out of it self; for an affliction, like a dimension, may be so divided, as, if not indivisible, at least to become insensible. Now with my friend I desire not to share or participate, but to engross, his sorrows; that, by making them mine own, I may more easily discuss them; for in mine own reason, and within my self, I can command that which I cannot intreat without my self, and within the circle of another. I have often thought those noble pairs and examples of friendship not so truly Histories of what had been, as fictions of what should be; but I now perceive nothing in them but possibilities, nor any thing in the Heroick examples of Damon and Pythias, Achilles and Patroclus, which methinks upon some grounds I could not perform within the narrow compass of my self. That a man should lay down his life for his Friend, seems strange to vulgar affections, and such as confine themselves within that Worldly principle, *Charity begins at home.* For mine own part I could never remember the relations that I held unto my self, nor the respect that I owe unto my own nature, in the cause of GOD, my Country, and my Friends. Next to these three, I do embrace my self. I confess I do not observe that order that the Schools ordain our affections, to love our Parents, Wives, Children, and then our Friends; for, excepting the injunctions of Religion, I do not find in my self such a necessary and indissoluble Sympathy to all those of my blood. I hope I do not break the fifth Commandment, if I conceive I may love my friend before the nearest of my blood, even those to whom I owe the principles of life. I never yet cast a true affection on a woman; but I have loved my friend as I do virtue, my soul, my GOD. From hence me thinks I do conceive how GOD loves man, what

happiness there is in the love of GOD. Omitting all other, there
are three most mystical unions: 1. two natures in one person;
2. three persons in one nature; 3. one soul in two bodies; for
though indeed they be really divided, yet are they so united,
as they seem but one, and make rather a duality than two
distinct souls.

There are wonders in true affection: it is a body of *Enigma's,*
mysteries, and riddles; wherein two so become one, as they
both become two. I love my friend before my self, and yet
methinks I do not love him enough: some few months hence
my multiplied affection will make me believe I have not loved
him at all. When I am from him, I am dead till I be with him;
when I am with him, I am not satisfied, but would still be
nearer him. United souls are not satisfied with imbraces, but
desire to be truly each other; which being impossible, their
desires are infinite, and must proceed without a possibility
of satisfaction. Another misery there is in affection, that
whom we truly love like our own selves, we forget their looks,
nor can our memory retain the Idea of their faces; and it is
no wonder, for they are our selves, and our affection makes
their looks our own. This noble affection falls not on vulgar
and common constitutions, but on such as are mark'd for
virtue: he that can love his friend with this noble ardour,
will in a competent degree affect all. Now, if we can bring
our affections to look beyond the body, and cast an eye upon
the soul, we have found out the true object, not only of friendship, but Charity; and the greatest happiness that we can
bequeath the soul, is that wherein we all do place our last
felicity, Salvation; which though it be not in our power to
bestow, it is in our charity and pious invocations to desire, if
not procure and further. I cannot contentedly frame a prayer
for my self in particular, without a catalogue for my friends;
nor request a happiness, wherein my sociable disposition doth
not desire the fellowship of my neighbour. I never hear the
Toll of a passing Bell, though in my mirth, without my prayers
and best wishes for the departing spirit; I cannot go to cure
the body of my patient, but I forget my profession, and call

unto GOD for his soul; I cannot see one say his prayers, but, in stead of imitating him, I fall into a supplication for him, who perhaps is no more to me than a common nature: and if GOD hath vouchsafed an ear to my supplications, there are surely many happy that never saw me, and enjoy the blessing of mine unknown devotions. To pray for Enemies, that is, for their salvation, is no harsh precept, but the practice of our daily and ordinary devotions. I cannot believe the story of the Italian: our bad wishes and uncharitable desires proceed no further than this life; it is the Devil, and the uncharitable votes of Hell, that desire our misery in the World to come.

To do no injury, nor take none, was a principle, which to my former years and impatient affections seemed to contain enough of Morality; but my more setled years and Christian constitution have fallen upon severer resolutions. I can hold there is no such thing as injury; that, if there be, there is no such injury as revenge, and no such revenge as the contempt of an injury; that to hate another, is to malign himself; that the truest way to love another, is to despise our selves. I were unjust unto mine own Conscience, if I should say I am at variance with any thing like my self. I find there are many pieces in this one fabrick of man; this frame is raised upon a mass of Antipathies. I am one methinks, but as the World; wherein notwithstanding there are a swarm of distinct essences, and in them another World of contrarieties; we carry private and domestick enemies within, publick and more hostile adversaries without. The Devil, that did but buffet St. Paul, plays methinks at sharp with me. Let me be nothing, if within the compass of my self I do not find the battail of Lepanto, Passion against Reason, Reason against Faith, Faith against the Devil, and my Conscience against all. There is another man within me, that's angry with me, rebukes, commands, and dastards me. I have no Conscience of Marble to resist the hammer of more heavy offences; nor yet so soft and waxen, as to take the impression of each single peccadillo or scrape of infirmity. I am of a strange belief, that it is as easie to be forgiven some sins, as to commit some others. For my Original sin, I hold it to be washed away in my Baptism: for my actual transgressions, I compute and reckon with GOD but from my last repentance, Sacrament, or general absolution; and therefore am not terrified with the sins or madness of my youth. I thank the goodness of GOD, I have no sins that want a name; I am not singular in offences; my transgressions are Epidemical, and from the common breath of our corruption. For there are certain tempers of body, which, matcht with an humorous depravity of mind, do hatch and produce vitiosities, whose newness and monstrosity of nature admits no name: this was the temper of that Lecher that fell in love with a Statua, and the constitution of Nero in his Spintrian recreations. For the Heavens are not only fruitful in new and unheard-of stars, the Earth in plants and animals, but mens minds also in villainy and vices. Now the dulness of my reason, and the vulgarity of my disposition, never prompted my invention, nor solicited my affection unto any of these; yet even those common and quotidian infirmities that so necessarily attend me, and do seem to be my very nature, have so dejected me, so broken the estimation that I should have otherwise of my self, that I repute my self the most abjectest piece of mortality. Divines prescribe a fit of sorrow to repentance: there goes indignation, anger, sorrow, hatred, into mine; passions of a contrary nature, which neither seem to sute with this action, nor my proper constitution. It is no breach of charity to our selves, to be at variance with our Vices, nor to abhor that part of us which is an enemy to the ground of charity, our GOD; wherein we do but imitate our great selves, the world, whose divided Antipathies and contrary faces do yet carry a charitable regard unto the whole, by their particular discords preserving the common harmony, and keeping in fetters those powers, whose rebellions, once Masters, might be the ruine of all.

I thank GOD, amongst those millions of Vices I do inherit and hold from Adam, I have escaped one, and that a mortal enemy to Charity, the first and father-sin, not onely of man, but of the devil, Pride: a vice whose name is comprehended in a Monosyllable, but in its nature not circumscribed with a World. I have escaped it in a condition that can hardly avoid it. Those petty acquisitions and reputed perfections that advance and elevate the conceits of other men, add no feathers unto mine. I have seen a Grammarian towr and plume himself over a single line in Horace, and shew more pride in the construction of one Ode, than the Author in the composure of the whole book. For my own part, besides the *Jargon* and *Patois* of several Provinces, I understand no less than six Languages; yet I protest I have no higher conceit of my self, than had our Fathers before the confusion of Babel, when there was but one Language in the World, and none to boast himself either Linguist or Critick. I have not onely seen several Countries, beheld the nature of their Climes, the Chorography of their Provinces, Topography of their Cities, but understood their several Laws, Customs, and Policies; yet cannot all this perswade the dulness of my spirit unto such an opinion of my self, as I behold in nimbler and conceited heads, that never looked a degree beyond their Nests. I know the names, and somewhat more, of all the constellations in my Horizon; yet I have seen a prating Mariner, that could onely name the pointers and the North Star, out-talk me, and conceit himself a whole Sphere above me. I know most of the Plants of my Countrey, and of those about me; yet methinks I do not know so many as when I did but know a hundred, and had scarcely ever Simpled further than *Cheapside*. For, indeed, heads of capacity, and such as are not full with a handful or easie measure of knowledge, think they know nothing till they know all; which being impossible, they fall upon the opinion of Socrates, and only know they know not any thing. I cannot think that Homer pin'd away upon the riddle of the fishermen; or that Aristotle, who understood the uncertainty of knowledge, and confessed so often the reason of man too weak for the works of nature, did ever drown himself upon the flux and reflux of Euripus. We do but learn to-day what our better advanced judgements will unteach to morrow; and Aristotle doth but instruct us, as Plato did him; that is, to confute himself. I have run through all sorts, yet find no rest in any: though our first studies and *junior* endeavours may style us Peripateticks, Stoicks, or Academicks; yet I perceive the wisest heads prove, at last, almost all Scepticks, and stand like Janus in the field of knowledge. I have therefore one common and authentick Philosophy I learned in the Schools, whereby I discourse and satisfy the reason of other men; another more reserved, and drawn from experience, whereby I content mine own. Solomon, that complained of ignorance in the height of knowledge, hath not only humbled my conceits, but discouraged my endeavours. There is yet another conceit that hath sometimes made me shut my books, which tells me it is a vanity to waste our days in the blind pursuit of knowledge; it is but attending a little longer, and we shall enjoy that by instinct and infusion, which we endeavour at here by labour and inquisition. It is better to sit down in a modest ignorance, and rest contented with the natural blessing of our own reasons, than buy the uncertain knowledge of this life with sweat and vexation, which Death gives every fool *gratis,* and is an accessary of our glorification.

I was never yet once, and commend their resolutions who never marry twice: not that I disallow of second marriage; as neither, in all cases, of Polygamy, which, considering some times, and the unequal number of both sexes, may be also necessary. The whole World was made for man, but the twelfth part of man for woman: Man is the whole World, and the Breath of GOD; Woman the Rib and crooked piece of man. I could be content that we might procreate like trees, without conjunction, or that there were any way to perpetuate the World without this trivial and vulgar way of union: it is the foolishest act a wise man commits in all his life; nor is there any thing that will more deject his cool'd imagination, when he shall consider what an odd and unworthy piece of folly he hath committed. I speak not in prejudice, nor am averse from that sweet Sex, but naturally amorous of all that is beautiful. I can look a whole day with delight upon a handsome Picture, though it be but of an Horse. It is my temper, and I like it the better, to affect all harmony; and sure there is musick even in the beauty, and the silent note which Cupid strikes, far sweeter than the sound of an instrument. For there is a musick where ever there is a harmony, order, or proportion: and thus far we may maintain the music of the Sphears; for those well-ordered motions, and regular paces, though they give no sound unto the ear, yet to the understanding they strike a note most full of harmony. Whosoever is harmonically composed delights in harmony; which makes me much distrust the symmetry of those heads which declaim against all Church-Musick. For my self, not only from my obedience, but my particular Genius, I do embrace it: for even that vulgar and Tavern-Musick, which makes one man merry, another mad, strikes in me a deep fit of devotion, and a profound contemplation of the First Composer. There is something in it of Divinity more than the ear discovers: it is an Hieroglyphical and shadowed lesson of the whole World, and creatures of GOD; such a melody to the ear, as the whole World, well understood, would afford the understanding. In brief, it is a sensible fit of that harmony which intellectually sounds in the ears of GOD. I will not say, with Plato, the soul is an harmony, but harmonical, and hath its nearest sympathy unto Musick: thus some, whose temper of body agrees, and humours the constitution of their souls, are born Poets, though indeed all are naturally inclined unto Rhythme. This made Tacitus, in the very first line of his Story, fall upon a verse; and Cicero, the worst of Poets, but declaiming for a Poet, falls in the very first sentence upon a perfect Hexameter. I feel not in me those sordid and unchristian desires of my profession; I do not secretly implore and wish for Plagues, rejoyce at Famines, revolve Ephemerides and Almanacks in expectation of malignant Aspects, fatal Conjunctions, and Eclipses. I rejoyce not at unwholesome Springs, nor unseasonable Winters: my Prayer goes with the Husbandman's; I desire every thing in its proper season, that neither men nor the times be put out of temper. Let me be sick my self, if sometimes the

malady of my patient be not a disease unto me. I desire rather
to cure his infirmities than my own necessities. Where I do
him no good, methinks it is scarce honest gain; though I confess 'tis but the worthy salary of our well-intended endeavours.
I am not only ashamed, but heartily sorry, that, besides death,
there are diseases incurable: yet not for my own sake, or
that they be beyond my Art, but for the general cause and
sake of humanity, whose common cause I apprehend as mine
own. And to speak more generally, those three Noble Professions which all civil Commonwealths do honour, are raised
upon the fall of Adam, and are not any way exempt from their
infirmities; there are not only diseases incurable in Physick,
but cases indissolvable in Laws, Vices incorrigible in Divinity.
If General Councils may err, I do not see why particular
Courts should be infallible: their perfectest rules are raised
upon the erroneous reasons of Man, and the Laws of one do
but condemn the rules of another; as Aristotle oft-times the
opinions of his Predecessours, because, though agreeable to
reason, yet were not consonant to his own rules, and the
Logick of his proper Principles. Again, (to speak nothing of
the Sin against the HOLY GHOST, whose cure not onely, but
whose nature is unknown), I can cure the Gout or Stone in
some, sooner than Divinity, Pride, or Avarice in others. I can
cure Vices by Physick when they remain incurable by Divinity, and shall obey my Pills when they contemn their
precepts. I boast nothing, but plainly say, we all labour against
our own cure; for death is the cure of all diseases. There is
no *Catholicon* or universal remedy I know, but this; which,
though nauseous to queasie stomachs, yet to prepared appe-
tites is Nectar, and a pleasant potion of immortality.

For my Conversation, it is like the Sun's, with all men, and
with a friendly aspect to good and bad. Methinks there is no
man bad, and the worst, best; that is, while they are kept
within the circle of those qualities wherein they are good:
there is no man's mind of such discordant and jarring a temper, to which a tunable disposition may not strike a harmony.
Magnæ virtutes, nec minora vitia; it is the posie of the best

natures, and may be inverted on the worst; there are in the most depraved and venomous dispositions, certain pieces that remain untoucht, which by an *Antiperistasis* become more excellent, or by the excellency of their antipathies are able to preserve themselves from the contagion of their enemy vices, and persist intire beyond the general corruption. For it is also thus in nature: the greatest Balsomes do lie enveloped in the bodies of most powerful Corrosives. I say, moreover, and I ground upon experience, that poisons contain within them-selves their own Antidote, and that which preserves them from the venome of themselves, without which they were not deleterious to others onely, but to themselves also. But it is the corruption that I fear within me, not the contagion of commerce without me. 'Tis that unruly regiment within me, that will destroy me; 'tis I that do infect my self; the man without a Navel yet lives in me; I feel that original canker and corrode and devour me; and therefore *Defenda me* Dios *de me*, "Lord deliver me from my self," is a part of my Letany, and the first voice of my retired imaginations. There is no man alone, because every man is a Microcosm, and carries the whole World about him. *Nunquam minus solus quam cum solus,* though it be the Apothegme of a wise man, is yet true in the mouth of a fool. Indeed, though in a Wilderness, a man is never alone, not only because he is with himself and his own thoughts, but because he is with the Devil, who ever con-sorts with our solitude, and is that unruly rebel that musters up those disordered motions which accompany our sequestred imaginations. And to speak more narrowly, there is no such thing as solitude, nor any thing that can be said to be alone and by itself, but God, Who is His own circle, and can subsist by Himself; all others, besides their dissimilar and Heter-ogeneous parts, which in a manner multiply their natures, cannot subsist without the concourse of God, and the society of that hand which doth uphold their natures. In brief, there can be nothing truly alone and by it self, which is not truly one; and such is only God: all others do transcend an unity, and so by consequence are many.

Now for my life, it is a miracle of thirty years, which to relate, were not a History, but a piece of Poetry, and would sound to common ears like a Fable. For the World, I count it not an Inn, but an Hospital; and a place not to live, but to dye in. The world that I regard is my self; it is the Microcosm of my own frame that I cast mine eye on; for the other, I use it but like my Globe, and turn it round sometimes for my recreation. Men that look upon my outside, perusing only my condition and Fortunes, do err in my Altitude; for I am above Atlas his shoulders. The earth is a point not only in respect of the Heavens above us, but of that heavenly and celestial part within us; that mass of Flesh that circumscribes me, limits not my mind: that surface that tells the Heavens it hath an end, cannot persuade me I have any: I take my circle to be above three hundred and sixty; though the number of the Ark do measure my body, it comprehendeth not my mind: whilst I study to find how I am a Microcosm, or little World, I find my self something more than the great. There is surely a piece of Divinity in us, something that was before the Elements, and owes no homage unto the Sun. Nature tells me I am the Image of God, as well as Scripture: he that understands not thus much, hath not his introduction or first lesson, and is yet to begin the Alphabet of man. Let me not injure the felicity of others, if I say I am as happy as any: *Ruat cœlum, fiat voluntas Tua*, salveth all; so that whatsoever happens, it is but what our daily prayers desire. In brief, I am content; and what should Providence add more? Surely this is it we call Happiness, and this do I enjoy; with this I am happy in a dream, and as content to enjoy a happiness in a fancy, as others in a more apparent truth and realty. There is surely a neerer apprehension of any thing that delights us in our dreams, than in our waked senses: without this I were unhappy; for my awaked judgment discontents me, ever whispering unto me, that I am from my friend; but my friendly dreams in the night requite me, and make me think I am within his arms. I thank God for my happy dreams, as I do for my good rest; for there is a satisfaction in them unto reasonable desires, and such as can be content with a fit of happiness: and surely it is not a melancholy conceit to think we are all asleep in this World, and that the conceits of this life are as meer dreams to those of the next; as the Phantasms of the night, to the conceits of the day. There is an equal delusion in both, and the one doth but seem to be the embleme or picture of the other: we are somewhat more than our selves in our sleeps, and the slumber of the body seems to be but the waking of the soul. It is the ligation of sense, but the liberty of reason; and our waking conceptions do not match the Fancies of our sleeps. At my Nativity my Ascendant was the watery sign of Scorpius; I was born in the Planetary hour of Saturn, and I think I have a piece of that Leaden Planet in me. I am no way facetious, nor disposed for the mirth and galliardize of company; yet in one dream I can compose a whole Comedy, behold the action, apprehend the jests, and laugh my self awake at the conceits thereof. Were my memory as faithful as my reason is then fruitful, I would never study but in my dreams; and this time also would I chuse for my devotions: but our grosser memories have then so little hold of our abstracted understandings, that they forget the story, and can not relate to our awaked souls, a confused and broken tale of that that hath passed. Aristotle, who hath written a singular Tract *Of Sleep,* hath not, me-thinks, throughly defined it; nor yet Galen, though he seem to have corrected it; for those Noctambuloes and night-walkers, though in their sleep, do yet injoy the action of their senses. We must therefore say that there is something in us that is not in the jurisdiction of Morpheus; and that those abstracted and ecstatick souls do walk about in their own corps, as spirits with the bodies they assume, wherein they seem to hear, see, and feel, though indeed the Organs are destitute of sense, and their natures of those faculties that should inform them. Thus it is observed, that men sometimes, upon the hour of their departure, do speak and reason above themselves; for then the soul, beginning to be freed from the ligaments of the body, begins to reason like her self, and to discourse in a strain above mortality.

We term sleep a death; and yet it is waking that kills us, and destroys those spirits that are the house of life. 'Tis indeed a part of life that best expresseth death; for every man truely lives, so long as he acts his nature, or some way makes good the faculties of himself. Themistocles, therefore, that slew his Soldier in his sleep, was a merciful Executioner: 'tis a kind of punishment the mildness of no laws hath invented: I wonder the fancy of Lucan and Seneca did not discover it. It is that death by which we may be literally said to dye daily; a death which Adam dyed before his mortality; a death whereby we live a middle and moderating point between life and death: in fine, so like death, I dare not trust it without my prayers, and an half adieu unto the World, and take my farewel in a Colloquy with GOD.

> The night is come, like to the day,
> Depart not Thou, great GOD, away.
> Let not my sins, black as the night,
> Eclipse the lustre of Thy light:
> Keep still in my Horizon; for to me
> The Sun makes not the day, but Thee.
> Thou, Whose nature cannot sleep,
> On my temples Centry keep;
> Guard me 'gainst those watchful foes,
> Whose eyes are open while mine close.
> Let no dreams my head infest,
> But such as Jacob's temples blest.
> While I do rest, my Soul advance;
> Make my sleep a holy trance;
> That I may, my rest being wrought,
> Awake into some holy thought;
> And with as active vigour run
> My course, as doth the nimble Sun.
> Sleep is a death; O make me try,
> By sleeping, what it is to die;

And as gently lay my head
On my grave, as now my bed.
Howere I rest, great GOD, let me
Awake again at last with Thee;
And thus assur'd, behold I lie
Securely, or to awake or die.
These are my drowsie days; in vain
I do now wake to sleep again:
O come that hour, when I shall never
Sleep again, but wake for ever.

This is the Dormative I take to bedward; I need no other
Laudanum than this to make me sleep; after which I close
mine eyes in security, content to take my leave of the Sun, and
sleep unto the Resurrection.

The method I should use in distributive Justice, I often
observe in commutative; and keep a Geometrical proportion in both, whereby becoming equable to others, I become
unjust to my self, and supererogate in that common principle,
Do unto others as thou wouldst be done unto thy self. I was
not born unto riches, neither is it, I think, my Star to be
wealthy; or, if it were, the freedom of my mind, and frank-
ness of my disposition, were able to contradict and cross my
fates: for to me, avarice seems not so much a vice, as a deplor-
able piece of madness; to conceive ourselves pipkins, or be
perswaded that we are dead, is not so ridiculous, nor so many
degrees beyond the power of Hellebore, as this. The opinions
of Theory, and positions of men, are not so void of reason as
their practised conclusions. Some have held that Snow is
black, that the earth moves, that the Soul is air, fire, water;
but all this is Philosophy, and there is no delirium, if we do
but speculate the folly and indisputable dotage of avarice to
that subterraneous Idol, and God of the Earth. I do confess
I am an Atheist; I cannot perswade myself to honour that
the World adores; whatsoever virtue its prepared substance
may have within my body, it hath no influence nor operation
without. I would not entertain a base design, or an action that

should call me villain, for the Indies; and for this only do I love and honour my own soul, and have methinks two arms too few to embrace myself. Aristotle is too severe, that will not allow us to be truely liberal without wealth, and the bountiful hand of Fortune. If this be true, I must confess I am charitable only in my liberal intentions, and bountiful well-wishes; but if the example of the Mite be not only an act of wonder, but an example of the noblest Charity, surely poor men may also build Hospitals, and the rich alone have not erected Cathedrals. I have a private method which others observe not; I take the opportunity of my self to do good; I borrow occasion of Charity from mine own necessities, and supply the wants of others, when I am in most need my self: for it is an honest stratagem to take advantage of our selves, and so to husband the acts of virtue, that, where they are defective in one circumstance, they may repay their want and multiply their goodness in another. I have not Peru in my desires, but a competence, and ability to perform those good works to which He hath inclined my nature. He is rich, who hath enough to be charitable; and it is hard to be so poor, that a noble mind may not find a way to this piece of goodness. *He that giveth to the poor, lendeth to the* Lord: there is more Rhetorick in that one sentence, than in a Library of Sermons; and indeed, if those Sentences were understood by the Reader, with the same Emphasis as they are delivered by the Author, we needed not those Volumes of instructions, but might be honest by an Epitome. Upon this motive only I cannot behold a Beggar without relieving his Necessities with my Purse, or his Soul with my Prayers; these scenical and accidental differences between us, cannot make me forget that common and untoucht part of us both: there is under these *Centoes* and miserable outsides, these mutilate and semi-bodies, a soul of the same alloy with our own, whose Genealogy is God as well as ours, and in as fair a way to Salvation as our selves. Statists that labour to contrive a Common-wealth without poverty, take away the object of charity, not understanding only the

Common-wealth of a Christian, but forgetting the prophecie of CHRIST.

Now, there is another part of charity, which is the Basis and Pillar of this, and that is the love of GOD, for Whom we love our neighbour; for this I think charity, to love GOD for Himself, and our neighbour for GOD. All that is truly amiable is GOD, or as it were a divided piece of Him, that retains a reflex or shadow of Himself. Nor is it strange that we should place affection on that which is invisible: all that we truly love is thus; what we adore under affection of our senses, deserves not the honour of so pure a title. Thus we adore Virtue, though to the eyes of sense she be invisible: thus that part of our noble friends that we love, is not that part that we imbrace, but that insensible part that our arms cannot embrace. GOD, being all goodness, can love nothing but Himself; He loves us but for that part which is as it were Himself, and the traduction of His Holy Spirit. Let us call to assize the loves of our parents, the affection of our wives and children, and they are all dumb shows and dreams, without reality, truth, or constancy. For first there is a strong bond of affection between us and our Parents; yet how easily dissolved! We betake our selves to a woman, forget our mother in a wife, and the womb that bare us, in that that shall bear our Image. This woman blessing us with children, our affection leaves the level it held before, and sinks from our bed unto our issue and picture of Posterity, where affection holds no steady mansion. They, growing up in years, desire our ends; or applying themselves to a woman, take a lawful way to love another better than our selves. Thus I perceive a man may be buried alive, and behold his grave in his own issue.

I conclude therefore, and say, there is no happiness under (or, as Copernicus will have it, *above*) the Sun, nor any Crambe in that repeated verity and burthen of all the wisdom of Solomon, *All is vanity and vexation of Spirit*. There is no felicity in that the World adores. Aristotle, whilst he labours to refute the Idea's of Plato, falls upon one himself; for his *summum bonum* is a Chimæra, and there is no such thing as his Felicity. That wherein GOD Himself is happy, the holy Angels are happy, in whose defect the Devils are unhappy, that dare I call happiness: whatsoever conduceth unto this, may with an easy Metaphor deserve that name; whatsoever else the World terms Happiness, is to me a story out of Pliny, a tale of Boccace or Malizspini, an apparition, or neat delusion, wherein there is no more of Happiness than the name. Bless me in this life with but peace of my Conscience, command of my affections, the love of Thy self and my dearest friends, and I shall be happy enough to pity Cæsar. These are, O LORD, the humble desires of my most reasonable ambition, and all I dare call happiness on earth; wherein I set no rule or limit to Thy Hand or Providence. Dispose of me according to the wisdom of Thy pleasure: Thy will be done, though in my own undoing.

The Best of the World's Best Books

COMPLETE LIST OF TITLES IN

THE MODERN LIBRARY

For convenience in ordering use number at right of title

MODERN LIBRARY GIANTS

*A series of full-sized library editions of books that formerly
were available only in cumbersome and expensive sets.*

THE MODERN LIBRARY GIANTS REPRESENT A SELECTION OF THE WORLD'S GREATEST BOOKS

These volumes contain from 600 to 1400 pages each